Bad Habits

The American Social Experience
S E R I E S

General Editor:
JAMES KIRBY MARTIN

Editors:
PAULA S. FASS, STEVEN H. MINTZ, CARL PRINCE,
JAMES W. REED, AND PETER N. STEARNS

Bad Habits

*Drinking, Smoking, Taking Drugs,
Gambling, Sexual Misbehavior,
and Swearing in American History*

J O H N C . B U R N H A M

N E W Y O R K U N I V E R S I T Y P R E S S
New York and London

New York University Press
New York and London

Library of Congress Cataloging-in-Publication Data
Burnham, John C. (John Chynoweth)
Bad habits : drinking, smoking, taking drugs, gambling, sexual
misbehavior, and swearing in American history / John C. Burnham.
p. cm. — (The American social experience series ; 28)
Includes bibliographical references (p.) and index.
ISBN 0-8147-1187-1 (acid-free paper)
1. United States—Social conditions. 2. United States—Moral
conditions. 3. Vices—Public
opinion. 4. Deviant behavior—Public opinion. 5. Public opinion—United States. I. Title.
II. Series.
HN57.B87 1993
306'.0973—dc20   92-34840
                              CIP

New York University Press books are printed on acid-free paper,
and their binding materials are chosen for strength and durability.

Manufactured in the United States of America

c   10   9   8   7   6   5   4   3   2   1

This book is dedicated
to
Leonard
Abigail
Peter
Melissa

Contents

Illustrations

Following page 100

Following page 196

Preface

This book is a history of drinking, smoking, taking drugs, gambling, sexual misbehavior, and swearing in the United States. Early in the nineteenth century, each one was a common social misdemeanor in American society, a personal "bad habit" subject to various local and mostly informal social restraints. At different times in the late nineteenth century or early in the twentieth, these "minor vices" interacted with regional and then large-scale national business enterprise. In the process of becoming commercialized, the rituals of indulging in some simple misdemeanors became transformed and acquired important historical power. Ultimately, they converged and played a large part in shaping American society and culture. By late in the twentieth century, it had become inappropriate to continue to conceptualize this group of commonplace misbehaviors in nineteenth-century terms. Instead, they were best viewed as components of a social and business complex of enormous influence.

But this book, it is only candid to say, is something else also. In the course of assembling my material, I was forced to adopt a perspective on American history somewhat different from that which is customary.

I did not intend to write a book with a shifted historical orientation. I started out instead with a different purpose, but as I reviewed the evidence, the new perspective emerged inexorably from the material. My own view of the history of American society will never be the same again, and I hope that my account will permit others to see how the evidence fell into place. Indeed, I hope that it will show why I was surprised and constrained by the evidence once I was willing to open myself to a new vantage point. The evidence in fact contradicts much of late-twentieth-century common wisdom and media portrayals of the place of the "bad habits" in American society.

My original purpose in writing this book, and one to which I still adhere, was to try to explain to the four young adults whose names appear on the dedication page how it came to be that they grew up in a society in which so many "good" people would do—and even advocate—things that they knew, and everybody else knew, were conventionally "bad." (As late as 1970, for example, a substantial majority of Americans, even those who were heavy drinkers, believed that "drinking does more harm than good."[1]) The quest for explanations for that paradox took me to the historical record. I have therefore written this book primarily to tell at least four Americans how their world came to be as it was and is.

As the reference notes indicate, my shifted perspective is based on conventional scholarly evidence. In some cases, the notes serve merely to document materials that are generally known and to confirm common wisdom. But in other cases, the notes should reassure readers as they may find parts of the narrative that are fresh and perhaps startling. Sometimes I have had to correct my own evaluation of assertions dismissed years ago. In the context of my new perspective, many contentions have presumptive validity that I would not have accorded them earlier.

My intention in this book is to establish profiles and general patterns and give illustrative examples, rather than to provide exhaustive histories. The notes therefore indicate also that many more details are available than I have included in my account. Because the notes serve as a guide to further reading, in lieu of a formal bibliography or bibliographical essay, I have sometimes commented in the notes on both sources and technical historical problems. Using the index and the notes together should furnish a literature guide for anyone interested.

Finally, as the book came together, I became aware of another dimension: what this account might mean beyond my immediate intentions.

Many of the people who today and in the past have opposed drinking, smoking, taking drugs, gambling, sexual misbehavior, and swearing have done so as a matter of unreasoned faith, or even simple prejudice explained as "the way I grew up." My book turns out in effect to constitute an inquiry as to whether or not historical evidence might justify those who disapproved of the so-called bad habits, at the very least showing that historical understanding does *not* justify supporting the "bad habits"—not even, perhaps, just tolerating them. Much of my surprise came from the realization that such a case can be made. It can be made, I found, in substantial measure by tracing how the *opposite* assumption grew: that everyday, pleasurable "misdemeanors" are (within very broad extremes) harmless, natural, spontaneous, sociable, and without significance.

People have strong feelings about their own personal rituals and beliefs in the realms of drinking, smoking, gambling, drug taking, swearing, and especially sexual practices. These rituals are even more potent in generating emotions when a person's family and family traditions are involved. In approaching these subjects in a way that sometimes casts doubt upon customary and common rationalizations, I have therefore found that the material in this book elicits substantial personal reactions, both negative and positive. Such personal reactions are complicated by the fact that most people maintain a mix of personal identifications concerning the various "bad habits." I do myself. A horror of drugs but devotion to beer and swearing would be a common combination, but others are obviously possible, such as an abstemious household who happened to be dedicated to sexual activities or arrangements that their neighbors might not approve of. Problems arise particularly because people rationalize their own behaviors with myths, and in the area of the "bad habits," many myths do not, in fact, wholly square with the record of what actually happened. Such news can be unwelcome. Even worse, as I think my findings demonstrate, disturbing moralistic assertions that people have confidently discredited in their own minds on the basis of what happened in the past may turn out to have some level of secular validity. Against reactions of personal discomfiture to the narrative that follows, I can appeal only to intellectual curiosity and candor. My hope is at least to open up discussion.

Many people will nevertheless insist on reading this history in terms of personal choices, and often moral choices. That is their privilege. My intention, however, is not to suggest that drinking or smoking or any of the other actions is in and of itself "bad." Generations of Americans found that some ordinary rebelliousness or personal misbehavior or violation of the strictest standards was not necessarily subversive of society or values.

But in the United States, at least, the "bad habits" became more than personal matters. As I shall explain, they came to constitute a social phenomenon. As a consequence, they became not just matters of personal choice or prejudice but matters for social decision and social responsibility. My focus in what follows, therefore, will be the history of the *social* aspect of moral choices—values that various groups of Americans held, as shown in what they said were their standards of behavior and in their actual conduct.

The conclusion that I set forth in this book is therefore this: it is a common belief that earlier Americans paid too much attention to the "bad habits" and invested in them too much emotion and concern. The truth is, the descendants of those Americans, by moving attention and concern away from the way each of these minor vices interacted with other aspects of society, for generations lost awareness of one of the major determinants of their lives.

Bad Habits

CHAPTER ONE

Introduction

My narrative is largely about the struggle between what emerged in the nineteenth century as "respectability" and "unrespectability"—a struggle that focused on the conventional minor vices of my title. But what I shall describe was not a simple clash between the forces representing two cultural standards. In the twentieth century, unrespectability began to take on special attributes. It drew upon transformations in commerce and demography and interacted with many other important social and cultural changes, with the result that by the late twentieth century, unrespectability overwhelmed traditional respectability in American society.

In a social context, the "bad habits" were anything but simple. Not least curious, as it turned out, was the way in which they constituted a cultural unit. This introductory chapter provides the reader with definitions, strategies, and themes in the narrative that make possible discussion of this peculiar unit of minor personal vices. After identifying a critical change in standards in the period around the 1920s, I shall introduce the core countercultural force, the Victorian underworld, and the respectability against which the people in the underworld contended. I shall then alert the reader to the salient motives that animated a very complex social change—motives that I shall identify as greed, parochialism, and rebelliousness.

The Subject of the Bad Habits

Drinking, smoking, sexual misbehavior (mostly activity outside of marriage), taking drugs, gambling, and swearing are vices that have the label vice and yet traditionally have been attractive, indeed, have been recreational and gratifying activities. Moreover, for generations, virtually everyone knew what the "bad habits" were and knew that parts of the population labeled them vices or bad habits. As vices, each one often involved not only some level of malicious intent but, above all, a quality that engendered and still engenders reactions that are ambivalent.[1] (Because the nineteenth-century category of "bad habits" and the more recent description of them as "minor vices" are clear as to content, I am employing them as non-pejorative, substantive terms.)

The bad habits also possessed and possess another fundamental attribute: they have ritualistic aspects. Users of tobacco, for example, from the beginning tended to consume it in the same, repetitive way, over and over. From the middle of the twentieth century, there have existed prescriptions for permissible and impermissible actions in organized group sex activities, including, in some organizations, the way the furniture was to be arranged. More than other personal habits, such "rituals of transgression," as anthropologists have designated them, signified that the actions had substantial cultural significance. The bad habits, from the nineteenth century on, were ritual transgressions subject to moral judgments. But as will appear in this book, in the twentieth century, indulging in those minor vices produced profound social effects that endowed them with another kind of cultural significance. Indeed, when I first began my research on this subject, I tended to view the bad habits as essentially laughable misdemeanors. By the time I had traced them into the twentieth century and realized the power of the social forces that they generated, I had stopped laughing.[2]

When historians have written about drinking, smoking, taking drugs, gambling, sexual misbehavior, and swearing, almost invariably the focus has been on attempts to control and repress these bad habits. I have found few works focusing on efforts to spread and expand such commonplace behaviors, much less to explain the social momentum that they developed. And that is no wonder, because, until recently, proponents of the bad habits rarely left records. Seldom did an agenda or a platform for a bad habit surface. Moreover, when advocates did speak up, they usually offered not a reasoned defense and civilized discourse, but distraction or defiance. In the mid twentieth century, a publisher who was criticized for what appeared at that time to be the provocatively erotic content of his comic books replied insolently: "I don't see a child getting sexual stimulation out of it. Looking at those enlarged mammary glands, he'd remember that not long ago he was nursing at his mother's breast."[3]

Because hardly any scholars have focused on the proponents of the bad habits, I am in this volume, it should be frankly recognized, pioneering. I had to ask new questions, and I have followed the evidence to conclusions that are unusual.[4] People who over a period of decades have kept up with reports of consumer groups and a certain type of journalistic exposé and social criticism will be familiar in a different context with a substantial fraction of the examples that I cite, if not with some of the argument. Yet no one before has laid out the histories of the minor vices parallel to one another. My contribution is, then, to call attention to the direction in which the various types of evidence point so that the outlines of major social change appear.[5] And one major aspect of my findings is that combining the subject of the constellation of the attractive minor vices with the historical record produces a striking pattern.

An Inversion of Values

My own reorientation to this subject matter took place particularly as I eventually adopted two strategies. The first was to follow the agents and proponents of the minor vices as if they were protagonists in a story. Tracing a point of view is, after all, a venerable narrative device. In this case, it is a very enlightening one. The second strategy was to use this focus in an unpretentious way in the framework that sociologists have offered for at least a generation, deviance theory.

What I discovered was that American values had turned upside down in the twentieth century, and, moreover, that many observers had long been aware of the reversal. Some writers, for example, have quoted Willa Cather's succinct observation: "The world broke in two in 1922 or thereabouts. . . ." To more recent witnesses, the larger part of the change appeared to have taken place only after midcentury. A University of Michigan researcher noted in 1979 that "norms about marriage and parenthood have changed dramatically over the last twenty years. Today marriage and parenthood are rarely viewed as necessary, and people who do not choose these roles are no longer considered socially deviant." But the beginnings of the transformation tended to show up, as Cather suggested, around the 1920s.[6]

The change was so great that in public discourse people began well before World War II to speak of the conduct that had previously appeared "bad" as "good." More specifically, activities such as gambling and public swearing that previously had been labeled deviant frequently came to enjoy positive valuing. Conversely, to a greater and greater extent, the practitioners and advocates of commonplace virtues began to appear to other Americans to be the social deviants, indeed sometimes serving as a negative reference group who set a bad, rather than a good, example. Moral righteousness went out of style. A standard of no restraints—particularly in indulging in the bad habits—came into vogue. This book, then, is an effort to show in developmental terms when, how, and why this inversion of values and attitudes toward the bad habits came about.[7]

Reformers and the Constellation of Minor Vices

Historians of the United States have traditionally followed as a major theme, if not the organizing theme, the rise and fall of reformers. For generations, various investigators have asked why the reformers were repeatedly frustrated in their efforts to reap the promise of American life. My inquiry suggests that the best understanding of American society comes from searching out not the weaknesses of the reformers but, rather, the *strengths of the forces* against which reformers contended. And, no doubt, any cautious person should at least consider that when talented people of the past were frustrated in their finest efforts, the primary explanation for events was not the deficiency of the uplifters but rather the power of the groups, formal and implicit alike, arrayed against those reformers.[8]

I continue to find it astonishing that historians have so far not identified and analyzed the opponents of reformers. Corrupters of some political and social institutions—such as Boss Tweed in New York and other city bosses—and to some extent blatant exploiters like the robber barons have received at least desultory attention. But the forces of traditional moral dissent and misbehavior have not had even that much attention except under the headings of violence and crime—or, perversely, as "reform."[9]

In the nineteenth and early twentieth centuries, the Americans who worked against conventional misdoings and for "morality" knew what they opposed. They tied urban disorder to the obvious, recognizable, and familiar minor vices. In the nineteenth century, disorder was a real and constant problem in the developing cities, and reformers' efforts, negative and positive, to impose social control involved both personal behavior and attempts to shape public demeanor.[10] Everyone knew that saloons were centers of crime and vice in most communities, sites from which disorder spread. Brothels were called "disorderly houses," a euphemism embodying true social significance. This book focuses on the constellation of those disorderly bad habits that everyone knew and talked about for many generations.

Virtually all commentators agreed that a number of common vices (questionable habitual behaviors) embodied some level of sinfulness (but, of course, again, not all sin), and they identified in the nineteenth century, if not before, that single social constellation that included drinking, smoking, gambling, sexual misbehavior (again, generally understood for centuries as activities outside of strictly monogamous marriage), swearing, and taking drugs, plus some subordinate conventional misdeeds, such as, in an earlier day, Sabbath-breaking. This constellation, moreover, was at the heart of the conduct and standards that so many Americans believed had been transformed in the twentieth century—"the average American's value scale—turned inside out," as a journalist put it in 1958.[11] Even though they did not agree about whether or not the change in public attitudes toward the minor vices was or is desirable, a wide range of observers has confirmed that the change occurred.

The constellation is even today so commonplace as to need little explication except to observe that it was a commonplace in the nineteenth as well as the twentieth century. The juxtaposition of "cigareetes and whusky and wild, wild women" in the satirical mid-twentieth-century song could be matched in the nineteenth by the way in which ex-gamblers connected gaming with alcohol and cigars. Tom Sawyer and Huck Finn knew exactly what was naughty, and how all of the naughtinesses were generally found in the same individuals, such as Huck's father. Even before that, in 1790, Benjamin Rush had devised "A Moral and Physical Thermometer, Or, A Scale of the Progress of Temperance and Intemperance" (see fig. 1.1). And as early as 1691, Virginia passed "An act for the more effectuall suppressing the severall sins and offences of swaring, curseing, profaincing Gods holy name, Sabbath abuseing, drunkenness, fornication, and adultery." There was from the beginning a continuing and almost universal cultural belief that the various minor vices manifested themselves in company with one another, and many people believed that the affinity was simply in some sense natural.[12] Moreover, the bad habits had in common associating nonproductive behavior and the spending of money with pleasurable activity.

But the persistence with which Americans over many generations connected the minor vices into a constellation raises the question if there was not more to the association than having in common the quality of violating the work ethic in a gratifying way. I shall explore some other cultural connections in Chapters 9 and 10, but for the time being I simply record and note that the association existed from the first days of North American colonization.

Personal Habits and Social Phenomena

In the nineteenth century, thinkers typically explained the occurrence of smoking, drinking, gambling, and other misbehavior in one person with the concept of habit. In 1838, for example, the author of *Temperance Tales* hoped to break "the chain of evil habit" involved in drinking. It was at about that time that "bad habits" came to be a specific euphemism for this whole range of misbehaviors that were roughly interchangeable. By the late nineteenth century, reformers were talking about the system within which drinking and prostitution, not to mention gambling and various crimes, seemed to be allied in society, as well as in individuals, with bad character.[13]

Many nineteenth-century moralists, such as the authors of the McGuffey readers, believed that people had chosen one path—right or wrong—and were consistent in their behaviors. In the 1853 *Third Eclectic Reader*, for example, Uncle Philip tells a story to the boys:

"Do you know poor old Tom Smith?"
"Know him! Why, Uncle Philip, every body knows him. He is such a shocking drunkard, and swears so horribly, that no one can forget him."
"Well, I have known him ever since we were boys together. There was not a more decent, well-behaved boy among us.
"After he left school, his father died, and he was put into a store in the city. There, he fell into bad company.
"Instead of spending his evenings in reading, he would go to the theater, to balls, and to suppers.

"He soon learned to play cards, and of course to play for money. He lost more than he could pay. . . .

"But one thing, boys, one single thing ruined him forever. In the city, he had learned to take strong drink.

"I remember he said to me once, that when a man begins to drink, he never knows where it will end. 'Therefore,' said Tom, 'beware of the first drink!' "14

Such people as Uncle Philip relied on the idea of character—which did consist of patterns of consistent behavior—and included the subordinate idea of habit in it.

What is perhaps most striking is the fact that in the mid twentieth century, sociologists found that the connections between the various bad habits were neither fictitious nor accidental. High school students who did not smoke tended not to drink, either. Moreover, those who neither drank nor smoked virtually never used marijuana. And, finally, as if to confirm popular prejudices, users of hard drugs had invariably come to them only by way of marijuana—or at least by way of smoking and drinking. The statistical exceptions to this pattern were so small as to suggest that a genuine social phenomenon was still involved in the interconnection of these conventional minor vices.15

It is this combination of the substantive nature of the constellation with the fact that it persisted remarkably over time that provides the subject of this book. Few social realities are so clear and so constant as this constellation. Advocates of any of the bad habits, together or singly, then— the proponents of the minor vices—were people all pushing, as it turned out, in the same direction, and in so doing, they collectively affected the direction of the flow of history. Although the effects of their actions can be described in generalizations, these proponent forces were entirely real as they functioned in specific times and places: in Progressive-era San Francisco, for example, clearly identifiable people and organizations and interests operated together as a very tangible and particular historical entity working to protect and perpetuate prostitution there.16

As my narrative will show, no such proponent forces were discernible when bad habits first showed themselves among American populations. Writing, for example, about Middlesex County in Massachusetts in the seventeenth century, historian Roger Thompson recently noted that even after the most thorough examination of the evidence, he could find no substantial evidence "of a thriving counterculture" subversive of Puritan respectability.[17] Only later did the forces supporting the constellation come together sufficiently so as to be detectable as they generated patterns of actions and pressures in American culture contrary to a whole set of social standards that restrained individual behavior.

The Victorian Underworld as Counterculture

Although there may have been precursors here and there, initially the form in which the combined supporters of the minor vices appeared was the Victorian underworld. The underworld had two existences. One was in the minds of journalists and social leaders who used the people and activities in the underworld to define and label what was deviant—a negative reference group for the "respectables." The other existence was the actual world of crime and disorder, a world that developed the power and character of a counterculture, standing for and working for a set of values at odds with those of the dominant respectable culture.

Beginning in the nineteenth century, the underworld consisted primarily of criminals and what used to be called ambiguously "sports" and "idlers"— typically, unattached males who were looking for fighting, betting, drinking, and sexual adventures. In addition, those who served the underworld were at the heart of it: typically, alcoholic-beverage vendors, gamblers, and prostitutes. All these classically "antisocial" people grouped together, with at least some sense of common identity, partly imposed by a hostile society, partly developed out of shared goals and attitudes.[18]

But there was a second aspect to the underworld. The underworld included very large additional numbers of people who were only loosely attached to it or just passed through it from time to time. One such group consisted of itinerant workers, who often were also hobos and tramps. They took on an underworld identity to the point that they all even used common identifying argots. In 1927, for example, folklorist Elisha K. Kane, an eyewitness for many years, explained why language bound such populations together at the beginning of the twentieth century:

> Tramps learn the ways of crime in prison; criminals taking to the road to avoid detection, pick up the tricks of vagrancy; the pimps and lovers of prostitutes are usually criminals, while these unfortunate women, together with all the misfits and flotsam of society, ultimately gravitate down the ways

of vagrancy. . . . Knavery, filth, and despair speak, therefore, the same jargon.[19]

In urban centers, the underworld had a real, largely geographical existence, usually originally called the segregated district, in which houses of prostitution, drinking places, gambling dens, opium dens, and disreputable people in general all tended to locate. Being localized helped bring in still other groups, people who lived in the cheap boardinghouse areas, which often contained disreputable drinking places and which characteristically overlapped disorderly districts. Boarders were usually poor single people, at first male—the bachelor subculture. In antebellum New York, for example, young single males were typically recent immigrants who would soon move on. But increasingly the boardinghouse areas included larger populations of females, many of whom in one way or another sought what they believed was "freedom" and independence—and, like the men, showed in practice what that meant by moving away from people with conventional or bourgeois standards. Single women workers in the boardinghouse areas, for example, found that peers in work and living groups were contemptuous of young women who did not enter into profitable and casual sexual arrangements. In similar ways, other poor people found themselves moving in and out of the geographical underworld and often identifying with it. Later, in the twentieth century especially, important components came from vulnerable ethnic neighbors who had cut many traditional social ties that might have protected them from underworld influences. Altogether, a substantial fraction of the total population meshed at least in part with the underworld way of life.[20]

The underworld in its original form included, therefore, not just the brothels, betting parlors, and saloons and the activities that flourished in and around them. The underworld universe included people in the sporting world, "roughs," and many unattached males and just plain impoverished people, large numbers of whom moved frequently from place to place and from job to job, and whose occupations often included begging, prostitution, and thievery as well as respectable labor. In the cities, poor people and people with dubious intentions lived alongside each other in the slum and boardinghouse areas. A proper boardinghouse could occupy the same building as a brothel. Substantial numbers of children grew up in these corrupting neighborhoods, often to the distress of their impoverished parents. "Newsies," for example, gathered in Hearst Alley in Chicago at the beginning of the twentieth century: "We had a regular racket of 'jack-rolling' and breaking into homes, and made more money than we needed . . . but we got rid of most of it . . . at the newspaper alley" where "there was a continuous crap game going on" and all kinds of delinquents preying on the youngsters.[21]

It was of great significance that the underworld furnished for at least parts of society some or all of their leisure-time activities, legal and illegal. But the underworld also came to function as a counterculture. Initially, in addition to informal group pressures on people in and around the area, the underworld fostered bands of rowdies and mobs. In Philadelphia, for example, the Christmastime "callithumpian" revels of costumed gangs alarmed nineteenth-century property owners, who not only suffered outrage and damage but also feared for public order, and rightly so: class and ethnic dissidents used the occasion to extend outside of unrespectable sites the riotous misbehavior of the developing underworld. By 1900, the custom was tamed to some extent as a Mummers Parade; but all along, people correctly recognized the countercultural power of the rowdies. In southern rural towns of the late nineteenth century, there existed a somewhat variant pattern that involved a substantial proportion of the male population. Defiant anti-society rowdies took over the small business centers and moved them outside normal moral boundaries with drinking, fighting, gambling, and swearing—but only on Saturdays or holiday occasions. Afterward, the ruffians largely disappeared into the surrounding houses and farms.[22]

In most cities, underworld groups wielded much political power even in the nineteenth century. Urban history is replete with victories of champions of saloons, gambling, and "wide-open" operations. Moreover, from the beginning, members of the underworld generated recognizable gangs, which operated with great effectiveness into the mid twentieth century, particularly as large, often alienated, ethnic populations replaced the bachelor subculture in many questionable neighborhoods. In Los Angeles, for example, by the 1920s, the gangs, instead of resisting uplifters' institutions by playing truant or breaking windows, took over the playgrounds and schools and imposed their own standards there as well as in other public areas such as movie theaters and racetracks.[23]

The sheer number of people in the heart of the underworld increased with urbanization and immigration. Writing as early as 1868, James Dabney McCabe, Jr., claimed that, for example, there were as many prostitutes in New York City as there were members of the Methodist Church.[24] But the number of Americans who were forced to live and work in bad neighborhoods or who chose to go slumming—the groups who constituted the fluid border between the underworld and the larger community—increased even faster than the regular residents of the segregated districts. Those who willingly or unwillingly mixed and allied with the underworld proper, including very substantial groups of people who could move from working class to underworld as circumstances changed, were what earlier generations referred to as the lower orders of society. The lower orders of society constituted the wider popular base that, through most of American history, furnished support for the proponents of the minor vices. I shall therefore use that term, *lower order*, which continues to suggest the changing identities of many citizens as they entered into or temporarily allied with the core underworld counterculture.

Unrespectability and Respectability

The underworld was well known for generations. Adventurous middle- and upper-class people had been going slumming since the mid nineteenth century. Moreover, the very term "underworld" recognized that within American society, a moral universe existed that was not part of the public face of that society. As dominant population groups worked out the definition of what was "respectable" and what was not, the constellation of minor vices occupied a central position. Historian John Kasson, one of the few scholars to take these activities and distinctions seriously, has noted that the deviant groups of the underworld, along with their allies in turn-of-the-century society, "constituted the counterculture of Victorian America: their activities, an inversion of genteel cultural norms."[25]

In the chapters that follow, then, I shall be describing as a theme of this book the way in which the bad habits were embedded in the values and people of the underworld and worked as a cultural force that, with the help of the rest of the lower orders, ultimately won out in the larger American society.

In the United States, the respectability from which the underworld dissented was what was generally understood as middle-class, bourgeois, Old Testament respectability. The chief proponents of respectability were originally powerful nineteenth-century evangelicals. For generations, they either constituted or influenced the people who dominated society as their values were picked up by advocates of public order and sobriety such as industrialists. Core supporters of respectability were at first mostly descended from English and Scottish Protestants, although in fact their values and standards were widely shared by middle-class nonwhites and non-Protestants (as reflected in many parts of the immigrant press). The middle classes were in general those who held some property or hoped to. They included, most conspicuously, professionals, but also skilled laborers and modest farmers. Propertyless workers and clerks often shared middle-class values even though they were part of the *economically* lower classes. As Lewis Perry, another historian who uses the term and concept of respectability, points out, early in the nineteenth century, the meaning of respectability changed. Before, it had referred to the upper, aristocratic groups in the social hierarchy. Now, it came to refer to those who criticized the conduct of anyone, high born or low, who was gambling or drinking or whatever. The terms "lady" and "gentleman" came to refer to deportment, not birthright.[26]

Beginning before the Civil War, people who advocated the values of the respectables also usually controlled public expressions of values: in the press, on the speaker's platform, and in the pulpit. The respectables in addition controlled the institutions that trained and constrained behavior, particularly the schools and Sunday schools, and they had great influence in institutions that operated to discourage behavior that deviated from the usual standards, particularly informal patterns of association and the legislatures, police, and courts. (Again, many high upper-class people, like members of the underworld, resisted the influence of respectability and were only occasionally part of it.) Until the early and mid twentieth century, then, it was the forces of respectability who effectively set the general standards for American society, and because of their monopoly on public expressions of opinion, they developed an effective consensus across the country at large.

Even late in the twentieth century, people talked about "prosocial" actions and attitudes that not only supported generally accepted ethics but also made society a better place by those standards (prosocial as the opposite of antisocial). Indeed, in an extreme form, prosocial attitudes shaded into moral righteousness. Respectable people therefore could become quite unlovely—bigoted and narrow-minded and of course parochial in their own way. But in contrast to the negativism of the lower orders, the respectables fumbled toward some sense that a social order could improve the condition of all citizens.[27]

The basic issue in traditional respectability could appear to be the work ethic. The moral stance of the McGuffey readers and most other cultural productions for a century, at least, emphasized the value of being a productive worker. Even many generations later, the bulk of Americans still found that activities that were unproductive and particularly that were based on easy, immediate gratification—like those in the constellation of minor vices—could arouse disapproval from others and unease and ambivalence in oneself. Such terms as "lazy" and "good-for-nothing" still carried a sting in most social groups. And yet, at the same time, people could and did argue that in their postindustrial, consumer-oriented world, the work ethic was not necessarily functional any longer.

But there was more to the minor vices. Even in a consumer society, advocates of the bad habits could function as antisocial forces, as opposed to defenders of prosocial activities designed to carry out and reinforce common values and activities that made society both protective and compassionate. People in the past used such terms as "public spirited" and "socially responsible" to convey what being prosocial meant. Antisocial people used other terms or, most frequently, simply denied the validity and relevance of respectability. The distinction between prosocial and antisocial was therefore carried in this label of "respectability" that for generations marked tensions between proponents and opponents of the bad habits.

One of the results of the post-World War I change in standards was the separation of moral reform from other kinds of social reform in the United States. Prosocial "good" people no longer presented a single front of both moral and social uplift. The "respectables" often lost touch with other kinds of reformers and hence were vulnerable to arguments that they ignored social wrongs. One of the implicit arguments for good people to tolerate pleasurable vices was that miserable workers and exploited people deserved some gratification, however flawed. Some reformers therefore tended to jettison moral uplift and deemphasize respectability in favor of working for social justice. All this furnished a milieu that complicated struggles over the minor vices during and after the 1920s.

For many people who grew up in the late twentieth century, it may be difficult to evoke the power of old-fashioned respectability.[28] People in the age of respectability joked about the standards, but the bulk of the population lived in communities (even in cities) in which, in public at least, a substantial consensus viewed the actions of indulgers in the bad habits as somewhere between unfortunate and deplorable. To be clean, pure, wholesome, upstanding—indeed, respectable—was a status that would have given most Americans a happy sense of self-worth.

It should be noted that respectability involved both standards of conduct and community labeling. From the beginning, there was a certain amount of misbehavior in all departments of the constellation, and there was community suppression of that misbehavior. Often people were reluctant to acknowledge that some specific action was an affront to community standards, and they could ignore it, disguise it, and even excuse it, sometimes in the most hypocritical way. But by confronting and suppressing the bad habits, or papering them over with hypocrisy, the respectables were for generations able to restrain the extent to which they and their neighbors indulged in or abetted the minor vices—despite frequently expressed alarms that antisocial behavior and attitudes were rampant.

Deviance

Sociologists have explained the idea of deviance by pointing out that every group developed institutions through which members stigmatized both behaviors and persons. The process of stigmatizing defined the relationship of those persons to the rest of the group. When a thief or a heretic or a brothel keeper was labeled, and sanctions applied, the institutions through which controlling members of the group—originally the respectable people—carried out the labeling and sanctioning served to define the group's standards. Individuals who did not hew to those standards were outside of the group, or they existed within the group as deviants. In so far as the standards applied to people, rather than to abstract actions, those people still belonged to the group—even as their behavior drew negative sanctions.[29]

In the United States, labeling an activity deviant sometimes occurred within formal institutions, as when a deviant was judged and institutionalized (a sex offender or drunkard or drug dealer) or when widely shared publications carried statements about proper behavior. The results of labeling also showed up in the informal institutions of disapproval, avoidance, and similar social niceties (nice boys and girls did not play with children who swore). The social consequences of a label could in fact be extensive, as "alcoholics," for example, have found. Throughout the nineteenth and early twentieth centuries, the most common label to indicate informal social sanctioning was, obviously, "respectable." In the case of the underworld, by labeling and romanticizing the unrespectable subculture, typically in exposés and discussions of the mystique of the lower-order folk, opinion makers reinforced the standards of the respectables. Late-nineteenth-century readers could be titillated, for example, by books on *The Secrets of the Great City*, *The Dangerous Classes of New York*, or, regarding Chicago, *The Masque Torn Off*—all suggesting mystery, allure, danger, and condemnation.[30]

My story begins, then, with a time when the bad habits represented deviance, and the narrative goes on to trace the way in which disapproval and sanction were lifted from them, and how in dominant sectors of American society, opposition to the bad habits in itself became deviant—a remarkable sign of that complete inversion in values.

This inversion did not happen easily, and most of the principals in it ultimately were unaware that they held to standards that were other than "conventional," that is, respectable, save that they were adjusting slightly to fit in with "changing times." Basically the shift amounted to denying either that old-fashioned minor vices were bad or that the bad habits had consequences of any importance.

Curiously enough, during the 1970s, attitudes toward one of the bad habits, smoking, reversed again, dramatically, inspiring two sociologists, Ronald J. Troyer and Gerald E. Markle, to use deviance theory in a major study explaining this remarkable phenomenon.[31] As Troyer and Markle have demonstrated in the case of smoking, and as I found to be valid in the histories of the other minor vices, the deviancy model is particularly useful because it helps make sense of changing patterns in public actions that embodied values. Within human groups and institutions, labeling and condemning provide specific measures of values.

Energizing Factors

The specific motives that drove the minor vices in the United States came from diverse sources in history and American society, beyond the mere existence of an underworld. One motive was simple greed—immoderate and to some extent reckless attempts to make money, profit seeking that reflected a decidedly more than ordinary desire for gain. This unusual strength of the pursuit of profits was a distinctive characteristic of people who stood to make money from the bad habits. In their greed, those profiting from the minor vices worked in such a way as to alter historical events, and when, eventually, there were enough such people, and particularly when they were organized, the merchants of the minor vices constituted an awesome historical influence.[32]

A second motive that energized the proponents of the minor vices was the parochialism of the lower orders of society. Critics of American reform have pointed out that reformers wanted to impose on all the world their own bourgeois, middle-class, uplift standards—in making the South over in the image of New England and in forcing all population groups into a WASP (white, Anglo-Saxon, Protestant) mold. What such critics have not spelled out, for the most part, is that another parochialism was also operating, namely, that of non-middle-class groups. In nineteenth- and early-twentieth-century Worcester, Massachusetts, for example, working-class people developed persistent programs to try to gain control over their space and activities. They wanted not to be uplifted but, rather, in their own terms and traditions to engage in play and other activities of non-middle-class culture. Similar resistance efforts showed up in Pittsburgh among non-middle-class groups, who insisted on spending their money for commercial amusements and not being uplifted.[33]

In Worcester, in Pittsburgh, in Los Angeles—in American cities everywhere—non-middle-class groups resisted uplift and pursued various kinds of leisure activities. Many elements in these same groups defended saloons and other institutions and activities that shaded over into the underworld culture/counterculture. At that point, they all operated under what I shall designate as *lower-order parochialism*. Leonard Ellis has described how, in the late-nineteenth-century city streets, gangs of boys carried out antisocial acts, such as teasing the policeman on the beat, and did so with covert parental support. These boys did not go on into respectable young manhood as did the alumni of middle-class neighborhood gangs, who also sometimes committed delinquent acts. Street-gang boys instead graduated into the poolrooms and saloons where all the bad habits flourished, along with substantial dissent from middle-class standards, and became part of the lower orders of society and bearers of lower-order parochialism.[34]

In one regard, lower-order Americans were no different from their uplifting fellow citizens: people in each element believed that their way of life was correct and should be imposed on the whole world. Parochialism has always been a powerful social determiner, and it would be a particularly serious error to underestimate the power of lower-order parochialism in the United States, for it was based in growing population groups. And it accounts for otherwise apparently inexplicable phenomena, including, in part, the impact of the increasingly profit-oriented mass media.

A traditional way of describing the lower-order parochials is to note that they were lower class or even working class (as opposed to middle class). The description of lower-order grouping is functionally precise. The usual concept of social class, however, is not useful in understanding the power of the minor vices, especially because of the many non-middle-class people, particularly in the working class, who allied and identified with the dominant respectable elements and promoted respectable values. It is true that most of the population groups who instead allied with the Victorian underworld were economically lower class. By the twentieth century, the bulk of low-paid and often exploited workers came through the world labor market, typically from southern and eastern Europe (and, as late as about 1910, from Ireland). Yet the workers varied greatly in culture, whatever their economic and geographical origins. A substantial number continued to hold thoroughly middle-class values (typically, for example, many Jews). It is also true that at least at some points in time, a very large proportion of the least-prosperous (or most-exploited) workers and their families allied with the people who most often furnished them commercialized amusement—chiefly the underworld. On those occasions, they functioned as part of the lower orders. But they were responding *culturally*, not economically, as part of the lower orders of society and shared that parochialism. Moreover, although sometimes ethnic identities had importance in specific circumstances, at least until well into the twentieth century, ethnic differences were not substantial in defining or determining lower-order antisocial activities.[35] Responsiveness to underworld values was.

Why did so many different kinds of people come to ally with the core underworld and support lower-order parochialism? I have already suggested the simple pressure of the geographical overlap in the segregated districts, the bachelor groups, and the slums in general. But the parochialism of those who resisted being uplifted by the respectables was the powerful social dynamic, as self-justification was reinforced in various social settings—not least the saloons before World War I. In the face of pressures from the respectables' own parochialism (as in Americanization programs of the first decades of the twentieth century), many humble people asserted their different parochial standards of conduct and attitudes. What may have come from either dignified family tradition or immediate

socializing influences therefore melded into the self-justification of alcoholic-beverage vendors, gamblers, and idlers of the underworld and in this
way became a potent force to counter the standards that the respectables
thought should hold universally.

I have already warned about a necessary reorientation of viewpoint, and
I do not want to take the reader unawares about other matters. I am
speaking bluntly about the way in which the underworld replaced the
respectables in setting standards. It is true that the initial hegemony of the
respectables had additional negative aspects (such as disrespect and prejudice), suffered especially by population groups who were economically
disadvantaged. Nevertheless, in *this* book I am—besides describing change—
calling attention to the social costs that were incurred as the standards of
the lower orders replaced the standards of the respectables. Those costs
were not trivial. Indeed, they turned out to be enormous and even fundamental.

It should by now be evident why a fresh look at the history of social
standards may activate various kinds of subjective reactions. Yet I write
in the belief that the fact that one's ancestors were involved on one side
or the other, or that one's grandmother held dear one set of standards or
another, is no reason to close one's eyes to what happened decades ago.
In particular, the way in which a person was manipulated by proponents
of the minor vices, or used by those proponents, can be unwelcome news.
That a person should be a product of his or her culture, even subculture,
is hardly surprising or blameworthy (although to this day many well-informed people still appear ashamed of being descended from folks who
were poor and ignorant). But people are very likely to want to avoid
believing that some vendor—or, worse, media image—directly or indirectly
made fools of those, including admired forebears, who thought they were
making praiseworthy, independent decisions.

Moreover, even the most active individual agents of the change from
"respectability" to "unrespectability," I need hardly say, were real, complicated human beings, few of whom were entirely and consistently dedicated to either all the bad habits or none. Many people, in addition, acted
as transitional figures, and therefore their actions in particular should have
been, and were, contradictory. This book is not, however, about individuals. It was in American society and culture as an aggregate, judged by
dominant spokespeople and institutional expressions, that attitudes toward
the bad habits were inverted. Moreover, it was not only greed and lower-
order parochialism in their complex settings that conditioned the shift;

there was the other great motivating force, rebelliousness, that in all population groups moved some citizens.

Rebelliousness

Rebelliousness was a particular pattern of behavior that appeared constantly, and it connected with both deviance and lower-order dissent. Deviance functions in part by means of individuals' testing the limits of social tolerance. One way of testing is simple rebelliousness, and it was common for (usually) young people, even before the term "adolescence" came into vogue, to commit deviant actions or make assertions contrary to local standards. In so doing, the rebels would trigger the usual containment mechanisms found in any society. Moreover, in all groups, people create humor by joking about acceptable limits, by saying shocking things—which is both a rebellious action and a reassuring confirmation of social limits, because people laugh and know that the rebelliousness is not a serious challenge.

Every society, in fact, has rebels and rebelliousness even in the midst of the most stable culture and secure standards. In the United States, two special types of rebelliousness had special relevance to the constellation of the minor vices. One was intellectual and artistic, a roguish rebelliousness that could extend to lifestyle and for a long time was a major source of Victorians' condemnations of the hypocrisies of the respectables. The other rebelliousness came out of subcultures, not only ethnic and class groups, whose parochialism could change from mere cultural differences to active lower-order dissent, but also regional groups who remained disaffected from many of the larger American cultural norms. The lower-order rebellious subculture in early-nineteenth-century New York, for example, was defined at least in part in terms of dominant respectability. There the use of parody was employed to take known cultural standards and reverse and make fun of them ("You Never Miss Your Water Till the Well Runs Dry" became "You Never Miss de Lager Till de Keg Runs Dry"). Both types of rebelliousness, high culture—as later stereotyped in Greenwich Village bohemians—and parochial subgroup dissent, were well established in the nineteenth century. Both also offered important assistance to the proponents of the minor vices in the general inversion of social standards, once the advocates of the bad habits took the lead. Indeed, in Chicago, early-twentieth-century bohemian elements who lived in lower-order neighborhoods learned from their lower-order neighbors exactly how to rebel against respectability.[36]

Rebelliousness was particularly useful to the proponents of the minor vices because it was chiefly negative in aim. Even reformist bohemians of Greenwich Village were preoccupied with rejecting the predominant respectability and conventional materialism of the early twentieth century. They resonated with the individualist who growled constantly about "goddamned bourgeois" restraints.[37] Advocates of the bad habits were also in effect advocating negative, defiant actions in ways that meshed with the provocativeness of all the other social rebels. Indeed, the implicit ultimate objective of the proponents of the minor vices was a society best characterized as one with *no restraint.* Unfocused or focused, rebellious negativism could lead to a no-restraint standard.

The Transformation of the Minor Vices

My story begins, then, in the early nineteenth century, when drinking, smoking, sexual misbehavior, gambling, swearing, and, later, nonmedical drug taking were, for dominant groups in the United States, deviant behavior—with all the shades and ambivalences engendered by any social labeling—but behavior that nevertheless constantly appeared among a variety of citizens. Manifestations of these minor vices, either individual or group, at that time did not have any particular social consequences.

Minor vice misbehavior was therefore common, indeed, endemic, but it had no special power. In fact, most Americans collaborated in attempts to keep such misbehavior more or less under control. City dwellers from the early nineteenth century on who missed the immediate controls of the rural community devised new methods to combat "temptation" and contain the behaviors and the people involved in the constellation of minor vices. Various social groups formed—primarily among religious evangelicals—to work on behalf of respectability. They in turn came to constitute new power groups in the nineteenth century, and it was these respectables who paid a great deal of attention to each of the elements of the constellation and attempted to suppress them all.[38]

And then industrialism intruded and upset the balance. The struggle of respectability to suppress endemic tendencies to indulge in bad habits was resolved in favor of the bad habits. Industrialization provided the profit motive with a much larger arena, as marketing and distribution became national rather than local. Moreover, as the population changed in composition and concentrated in cities, new or changed institutions, too, contributed to upsetting the old balance. The most conspicuous destabilizing institutions were the mass media, which developed directly out of yellow journalism and advertising, playing to a market expanding in non-middle-class groups just at the end of the nineteenth century and the beginning of the twentieth.

The changes that came with industrialization energized the proponents of the minor vices. As the twentieth century proceeded, then, those proponents, rather than the supporters of conventional respectability, became dominant in shaping American values and behavior, as elements among the advocates of the bad habits coopted each other and ultimately the larger part of American society.

One event both symbolized and decisively accelerated the victory of these new historical influences: the repeal of national Prohibition in 1933. Repeal touched each of the component minor vices of the constellation and is taken up in the next chapter to set the stage for all of them. But before and after Prohibition, each of the bad habits had had an origin different from the others and followed a course of development different from the others. Yet, in the end, they all converged. Indeed, they all by degrees contributed to the powerful minor vice-industrial complex that came into place in the last half of the twentieth century.

Recapitulation

Therefore in the chapters that follow, I shall go from the repeal of Prohibition to the full history of drinking and then continue with parallel histories of the other components, showing differences in circumstance and timing. I have now indicated the basic elements that were involved in the transformation of the bad habits. One was the existence of an underworld with, eventually, a subculture of values that spread into the lower orders. Still another was the conventional respectability of middle-class evangelicals. Those were the respectables who at first effectively labeled as deviant either indulging in, or pandering to, the bad habits.

Viewed another way, the components in this inversion of respectable and unrespectable consisted of two constants and three changes. The constants were, first of all, the bad habits that were endemic in the population, such as the common tendency to gamble or to misbehave in the sexual realm. The second constant was the tendency of individuals to rebel. The rebellions were of various levels of seriousness, and to some extent, a teasing testing of social standards actually served to reinforce the standards. The most formidible rebellion came out of sincerely subversive parochial groups who identified with the lower orders.

There were of course general social changes that played into the transformation, such as the growth of towns and cities and the increase of various non-English ethnic groups. But the three changes that specifically affected the minor vices were industrialization, which transformed the scale of the profiteering involved in the bad habits; the cooptation of many cultural and population elements by the now-energized proponents of the minor vices; and the beginnings of the coming together of the whole combination in the campaign to repeal Prohibition and establish new standards of deviant and nondeviant behavior. Central to the new standards was the idea that individual, not community, standards should be the basis for judging conduct. The self-righteousness of that idea obscured the process through which the dominant elements in society finally came to be dedicated to no-restraint and to the antisocial.

The Turning Point: Repealing Prohibition

Merchandisers of alcoholic beverages were always the most important element among the American proponents of the minor vices, and they usually took a leadership role as well among the cultural groups with an interest in drinking. But in the early twentieth century, alcoholic-beverage makers and sellers suffered a great defeat when reformers got the business outlawed (but not drinking itself), first in many states and localities and then, by means of federal law and the Eighteenth Amendment, throughout the country. As soon as the court appeals and other hopes of escaping the law had ended, those with a financial stake in the business set about to regain their markets. Campaigns to change the law succeeded in the early 1930s. The merchandisers of alcoholic beverages suffered no major defeats after that time.

In the course of rolling back Prohibition, the makers and sellers of alcohol for a brief moment in time appeared transparently in their role as the vanguard of the advocates of the attractive minor vices. Alcoholic-beverage-industry people united with one another to manage vigorous efforts to bring the beverages back.[1] Moreover, they mobilized many allies, including some otherwise uninvolved intellectuals and leading citizens concerned about the power of government. Above all, the proponents of beverage alcohol helped manipulate the new mass media to create a climate favorable to the reintroduction of alcohol. In creating that climate, they profoundly affected American life in many ways that went far beyond establishing the legal status of the alcoholic-beverage business.

The Transformation of Standards

Accompanying and following repeal was the major shift that began the change in standards of behavior, expressed in public actions and words. One is usually skeptical that any particular period was a time of critical change; in the realm of standards regarding the bad habits, however, the testimony of people then and afterwards reinforces vividly the evidence that ideas of dominant groups of Americans about what was acceptable and respectable began to turn upside down as the campaign to undermine Prohibition gathered momentum, with effects that were decisive by mid-century.[2]

"We are at one of those turning-points in human history at which stability and complacent assurance are giving way to criticism and change," wrote Durant Drake in *The New Morality* in 1928; and there was in fact a wider cultural context within which views about the bad habits changed. Journalist and pundit Walter Lippmann, always sensitive to currents of his times, wrote a whole "preface to morals" in an attempt to sketch the challenge that faced people of the late 1920s who were watching traditional bases for behavior disintegrate under new conditions. Lippmann and others found that serene beliefs, such as had undergirded dominant values in previous times, had given way. Now, in the 'twenties, thinking people emphasized doubt and the individual, rather than social needs and responsibilities.[3]

Many commentators conceptualized what happened in the Jazz Age as a loss of standards. But it was in fact not a loss but a substitution, or inversion. Signs of the inversion became ever more numerous during the 1920s and 1930s and were, as it turned out, significantly connected with the repeal of Prohibition. Within another generation, the forces of change began to dispense with even a pretense of the old respectability as new, inverted standards became better established in American society in a new urban culture.[4]

One thing that was new in the 1920s and 1930s was the fact that a number of commentators began to talk about changes in American values and behavior in a way that was different from the usual handwringing over the way the younger generation was going to the dogs or over the prevalence of sin in general. Based on his distillation of journalists' pictures of their own times, Frederick Lewis Allen in 1931 wrote a much-quoted description of "The Revolution in Manners and Morals" of the 1920s. Many other writers made similar observations about the "flaming youth" who, according to media sensationalists, were setting new standards for the whole country. Allen connected a much more open toleration of smoking and drinking—especially women's smoking and drinking—and use of strong and even offensive language with the scandalous new dancing (nothing but a "syncopated embrace") and myriad changes involving sexual mores. Much discussed, too, was the role of consumer goods—the automobile, which greatly aided youthful misbehavior; cosmetics; short skirts; confession magazines; motion pictures. Altogether, the new ideals, in so far as they appeared in public discussion, involved unrestrained frankness and irresponsible searching for pleasure—as well as consumption linked to such behavior as smoking and drinking. Indeed, one of the major evidences of change was not only shifts in moral standards but also widespread acceptance of the idea of installment buying. Both represented breaching the work ethic. "*Mores are in flux*," wrote Ross L. Finney, a sociologist in 1930; ". . . Almost every item of the moral code is subject to skepticism, discussion and nonconformity." In this "great transition," Finney noted that large numbers of "people in good social acceptance" embraced views decidedly at variance with previously established respectability and thereby confused both young and old who were searching for standards.[5]

World War I

Allen and the other commentators correctly associated the controversy over Prohibition with the change in standards.[6] Although the evidence confirms the conclusions of the eyewitnesses, there was a major complicating factor: World War I. The wartime service experiences of millions of mostly young Americans provided a trial run of the inversion of values. In the service, both respectables and unrespectables found themselves in a setting in which lower-order parochials largely set the standards. In the name of comradeship and tough-guy manliness, they either tolerated or embraced drinking, smoking, gambling, sexual misbehavior, and swearing. For the substantial and influential portion of the men from "nice" homes, the service experience represented a radical reversal of standards from the respectability that they had—in their own parochialism—known.

After the war, many influential citizens definitely not from underworld or even working-class backgrounds continued at least some of the bad habits—particularly smoking and swearing—and were willing, it turned out, to defend the whole constellation in the name of masculinity. Moreover, when commercial, rather than cultural, forces came into play, large numbers of war veterans constituted a formidable, organized group who would noisily oppose restrictions on their behavior—and on the commercial activity that supported that behavior.[7] Moreover, because Prohibition had in fact begun during the war, the impact of the war blurred into the impact of the forces working to repeal Prohibition. Both the war experience and repeal agitation therefore pushed Americans to turn standards upside down.

Prohibition and Repeal

Prohibition resulted in the first place because for Americans at the turn of the century, many social problems were directly rooted in one particular institution: the saloon—the retail outlet for alcoholic beverages. Saloons furnished an arena within which gambling and prostitution could flourish. Crime and political corruption as well were centered in saloons. Indeed, all the problems connected directly with alcohol in American culture flourished in saloons and were symbolized for most citizens in the drunkenness and irresponsible, destructive behavior that were exactly the opposite of the careful, controlled, future-oriented conduct that connoted civilization among dominant groups at that time. Mark Matthews, a respectable and responsible moderator of the Presbyterian General Assembly, wrote in 1912 that the liquor traffic was "the most fiendish, corrupt and hell-soaked institution that ever crawled out of the slime of the eternal pit." Even allowing for rhetoric, those are strong words, and it behooves later generations to attend to eyewitnesses such as Matthews who concluded that saloons and the alcoholic-beverage business behind them were institutions that profoundly corrupted both individuals and society.[8]

As historians now recognize, prohibitionists at that time represented the mainstream populations of the country. In the early years of the twentieth century, traditional temperance groups attracted the support of other reformers and drew in business elements who believed that a sober worker was both a better, happier, and more prosperous worker. Indeed, the brewers' blacklist of 1915 included (in some cases without justification) the Pennsylvania Railroad, the United States Steel Corporation, Wanamaker's department store, and the Goodyear Rubber Company, among others. Finally, a well-organized pressure group, the Anti-Saloon League (ASL), arose to lead the "dry" coalition to ultimate success in obtaining the Eighteenth Amendment.

The ASL exerted political pressure particularly through local churches, and by using that and other political leverage, the organization achieved a series of votes in favor of Prohibition at all levels of government so that before World War I, about half of the territory of the United States (but not half of the population) came under prohibitory local laws. Finally, in the Congressional elections of 1916, enough candidates pledged to national Prohibition were elected to Congress (more than a two-thirds majority) that a Constitutional amendment appeared to be assured. In 1919 such an amendment was ratified by the states.[9]

Exactly how the amendment would work out in practice was uncertain in 1916. No one was sure that, for example, light wines and beers would not still be legal. Moreover, another circumstance intervened: the United States entered World War I and needed grain for food (as opposed to alcoholic beverages). Therefore federal restrictions on the industrial production of alcoholic beverages increased until, by 1918, the United States had de facto Prohibition, which Congress extended to cover the period until the newly passed Eighteenth Amendment came into force in 1920.

The amendment ultimately forbade "the manufacture, sale, or transportation of intoxicating liquors" and charged the states as well as the federal government with enforcing the law. Congress passed the Volstead Act to implement the amendment, stipulating that any alcohol content in excess of one-half of one percent was intoxicating. Most newspapers supported the measure in general, and reasonable people expected that, after some adjustment, alcohol would increasingly drop out of American life. As a writer in a New York newspaper hostile to Prohibition noted in 1919, "Prohibition seems to be the fashion, just as drinking used to be."[10]

Practice under the Volstead Act explicitly permitted religious groups to use wine, physicians to prescribe alcohol, and private citizens to own and drink it and even to make small quantities of wine and beer for home use. Wealthy citizens, should they have wanted it, never lacked liquor, because only a little foresight was necessary to lay in a very large store of it ahead of time. The production of wine grapes for home processing was so profitable in the early 1920s that there was ultimately serious overproduction in

California.[11] The law in fact affected primarily low-income consumers who could not readily buy drinks at a saloon any longer, and they were not politically potent enough to affect the legislation. Effective outrage came, rather, because a very profitable industry was being put out of business.

Contrary to myth, Prohibition was substantially successful. The saloon, the disreputable public drinking place, disappeared—the obvious goal of the Anti-Saloon League. Moreover, despite the many legal sources of intoxicating beverages, the per capita consumption of alcohol declined by the early 1920s to only a fraction (well under half) of the amount consumed in 1910. Medical conditions associated with alcohol consumption declined even more precipitously than total quantities drunk, and social conditions also showed definite changes. Billions of dollars formerly spent on alcoholic beverages went into other consumer goods such as automobiles.

Yet no level of government provided anything like adequate support for enforcement, and many entrepreneurs went into the business of furnishing illegal beverages so that slowly in the late 'twenties the total amount of alcohol consumed per capita increased slightly—but never to a level near the pre-Prohibition rate; indeed, that amount was not reached again until the early 1970s. The pattern of the illicit beverage supply system was such that eventually in the 1920s some regions were considered bone dry, but in others, such as New York City, illegally produced beverages were to some extent available, and in some cultural enclaves openly so. These striking geographical variations confused the issue of the overall effectiveness of Prohibition. Almost all the activity of alcoholic-beverage tradespeople was explicitly criminal and local or at most regional, and typically, as in Philadelphia, for example, the business proceeded on the basis of local conditions and corruption.[12] Unlike the pre-Prohibition brewers and distillers, the new traders had no immediate rational motive to advocate repeal or even modification of Prohibition. Yet, as in the case of drug pushers later, even unenforced laws discouraged trade, and bootleggers saw the possibility for ever-more profits if their business was legalized. Moreover, some of them became established figures in their communities and then longed for respectability for their erstwhile unlawful activities.[13]

Meanwhile, a number of the pre-Prohibition businesses campaigned openly for modification and/or repeal of the laws against engaging in the manufacture and distribution of intoxicating beverages. Some alcoholic-beverage manufacturing and distribution firms had simply gone out of business and disappeared. Others pursued different activities such as making yeast or industrial alcohol or just waited for their plants to become useful again. They clearly still had plenty of money, for they spent a great deal on repeal efforts. Those who had faith—and investments—in alcohol were rewarded: by the mid-1920s, a number of allies had appeared to assist the businesspeople in a vigorous propaganda campaign against Prohibition.

In 1923, in the course of partisan politics (to some substantial extent involving lower-order parochialism as well as ethnic partisanship), New York State repealed its "little Volstead" act providing for concurrent state enforcement of the Eighteenth Amendment.[14] This important symbolic event encouraged the scattered opponents of Prohibition. Thereafter, the media, dominated by New York publications, began to project a negative image of the working of the national law. At about the same time, 1923–1925, intellectual and artistic rebels mobilized in New York in favor of an additional cause, frankness in literature—an event that indicated that widespread "anti-Puritan" agitation of other kinds was also getting media encouragement and some backing from other groups.[15] It was in this setting that the formal campaign for repeal became effective.

In 1929, Herbert Hoover took office as president. Unlike his predecessors, he sympathized with Prohibition. The new prospect of truly effective enforcement, along with the increasing influence of the campaign against the Volstead Act, if not the Eighteenth Amendment, made it appear likely that some adjustments in the law would be made, probably in the direction of legalizing light wines and beers, with part of the distribution or manufacture to be kept in government hands so that only a very limited private alcoholic-beverage trade would develop. But what might have happened did not. After the Great Depression set in and became entrenched, large numbers of powerful Americans abandoned their support of Prohibition and joined the repealers. In very short order, Congress initiated the Twenty-First Amendment, repealing the Eighteenth. Thus in 1933 the question of Prohibition was returned to the states. Almost all the states, in fact, immediately permitted the alcoholic-beverage business to thrive legally—as everyone had expected.[16]

Repeal came about because a number of developments played into the hands of the repeal advocates. Some historians have contended that "public opinion" changed spontaneously, without manipulation. Such a naive statement obscures more than it reveals and, moreover, like most latter-day general wisdom about Prohibition, comes directly from the repealers' propaganda. Other historians have cited specific arguments that repealers used, assuming that if used, they were effective. In fact, no argument of the late 1920s-early 1930s was new. Anti-Prohibitionists had tried all of them for years. Only in the case of influential citizens who in the Great Depression hoped that the private manufacture of alcohol products would produce tax revenue—and so save them from paying taxes—was there any evidence that rational argument was effective—and then only because of new economic circumstances. As William P. Beaszell noted in 1932, Prohibition "has become primarily an economic question, with every indication that soon it will be wholly so."[17] Apart from anything to do with drinking, Americans were facing their worst domestic crisis since secession, and the repealers tailored their arguments to take advantage of this economic emergency.

The Campaign for Repeal

Those who had something to gain from the reestablishment of the alcoholic-beverage industry had meanwhile led campaigns that for a number of reasons altered the ways in which many Americans perceived reality. In those campaigns, repealers succeeded in utilizing the mass media in a remarkable way to propagate a series of assertions, symbols, and associations. Even personally observing someone break the law took on new meanings for many citizens after years of exposure to propagandizing and recruiting by repeal groups.

Because these groups and their arguments won repeal, their version of events prevailed afterward. The dry forces stood discredited. In public discourse, beginning in the 1930s, virtually no one listened to the dry side of the story any longer—a situation that had intensified by the mid twentieth century. Moreover, members of the groups who won repeal had a stake— sometimes financial, sometimes cultural—in perpetuating their versions of what happened, and the symbols and associations involved were those that ramified in other areas of the culture, beyond drinking arrangements.

The campaign for repeal went through two phases, one before and one after about 1925–1926. In the first—and largely unorganized—phase, those agitating against the Prohibition Amendment consisted of three groups: the essentially local organizations fronting for alcoholic-beverage business groups; a number of citizens doctrinairely opposed to extending the power of the federal government (or any government); and some important social sophisticates, including the usual bohemian rebellious elements. The sophisticates were by far the most conspicuous because they were able to publicize their views in fashionable publications. During the second phase, the opposition to Prohibition organized systematically and, using the elements already present, plus large amounts of money, developed the campaign that was ultimately effective.[18]

The confusion of economic and cultural elements in both stages is highlighted in an interview that Lavinia Larson reported in 1927. She found that George Eads, secretary of the Association Against the Prohibition Amendment (AAPA), had formerly done publicity work for the Anheuser-Busch brewery. When Eads held up a booklet by E. Clemens Horst, which presumably refuted the dry arguments of a book by Irving Fisher, Larson said,

> "But, Mr. Eads, I understand that Mr. Horst is one of the biggest hop-growers in the country. Would that not prejudice anything he had published and circulated at his own expense concerning the success of prohibition?"
>
> "No, I do not think so. Mr. Horst is much interested in all phases of the question. He is not prejudiced as is Professor Fisher, who is a radical dry."
>
> "But Professor Fisher has no money to lose if prohibition survives or fails."
>
> "No, but he's a radical dry."

Economic self-interest and cultural beliefs (fanaticism) clearly mixed into all of the repeal struggles.[19]

The chief organization working for repeal, the Association Against the Prohibition Amendment, was carefully designed to bring about modification of the law, particularly to increase the alcoholic content of permissible beverages—but only as a step to ultimate repeal. Therefore all the AAPA campaigns operated to discredit the entire experiment, regardless of immediate goals. The organizers implicitly believed that just as Prohibition had come step by step, so it would be necessary for repeal to come gradually. They were as surprised as anyone, then, when their implicit message advocating repeal, rather than their public campaign for modification, carried the day in the early 1930s. Part of the explanation was that by that time there was virtually no organized support for Prohibition. Although it was really not comprehended then, the Anti-Saloon League was divided and in fact for years had had virtually no money with which to counter the AAPA campaigns. In a culture in which organization and media control were coming to count for so much, the drys were therefore ineffectual, and this fact—unknown until recently—helps explain why the step-by-step repeal struggle that the wets imagined would mark repeal did not materialize. Repeal was, consequently, a result of the propaganda campaign of the wets, aided by the fact that the repealers' opponents offered only little opposition.[20]

The Transformation of Repeal Leadership

The Association Against the Prohibition Amendment had begun even before the Eighteenth Amendment was ratified. The founder was William H. Stayton, a former navy officer and lawyer who worked for the Navy League (which gave him a tie not only to the military but to the munitions makers, notorious for their egregious profit seeking). Stayton recruited business and professional men mostly from among members of his exclusive clubs. The bias of the membership was doctrinaire: to avoid federal-government activity in either business or what they considered private conduct (Stayton himself also opposed even legislation against child labor). The strategy was to recruit influential community leaders and to try to make dignified statements. In 1922, two of the Du Pont brothers joined Stayton's organization, and in 1925–1926, a third, the domineering Pierre Du Pont, also joined and then became active in the AAPA. Soon he had displaced Stayton and had his own group directing—and dramatically expanding and financing—the campaign to repeal the Eighteenth Amendment. At that point, the campaign entered the second phase.[21]

The increasing cleverness of the AAPA efforts was a reflection of the shrewdness and money that the new leadership brought. Much effort went into attitude and image in the manner of slick national advertising (as opposed to rational persuasion). By setting up sources for newspaper reporters, for example, and by making the copy moderate and plausible (although not necessarily accurate), the officials of the AAPA were able to manipulate the press in a remarkable way. Free boilerplate went out to local papers on a scale that the Anti-Saloon League could never achieve. Innocent-appearing stories, such as those suggesting that alcohol could benefit humanity by serving as automobile fuel along with gasoline, had their origin with AAPA publicists who saw that any material that would generate favorable associations in connection with alcohol would benefit the repeal cause (and in the case of alcohol for gasoline, appeal in the farm belt that was strongly dry). And of course the publicists kept up a high volume of releases that in one way or another called attention to violations of the law or suggested that Prohibition was a failure or had undesirable side effects. In these and many other ways, the AAPA staff worked the

American mass media until the drys were almost frantic with frustration, for they could see exactly what was happening.[22]

The campaign of the repeal groups, and especially of the AAPA, diverged from the methods that had brought about Prohibition. In a society in which the saloon was conspicuous in almost every community, the prohibitionists focused on local and regional organization and fund raising. Although myriad wet groups also worked in local arenas, the AAPA in particular developed a national campaign and tried to change national images. The nationalizing of the repeal campaign was of great significance. Whereas before Prohibition, cultural values—ethnic parochialism—had been a powerful cultural force resisting Prohibition, by the late 1920s, national symbols had coopted ethnic and even class arguments so that the cultural meaning of drinking and the right to drink took on additional meanings from the national campaign.

Moreover, the AAPA leaders deliberately attempted to utilize the propaganda techniques that had been so successful during World War I, that is, not reasoning with people or changing their values but, by controlling the perceptions that they had, manipulating the ways in which they applied their existing values—making Prohibition, rather than alcoholic beverages and the saloon, appear to encourage crime, for example. Again, the cultural effects resonated for decades afterward. Instead of concentrating on their own organs and publications, the AAPA leaders undertook to use the national mass media in what would later appear to be a remarkably modern—and telling—way.[23]

The AAPA leadership were not just rigidly trying to take the country back to prewar conditions. From the beginning, they conceded that the saloon had to go. The letterhead for some time bore the motto, "Beers and Light Wines NOW; But No Saloons EVER."[24] The saloon keepers were not an economic or cultural group with whom the AAPA powers concerned themselves. Instead, and particularly in their national campaigns, they operated on the more general level of the abstract act of drinking and, by implication, lifestyle.

It is therefore understandable that, to a large extent, the intellectual and symbolic strategy of the repealers was charted not only deliberately in the Du Pont offices but spontaneously and for a long time independently by a determined set of primarily New York intellectuals—not the earnest radicals, who believed that social and economic issues were serious and real, but, rather, other kinds of intellectuals, whose interests were esthetic and narrowly political and whose agitation was directed very largely at styles of living. Many who argued art for art's sake held art—and themselves, like the bootleggers—to be above the law. These repealers' work appeared in *Vanity Fair* and later the *American Mercury* and relatively highbrow humor magazines, and the major device that they used to undermine Prohibition was satire. In that way they avoided any social arguments and instead concentrated on personal values and on symbols, caricaturing as blue-nosed "anti's" the people who were repressively against drinking, sensuality, and art. Such artistic and literary advocates of lifestyle were able from the beginning to use part of the press, and the press in turn increasingly in the 1920s adopted their ideas.[25]

The Media

After Prohibition began, American newspapers and magazines—with only a few exceptions—had continued supporting the law into the 1920s. The exceptions ultimately were of great importance, however, for it was just such organs that drew on the rebellious anti-Prohibition sophisticates so that their work first appeared not only in highbrow magazines but also in influential dailies in New York City and Chicago and in an occasional other large metropolitan center. Of special significance was New York. "The New York press," noted a writer in the New Orleans *Times-Democrat* as early as 1919, "is making itself ridiculous in the extreme to which it has gone in its opposition to the legislation of Congress and the country in the matter of the prohibition of intoxicating liquors."[26]

The domination of New York City journalists particularly meant that the Associated Press played up any material that was unfavorable to Prohibition (and drys at the time counted the other two press services overtly hostile). The wire services thus undermined the avowed editorial stand of the press, which overwhelmingly otherwise continued for several years to be formally favorable to the Eighteenth Amendment. Around 1923–1924, the sophisticates' anti-Prohibition images began rather suddenly to dominate any press presentations of the issue, and after that, the dry side received short shrift in the nationally oriented newspapers and in a growing number of magazines.[27]

Structural changes also contributed to the ways in which the media eventually helped destroy Prohibition. As powerful and wealthy people took an active interest in repeal, they of course, as important advertisers, made editors aware that immediate economic interest might be affected by material sensitive to the repeal issue. (At least fifteen of the twenty-eight directors of General Motors—a corporation controlled by the Du Ponts—chose to become members of the AAPA.) Pierre Du Pont in 1928 was so indiscreet as to try a direct approach to the editor of the very widely read *Saturday Evening Post*, attempting to influence the content of the magazine. Drys had of course employed economic boycotts also, but the national economic clout that they commanded at any time was not comparable with that of the Du Ponts and other businesspeople alarmed by the implications of a successful Eighteenth Amendment.[28]

By the end of the 1920s, it was clear that editors and publishers, of newspapers at least, had another clientele in mind also—namely, the working-class and lower-order masses who were coming into power in the United States. For a big-city newspaper to advocate anti-Prohibition sentiments that fitted in with the lower-order parochialism that had always been aggressively wet was simply good business, for it flattered many lower-order parochials by giving at least some recognition to the values and lifestyles in those cultural enclaves.[29] And because editors perceived the tastes of the new audience to be low tastes, sensationalistic treatment of Prohibition news—invariably negative—also proliferated.

An important structural change of the 1920s, then, was the continued development of sensationalism and the growth of large urban newspapers as they, along with national magazines, increasingly set standards for the entire country. Especially after World War I, with the founding of a notorious new tabloid, the New York *Daily News*, newspaper editors played up the most emotional and distracting material, using illustrations freely. It was in this setting that Prohibition was big news only when it was being defied, not when it was working. Headlines such as "Dry Agent Accused," "Prohibition Graft," "Enforcement Farce," "Drunken Children," and even "Prohibition Failure" appeared consistently in metropolitan newspapers. As the decade progressed, lurid crime news tended increasingly to be associated with bootleggers and bootlegging. Thus was created the great crime-wave myth—a product of ingenious journalists looking for thrilling and simplistic news sensations. In fact, crime in the 1920s was not special, and bootlegging except in a few local circumstances (in which violence was featured by journalists) was largely incidental (as compared, for example, to gambling, which was not incidental). But in the press, it was otherwise. Stories of bootleg liquor and articles associating Prohibition with lawbreakers were so pervasive that the wets received a great boost in their campaign to convince people that 1) Prohibition was a failure and 2) Prohibition created rather than diminished crime.[30]

Magazines, which covered a great range of attitude and audience from the most avant-garde to extremely conservative, were on average somewhat slower than newspapers to swing against Prohibition, although a number of radical and libertarian periodicals were of course consistent critics of the whole idea, mostly from the beginning. Evidence from magazines suggests that at least as far as stereotyped propaganda was concerned, ordinary opinion leaders in general were not in the forefront of repeal propaganda. New York journalists and cultural rebels, who reinforced each other's wet sentiments, were.[31]

Moreover, and most significantly, writers and artists attacking Prohibition in the magazines displayed the most transparent—and ultimately successful—attempts to act as arbiters of social standards. They portrayed themselves as the nondeviant majority and the bearers of civilization—exactly the tone that other magazine writers of previous generations, with very different sentiments, had taken. So H. L. Mencken's technique, for instance, was to speak as if he were the most civilized person on earth and flatter his readers that they shared the civilized view that old-fashioned conventional standards and prejudices were ridiculous and, indeed, amusing. On one occasion, Mencken wrote:

> It was among country Methodists, practitioners of a theology degraded to the level of voodooism, that Prohibition was invented, and it was by country Methodists, nine-tenths of them actual followers of the plow, that it was fastened upon the rest of us. . . . What lies under it, and under all the other crazy enactments of its category, is no more and no less than the yokel's congenital and incurable hatred of the city man—his simian rage against everyone who, as he sees it, is having a better time than he is.[32]

Another influential arena in which such ideas were spread and even popularized was advanced fiction. In contrast to Jack London, who in 1913 criticized the effects of drinking in his famous *John Barleycorn*, F. Scott Fitzgerald in his novels pictured drinking as a great adventure, an activity that had particular effectiveness in enhancing subjective awareness and social activity. In Ernest Hemingway's novel about the 1920s "lost generation," *The Sun Also Rises* (1926), alcoholic beverages are mentioned on well over half of the pages in the book.[33]

In the meantime, writers and artists of all varieties had had a substantial effect on the increasingly important new medium, motion pictures. The motion picture industry exploited sensationalism in exactly the same way that journalists did, providing vivid images of the connection between crime and Prohibition and portraying violation of the Volstead Act as a large part of a sophisticated lifestyle. The plot of the first all-talking motion picture, *Lights of New York* (1928), revolved around bootleg whiskey. A 1930 survey of motion pictures showed that drinking played a part in four-fifths of all films. Clarence Brown, an M-G-M director, was quoted in 1933 saying,

> We took the position that motion pictures should depict and reflect American life, and cocktail parties and speakeasies were definitely a part of that life. We were able to prevail to a large extent, and I believe that it was the motion picture, showing that in spite of prohibition, liquor was an immense factor in American life, that had a great deal to do with changing sentiment on the question.[34]

Brown clearly believed that he, as wise as Mencken, knew from his own social circles what was normative, that is, nondeviant, in "American life," and, like Mencken, he was assuming a new authority to replace that of the respectables who had theretofore defined the normative.

The motion pictures had begun as decidedly unrespectable influences but before World War I had fallen into the hands of reformers. After about 1915, however, moviemakers, as in the Mack Sennett comedies, satirized goody-goody values and moral earnestness in general; their heroes and heroines gave in to temptation seductively portrayed on the screen. Temperance films almost disappeared in the 1920s, and in their place, filmmakers produced for their growing audiences pictures that in both content and symbolism favored drinking. When regulations were finally set up that discouraged actually portraying an actor's taking a drink, moviemakers devised teasing portrayals, even what sociologist Robin Room characterizes as "a pornography of drinking" (the actor, for example, turned his back to the camera—but everyone knew that the character was downing a snort of whiskey). Drinking was communicated as not only an act to accomplish for itself but as a symbol (particularly when women were imbibing) of sexual availability and, indeed, as part of the entire way of life popularized by Fitzgerald in the novel and by innumerable journalists who wanted to hobnob with the smart set in cabarets and clubs in New York. Room notes that after repeal, in the late 1930s, under a new set of rules, which he characterizes as essentially Roman Catholic, much attention was devoted to avoiding overtly sexual actions in films, but restrictions on drinking were lifted. Taking alcohol was thereafter understood to be conventional rather than deviant/rebellious.[35]

The Cabaret: An Alternative Standard

As the media campaign showed clearly, then, repeal involved both negative attacks on Prohibition and what appears to be a more general positive advocacy of an urban night-life lifestyle. In a most effective way, repealers portrayed sophisticated—and presumably desirable—urban life to be largely lubricated by drinking. The cabaret model had already developed before World War I in New York, when the night-club image of the city was in the making. Indeed, writers in the New York newspapers began paying attention to the enactment process that brought the Eighteenth Amendment only when, in 1919, it appeared that the favorite watering places of the reporters might actually close down and displace them and their friends, many of them from among the self-styled rebellious intellectuals. During Prohibition, Stanley Walker, the city editor of the New York *Herald-Tribune*, for example, contrasted "the honest speakeasy proprietor, who served good food and sound liquor," with the Prohibition lawman's "duplicity . . . bad manners . . . cheapness . . . occasional brutality."[36]

The first years of Prohibition slowed the development of the life of night-club sophistication only briefly. As New York City permitted such establishments to flourish, the night club per se, with alcoholic beverages—legal or illegal—became the definitive symbol of urban sophistication. Harold Ross, editor of the fresh organ of high-toned worldliness of the late 'twenties, the *New Yorker*, boasted that (still at the time of Prohibition) his readers would "be kept apprised of what is going on in the public and semi-public smart gathering places—the clubs, hotels, cafes, supper clubs, cabarets, and other resorts"—which anyone would have understood to have involved drinking.[37]

The journalists and sophisticates, therefore, tried to undermine the law not only by making fun of it but also by stressing the normality of illegal drink. For example, "Bringing bootleg licker in from Canada by aeroplane should be stopped," declared one upscale writer—"The stuff doesn't have time to age properly"—thus turning apparent moral indignation into an assumption that everyone drank liquor—and, it was hoped, with some discrimination.[38] Such advocates were of course assisted by the long-term demographic changes, so that there was an increase in following urban patterns of commercial leisure by larger parts of the population—at the expense of the church ice-cream social. Nevertheless, it was particularly through the media that the idea of the normality of drinking spread.

Inverting Respectability

In the repeal campaign, the big issue other than the supposed failure of Prohibition was not just the normality but the respectability of drinking. In the years just before World War I, business and professional leaders had turned markedly toward a dry standard of personal behavior. At the end of the nineteenth century in the Midwest, college students—presumably sensitive to cultural cues—were overwhelmingly dry in sentiment, and in 1917, even the national interfraternity conference resolved that intoxicants be banished from chapter houses and functions at colleges all around the country.[39]

Repealers, and particularly the Du Pont propagandists, attempted to convince middle-class people particularly that, bohemians aside, unmistakably respectable folks drank as a normal part of life. The success of the idea of respectable drinking was perhaps the most remarkable aspect of the propaganda campaign. The AAPA leaders mobilized women, and especially "society" leaders, with particular effect to show that even the putative guardians of respectability, ladies of high social status, thought that advocating the production and use of alcoholic beverages—or at least being part of the drinking smart set—was acceptable. Both sides set much store by this symbolic marshaling of the forces of "respectability."[40]

Underlying Negativism

Despite the repealers' quest for respectability, the underlying negative nature of their campaign appeared clearly in their symbolism. As the wet propagandists worked to deprive dry leaders of their moral authority, ridicule was particularly effective. In a nation increasingly beguiled by urban sophistication and consumer institutions, wets such as Mencken could be convincing when they portrayed the pro-Prohibition forces as bigoted, self-righteous, rural provincials (again, the exact opposite of most actual pre-World War I reformers who advocated Prohibition). In this case, a visible image, that of the blue-nosed, busybody Puritan, which had been a stereotype used occasionally for generations, became the relentlessly repeated cartoon embodiment of dry sentiment. Such a figure was, of course, made so unattractive that he or she was not someone with whom a viewer would want to identify—the symbol of a strong negative reference group. And so, once again, it was the drys who increasingly appeared to be deviant while the wets appeared in the media as reasonable and tolerant members of a majority, indeed, a bandwagon majority.[41]

The Puritan figure, although used primarily in the anti-Prohibition campaign, in fact stood for the whole attitude toward life that ultimately came to be characterized as oppressive middle-class morality. The figure was ambiguously a male clergyman and a pinched old maid, "Aunty Everything" (anti-everything). By 1920, the Puritan figure already embodied a set of characteristics that rebellious litterateurs were confusing with philistinism and, above all, with fanaticism (of crucial importance since the repealers were emphasizing their own moderation). "Philistinism, Harsh restraint, Beauty-hating, Stout-faced fanaticism, Supreme hypocrisy, Canting, Demonology, Enmity to true art, Intellectual tyranny, Grape juice, Grisley sermons, Religious persecution, Sullenness, Ill-temper, Stinginess, Bigotry, Conceit, Bombast" was Charles Beard's contemporary inventory of the stereotype that started with the rebellious intellectuals and flourished in the cartoons. Indeed, the Puritan stereotype itself changed in the cartoons over the years and helps suggest what was happening: the bluenose evolved eventually in the late 'twenties into a criminal or a bedraggled failure.[42] Altogether, getting people to rally against "anti's" was an important factor in attracting to the wet leadership other elements in the constellation of the minor vices. The wets took the offensive, advocating not the saloon but a vague alternative: moderate or even temperate—but of course stylish—use of alcohol. Prohibition, they claimed, was extreme and, like other extreme—deviant—behavior, a source of disorder and lack of respect for the law, so again turning the tables on the drys.[43]

Still another strategy of inverting the labeling of respectability came in the course of the venerable appeal to personal liberty. The original argument in principle against various aspects of Prohibition was that it infringed on the imagined personal liberty of a person to drink whatever he or she chose, and this argument set advocates of liberty against those who wished to use coercion to fight social ills. The pre-World War I reformers had in general used a variety of coercions and educational devices to try to bring about a better social environment. At that time, personal-liberty advocates opposed most social coercion, and when Prohibition came, it was such strong libertarians who joined with Stayton in the AAPA. Moreover, their concern was, as the enemies of Prohibition put it, "prohibitory laws" in general. In their hidden agendas, the real fear was compulsory social uplift of any kind.[44] Included was the fear on the part of businesspeople that Prohibition would set a dangerous precedent in destroying a business for social reasons.

Personal-liberty arguments, therefore, came to embody more than just the right to indulge private habits without regard for possible social consequences. Although many of them had alternative social models in mind, the repealers were consistently negative and destructive, whether talking about personal liberty or repressive Puritanism or a defiant sophistication. This negativism also appeared in campaigns against other restraints, as in the case of restraints on sexual misbehavior. One satirist, for example, foretold that within ten years, Prohibition would go so far that under the "Eighty-Seventh Amendment," movies would be forbidden, and later, he fantasized, so many types of actions would be prohibited that everyone would have to have prescriptions for alcohol to counter the hardness of life. So, in this way, the world would return to "normal," that is, drinking.[45] Some contemporaries even saw in the anti-Prohibition efforts a negativism so pervasive as to include advocacy of nullification of the law. The repealers, in short, were engaged in a full-scale assault upon not only standards of restraint but also aspects of society that upheld standards—all in the name of new fashions, as opposed to the older respectability.

With all these symbolic forces in place in the 1920s, the end of Prohibition came easily. Because the repealers were negative and offered no positive program that might have been divisive, it was easier to get them to work together and provide a vague alternative that raised little specific criticism in the rapidly changing political circumstances of the late 1920s and early 1930s. The pre-World War I brewers and distillers, at last united by the common goal of repeal, poured large amounts of money into action and agitation groups. The large number of their public organizations (at one point in the early 1920s more than forty) suggests that a great deal of money was involved. These business interests also made funds available to the AAPA, but for some years the AAPA refused such donations (unless suitably laundered) and then for a time restricted them to a fraction of the budget (obviously more was available). Meanwhile the advocates of "personal liberty" were at work in other formal organizations.[46]

Over the years, the opponents of Prohibition thus reinforced one another and in turn pulled in those representing more general cultural trends. As many journalists started out reacting against censorship, for example, so they brought an anti-government as well as aesthetic element along as they were taken into the personal-liberty campaign against Prohibition. In fact, sophistication came to include all the elements of the constellation of minor vices in one form or another. The journalist/smart set attack on Prohibition began as just a part of a general attack on prudery and blue laws of all kinds. Moreover, their activities took some time to reach the mass media. The targets of the "Sabbatarians and Comstockians" included not just alcohol but tobacco, obscenity/immodesty, Sunday secular activities, and certain types of entertainment, especially racing and poolroom activity—in short, the usual constellation. Conversely, the sophisticates who attacked the "Sabbatarians and Comstockians" favored such activities.[47] Regardless of elements of value or cultural conflict, the fact remains that the whole constellation was involved. The AAPA and other forces took sides and could not isolate themselves or their single issue as long as that issue was part of the constellation. Perhaps they did not want to.

Gathering in Other Forces

It may be that the profit motive of the controllers of the new mass media who pandered to sensationalism and lower-order taste would have succeeded without the AAPA campaign to destroy the credibility of traditional respectability in the backwash of World War I. But by drawing all the forces of the minor vices together, the anti-Prohibition campaign hastened the change in standards in a revolutionary way. An example may suggest the effectiveness of the campaign.

One of the elements in the traditional constellation of bad habits was the use of tobacco. As will be explained in Chapter 4, on smoking, despite the association of smoking and drinking, the "tobacco men" who dominated the trade considered themselves very respectable, and they aspired fervently to even more respectability. For some years early in the twentieth century, they faced growing opposition because of the introduction of cigarettes into the mass market. Indeed, beginning in the 1890s, there was a cigarette prohibition movement that succeeded in getting cigarettes (not other forms of tobacco) outlawed in a number of states for several years. Traditional tobacco men, who were interested primarily in manly cigars and pipes, were not necessarily unsympathetic to anti-cigarette sentiment. They showed surprisingly little alarm in the face of the anti-tobacco forces and even less regarding alcoholic-beverage prohibition. Indeed, they anticipated replacing the saloons to some extent, and many believed that a dry community might not be bad for cigar merchants. As for the fanatical anti-tobacco agitators, tobacco men really could not see themselves put into the same antisocial group with the alcoholic-beverage vendors. After all, wrote one journalist in 1919, "Who ever heard of a man committing murder or rape or felonious assault while under the influence of—tobacco? . . . Who ever saw a man so much a slave to tobacco that if he smoked three cigarettes in succession he was sure to go home—if at all—reeling, befuddled imbecile because he could not control his appetite and stop smoking?"[48]

Eventually, as cigarettes became more important in the trade, there was some apprehension and some sentiment for joining the repealers, but for some time, tobacco traders in general held back from allying with the pro-alcohol forces. Then as the anti-Prohibitionists began to gain control of the media, tobacco spokespersons converted. That they were coopted by the wet campaign is evident from the fact that there suddenly showed up in the tobacco trade papers telltale "personal liberty" arguments as well as accounts paralleling tobacco with alcohol prohibition, a parallel that only shortly before had been rejected by tobacco writers. By 1928 one writer could say that smoking was secure from the anti's, "and it is doubtful whether we shall ever see a tobacco speakeasy. . . . The cigarette is too firmly entrenched in the hearts of smokers for us to fear its prohibition."[49]

The major sign of the alliance of tobacco with alcoholic beverages, however, was the campaign in which cigarette advertisers had begun to portray women as smokers—unthinkable a few years earlier—and had joined the other repeal advocates in working for the self-indulgent standard that later would be called the consumer society. "In seeking alliance" against tobacco prohibitionists, wrote one tobacco man as early as 1919, "let the tobacco trade align itself with producers and handlers of so called luxuries such as coffee, tea, candy, chewing gum, trinkets and fancy dress."[50] But it turned out that the alcoholic-beverage advocates were successful in coopting the whole lot, including tobacco.

The Aftermath of Prohibition

In terms of drinking, Prohibition, even though it ended in 1933, was not an isolated historical incident. For many years after repeal, Americans drank much less per capita than before, which was a major lasting effect. Once wiped out, the old saloons in fact did not return. Some state governments reduced the influence of wholesalers and package retailers by taking over that part of the business. Reduction in the physical and institutional influence of drinking therefore was a continuing effect of Prohibition that repeal did not cut off. Nevertheless, the campaign for repeal did have the more profound effect of inverting many general values.

The changed standards were embodied in new ideals and heroes that came in during the 1920s and 1930s. As suggested above, the most obvious and most frequently commented upon new social model was the urbane sophisticate and even artist-bohemian—as opposed to the rural and provincial righteous type. Americans became familiar with the smart-set ideal as first the chic, and then the mass, media glorified the artist who was individualistic and took liberties with convention—indeed, defied convention. This figure merged then into the conventional consumer who did glamorous things imitating glamorous people in the media, who, as in the movies, drank and smoked and carried out other more or less naughty and defiant actions. The leading advertising agencies produced copy that pictured celebrities and obvious high-society figures lending desirability and mystique to the use of some product. It was no accident that the Du Pont publicists of the AAPA contemporary with those advertisers used the same technique to popularize alcohol and repeal, with the same implied appeal to consumerism and rebelliousness and to achieving social status through buying and consuming—the lifestyle. Indeed, Malcolm Cowley in his famous autobiographical account of the avant-garde of the 1920s spoke explicitly about the way in which self-expression, paganism, living only for the moment, and other goals in the fairly consistent program of the avant-garde intellectuals meshed with opposition to Prohibition and with what he called "the consumption ethic" that was flowering at that time.[51]

Beyond the sophisticate, another type of hero surfaced in the 1920s who served both sensationalistic media controllers and those interested in repealing the Eighteenth Amendment: the gangster.[52] The gangster combined rebellion against respectability with three attributes: he was individualistic (no laws or restraints other than his own feelings limited his behavior); he was the ultimate business entrepreneur (even defying governments to pursue commercial activities); and he was supermasculine in a way that appealed to all classes but embodied lower-order standards as they were then understood. Unlike earlier outlaw heroes, the gangster provided society with illegal services. His interest was personal profits rather than the overthrow of the existing formal system, and in that context his bravery and tough individuality did not endanger most other social arrangements.

In some ways, it was a harmless model. In a cartoon of 1929, an obviously respectable mother tells a clerk in a store, "My little boy wants to see an Al Capone outfit."[53]

The closely related tough-guy hero of the novels and motion pictures of the 1920s and 1930s was also often defiant of the law and of convention and propriety. Although the positively toned term "tough guy" came in only in the mid 'twenties, the stereotype drew on old American traditions, including the virility ideal of the earlier period of reform—as embodied in Theodore Roosevelt. The new American tough, however, as indicated by the bootlegger and gangster who were glorified in the media, took on a positive tone in part as a social leveler. Businesspeople and politicians who were tough won admiration in media presentations—and they never lost the implication that their toughness represented lower-order defiance of conventions, including conventions of decency. As early as 1918, in the shadow of World War I, Mencken tied the sophisticates' opposition to Prohibition directly to this tradition. The drinker, he wrote, "does the hard and dangerous work of the world. He takes the chances, he makes the experiments. He is the soldier, the artist, the experimenter." Clearly, toughness was useful to the repealers precisely because it licensed social irresponsibility and played up individual willfulness. Indeed, the amoral variety of the tough guy became markedly more prominent in the media in the 1920s. Furthermore, this stereotype and the association of drinking with it dominated the mass media into the late twentieth century so that depiction of admirable and instrumental alcohol consumption in the entertainment media was a permanent legacy of the victory of the wets in the repeal struggle.[54]

Why Did They Do It?

Those who put so much effort into repealing Prohibition were therefore involved in a great deal more than passage of the Twenty-First Amendment in 1933. They used the restoration of alcoholic-beverage sale and manufacture ever after as a self-evident justification for what they did. Moreover, legalizing the alcoholic-beverage trade appeared consistently as justification and symbol in discussions of legalizing gambling, drugs, prostitution, and pornography.

The agents of the whole multifarious set of changes that operated to bring about repeal became involved in ways that help elucidate and confirm the nature of the historical currents that prevailed. For their part, the lower-order parochials continued transparently to show resentment of any change from their standards. They welcomed the gangster heroes and sensationalistic journalism that catered to the belief that pretentious respectable people were flawed and hostile figures. Indeed, in 1919, the newspapers carried stories of threatened working-class strikes and riots protesting the destruction of the alcoholic-beverage trade. The slogan was to be "No Beer, No Work."[55] Many Americans from underworld and oppressed groups also obviously welcomed the open expression of the idea that those who abhorred lower-order standards were not a majority or their legislation legitimate. The anti-Puritan stereotype embodied a strong appeal to class prejudice.

The very wealthy (not middle-class) figures who effectively led the fight against Prohibition and against respectability resented the morality of the Methodists and Baptists and reformer professionals who had dominated those important aspects of American life in which middle-class standards had been set. Many of the new rich, especially, were frustrated in not being able to meet the "Puritan" demands that would have conferred on them petit-bourgeois respectability (recalling, for example, the prejudicial provision of the late-nineteenth-century Knights of Labor that anyone could join the Knights except bankers and saloon keepers).[56]

Moreover, the rich, as already suggested, were not above the motive of the simple, unprincipled love of money—as in the appeal that ending Prohibition would bring in tax money and so relieve property holders of some of their burden. If Prohibition were repealed, argued Pierre Du Pont in a radio talk in 1932, "the income tax would not be necessary in the future, and half of the revenue required for the budget . . . would be furnished by the tax on liquor alone."[57]

Such motives certainly fitted, to name the prime example, Pierre Du Pont himself, who reacted with alarm to what he saw as populistic threats to control his fortune and business. Prohibition appeared to members of the Du Pont family to be an entering wedge for Bolshevism. Various self-righteous Americans had made cruel, if often accurate, remarks about the Du Ponts as munitions makers and war profiteers. It was no accident that many such self-righteous people were also drys (such as Senator George W. Norris). Probably unaware of this aspect of his bias (he became active only after the mass media had shifted against Prohibition in the mid 'twenties), Pierre Du Pont as a repealer devoted a substantial part of his life to rendering socially ineffective the drys who had denied him full respectability. In the process, he was able to change their public image from that of definers of respectability to deviant fanatics, while "moderates," such as Du Pont pictured himself, could now set standards. The new standards, however, came to include a great deal more than moderate drinking.[58] Indeed, by their negative attacks on the old respectables, the repealers destroyed the legitimacy of moderation as a traditional virtue. Instead, it became a mask for a step toward full repeal and toward a society with no restraint on behavior.

Nothing demonstrated the importance of the Prohibition-repeal campaign as a turning point and effective symbol as did the changes in advertising. Before World War I, the advertising for alcoholic beverages, although advanced for the time, was very restrained and did not appear in many publications. In a 1908 ad for Schlitz beer, for example, the ad copy emphasized the healthfulness of the product, and a picture showed a man and woman clearly of very high social class in a probably romantic outdoor setting. Even there, it was unclear whether or not the lady was indulging. Already in October 1933, however, Pabst beer was running ads showing both an older and a younger woman drinking beer, albeit in a family setting. As early as December 1933, a magazine ad for cognac showed both a man and a woman drinking—the man in tails and the woman in a formal gown. And this idea of respectable and even upper-class behavior extended to other advertising as well. A November 1933 ad for toothpaste showed a hostess and maid with a dining table clearly set up for multiple alcoholic beverages. A year later, a food manufacturer was telling hostesses that "a canape of deviled ham makes *any* cocktail taste better." As the 1930s progressed, the upper-class stereotype in advertising increasingly came to include alcoholic-beverage consumption. The fact that after 1933 such ads eventually appeared in standard women's magazines underlines the impact of repeal, for such a thing would have been impossible fifteen years earlier. But of course by the 1930s, respectability had been turned upside down.[59]

Many scholars have pictured such changes as more or less self-determined events in various social groupings.[60] What they have not taken into account is the way in which the pursuit of profits interacted with cultural conflict. The forces of respectability, which had managed for generations to keep more or less within bounds the constant human tendency to indulge in the constellation of minor vices, were giving way. Particularly in the 1920s, what dominant middle-class people had believed was a whole social stability was being overturned by the rise of a self-indulgent consumer culture. So much is evident. But beyond that, the consumer culture operating on a mass scale made lower-order parochialism into a dynamic factor, especially when manipulated by predatory businesspeople. At that point, as I shall show in parallel narratives of all the minor vices, proponents of each one, pushed by greed and parochialism, became effective historical forces.

The change was epitomized in an ad for Spud cigarettes that appeared in 1930. A man and a woman, both dressed in the usual upper-class way, are being served hors d'oeuvres by a servant. Both are smoking, and the woman is drinking what is obviously a cocktail, probably a martini. The ad copy reads in part: "These charming people! Always so casually, yet so successfully pioneering in the realm of enjoyment. . . . Their trained senses were first to find that cooler smoke transforms tobacco enjoyment into enjoyment unburdened by limitation, or even moderation. . . ."[61] Three years before repeal, the advertisers knew well what standards the mass media could project in repeal propaganda that was pitched to the new consumer culture. Enjoyment unburdened by limitation or moderation represented the fresh set of dominant values.

The repeal struggles took place, then, in the midst of substantial social conflict. The artistic distaste for restraint was just beginning to interact with the cabaret ideal, with underworld interest, and with lower-order parochialism, particularly as it expanded in the World War I experience. Before the struggles were over, economic interest had enabled well-financed, organized groups, using the media, to challenge many conventional respectabilities and begin to turn them upside down. There was no halfway stopping point for moderate indulgence. Instead, moderation became not a virtue but a propaganda tool moving American society—in ways unanticipated by most repealers—toward the lifting of restraints on behavior.

In the 1920s and 1930s, the full force of the various attractive vices was still not developed, nor, despite the leadership of those interested in alcohol, had the forces all converged. Each of the elements in the constellation had an independent existence, conditioned by a history in some ways unique but, in other, and telling, ways, parallel to events in Americans' encounters with alcohol. But the symbolic action of repeal in 1933 left none untouched, and in each case the advocates were spurred in their quest for an unrestrained society freed from old-fashioned, conventional respectability.

The legislative repeal of Prohibition was therefore of double importance: it changed institutions, and it provided a public statement of what American standards of behavior were. In a few short years, the repealers had achieved a stunning public victory. Afterward, they declared the victory not one of economic issues or issues confused by propaganda, such as the issue of crime, but one of standards. Eventually most Americans followed suit in viewing repeal as a symbol of a change in standards.

But the negative nature of the victory was also of great significance, connoting change in the way in which implicit contractual arrangements constrain behavior. As Patricia Helsing observed in 1976 concerning a similar debate about legalizing gambling,

> A government that is willing to legalize some forms of gambling is in effect nullifying any moral, ethical, social or economic censure that may have been implied or stated prior to legalization. Once these restraints are removed, the public may be justified in its refusal to acknowledge the harm in other forms of gambling that have not received the official stamp of approval.[62]

Repealing Prohibition, in the context of the repealers' negativism, signified the repeal of many implicit contracts concerning behavior. That was the ultimate meaning of the goal of the forces of the minor vices: action without restraint, not only the restraints of explicit law but even informal social restraints.

CHAPTER THREE

Drinking

From the time of the first English settlements in America, drinking had been a traditional and accepted custom. Only as critics appeared in the early nineteenth century did it become possible to begin to identify certain groups as proponents of alcoholic-beverage production and consumption. Those working for temperance, rather than against it, have so far attracted almost all the attention. Writing in 1982 on the early history of temperance and prohibition in Massachusetts, Robert L. Hampel noted that "no work has ever examined the enemies of temperance—the anti-prohibitionists, the sellers, and the drunkards." Although it is true that most historians of the subject have concentrated on attempts to regulate and abolish alcoholic beverages, nevertheless there are in fact historical works on drinking as such, on manufacturers (but not wholesalers), on the Association Against the Prohibition Amendment, and even on aspects of alcoholic-beverage retailing. But advocates of drinking have not attracted serious historical attention, certainly not in a way sufficiently articulated to reveal the social impact of those opponents of temperance.[1]

The alcoholic-beverage business, both before and after Prohibition, influenced deeply the ways in which Americans used their leisure time and socialized with one another. As the commerce in such beverages developed, advocates of drinking built up an intimidating momentum and became ever more aggressive in pressing their viewpoint. In the course of expanding and defending their enterprises, even before the 1920s, pro-alcohol forces developed standard tactics to neutralize opponents. They pointed out as models prominent citizens who indulged. Supporters of drinking painted an unfavorable picture of prohibitory laws—just as they did again in the repeal efforts of the 1920s. And in the era of mass media, advocates also moved their campaigns into advertising. After 1933, especially, alcoholic-beverage vendors and their allies emphasized not only lifestyle advertising but also what might be designated a psychiatric approach to alcoholism and other problems connected with drink: any difficulties were all individual, not social, problems.

The tone and approach of alcohol advocacy had not always been negative and destructive. The negative element originated in the nineteenth century and grew parallel to both the temperance movement and the alcoholic-beverage business. And only in the late twentieth century did the negativism work itself out into an often open championing of total unrestraint. But by that time the commercial aspects of alcoholic-beverage merchandising had become gargantuan and had given special form to what had once been just an anti-temperance stand.

The Ubiquity of Hard Drinking in Early America

Records indicate that early Americans consumed an extraordinary amount of alcohol, especially in the decades after the American Revolution. Pioneer settlers had brought from England conventions and attitudes that held drinking various kinds of alcoholic beverages to be an ordinary, unremarkable action. Indeed, people viewed them as beneficial substances, good for the health. Moreover, until at least the mid nineteenth century, tea and coffee were more expensive than distilled beverages. If a person did drink too much, some rowdiness might develop, but Americans usually did not expect crime or violence to ensue, and this expectation had substantial social effects. Traditional sermons, both a means and a sign of social control, condemned intemperate drinking, as did, sometimes, local laws. And it is true that the proliferation of public-house drinking and a degree of associated antisocial behavior where they were living was a major factor in driving the Puritans away from England. But for many years, the use of intoxicants was not a serious threat in the colonies, because in the deferential society of that day, everyone was relatively easily controlled by the community. Drinking occurred not only at home each day but on all public festive occasions. A few taverns existed for travelers, and some members of the community gathered in such places to drink and socialize. For some time, however, most tavern keepers were allied with the controlling elements of the community even as the number of drinking places increased.[2]

Although high license fees usually guaranteed that only responsible citizens ran public drinking places, from the beginning, such institutions were a source of trouble, and the more so as time went on. Hardly anyone commented on the large amount of drinking that took place in private, but public drinking, either in taverns or on occasions such as election and muster days, caused many citizens concern. Various legislatures passed laws to try to curb unseemly proceedings. In 1751, a Virginia clergyman asserted that taverns

> are become the common Receptable and Rendezvous of the very Dreggs of the People; even of the most lazy and dissolute . . . where prohibited and unlawful Games . . . are . . . practiced, almost without any Intermission; namely Cards, Dice, Horse-racing, and Cock-fighting, together with Vices and Enormities of every other Kind and where . . . Drunkenness, Swearing, Cursing, Perjury, Blasphemy, Cheating, Lying, and Fighting, are . . . permitted with Impunity . . . as though . . . those Houses were enfranchised with unlimited Privileges; and neither subject to the Laws of Man, nor yet to the Inspection and Authority of God himself.

This chronic concern with the connection between alcoholic-beverage drinking and public spaces—such as the community tavern that attracted (chiefly male) people with time to kill—was a continuing feature of the history of drinking in American society.[3]

Before independence, but particularly in the decades after the American Revolution, an increase in the availability of distilled beverages—and a consequent decline in price—put strong drink within easy reach of working people. Gradually whiskey replaced rum. By 1830, the average American adult was drinking about 7 gallons of absolute alcohol per year (the 1970s figure was about 2.7 gallons). These hardy Americans drank chiefly hard cider and whiskey; whiskey accounted for over 60 per cent. This enormous rate of consumption joined with other changes to make the United States what William J. Rorabaugh calls "the alcoholic republic." An eyewitness, Ohio lawyer Darius Lyman, described the situation in 1830:

Public sentiment sustained individuals, in taking the daily dram and passing round the social glass; it went further it obstinately demand[ed] and required that people should do so; it exercised an inquisitorial search and required that every man should have his bottle in his cupboard; it was deemed necessary to sustain health good manners and hospitality. The Brewery Bottle and the Whiskey Jar were house hold gods in every family: and every member of every family were scrupulous in paying their devotions to them.

The fact that members of the controlling classes not only drank extraordinarily heavily themselves but also often profited from the trade made any change very difficult.[4]

The Rise of Commercial and Cultural Interests

The saloon rose in importance in the nineteenth century as the workplace became more formal and the casual mixing of work and recreation, including drinking and socializing on the job, receded before the forces of organization and factory discipline. In the saloons, activities were freed from the workplace discipline. There reciprocal "treating" underlined the social function of the retail drinking establishment and set the stage for the rise of antisocial forces and a struggle for control of leisure activities. Increasingly, the saloon became a main leisure-time space, particularly for the poorer workers and especially young urban males living in crowded boardinghouses. Moreover, newly arrived immigrants from Europe purchased alcoholic beverages as they purchased meat. In the Old Country, both were too expensive for humble folk. Both were relatively cheap in America.[5]

As transportation altered the grain market in the early nineteenth century, the price of whiskey (at times as low as 25 cents a gallon in the trans-Appalachian West) rose, and instead of myriad small distilleries throughout the agricultural regions, producers began to be concentrated in relatively few areas and firms. In 1825, there were 1,129 distillers licensed in New York State; in 1860, only 77.[6] Thus even though self-control, social control, and economics in a modernizing and urbanizing society ultimately began to restrain drinking in the United States, an increasingly concentrated business had an interest in maintaining and adding to the consumption of alcohol. Moreover, other factors transformed the traditional taverns into liquor-by-the-glass institutions, the owners of which had unusual motivation to get anyone and everyone to drink, especially after travelers, who had for generations helped sustain the taverns, began to bypass the inns and go by steamboat and train. By the 1830s in Massachusetts, both grocers and distillers in Boston were arguing that any legislation restrictive of alcoholic-beverage retailing was undesirable and anyway improper because it restricted their property rights to sell what they pleased.[7]

In nineteenth-century America, as middle-class evangelicals actually wielded power, they allied with other middle-class people who were concerned about public order, the work ethic, and national morals. Moreover, citizens of varied backgrounds were profoundly moved by the tangible damage that drink did to individual people and members of their families. Temperance movements thereupon developed that threatened both customary drinking and profits of the alcoholic-beverage trade. This clash between wets and drys was complicated when large numbers of working-class Irish and also largely middle-class Germans were added to the population in the 1840s and after. These new ethnic groups came from heavy-drinking cultures and resisted temperance movements. They therefore brought a powerful additional element of cultural clash into the drink question. These groups further confused the temperance issue with religious and school issues so that at times Roman Catholic churches lined up on the side of alcoholic-beverage dispensers because of the cultural questions in which all were entangled.[8] It was in this complicated context that the temperance movement goaded into the open the forces that alcoholic beverages engendered in American society—at least to the extent that the beverage supply and the suppliers' profits were threatened.

By the mid nineteenth century, then, as the United States became a more urban and commercial society, the stage was set for persons who promoted drinking to have major social impact. For one thing, the dominant drinking patterns tended to change early in the century from the daily drams taken at home to group binges, often in public spaces, and even solo binges, again often in public spaces.[9] As the drinking establishment more and more dominated the public spaces in which alcohol consumption occurred, the commercial interests involved in the saloons and taverns grew in number and influence, joining the producers in exerting powerful influences on the community and region and, finally, the whole society. Eventually a stable set of social alignments evolved, and the economic networks gathered allies from three important groups, all of whom tended to consider alcohol part of normal existence. The first were lower-order drinkers who were not touched by the middle-class concerns about sobriety, work, order, and evangelism. The second were high upper-class figures who considered temperance vulgar and drinking part of upper-class life—or who based their stand for alcohol on the political issue of personal freedom, particularly the freedom of the upper classes to do as they pleased. Finally, there were the cultural groups—particularly, numerically important Irish and German ethnics—in which patterns of alcohol consumption cut across class lines and provided important elements of group cohesion.[10]

During the last half of the nineteenth century, then, alcoholic-beverage producers, merchandisers, and consumers struggled against legal restrictions and moral suasion. *The Western Brewer* began in 1875 with a pledge to "preach the gospel of BEER, . . . against the Gospel of Puritanism, of Prohibition, of Personal Thralldom." Suppliers, particularly bottlers, also brought economic and social pressure to bear in support of the business— as of course did some labor groups directly affected. The brewers grew in numbers and influence. While the distillers did not grow proportionately, they survived numerous prohibition campaigns and even joined in one of the great national trusts of the 1890s in an attempt to stabilize overproduction. Altogether, alcoholic-beverage businesspeople, including the seldom-studied wholesalers, exercised a great deal of power in formal institutions on both the regional and national levels. In Virginia in the 1870s, for example, retail vendors could serve at any hour of the day or night and had also managed repeal of previous prohibitions against selling to drunks, incompetents, and students.[11]

In addition to their simple political maneuvering, traders worked to undermine any state and local anti-alcohol laws by furnishing beverages from outside the locality to colluding consumers and by crippling enforcement in various ways, legal, political, and illegal. Drys found that their opponents had large sums of money available from beverage businesspeople. Immediately after the very first women's crusade began in southern Ohio, targeting the business of drink and closing many of the saloons, the wholesale liquor dealers of Cincinnati furnished a young Irishman with five thousand dollars to go to the commercial center of the agitated district, Washington Court House, and open a saloon. Moreover, the alcoholic-beverage interests could stir up mobs of lower-order allies who abused and attacked temperance workers who were campaigning or attempting to use moral means to get drinkers to sign the pledge or saloon keepers to close their dram shops. In 1886, for example, a pro-drink crowd in Sioux City, Iowa, killed a Methodist minister who had led a campaign to enforce a dry ordinance there; a brewer had earlier offered a reward for the temperance agitator's death at a meeting of local saloon keepers.[12]

The political actions of the alcoholic-beverage traders reflected their general cultural goal: to have a society sufficiently without restraint as to be open to more or less unlimited marketing of alcohol. The president of the United States Brewers' Association, Hermann B. Scharmann, in 1884 stated the aim of the group plainly: "This Association contends, and always shall maintain, that society has no right to deny the use of intoxicants, or, indeed, to prevent by laws the abuse of them"—although he of course tempered his words by going on to favor moral suasion, which would of course be of limited effectiveness "in an imperfect state of society." Later, in 1906, members of the association wanted "to make beer a drink that can be taken in a soda water fountain or anywhere else without subjecting anyone to criticism." A trade publication editor in 1912 pointed out that the evils of the saloon could be alleviated by making the saloon licenses secure: "The saloonkeeper would not violate the law if it were more profitable for him to obey the law than it is to violate it." Clearly what key people in the trade wanted, beginning in the late nineteenth century as the business consolidated and expanded, was profits, without restraint.[13]

In an age of business enterprise in which profit making was honored, unrespectability tended to get pushed onto only parts of the alcoholic-beverage business. Makers of different beverages were often very hostile to one another, and the brewers considered the distillers a social menace except when the two groups had to cling together in opposing anti-liquor laws. The United States Brewers' Association noted in 1866 that "Free indulgence" in whiskey "is the fruitful cause of domestic misery, pauperism, disease and crime. . . . The remedy for national intemperance," they concluded, lay "not in the abolition or disuse of every beverage but cold water, but in the substitution for a hurtful beverage one which is harmless." The brewers assumed that beverage would be beer, which they sometimes portrayed as "liquid bread." But producers of all kinds of alcoholic beverages, and especially wealthy producers and traders, tended to escape at least some social condemnation, while the whole force of that condemnation fell upon the retailers and particularly the saloons—even though manufacturers and distributors were also corrupting politics and the press (at times to the point of bribery). But it was in fact the saloons that were altering the nature of the use of public space as the population was changing rapidly around the turn of the twentieth century.[14]

The Rise of the Saloon

The place of drinking in American society had been undergoing substantial transformation during all of the last half of the nineteenth century. Despite the sobriety movement, and despite especially middle-class revulsion from drunkenness, during the 1850s, enterprise in alcoholic beverages gained in social acceptability. The Civil War experience of significant numbers of soldiers also tended to sanction the use of alcohol in public, and many continued that habit after discharge. Another factor in further promoting alcoholic beverages was the continuing impact of Irish and German immigrants with their very powerful pro-alcohol sentiments. The Germans were spectacularly successful in promoting the use of malted beverages, particularly lager beer. In just a few decades, the amount of alcohol that a statistically average American consumed in hard liquor was replaced by the equivalent amount carried in brewed drinks. Beginning in the late 1880s, as noted earlier, immigrants from southern and eastern Europe, plus a renewed influx from Ireland, also added to variety in drinking habits and to pro-drinking attitudes among population groups that were increasing dramatically in numbers and influence.[15]

This late-nineteenth-century aggregation called into existence the pre-Prohibition saloons that moved so many people to support Prohibition. The brewers, to protect their markets, came to own 70 per cent or more of the retail outlets in the United States and brought great pressure to bear upon saloon keepers to move their goods. The saloon keepers in fact were already in a wildly competitive market in most areas and to a large extent operated marginally, surviving often only by the grace of the financing provided by the brewers. It was under these circumstances that retailers sold indiscriminately to any person or child—with money—and harbored criminal activities that brought in trade.[16]

Alcoholic-beverage businesspeople at all levels understood well how economic forces pushed retailers into unrespectable activity. One dealer in 1912, for example, noted that "we must create the appetite for liquor in the growing boys. . . . Nickels expended in treats to boys now will return in dollars to your tills after the appetite has been formed." In 1906, the editor of *Bar and Buffet* lamented:

> While the saloon has a legal status as well defined as any other business, it is the too general assumption on the part of the saloon man to consider his

own business in the outlaw class, and he accepts that dictum and takes upon himself the odium which is supposed to attach to such outlaw, just for the money that is in it. Few saloon men expect to continue long in the business. They are there to make a stake and retire. In too many cases the means by which the money is made becomes secondary. If it can be made by the infraction of the law, the law will be broken if the penalty can be evaded. That is the mood in which many men engage in the saloon business.

After the repeal of Prohibition, many alcoholic-beverage-industry figures admitted candidly "the abuses which existed prior to Prohibition," as one wholesaler put it.[17]

Many elements in the business advocated cleaning it up, even to the point that they collaborated with drys to get stronger control laws (laws that of course might also reduce the number of licenses and make each one more valuable). The United States Brewers' Association in 1909, for example, devoted much energy at the annual convention to the "Problem of the Saloon—The Clean-Up Movement." At that late date, much of the agitation was defensive. Large alcoholic-beverage associations were spending money to close the worst outlets so as to defuse prohibitionists' arguments.[18]

Economic factors, however, defeated most attempts to clean up the trade. In Chicago, for example, the political power of the saloon keepers prevented enforcement of a measure to limit games in saloons by licensing them. Moreover, when their economic interests were threatened, members of the trade continued openly to defy respectability, to go outlaw and set up an alternative standard. The editors of *Bar and Buffet*, for example, in 1907 started a regular feature, "Church News," containing press reports of all the misbehavior of church people, such as "Immoral Conduct Charged Against Chapman, But the Church Stands by Him," or "Preacher Beats His Child," or "Pastor Forced to Leave City," or "Minister and Girl Disappear"—all in the interest of showing that the drys' organized religion could harbor as much unrespectability as the alcoholic-beverage business.[19]

This tactic of saying that everybody does it—no matter what the "it" was—increasingly marked the technique by which not only advocates of drinking but all the proponents of the minor vices wittingly and unwittingly reversed standards in the United States.

Class and Ethnicity

There was a second element that reinforced the active resistance of members of the alcoholic-beverage trade to respectability: not only the increasing presence in the United States of ethnic groups but also new aspects of social-class groupings that grew out of an industrializing, urbanizing society. In the slums in the cities, the saloon as public space had obviously become an integral part of life. But that same social function of retail beverage dispensing also appeared anywhere that significant numbers of working-class people gathered, as historians of saloons in the pioneer West have shown. In the cities, the saloons often furnished the meeting place for unions and fraternal groups. In frontier Colorado in 1889, the legislature held official sessions in the White House Saloon in Denver.[20] Under these circumstances, it was difficult for respectables, particularly those in the working class, to avoid at least sometimes taking on the lower-order identity of the saloon patron.

One aspect of lower-order opposition to dry respectability was the power of male culture—the same culture that was nurtured among the drafted troops of the Civil War and World War I and that underlay the tradition of the tough guy. Everyone knew the stereotype of the young male who drank as part of proving his manhood and the vital ritual of one man's taking a drink with another man. Moreover, this tough manliness contained a strong streak of misogyny, which was easily mobilized in the interests of the alcoholic-beverage industry and saloons (as I have already noted happened after World War I), whether in mobs or in sociopolitical pressure. Wet writers, for example, referred to drys as "shriekers" or the "shrieking sisterhood"; real temperance, according to such journalists, required "men—not women—men, sane men, practical men," such as saloon keepers.[21]

When ethnic immigrants, especially the transient laborers of the late nineteenth and early twentieth centuries, brought with them similar traditions and attitudes, they reinforced the ambiguity of humble people's unrespectable, lower-order devotion to the use of alcoholic beverages. The German migrants provided only the most conspicuous example in which considerations of ethnicity far overcame those of social class. This tie was so tangible in the St. Louis German community at the beginning of the twentieth century that Prohibition actually undermined the continued existence of the group because of the extent to which fundamentals of the subculture revolved around alcoholic beverages. Other ethnics, too, utilized group consumption of alcoholic beverages as both symbol and substance of shared social attributes, particularly in public spaces. In Chicago, many turn-of-the-century working-class ethnics routinely gave their children beer; after all, one man remarked, "You can depend on the beer, but you can't tell about the milk you get down here." The temperance and Prohibition movements in the Roman Catholic Church were identified with the Americanization elements in the hierarchy, not with the ultramontane and ethnic elements that were wet and that ultimately won out in the church. In general, many ethnic groups defended alcohol consumption aggressively as a major part of resisting assimilation into non-working-class American culture, particularly where, as in, for example, Polish communities, the traditional belief was that manliness and drinking were closely associated. People of an Italian community in St. Louis, for instance, had had little respect for intrusive laws in the old country and were actually united by their similarly unlawful efforts to defy American Prohibition, which represented standards and authority that were different from those of their subculture and that they did not wish to recognize.[22]

The ethnic issue was complicated by a number of other issues. One was municipal corruption and the conspicuous place of ethnic saloon keepers in it (at one point in the late nineteenth century, one third of Denver's saloon owners had been born in Germany). The confusion between the alcoholic-beverage trade and ethnic politics continued for generations. Moreover, ethnic assimilation into mainstream culture involved patronizing the saloon. Public drinking could therefore constitute lower-order rather than ethnic behavior. Any number of Jewish parents were scandalized when their children began to frequent saloons or work in them, because in the parents' subculture only very light drinking, and that in a private setting, was acceptable. For Jews, therefore, saloons represented not ethnic bastions but assimilation into the American lower orders. Both class and ethnicity, then, undergirded popular support of drinking. And because drinking habits were so markedly a part of personal identity, members of such groups generally ignored the significance of the exploitative commercial nature of alcoholic-beverage distribution.[23]

From Saloon to Cabaret to Night Club

Even before World War I, the alcoholic-beverage business was beginning to move in new directions, directions that would supersede many ethnic pressures but reinforce and expand lower-order influence. To begin with, even though capital increased and the number of firms decreased, distilling was a relatively unhealthy industry as beer increasingly took a larger market share. After 1910, however, the brewers' markets also started to diminish as legislation continued to dry up the country. Finally, the saloon was already on the way out as the chief outlet for alcoholic beverages when the Anti-Saloon League did it in.[24]

From the end of the nineteenth century on, by means of a limited amount of stylish upper-class patronage, alcoholic beverages began to enter into the conspicuous consumption that evolved into the consumer culture. That patronage did not include workers' drinking places. Even in a city such as Denver, the respectable and middle-class people wanted an end to the lower-order saloon. In other cities, ads for stylish suburban real estate included the notation "No saloons."[25] That was one side of the decline of the saloon: most were just too unrespectable to tolerate.

The other side was that early in the twentieth century, the upper-class retail outlets began to change in character, with two results. First, as noted in the previous chapter, the consumption of alcohol was able to take on a stylish connotation connected with the fantasy world of the theater. Second, the social pacesetters eventually tried to move stylish liquor consumption and the fantasy connected with it into the home. All this was prerequisite to ordinary Americans' later coming to imitate upper-class conspicuous consumption, as the humble folk responded to the advertising and mass-media fantasies of the consumer society.

In part the pressure to make drinking respectable came from the large amounts of money that the business brought in. Wealth, no matter how acquired, still tended, over time, to become legitimate. As early as 1898, as a writer in the *Liquor Trades' Review* noted, the bases of respectability were changing:

> It used to be the very proper thing for the 400 to sneer at anyone connected with the liquor trade; this is no longer good form, since the two Ws—whisky and wine—have been made three by the addition of another W—wealth. An Astor has married a London whisky dealer, and a Vanderbilt nephew has become a Parisian wine dealer. More will follow; it is only a question of time when one will be enabled to order a cocktail compounded and dispensed by the enterprising son of a progressive millionaire.

In 1911, American liquor manufacturers alone were netting the huge sum of $1.5 billion each year (substantially more than the national debt at the time). All this wealth helped sanction the social position of people in the business.[26]

The cabaret that became so notorious in uniting drinking with the theater mode in New York was what most effectively legitimated the consumers. The cabaret built on a variety of precedents besides drinking and the theater. One was the upper-class saloon, which could be very elegant indeed, as, for example, the bars of the most prestigious hotels. Another was the tradition of providing entertainment in drinking places. The "concert saloon," for example, was known in Chicago from the 1870s, and dance halls—very often unrespectable—were a problem in pre-World War I urban centers. It was but a small step to the cabaret, in which the model of urban "night life" developed.[27]

Night life came to embody all the elements and aspirations of the new consumer society. At first, urban drinking-entertainment spots broke down the conventional barrier between the stage and the patrons and at the same time permitted members of the upper class to find a semi-public arena in which they could be exclusive but still mix with the theater crowd. Before long, respectable slumming by the upper classes also meant that dancing and intimacy with the entertainers gave entré to mixing with many kinds of people in a cabaret or, as they frequently came to be known, club—that is, night club. In all the settings, the spending, the worship of celebrities, the fantasy of the media and advertising worlds, and the development of feeling and indulgence, all aspects of the growing consumer culture, combined with the image of drinking—to the evident profit of the owners and suppliers.[28]

Thus the New York cabaret came to provide the ultimate image of the night life of the urban elite. But another element also entered in: the bohemians. One of the attractions of night life in cabarets was the chance to mix with not only people of the stage but, as in European cabarets, with the more-or-less tolerated rebels of Greenwich Village who challenged conventional standards (but, because they were segregated in bohemia and were understood to be deviant, did not really endanger the standards of the larger culture).[29] It was in this atmosphere of bohemian challenge and upper-class consumption and fantasy that the New York journalists wrote about drinking and the noble experiment of Prohibition.

Normalizing and Domesticating the Consumption of Alcohol

Prohibition did not slow down the development of the alcohol retailing institution as the ultimate fantasy of consumer culture. Indeed, the club atmosphere of the speakeasy intensified the patrons' sense of self-importance and gratification. The new dance bands and the movies popularized this image, and by the 1930s, the night club had spread all over the country, soon operating legally to associate drinking with gratification, with the idea of new standards of behavior, and with spending money. Some found these establishments of the 1930s to be "snappier, more entertaining, and better served" than the fabulous pre-Prohibition clubs.[30]

One aspect of the growing consumer culture was the use of the act of personal consumption as a symbol or surrogate for the public actions or status denied to most people. Before World War I, most saloons—at best workingmen's public space—were hardly setting a model for consumers. But in those outlets through which a prosperous alcoholic-beverage industry was entering into the consumption world, the very best retailing institutions were impressive and seductive, like other public institutions connected with consumption. At the turn of the century, a young lady of strong dry sentiments went for the first time to an elegant beer garden and after an hour exclaimed, "Isn't it beautiful? Can it be, is it possible, that after all our ideas are wrong and these people are right?"[31] Her experience encapsulated that of respectable people in general in the twentieth century. The department stores, the flagship institutions of consumption fantasy and impulsiveness, were major dispensers of alcoholic beverages, beginning at least in the late 1890s.[32]

By chance, Prohibition intensified greatly the importance of drinking as an act of consumption, beyond the speakeasy club-cabaret image publicized from New York. By increasing the cost of alcoholic beverages, the law made consumption obviously a badge of affluence. Moreover, the wealthy who had laid in a supply of good liquor before transporting it became illegal, continued to be able to use alcohol on whatever occasions they chose to. Thus the cocktail, consumed at home or in the semi-private night club, became a sign of economic distinction. It was unusual before World War I but showed up afterward in the novels of not only F. Scott Fitzgerald and Ernest Hemingway but also Sinclair Lewis and many others. *The Saloon in the Home* was the suggestive title of a lighthearted cocktail-recipe book published in 1930. By the time of repeal, the president of the

United States, Franklin D. Roosevelt, was popularizing the custom of the cocktail hour before dinner—at home (although his martinis were said by friends to be notoriously bad). As early as January 1934, the Biltmore Hotel in New York was advertising a glamorous "Cocktail Hour in the Madison Room of The Biltmore."[33]

Implicitly the repealers advocated private drinking at home or in a night club, exactly the same action that novelists and motion-picture producers of the 1920s and 1930s were portraying with alluring images. As a Golden Wedding Whiskey ad of 1935 put it: "At swank bars and hotels. . . . At the homes of friends. . . . At the busiest liquor stores." And in fact in the years after repeal, sales of alcoholic beverages shifted overwhelmingly away from drinking places to supplies purchased for private consumption.[34]

The marketing symbols of the new age became, then, the cocktail lounge, canned beer (first available in the 1930s), and, eventually, the supermarket (also new in the 1930s). In the continuing revulsion from saloons, off-premises sales looked relatively innocuous to many members of the post-repeal generation. Moreover, drinking at home became increasingly easier and attractive as more and more people owned refrigerators. Finally, packaging beer and other alcoholic beverages in the same way that grocery items were being packaged was an important factor in normalizing the purchase of alcoholic beverages in American life.[35]

After Repeal: Business and Politics as Usual

Early in the 1930s, as the repeal bandwagon gathered momentum, the repealers talked vaguely about "control" of alcohol, a concept virtually unheard of before 1918. The positive program of the wets still was remarkably unsubstantial except that they promised that the saloon would not come back, only a lot of individuals who were drinking—or manufacturing and selling—in some high-toned and glamorous way. But as other reluctant leaders joined the repeal forces, they gave serious consideration to control. One of the most reluctant, John D. Rockefeller, Jr., spoke for the concerned converts in recognizing that the post-repeal control system had to cope with greed in order to avoid disastrous consequences. "Only as the profit motive is eliminated," wrote Rockefeller, "is there any hope of controlling the liquor traffic in the interest of a decent society."[36] As events proved, Rockefeller and his allies were doomed to be disappointed. The record of the repeal decades shows that the profit motive—with much encouragement from federal as well as, over time, state governments—in fact shaped the subsequent history of alcoholic beverages. But after the destructive and negative campaign for repeal, and in the light of the earlier history of the alcoholic-beverage business, no one should have been surprised.[37]

Profit making went out of control immediately in 1933 because repeal was inextricably connected with the Great Depression of the 1930s. Large numbers of Americans were under special financial pressure, and the advent of legal alcohol in most of the states offered a fresh chance for some people to make money fast, even in states that kept wholesaling and package retailing under state ownership in an attempt to hold corrupt forces within bounds. Already before repeal had passed and all beverages had been legalized, in a typical county in Montana, one out of every five hundred citizens had applied for a tavern license. By 1935, there were in the United States 225,000 retail outlets for alcoholic beverages and constant pressure for more. One industry analyst, using a different definition of outlet, figured there was "one liquor vendor for every 189 persons" in the United States that year.[38]

Retailing alcoholic beverages appeared to offer a great opportunity because for some time people actually saw profits—a rare phenomenon in those years—appear in many places. For months before the ratification of the Twenty-First Amendment, Congress legalized both 3.2 per cent beer sold anywhere and hard liquor dispensed through drug stores. Then state laws and special licensing came into place, and the new merchandising groups appeared, although of course to a substantial extent they were not new at all. Many bootleggers, especially those who were small scale and local, stayed in the business, and they financed many campaigns to defeat the state-store system that could have destroyed the private business in which illegal suppliers hoped to continue. The larger economic units in the alcoholic-beverage business, too, tended to represent previous liquor selling—very often criminal in nature. This tradition in the business of pervasive disrespect for the law (which most people believed was characteristic of lower-order groups) as well as disregard for evangelical standards therefore affected deeply the ways in which the alcoholic-beverage businesspeople would influence the culture. As early as 1934, brewer Jacob Ruppert noted, as beer became legal, "In many instances Federal permits were issued to racketeer brewers, the true ownership concealed behind the names of dummies, and thus a legal standing given to racketeers. . . ."[39] Ruppert believed or affected to believe that undesirable elements soon diminished greatly in the industry. They were in fact frequently absorbed, not forced out.

An obvious real (and not mythical) failure of Prohibition was that the alcoholic-beverage industry actually never went out of business. Not only was the industry still remarkably intact, but those brewers and distillers who stayed in business making nonalcoholic beer or commercial alcohol during the 1920s typically also became involved in diverting their products into the bootleg market. This was true even of producers who were apparently pillars of society, such as the family-owned and otherwise super-respectable Cream City Brewing Company of Milwaukee. Curiously, a number of the more successful bootleggers ended up in the legal gambling business. For those who continued purveying alcoholic beverages, the style of choosing profits over respectability did not disappear with repeal, and it is no wonder. The largest distillers after repeal had themselves been engaged in illegal activities in previous years. Seagram and Hiram Walker grew out of profits amassed by smuggling in collusion with criminals. Schenley Distillers Corporation was based more on ownership of large existing stocks supposedly held for medicinal purposes. With such a background, it was natural, then, that in the mid-1930s, Schenley, for example, did not scruple at employing a disreputable convicted bootlegger as the corporation broker in Montana. As one notorious crime figure, Moe Dalitz, put it some time later, "I did nothing more than the head of Seagram's, than the head of G & W [Gooderham and Worts], the head of Canadian Club. They assembled all this merchandise for runners to bring it across. . . ."[40]

Yet such were conditions at the time that beginning in 1933 all major alcoholic-beverage figures were suddenly transformed into apparently respectable businesspeople. When a grand jury in Minneapolis found that almost a third of the people holding local liquor licenses were criminals, for example, the city council pardoned them so as to keep them in business. Of course that was a time, too, when Pierre Du Pont carried his anti-government sentiments to the extreme of advocating that retailers govern their own hours without regulation. Officials had found that any restraints on the trade led to violations, and so, many like Du Pont reasoned, it was better not to attempt any regulation! The Du Pont repealers continued after 1933 to favor unimpeded commerce in all commodities, including alcoholic beverages. To what extent the motive was defending business and to what extent hoping to raise revenue through liquor taxes remained unclear.[41]

This lesson of repeal was not lost on a later generation of criminal profiteers. In 1976, *High Times*, a publication dedicated to drug taking, carried a story titled "How to Make a Fortune After Legalization" (referring to the expected legalization of marijuana), in which the author focused on the tactics used by the owners of Seagram and Schenley and by Joseph P. Kennedy (father of President John F. Kennedy) in evading and manipulating the Prohibition laws in order to make fortunes that they later tried to deodorize. Indeed, one writer in that same magazine, perhaps the founder, drug dealer Tom Forcade, worried that the criminal dealers' expertise would get lost after what he considered to be the inevitable repeal of marijuana prohibition. He hoped that such businesspeople, as in the 1930s, would also quickly attain social acceptability—and leadership.[42]

Other forces of the Great Depression helped propel the alcoholic-beverage business to sudden respectability. Not least was the greed of wealthy taxpayers who, like Du Pont, had wanted to avoid paying so much in taxes. But then a new group of proponents appeared: government officials who faced taxpayer strikes at the same time that demand for services increased. For both wealthy taxpayers and officeholders, liquor excise taxes offered an easy solution, both before and after repeal. Large revenues from liquor taxes (not to mention local payoffs to officials for licensing and enforcement favors) not only converted many politicians but also cemented the collective loyalty of government to programs that would facilitate, not discourage, the sale of alcoholic beverages. Those revenues also tied government officials to reinforcing, not opposing, demands of businesspeople intent on expanding consumption of alcoholic beverages—contrary to the promise of many repealers and the letter of the law in most states. The failure of the federal government to protect dry areas—as promised in the Twenty-First Amendment—was just one sign of the new political power of the beverage merchandisers. At the same time, state and federal taxes on alcohol increased 125 per cent, from the first legalized imposts to 1940.[43]

The desire of other groups for profits allied them, too, with the alcoholic-beverage businesspeople, just as before Prohibition. Both American Can and Continental Can were major new beneficiaries of the beer industry in the 1930s, and many additional suppliers, such as sugar refiners who supplied distilleries, were enlisted as before Prohibition except with much greater intensity because of Depression conditions.

Suborning the Media

By far the most significant group to profit was the print media, because alchoholic-beverage advertising represented salvation for many publishers in a rapidly consolidating industry. The December 1933 issue of *Vanity Fair*, for example, issued the same month that repeal was effected, carried six full pages of ads for spirits. Both the potential for revenue and the corrupting influence of having the press dependent upon alcohol advertising were points well understood among all the relevant parties as soon as repeal appeared likely, and everyone was well aware of the economic pressure of the Depression upon publishers. The impact of the advertising grew as time went on. By 20 September 1935, for example, out of 2,489 column inches of display advertising in the *New York Times*, 515—more than 20 per cent—were devoted to spirits and wine advertising alone, not counting those for beer and ale. And advertising was important also for alcoholic-beverage sellers who were simply trying to market their goods. As early as 1934, one industry representative estimated that the liquor industry had productive capacity of eight to ten times the then-current production.[44] (Industry leaders had not counted on the long-range effects of Prohibition in reducing drinking but had apparently believed their own propaganda that there was a deprived public out there somewhere demanding alcoholic beverages.) Clearly, aggressive marketing was in order for economic reasons, without regard to sentiment. Just through their impact on suppliers and the media, the profit motive alone made manufacturers and distributors of alcoholic beverages substantial cultural influences.

Such critics of alcohol as were left objected at least to the conspicuous side of aggressive marketing, national advertising. There was a running battle to keep alcoholic-beverage advertising off the new electronic media, so that before World War II the radio networks had agreed to carry beer and wine advertising but not advertising for strong drink. Exactly what should appear in ads was also controversial, even within the industry— should advertisers depict people (as opposed to bottles and scenery) in spirits ads, for example? In addition, for years, many magazines and small newspapers on their own continued to refuse to carry alcoholic-beverage ads, or at least spirits ads.[45]

Throughout the late 1930s, newspapers and magazines, one after the other, capitulated to economic pressure. The most notable surrenders were those of women's magazines—a symbolic as well as substantive victory for the wets. In 1942, one editor claimed that some American magazines were "little else than whisky announcements." Typical was *American Magazine*, the editor of which justified taking beer ads in 1934 by saying, ". . . we regard beer drinking as thoroughly consistent with true temperance and decent living." But about hard liquor ads, he said flatly, "They're out." Yet within a year, *American Magazine* was carrying an ad for Four Roses whiskey, and of course others followed. In 1945, *Life*, the most important popular publication in the country, contained 387 liquor ads covering a total of 318 pages and costing $4,409,175; sister publication *Time* had liquor ads worth $1,335,266—enormous sums for that day.[46]

For twenty years after repeal, alcoholic-beverage businesspeople were preoccupied with the idea that Prohibition might come back. They therefore continued their campaign against the increasingly impotent drys and followed strategies left over in many cases from the pre-World War I era. They made sure that every local vote for or against local option had vigorous wet representation. By the 1940s, the Distilled Spirits Institute was triumphantly charting how the areas that still had dry laws were decreasing. Representatives of the beverage industries organized economic boycotts against the drys. Their allies attacked any scholar or scientist, much less reformer, who appeared to be at all dry so that anyone who was the least bit vulnerable would have thought twice before criticizing drinking or any part of the alcoholic-beverage business.[47]

The trade itself undertook a vigorously publicized self-policing campaign in the late 1930s to clean up the worst dives that had opened, hopeful that the saloon image would not come back. California beverage merchants, for example, were alarmed when some brewers surreptitiously began financing retailers as in the old saloon days, and once again gambling and other illicit activities came to be associated with retail drinking establishments. "We are aware of the outlaw element in the industry," wrote Harry J. Krueger, president of the National Beer Wholesalers Association of America. He and other leaders redoubled their efforts to use self-regulation—both real and public relations—to negate any effort to prove that repeal, like Prohibition, had "failed." "Every offensive action by any retailer becomes ammunition for the Drys," warned one industry editor.[48]

The powerful advertising and public-relations efforts of the reborn alcoholic-beverage industry were supplemented by some at least ostensibly private groups, including a successor organization to the AAPA, the Repeal Associates.[49] The repealers ended up defending the industry that they had helped bring back into legal existence. Indeed, the personal-liberty repealers worked actively to expand the market for merchandisers of alcoholic beverages. In 1937–1938, the Repeal Associates revealed that the organization was working to get the state laws mandating alcohol education repealed or modified so that children would be taught to drink. The adverb employed was always "moderately"—masking the fact that such teaching would actively assist the industry, not to mention make drinking respectable in a setting in which it had not theretofore been acceptable. To suggest that alcoholic beverages were undesirable, the repealers argued, was "political" and therefore unsuitable for school curriculum materials. Indeed, when repealer publicists sought to take over the term *temperance* and give it connotations favorable to alcohol consumption rather than the traditionally negative dry association, the attempt backfired because a number of their less subtly minded business allies thought that their customers should not be exposed to temperance of any kind. When a Rockefeller plan to advocate moderation appeared shortly after repeal, the industry refused to cooperate. Their own pleas for moderation thereafter had, consequently, difficulty commanding credibility.[50]

World War II and Postwar Business

This approach by the alcoholic-beverage industry, combining public relations, advertising, and ostentatious self-policing to prevent the return of Prohibition, continued until well after World War II.[51] Nothing could demonstrate better the effectiveness of the advertising, propaganda, and public-relations efforts of the industry and the repealers than the record of events during that war.

The war itself once again raised fears of Prohibition as drys worked to keep draftees away from alcoholic beverages. Because Congress in 1933 had declared light beer to be nonintoxicating, soldiers in fact could obtain beer, but not spirits, at army canteens. Measures against drinking places near military establishments were reduced to merely policing, not controlling (in contrast to those aimed at prostitution). Leaders of the military forces in fact consistently favored making alcoholic beverages available, and military and wet came to be synonymous. Despite the war, beer makers, in contrast to distillers, stayed in the beverage business. As one industry spokesperson was so indiscreet as to note (correctly) in 1941, the army camps represented "a chance for brewers to cultivate a taste for beer in millions of young men who will eventually constitute the largest beer-consuming section of our population." Beer sales in fact increased over 50 per cent per capita, from 12.1 to 18.7 gallons, just between 1940 and 1945, and women, many of whom were now working in men's jobs, were among the new drinkers. The distillers were not converted to war production entirely until late 1942. Already by August 1944, they had obtained permission to resume production of beverages for a month despite the wartime demand for alcohol to make synthetic rubber. With their four-year inventory, distillers became war profiteers doubly, especially as they held back stocks of liquor waiting for higher prices. The distillers doubled their productive capacity during the war years, adding to already excessive capacity and therefore, of course, pressure to sell—although the industry seemed able to control output and avoid price wars. The beer industry ended the war in a particularly strong financial position. The U.S. government, in short, under great pressure from the businesses, was treating alcoholic beverages as necessities even in a "total" war, to the point of giving draft deferments to brewery workers. The effects of the political influence and money of the industry therefore showed up transparently during World War II. For a luxury industry, it was an awesome demonstration of power. Responsible officials, both military and civilian, merely mouthed industry propaganda and slogans in explaining their actions. John B. Smiley, an official of the War Production Board, had his staff put written objections from those who condemned alcoholic-beverage production during a total war into what was called a "Crank File."[52]

After the war, the business began to take on a new look, although the alcoholic-beverage trade was still concerned about trying to "make repeal work," as leaders put it. Over several decades, the profitability of the beverages attracted the attention of many types of businesspeople (retailers enjoyed a 30 to 40 per cent markup on whiskey), and closer ties than ever developed to various investment segments. The spirits business continued to be dominated by a few distilling and importing firms that increasingly absorbed small, independent distilleries. The number of breweries declined as the largest ones went national and drove local firms out of business, beginning with Pabst's purchase of a Newark establishment in 1945. There were 750 brewers in 1935, 457 in 1945, 231 in 1955, 113 in 1965, and 54 in 1975. The new national firms were therefore beginning national advertising campaigns just as television appeared. By 1954, packaged beer, notably a supermarket item, accounted for 75 per cent of beer sales.[53]

The actual business changed in many ways after midcentury. Schenley, for example, bought Blatz Brewing Company in 1944 and by 1949 had arranged major loans with Prudential, New York Life, John Hancock, and other major insurance firms—and all the time was into cooperage, farm feeds, and pharmaceuticals, with a major role in the production of the then-new wonder drug, penicillin. By the 1970s, in addition to beer and whiskey firms, the wine industry had become part of the more generalized alcoholic-beverage marketing effort and represented the major expansion of alcoholic beverages, although distillers still dominated social policies and advertising. All the producers were in turn combined directly not just with economic ties but in actual ownership with a large variety of other major American firms of all kinds.[54]

The alcoholic-beverage business involved not only manufacturers but also wholesalers and retailers. Retailers who misbehaved caused most of the public-relations problems of the industry, and in fact post-World War II bars had a number of features in common with the old saloon because of pressure to move the goods. Wholesaling was very lucrative, and whole-sale salespeople continued to pressure retailers. Distributors' representatives helped retail outlets coordinate with national advertising—one of many additional ways in which manufacturers exerted influence directly on retail outlets. In particular, retailers were urged to feature heavily advertised national brands. In some states, the distillers furnished and installed window displays once a month without charge. But always the advice was to push drink relentlessly. As two distillery officials counseled in 1947: "Since the most profitable end of the restaurant business is in the serving of alcoholic beverages, waiters and waitresses should be instructed *always* to recommend drinks with food"—perhaps with reminder signs on the "out" door of the kitchen, they suggested. The idea that alcoholic beverages were more profitable than food, frequently repeated among food-industry workers, of course benefited the alcohol sellers, not necessarily the restaurateurs.[55]

Retailers of the beverages in fact constituted a rapidly changing group. About a quarter of the bars changed hands each year. One of the problems in the business was that few retailers of any kind did any marketing. Instead, as one student of the industry noted, they operated as mere "order-takers rather than as promoters." The result was to make illegal sales (typically to minors and drunks, or after hours) more attractive to retailers who had few sales skills—and at the same time to shift the responsibility for marketing to national manufacturers and importers.[56]

The business prospered under these circumstances during the last half of the twentieth century. As national income rose and large parts of the population tended to move to suburbs, home consumption of alcoholic beverages continued to increase proportionately, fulfilling the mass-media images of the 1930s and after. Home ownership, so-called outdoor living, and television all combined to create private drinking patterns that made industry journalists talk in terms of the coming of age of the alcoholic-beverage industry.[57] In the suburbs, there was no bachelor subculture such as once sustained the saloon in "bad" neighborhoods, and public drinking places became dispersed throughout urban areas. In the late 1960s, further social changes once more led to relative increases in on-premises public consumption. But by that time, the change occurred in the context of drinking that was accepted and even normalized and, particularly, domesticated, among very large parts of the population.[58]

The Campaign to Normalize Drinking

During the 1950s, it became obvious that the place of the alcoholic-beverage business in the United States had shifted decisively. In 1936, an industry journalist expressed alarm that the WCTU had placed anti-liquor advertising in New York papers. Within twenty years, however, any such anti-drinking activity had receded from the attention of even alcoholic-beverage marketers and was almost absent from the mass media. Although concern about "repeal" and "the drys" still showed up in industry publications as late as the 1960s—along with information about local option elections—industry leaders' perceptions had already changed. Soon after World War II, even sensitive merchandisers realized that the initial public-relations and propaganda campaign of the industry had succeeded. "Through the industry's public relations and educational promotion, 70% of the American people are now opposed to prohibition—an increase of 7% in just the last six years," crowed one wholesale liquor spokesperson in 1952. In Kansas, two-thirds of the veterans who came back after World War II opposed the state prohibition law (which was repealed in 1948), and elsewhere polls showed a sharp increase in actual drinking behavior in the 1950s and after, especially among younger people and women.[59]

The post-1933 alcoholic-beverage makers and sellers tried to establish certain fundamental beliefs among Americans: that the business was a respectable and responsible business; that the act of drinking was a respectable act that occurred in a respectable and acceptable, nondeviant setting, particularly the home; and, finally, that any abuse was a problem for the individual who abused the substance, not for the alcoholic-beverage business. After the successes of the industry in the 1950s, those themes of advertising and public relations continued but tended to become relatively muted, especially as the business became more and more integrated into all aspects of American life—or, more accurately, American life became more and more integrated into the business. Only the idea of individual responsibility grew in importance.

In their public relations and advertising, therefore, the alcoholic-beverage merchants began to turn away from political content, the fear of anti-liquor laws, that had animated them for so long. Moreover, as one industry leader remarked, "Saintly ads intended to placate 'drys' and at the same time sell whiskey fool no one." Instead, a new kind of advertising and public relations developed, pioneered during World War II by the brewers. While the distillers were still preoccupied in their public relations with political stance and continued talking about their patriotism and the way liquor taxes supported government, the brewers emphasized in their advertising the idea that beer was an integral part of American life. By 1953, the U.S. Brewers Foundation ads asserted, "In this friendly, freedom-loving land of ours—Beer belongs . . . enjoy it!" As one church group noted in 1945, "The advertising of alcoholic beverages . . . is no longer promoting the sale of products and services but has become a strong weapon in the sale of economic and social ideas—ideas about alcoholic beverages which are as destructive to the people and the nation as the product itself."[60]

This process of normalization of drinking proceeded ever more rapidly from midcentury on. By 1958, the beverage merchants tallied the backing of the Episcopal Church for social drinking. Later, even the Methodists began turning soft on the alcohol question. By the late 1960s, the U.S. government was supporting alcoholic-beverage retailers with bank-loan guarantees through the Small Business Administration, just as after World War II the government had in a similar way guaranteed loans to veterans to go into alcoholic-beverage retailing.[61]

The major factor in normalizing the place of alcoholic beverages in American life after World War II was the advertising of the producers. "Normalizing" or "universalizing" drinking paid off for them in increasing overall sales, and the industry came to depend upon advertising to an extraordinary extent. By 1960, among the top 100 advertisers of all products and services, five were distillers, and their advertising had increased five times while their production only doubled. In 1981, alcoholic-beverage marketers were spending at least a billion dollars a year for advertising.

Whether it was beer in the World War II period or wine in the 1970s, both proponents and opponents of drinking believed that advertising was effective in stimulating sales—and not just of one particular brand but in expanding the market for alcoholic beverages. The best-known example was the success of the cigarette maker, Philip Morris, which bought the Miller Brewing Company, and in expanding the market segment of the Miller brand in the 1970s decisively expanded purchases of all beer.[62]

It was with advertising, then, that the merchandisers of alcoholic beverages attempted continuously to expand the market of which each held some segment. At the same time, for public-relations purposes, the alcoholic-beverage firms denied that they had any intentions of creating new drinkers, claiming instead that they were doing no more than enlarging the market share of an individual firm. Such a stance of course ignored the fact that the market was not just among one kind of alcoholic beverage but included all beverages. But few people outside of interested law and advertising firms took seriously at any time the self-denying claims of the merchandisers. As a writer in *Advertising Age* noted in 1979, "People spending millions on advertising must do their best to prove that advertising doesn't do very much!" In candid moments, alcoholic-beverage businesspeople agreed with the sentiments of Roy W. Stevens, president of Hiram Walker, when he was quoted in 1977 as saying, "We've got to persuade more people to drink whiskey." From the 1950s to the 1980s, the tactics of the merchandisers showed that they intended to convey as much output to as many people as possible. In fact, when vendors intensified their aggressive marketing in the 1970s, they succeeded in holding their sales relatively high for a number of years.[63]

The marketing efforts of the alcoholic-beverage industry proceeded along several lines in the post-World War II decades. In their advertising, the firms tied drinking to the upscale consumption that was becoming ever more conspicuous in advertising and the media. They associated themselves not only, as before, with famous—and presumably respectable—public figures but also with institutions and other consumer goods. It was a great breakthrough in 1952 when *Vogue* magazine, for example, took Miller Brewing Company ads or when Pabst beer was teamed up in a "Picnic Values" promotion with otherwise respectable Armour's Treet, Campbell's pork and beans, Borden's cheese, Swift's franks, and National Biscuit's Ritz crackers. Eventually, magazines seeking alcoholic-beverage ads boasted about how much money their readers made—surveys showed that affluence begot alcohol consumption—and how much their readers entertained, because entertainment was a major part of consumption. Even the *Smithsonian* magazine (supposedly popularizing knowledge) in 1977 noted that "700,000 of our subscribers served their guests Scotch, 315,000 broke the ice with rum and another 240,000 poured a cordial or two. Although nearly everyone served wine with dinner, a quarter of a million big spenders popped for champagne." These were, the ad continued, "the most affluent ($34,000 average income), best educated (85% college) subscribers of any million-plus magazine published in America."[64]

The alcoholic-beverage advertisers pushed as hard as they dared to breach restrictions on advertising, a movement in which media executives cooperated. In 1958, the distilled-spirits industry boldly began to introduce women into advertisements, and by 1963, ads showed women actually holding drinks. In 1958, radio station WOMT in Manitowoc, Wisconsin, began broadcasting spirits-beverage ads. Soon big-city stations were carrying plugs for major distillers' products. In the meantime, not only did the foremost women's magazines accept advertising for alcoholic beverages, but they were also joined by other holdout media, such as, in 1962, the *Catholic Digest*.[65]

Merchandising to the Vulnerable

In their quest for sales, alcoholic-beverage vendors continued in the last part of the twentieth century to target all vulnerable groups—particularly heavy drinkers, ethnics, women, and young people. Women constituted a particularly promising market. Although advertising pitched to men was often effective with women as well, late in the century, merchandisers very noticeably targeted independent women. *Ms.* magazine, for example, at one point lost some credibility because of the number and manipulative content of its liquor ads. Polls continued to show dramatic increases in women's drinking from the 1950s to the 1970s.[66]

Drinking, especially among humbler folk, in the last half of the century still constituted a major method by which members of ethnic groups began to become homogenized into American culture. Even more than earlier, Americans' identities as members of the consumer culture tended to preempt ethnic drinking customs by midcentury. Typically that meant either confirming a tendency to consume much alcohol, as in the case of many Irish-Americans, or shifting people to patterns of higher consumption of alcohol, often consumption that was conspicuous in one social setting or another—the pattern noted earlier for Jewish groups but applicable to a wide range of other ethnics, most notably, later, Hispanics. Merchandisers found that ethnics were extremely vulnerable to marketing pressures, particularly as new media came in after the 1920s. After observing that the 10 per cent of the population that was black consumed 15 per cent of all spirits, liquor-marketing expert Henry Bretzfield noted in 1955 that "Negroes, to a greater extent than whites, gravitate toward brands which are used by leaders in their individual social circles. Many important brands today first rose to popularity in the Negro market." In 1970, one brewery had a "Great American Negro" calendar, and the Black Newspaper Network advertised to alcoholic-beverage merchandisers, "Black people drink too much. . . . Too much, that is, for you to ignore."[67]

In many clever ways, merchandisers also directed advertising and packaging to the heavier drinkers who were such an important part of the market. Investigators in the 1980s found that over half of alcoholic beverage consumption was accounted for by heavy drinkers. Hence it was no surprise that shrewd marketers produced advertising that was strongly oriented toward males who drank heavily and copy that urged people to drink at all times of the day. Extensive introduction of the beer six-pack was held up by World War II, but it came on in full force afterwards. Six-pack cans became even more attractive with flip-top openers and other innovations—"all aimed at making the home use of beer easier and more pleasant," as one industry writer put it. Marketers' emphasis on larger containers clearly moved spirits as well as other alcoholic beverages. A stream of promotions over the last half of the twentieth century, such as the Budweiser "Pick a *Pair*" (of beer containers) advertising campaign of 1960 or Schaefer's "The one beer to have when you're having more than one" obviously cultivated the tendency to drink heavily.[68]

Like their predecessors of the late nineteenth century, alcoholic-beverage marketers tried to get young people into the habit of using alcoholic beverages. "Get the youth market and you're halfway home," noted one brewery official in 1979, adding explicitly: "The 18–34 age bracket is very important to us." Marketers envied the cigarette people who used coin dispensing machines, which were hard to police, to invade the youth market. But from the beginning, purveyors of alcohol connected advertising with the youth market at the same time that they favored low legal drinking ages. Throughout the last half of the twentieth century, well-informed people knew of various studies that showed the ways in which alcoholic-beverage advertising was pitched to the young (including the underage), particularly as advertisers tied alcoholic beverages to sports. In 1952, for example, a Philadelphia brewer sponsored Police Athletic League boxing television broadcasts, tied in Navy recruiting on the program, and announced scholarships sponsored by the company. In later years, consumer groups systematically exposed innumerable instances of alcoholic-beverage marketers' targeting of children and young people. Some targeting was very subtle, like the 1980s Miller beer ad on the Snap Tite model pickup truck (for ages ten and up). Much was just plain advertising. One way of appealing to younger people was to pitch ads to them, not only in connection with sports but also with the theme of growing up. In particular, alcoholic-beverage ads often showed adult behavior—of course including drinking—in a seductive way. After midcentury, industry ad dollars flooded rock-and-roll stations and such publications as *Rolling Stone* and the *National Lampoon* that appealed to young readers. By the 1970s, more than half of the national advertising in college newspapers was for alcoholic beverages, and a number of the ads, as one group of researchers noted, ridiculed studying, science, and even graduating. One marketing executive commented, "Let's not forget that getting a freshman to choose a certain brand of beer may mean that he will maintain his brand loyalty for the next 20 to 35 years. If he turns out to be a big drinker, the beer company has bought itself an annuity."[69]

Increasingly sophisticated studies showed that as traditional standards gave way to pluralism and consumerism, alcoholic-beverage advertising was effective in socializing children and young people into drinking. At the *very* least, it helped reinforce tendencies that an individual youngster might have to want to drink. And this effect was clearly deliberate. In the 1970s and 1980s, in alcoholic-beverage ads in *Rolling Stone*, a magazine still oriented toward juveniles, recipes for cocktails appeared with very great frequency (in contrast, for example, to those in the *New Yorker* at the same time).[70]

New Advertising Content, with Spillover into the Media

All alcoholic-beverage advertising conveyed the message that drinking was acceptable and, by implication, abstinence deviant. Some earlier alcoholic-beverage advertising themes continued, such as the quest for respectability and the attempt to portray consumption as upper class or masculine. But after World War II, a steady direction of change was clear. The beer-industry ads, for example, for years continued to emphasize the nondeviant nature of the beverage: "Beer belongs . . . enjoy it," with a picture of a family or group of friends, typically middle-class people in a congenial setting. But by the mid-1960s, the campaign had changed to "Beer Party/ USA," with an emphasis on a party setting (and, obviously, more drinking than in a strictly family environment).[71]

In this new style of advertising, marketers of alcoholic beverages began openly to reinforce the association of their products with ways of life that defied the old respectability. They did not scruple, for example, to use suggestive ad copy. Red Satin whiskey was touted as "Whiskey created simply to please a man . . .—a man *and* his closest friends," with a picture of a woman in an unmistakably provocative pose giving double meaning to the printed message. One vodka marketer employed well-known female stars in sexually suggestive advertising. For years, advertising trade journals in fact carried discussions of just how far advertising might go, for in this industry, sexual motifs in advertising had special significance. By the 1970s, not only sex but also lifestyle and risky—usually macho—activity constituted the most conspicuous themes in alcoholic-beverage advertising, in large part carrying to an extreme the pioneer efforts of the late 1920s lifestyle advertisers.[72]

The entire advertising and wider social-impact questions were greatly intensified by the arrival of television in the 1950s. Beer was soon a major factor in television advertising, with at least somewhat proportionate sales. As early as 1956, Pabst was advertising "It's Beer, Mama, and TV . . . 3 ingredients of a recipe for successful living." But numerous studies showed that, apart from the ads, the content of television programs was equally potent in making not only beer but also any alcoholic-beverage consumption a part of normal American standards. One investigation, made in 1979, found in prime-time network "entertainment" shows almost four drinking "incidents" per hour—hardly any of which involved abstentions. In another study of top dramas and situation comedies alike, 40 per cent of the incidents involved hard drinking, and virtually no drinking appeared to produce undesirable consequences. Drinking frequently was depicted as a response to both social and personal pressures, including crisis management, and good characters drank much more often than villainous characters.[73]

Motion pictures, usually shown on television shortly after theater release, not only involved similar drinking standards but also included brand names when marketers paid for the privilege. But of course movies contained influential prototype drinking even before television took over the convention, and advertising was not necessary to make generic drinking part of the tough-guy hero stereotype who continued to be so important a figure in novels, movies, and television for half a century and more.[74]

Although television and motion-picture writers did not invent the culture of hard drinking or the tough-guy convention, midcentury fiction writers did include more drinking than earlier authors and went into great descriptive detail to show exactly how drinking was done. Moreover, they tended to portray drinking positively, especially as an important social instrument—a quick technological fix for facilitating and sustaining social relationships—and obviously one that could be purchased. It was this same image that continued to show up in television, motion pictures, and other media: drinking, and even heavy drinking, had become a norm, with few negative consequences.[75]

As early as the 1960s, advertising analyst William H. Boyenton could summarize the media message about drinking:

> Serving and using alcoholic beverages enhances our social status. Women have a social responsibility to provide family guests with alcoholic drinks. When a man is tired and overwrought, what he needs is a drink. His wife's duty is to see that he gets it. When a single woman is tired, she should go home to a drink. A mother should drink with her daughter. Liquor belongs in romance. A young woman should serve her male companion alcohol; vice versa, the man should provide for his girl. A tavern is a good place to make love. Drink plenty [there]. Activity requiring fine judgments is helped by alcohol. If you admire show business people (as probably most people do)— they drink, and you should too. Drinking is sophisticated, the sign of social maturity. "Whatever we do, alcohol makes us do it better."[76]

Television images, particularly, had powerful effects on generations of young people. As early as 1965, the adolescent standard was, according to one journalistic account, "It's all right to get blasted, if you can be witty or brave, . . . but if you get sloppy you're way out." For decades, the media encouraged this and similar images, plus the more sophisticated hedonistic and affluent-lifestyle approach to drinking and everything else.[77]

Individual Responsibility

The issue of individual responsibility was the most political and most dangerous one for the alcoholic-beverage marketers and advocates. Shortly after repeal of Prohibition, both repealers and industry leaders knew that they had to deal with two issues: overindulgence and alcoholism, on the one hand, and drunken driving, on the other. A conspicuous amount of both in the late 1930s media made the repeal experiment tenuous and—the nightmare of the alcoholic-beverage businesspeople and the repealers alike—threatened to show repeal to be a failure just as their propaganda had depicted Prohibition a failure. The content of the public-relations blitz to counter bad publicity about both alcoholics and drunk drivers was the same as that used in pre-Prohibition days and did not change over the succeeding decades: the substance and the marketers of the substance were blameless. Rather, responsibility lay with those who used alcohol. This argument was especially congenial to many of the repealers, who had acted in the name of individual responsibility in the first place. "We believe that every man and woman should be allowed to exercise his or her own judgment" was the initial statement of a California repeal group in 1936.[78]

The strategy of the alcohol sellers to divert blame from themselves and to avert any move toward social solutions to the drunk-driving and alcoholism problems was extremely clever and a bit subtle. Their spokespersons issued many sanctimonious statements about the virtues of individual moderation. At the same time, firms and trade groups supported apparently disinterested educational and rehabilitation programs aimed at individuals with alcohol problems.

Alcoholic-beverage-industry funds early on helped the National Safety Council with campaigns to cut down on drinking and driving. When the problem became too acute to be swept aside any longer, especially in the late 1970s and early 1980s, industry money backed organizations like Mothers Against Drunk Driving (MADD, founded in 1980) that focused on individual behavior and responsibility and campaigned successfully to use individual legal penalties to try to dissuade anyone from drinking too much—whatever that might be—and then driving. MADD was particularly successful because the media used the MADD individual-responsibility laws as a distraction from the 1980s campaign to limit or ban alcoholic-beverage advertising—a drive that of course threatened the media. The ideal group was Students Against Driving Drunk, which permitted propaganda to reach young people urging them to drink—but just not to drive at the same time. Beer merchandisers, including Anheuser-Busch, backed this group heavily.[79]

The alcoholic-beverage sellers began their most daring and successful program shortly after repeal: helping to build up a large community of experts who dealt with the national problem of habitual drunkenness and alcohol addiction. These experts gradually coalesced into two overlapping groups at the end of the 1930s: those who did therapy and rehabilitation work with individuals habituated to alcohol and those who did scientific investigation into the use of alcoholic beverages. The Research Council on Problems of Alcohol was founded in 1938, and by the 1940s, a series of professional groups had organized and increasingly preempted the public role of spokespersons on the subject of alcohol use. They were supposed to produce facts, not programs.[80]

Beverage vendors began almost immediately after repeal to attempt to contribute substantially to alcohol professionals' efforts. In 1939, reformers who wanted to upgrade and update alcohol education were coopted by research scientists who were willing to accept "funds from liquor organizations." Between the large amounts of money that the beverage industry supplied in Depression times, when researchers were desperate for support, and repealers' jeering denigrations of dry scientists, scientists and therapists were careful to avoid any sign of social criticism of the industry and affected to maintain a strictly neutral stance on social issues. Their focus was on the individual drinker, and particularly the alcoholics, not the social problems around alcohol. Moreover, industry representatives were conspicuously present at all of the professionals' organizational activities. "The work of these committees," noted one alcohol trade journalist in 1944, "is not in any way associated with the Drys, and their sponsors are emphatically opposed to prohibition."[81]

Even before World War II, the Distilled Spirits Institute was cooperating with the American Association for the Advancement of Science in a conference on treating alcoholics, and in fact for decades no major conference on the subject of alcoholism was without industry funding to some extent. Research programs at both Yale and Rutgers enjoyed industry support. As Randolph W. Childs, a wet writer, noted in 1947, the propaganda of the WCTU contrasted with "the dispassionate investigations being conducted at the Yale School of Alcohol Studies. . . . The danger of excessive drinking is realistically displayed. The harmlessness of temperate indulgence is convincingly demonstrated." Most alcoholic-beverage-industry observers perceived that Alcoholics Anonymous (founded in 1935) was no threat to alcohol and that the scientists would be useful—"potentially valuable allies," in the words of one industry report to the distillers in 1947. And so they were.[82]

Using Alcoholism to Make Drinking Nondeviant

The great victory of the alcoholic-beverage business was to turn the idea that there is an illness, alcoholism, into the negative of social action that might diminish the profits on the sale of the beverages. As Thomas F. McCarthy, president of Licensed Beverage Industries, Inc., noted in 1947, specialized scientists generally agreed that "the root of the 'problem drinker's disease' lies in the man and not in the bottle. The 'problem drinker' is a *medical* problem—and he won't be cured until the scientists and doctors figure out a way." The money spent on individualizing the problem paid off handsomely over the years—not in solving drinking problems but in diverting public attention away from the industry.[83]

By defining "problem" drinkers as deviants, then, the alcohol-treatment and research personnel established the fact that nonproblem drinking was normal, that is, an acceptable and nondeviant standard. As a Yale researcher put it in 1960, "alcohol, taken in moderate amounts, may . . . [tone] down some unspecific anxiety or some specific fear. This . . . cannot be considered harmful." Moreover, in such a view, any social action should be limited strictly to deviant drinkers, those who brought attention to themselves by being either alcoholics or drunk drivers, which were strictly individual conditions. In this way, the alcoholic-beverage marketers got experts to endorse drinking—a reversal of the way in which most professionals lined up in the early twentieth century.[84]

Beginning in the late 1940s, another group came in to second the industry interest in emphasizing the individual alcoholic: the alcoholics themselves. Despite their initial deviant status, they soon formed a powerful pressure group and dominated not only private ventures but also government alcohol programs. One of their notable victories was separating the federal alcoholism programs from the National Institute of Mental Health into an independent National Institute on Alcohol Abuse and Alcoholism—to avoid the suggestion that alcoholics were mentally ill. And obviously this agenda well suited industrial sponsors as well. One of the obvious processes going on was talking about alcoholism as an illness the presence of which one could deny, that is, a drinker could deny that his or her drinking was deviant—so that, again, drinking, not abstinence, was a norm, that is, not deviant.[85]

The alcoholic-beverage merchandisers were also able to use their ties to the scientific and medical communities to influence educational materials made available to the general public and most especially to young people. Because alcohol vendors furnished so much money and had industry representatives among the specialists, they were able to object effectively should any anti-drinking material show up. As early as the 1930s, educators increasingly began to avoid moral stances in favor of what came to be called objective and scientific fact—based of course on research that was not objectionable to alcoholic-beverage merchants. Alcohol education became drinking education, not abstinence education. Moreover, alcohol advocates gained entrance to otherwise-inaccessible channels of communication, as on college campuses where presumably valuable alcohol-education programs were presented. In one instance in the late 1970s, the distilled-beverages group gained exposure on television—in connection with football games—in making announcements about the responsible use (not avoidance) of alcoholic beverages.[86]

The Continuing Pattern

Throughout the last half of the twentieth century, the alcoholic-beverage producers and merchandisers persevered. Their public relations and advertising continually suggested that drinking was a normal part of life, that everyone did it. Where there were no formal barriers to the extremes of advertising, as on cable television, merchandisers observed no limits. By the 1970s, public-relations personnel were trying to change the public terminology from "alcoholic beverage" to "beverage alcohol" to get away from new publicity about alcoholics. In the press, allies suppressed negative items about drinking (there were, proportionately, as one study found, strikingly fewer such unfavorable items in the 1970s than in the 1950s).[87]

Purveyors of alcoholic beverages therefore were substantially successful in their attempt to make the business seem normal, to insist that what they did was a part of everyday existence. As the sales manager of a whiskey importer noted in 1975, "Scotch is no harder to sell than shoestrings or overalls." Yet the beverage manufacturers and vendors remained in an institutional setting that was, as sociologists of midcentury and after noted, "criminogenic." Businesspeople had contempt for even the weak regulations that attempted to control alcoholic-beverage marketing. They were able to manipulate the relationships among retailing, wholesaling/distributing, and manufacturing. The push for easy profits took virtually all parts of alcohol-beverage merchandising into various levels of illegal activity and subversion of all attempts to enforce standards, from bribery for licenses and sales to minors to illegal business ties and versions of racketeering. As a high-ranking distillery official of the 1970s expressed the attitude that put his actions beyond community control, "We break the laws every day. If you think I go to bed at night worrying about it, you're crazy. Everybody breaks the law. The liquor laws are insane anyway." The basic contention of the proponents of the minor vices, that restrictive community standards had no validity and that anyway everyone else violated them, continued to animate merchandisers of alcoholic beverages whom media messages were portraying as respectable, indeed, model citizens.[88]

In the United States, historical factors within society shaped the ways in which drinking behavior interacted with other aspects of social functioning. From the well-defined customs of English settlers and various later ethnic arrivals to the media blitzes of the twentieth century, the influences conditioning drinking behavior were public and social—including the expectations, symbols, and constraints that anthropologists and other social scientists employ in explaining cultural peculiarities.[89] But economic and cultural factors, particularly an inordinate quest for profits and lower-order parochialism, in turn determined the social environment, in the end one that was particularly conducive to a flourishing trade in alcoholic beverages. These same factors and forces in turn affected the other behaviors that Americans for so many generations recognized, along with drinking, as elements in the constellation of minor vices.

CHAPTER FOUR

Smoking

The history of smoking is substantially different from that of drinking. Yet opponents—and to a remarkable extent proponents—of the two associated alcohol and tobacco together in the traditional constellation of minor vices, an association that continued in the consumer society of the twentieth century. But only relatively late, as tobacco people continued to use the traditional arguments that individual responsibility would take care of all problems, and as they defied a new public-health consensus, did they develop antisocial identities.

Smoking—and the use of tobacco generally—had even before the nineteenth century had what later became the stigma of a "bad habit": offensive primarily as a hazard to health, manners, and thrift. In the nineteenth century, use of the substance also took on gender connotations: men smoked and chewed. But the introduction of cigarettes in the 1880s began slowly to push tobacco into a new social role. In the twentieth century, it was advertising that pulled both the industry and the users increasingly to support and contribute to the other bad habits and the cultural changes that helped them prosper.

The Social Acceptance of the Tobacco World

Generations of tobacco growers, merchants, manufacturers, and retailers did not suffer the social stigma that saloon keepers, prostitutes, and printers of pornography did in the nineteenth and early twentieth centuries. Instead, tobacco people enjoyed a world of their own in which providing tobacco was a useful and respectable social service and in which tobacco became virtually a way of life, with mores enforced by social networks that applied high standards to a very extensive industry (in 1899, there were almost 15,000 manufacturing units of various sizes in the business, and as late as 1947 still almost a thousand, mostly small cigar makers). Moreover, most people in the business themselves had no sense of identity with antisocial forces. Around the turn of the twentieth century, for example, local civic leaders in North Carolina developed boys' clubs in which for uplift purposes the boys were taught to grow tobacco. Tobacco provided a positive, relatively stable, and morally secure world for the people who furnished it to the public. Trade papers reflected the existence of a sense of mutual social reinforcement among tobacco people in all parts of the business. Such attitudes also appeared among parts of the educated public.[1] "No man can understand the nineteenth century," observed a writer in the *Knickerbocker* magazine in 1859, "unless he be either a smoker or a snuff-taker ... no one can sympathize with the essential ideas and instincts of our time, unless he be experienced in the important psychological and sentimental modifications that result from the use of tobacco."[2]

It is true that a substantial and, during the nineteenth century, growing fraction of the population did not approve of the use of tobacco—including many people who nevertheless did use "the filthy weed." But much of the opposition focused on personal concern about health, and smoking or chewing without any other vices was—except among naughty boys and, in most places, women—not a deviant action.

With such a confident community of producers and friendly public, eyewitnesses who wrote about the tobacco industry tended to assume that everyone knew that "tobacco men" (a term that included the women in the business) were respectable and enjoyed a special and presumably admirable culture, a culture that carried substantial social status, especially in tobacco-growing and manufacturing areas. This assumption could have bemused outsiders, but it was so strong that until well into the twentieth century, at least until the campaign to repeal Prohibition began, even reformers tended to criticize tobacco *substances* as evil rather than the human beings who purveyed such things. Even the legendarily sharp salesmen who proliferated over the countryside trying to persuade retailers to sell more of a particular maker's tobacco escaped serious social stigma—in marked contrast with the fate of the marginal wholesaler of alcoholic beverages.

Only in one area did the traditional affinity of tobacco for the other bad habits show up in a notable way before the World War I era. That area was manufacturers' merchandising. Among premiums offered in the late nineteenth and early twentieth centuries in packages of tobacco products, and particularly of cigarettes, were small cards containing illustrations. Buyers presumably became repeat customers because they collected the pictures, which came in sets. A number of sets depicted "actresses" or other comely women in costumes that were daring and in poses that were provocative, to say the least, to the male tobacco clientele of that period. The founder of the American Tobacco Company was shocked by some of the "lascivious photographs" distributed thus by his son, James B. Duke, and there was some contemporary opinion that men discarded such material but that it was avidly sought by boys.[3] This material foreshadowed later advertising that brought the industry into disrepute.

The Evolution of the Tobacco Business

Before 1800, Americans had used tobacco chiefly in two forms, snuff and leaves smoked in pipes. Snuff was the substance of choice of the upper classes, and the tobaccos available for smoking were often strong and unpleasant. By the early nineteenth century, a number of changes were occurring. First, tobacco use became less fashionable, especially among women, and the amount of tobacco that Americans used actually declined. Second, new types of use began to come in. The first was chewing tobacco, the increasing sales of which peaked only about 1890 as it largely replaced snuff; indeed, in terms of pounds of tobacco, smoking tobacco surpassed chewing tobacco only in 1908. Cigar smoking was the other innovation. It came in, via England, particularly with the Spanish campaigns of the Napoleonic wars and continued to increase until the 1920s. In 1850, Americans bought ten cigars per capita; in 1860, 26. Between 1870 and 1890, the cigar became the dominant mode of tobacco use, particularly as smoking cigars took on upper-class connotations. Cigars were in fact expensive, part of the conspicuous consumption of the post-Civil War decades, and, in America, cigars were decisively masculine. Uses more common among the lower classes, pipe smoking and chewing tobacco, which had increased with the population, peaked around 1910 but continued to have substantial sales through the 1930s. Chewing tobacco, for example, declined in per capita consumption from 2.8 pounds in 1890 to .53 pounds in 1937.[4]

The respectable tobacco trade of the late nineteenth and early twentieth centuries, then, was oriented toward the cigar, which was relatively costly (although still widely used), and to a lesser extent toward pipe and chewing tobaccos. The element that upset this idyllic picture was the cigarette and, eventually, cigarette advertising.

The cigarette started out in the nineteenth century as the smoke of fringe and deviant groups. No "real man" would smoke a cigarette, and no one who could afford a cigar would have taken a cigarette. A writer in 1854 in New York deplored a few unconventional women who "are aping the silly ways of some pseudo-accomplished foreigners in smoking tobacco through a weaker and more feminine article, which was most delicately denominated cigarette" (i.e., cigar with a feminine diminutive). But after both the Crimean War and the American Civil War, some Englishmen and Americans who had made do with the quick smoke of a cigarette on the battlefield continued to use cigarettes and spread the custom. Consumption increased also during the depressions of the late nineteenth century, when economically hard-pressed men substituted cigarettes for the more expensive cigars. Indeed, as the decades passed, smaller cigars and some large forms of cigarettes helped a transition, especially in the summer, when even a respectable man might at times have smoked a cigarette rather than the customary heavy cigar.[5]

During the 1880s, new circumstances brought cigarettes into the marketplace in a dramatic way. The Bonsack cigarette manufacturing machine changed the economics and logistics of cigarette making. At the same time, a federal tax on cigarettes was drastically reduced. On top of that, James B. Duke introduced particularly aggressive marketing techniques. Sales of cigarettes grew dramatically, especially just after the turn of the century. Production skyrocketed from about two billion cigarettes in 1889 to almost 400 billion in 1949.[6]

The Cigarette as a Moral Issue

Throughout the nineteenth century, smoking earned two kinds of moral condemnation. Both narrowly moral and many other people viewed the habit as an expensive and unhealthy indulgence and also believed that smoking went with drinking and other bad habits. Yet respectable men who smoked pipes and cigars defended the habit and pointed out that it was not only a male prerogative but a harmless and pleasurable practice. An appalling amount of sentimental prose and poetry praised smoking while fulminations about health and morals condemned it. As upstanding a person as writer and historian John Fiske could say that "there is no physical pleasure in the long run comparable with that which is afforded by tobacco. If such pleasure is to be obtained without detriment to the organism," as Fiske believed, "who but the grimmest ascetic can say that here is not a gain?"[7]

There was, however, another element in smoking, one that had connected it from the beginning to the constellation of the minor vices: many people considered any use of tobacco naughty and rebellious in some sense. A Johns Hopkins physician writing in 1913 expressed the traditionally defiant element in smoking, classifying it with any activity that bothered moralists because it brought pleasure—so that "Puritans" felt a

> horror of tobacco, of boxing, of horse-racing, of the Continental Sabbath, and of the army canteen. Tobacco, in brief, is morally a hissing and a mocking, not because it does any normal man damage, but because it gives its users contentment, peace, and a healthful, animal sort of enjoyment, a sublime callousness to the ethical and theological puzzles which fret and frazzle its enemies, a beautiful and irritating indifference to all but pleasant things of life.

A comic poet of that time summarized the naughtiness and irrationality of tobacco use with

> Tobacco is a dirty weed,
> I like it.
> It satisfies no normal need,
> I like it.
> It makes you thin, it makes you lean,
> It takes the hair right off your bean;
> It's the worst darn stuff I've ever seen,
> I like it![8]

A man's assertive and ambivalent use of tobacco—presumably in a pipe or cigar—most Americans understood, but the low price of the cigarette brought not only a special market but a particular moral impact.

Low cost made the cigarette more available to poor people and, significantly, to children. As the editor of the *New York Times* observed in 1882, "Where the danger of cigarettes comes is from their cheapness, which permits too many of them to be smoked, and because they are getting into use by urchins of all ranks who are not more than 10 years old. Smoking, when indulged in by boys[,] is as pernicious as if they commenced to tipple."[9] Already in the late nineteenth century, then, the "cigarette-smoking boy," typically an urban urchin and rowdy and probably identified at least part of the time with the Victorian underworld, became a symbol of danger for moral reformers. The first anti-cigarette laws began to appear in the 1890s.

Much of the concern about the cigarette-smoking boy derived from the common observation that youngsters who were in trouble were almost invariably cigarette smokers. In 1915, for example, the Cadillac Motor Car Company announced that managers would not employ in the factory boys who smoked. "We may not know exactly what is wrong with the cigarette," wrote Lucy Page Gaston, the most conspicuous anti-tobacco crusader, "but we soon discover that something is the matter with the boys who smoke them." Truancy could result concretely from surreptitious smoking excursions, and if the relation of cause to effect in other cases of delinquency was not clear, the health hazards of smoking as understood then made laws to prevent furnishing cigarettes to children rational and sensible. (Many hygienists believed that tobacco not only stunted growth but caused various diseases and shortened life.) Tobacco interests in fact cooperated in obtaining and often in urging enforcement of laws forbidding the sale of cigarettes to minors.[10]

The respectable tobacco traders simply did not consider the juvenile cigarette customer part of their universe. But they reckoned without the lawless element among the youngsters, who continued to buy and smoke. One retailer in New York at the end of the 1880s, for example, hung out a glass sign, "No cigarettes sold to boys," and the boys of the area threw rocks at it and broke it. When the state passed a law outlawing selling such products to those under sixteen, one trade writer noted that respectable dealers had never been in the child trade. "There are numbers of small dealers, candy stores, and news stores who have sold cigarettes and tobaccos to boys of any age so long as they brought the necessary cash," he noted. He continued, "Nothing but good can possibly ensue" from legal actions against such elements.[11] Nevertheless, as much evidence shows, because of the merchandising pressures on many layers of salespeople in the business, indiscriminate sales at the retail level persisted in spite of the best efforts of industry leaders.

Unlike those in the alcoholic-beverage industry, the tobacco people did not have the kind of ties to unrespectable retailing that might have brought opprobrium upon the industry as a whole. In Chicago in 1906, for example, there were "approximately 20,000 places . . . where cigars are sold at retail, an average of practically one cigar stand to every 120 inhabitants, including women, children and other non-smokers." Mostly, of course, these retailers consisted of barber shops and stationery, candy, drug, and grocery stores that sold but a few cigars a day. There were also many cigar stores as such, some with the traditional wooden Indian statue in front. One smoker remembered those old stores with their friendly and cozy atmosphere and casual tables and chairs: "It was a place for neighborhood gossip, checker, domino, and card playing. Checker championships were held there. Cigarettes were hardly known. A nickel cigar was the standard smoke." With this respectable alternative to the saloon, it was no wonder that tobacco spokespersons thought that it might not be bad for Prohibition to come and redound to the benefit of the cigar store. And tobacco men and women were alarmed when a cigar store was used as a front for illegal drinking or for gambling. Gambling did constitute a constant temptation for tobacco retailers. But as drug stores and other more efficient retail outlets took more of the trade, the gambling problem naturally diminished with the eclipse of the tobacco store, and tobacconists in general maintained their sense of respectability. In 1919, the Independent Retail Tobacconists resolved, "We are doing all we can to show that the tobacco industry is a legitimate occupation and is not conducted by thugs, gamblers or men who are not good members of society."[12]

The more general moral attack on smoking that the cigarette-smoking boy generated caused tobacco people considerable perplexity, but they wrote off the opposition as mostly harmless extremists. They did so even though for a few years, in the 1890s, the general anti-cigarette laws—in some states involving actual prohibition of cigarettes (but, again, not other forms of tobacco)—may have contributed along with the depression of that period to a decline in consumption of cigarettes.[13]

The Goal of Tobacco People

The prohibitory movement appeared to one industry writer in 1889 to be so unproductive that he fancifully projected into the future how it would produce a tobacco person's utopia. In his scenario, in the year 1910 a new law would have become necessary. Enforcement of anti-tobacco legislation, he asserted, would have become very costly by that date, and not only did naughty boys still then smoke the prohibited item but also, when finding it in short supply, a youthful miscreant would turn to "tea, herbs, and other noxious substances, which [decimated] his hitherto healthy constitution." The government, now in 1910, the utopian writer imagined, decided to choose a lesser evil: "Smoking will not only be permitted to the small boy, but a school for teaching the proper manipulation in smoking will be established in every center." There, smoking would be blended with the three R's, the writer continued.

> Primary instruction, for children from four to eight, will treat of the virtue and good effect of the immoderate [*sic*] use of the weed; secondary instruction, for children from eight to fourteen, will demonstrate practically the rolling of cigarettes, and the first principles of inhaling, and a finishing class of higher instruction will treat of the history of the cigarette, the development of the album [cigarette case], and the political power of the cigarette, and the results of not smoking. Southern schools will have a special course embracing snuff-taking and eating, with a fully developed practical course of the use of the "stick" [dipping snuff]. Chewing will also be considered as a thing apart. All masters, professors, and teachers will smoke in and out of school hours. . . . Rewards and diplomas will consist of supplies of tobacco, and any pupil who is seized with vomiting more than once in a term will be expelled. It will be obligatory to erect over each school-house, and to be hung in each school room, and used upon all papers, the motto, "The useless man is he who never smokes." The benefits of such a system are tangible, and will soon appear in the Budget. New generations will create a large surplus, which will permit of other taxes more keenly felt being dispensed with.[14]

This satirical utopia suggests the social acceptability of men's smoking, at least, in the late nineteenth century, as a harmless and, at worst, perhaps rebellious bad habit. Yet it bears an uncanny resemblance to actual drinking-education programs that the alcoholic-beverage industry seriously and ultimately largely successfully urged on much later generations. Even a utopian, however, could not have foreseen the future of cigarette use and the cultural transformations that accompanied it.

World War I and the Metamorphosis of Cigarettes

Even before the United States actually entered World War I, cigarette smoking among British military personnel after 1914 had had a substantial impact on standards in the United States. As in nineteenth-century wars, service personnel adopted the cigarette because it was fast, convenient, and cheap. New types of matches made cigarettes even more convenient. Moreover, great changes had taken place in the trade, by chance just as war was coming on. Even under the tobacco trust that had largely monopolized the business around the turn of the century, there were many hundreds of brands of cigarettes produced by myriad local concerns. Then in 1914, after the breakup of the trust, the R. J. Reynolds Tobacco Company concentrated on a new cigarette, Camels. With a spectacular advertising campaign, Reynolds quickly won more than a third of a growing market. By 1917, when the United States entered the war, there were three heavily advertised standard brands of cigarettes that dominated American consumption: Camel, Lucky Strike, and Chesterfield.[15]

Advertising had already become important in the tobacco business in the late nineteenth century. Trade papers promoted everything from window displays to display ads that retailers could use to stimulate sales, and manufacturers and distributors employed regional and national advertising. The Camels campaign, however, involved new elements. It was patterned on Reynolds's earlier success in establishing Prince Albert pipe tobacco by concentrating on one brand. As a result, advertising changed in intensity. Moreover, accumulated profits by 1914 permitted extraordinary advertising budgets. Altogether cigarette advertising as advertising had a new kind of social impact. The first ad for a tobacco product to appear in the *Saturday Evening Post*, for example, was a two-page display for Camel cigarettes on December 12, 1914. It contrasted with the customary small, dignified newspaper ads for cigars for men. Almost every man, woman, and child learned about Camels as Reynolds saturated the media of that day with clever, teasing copy ("The Camels Are Coming!"). Most significantly, the Camels campaign convinced tobacco marketers—and other Americans— that advertising worked. The Reynolds budget for advertising grew to the then-immense sum of almost $2 million in 1916. In just four more years, it had tripled to over $6 million. In newspapers, magazines, and billboards, tobacco and especially cigarette advertising in remarkable quantity reached virtually all Americans.[16]

It was in the midst of these new advertising campaigns that manufacturers used World War I to extend the use of cigarettes in American culture. American military authorities cooperated with the companies and with charitable groups in furnishing either free or very inexpensive cigarettes in all military settings. An eyewitness, William D. Parkinson, writing in the Boston *Herald*, described what happened:

> There is something almost inspiring in the spectacle of a great industry capitalizing [on] war as did the tobacco industry. Every recruiting poster [showing a manly figure with a cigarette] was a gratuitous advertisement for the cigarette. The Y.M.C.A., the K. of C. and the Salvation Army were its zealous and generous distributors. Free samples were paid out of helmets into which we all tossed our cash lavishly whenever we were given opportunity. W.C.T.U. mothers sent their sons cigarettes and urged them to learn to smoke. . . . The armistice brought no diminished demand. The returning heroes were themselves models for younger youth to copy. . . .[17]

World War I therefore did two things. First, it masculinized the cigarette far more than delinquent boys could and set the stage for making the cigarette an indelible part of the new tough-guy image. Citing the British war example, cigarette advocate William W. Young noted in 1916, "As it was on the *Titanic*, so it was in the days of our Wild West with the cowboy who maintained life and law and order on the frontier. . . . Then as now, a case of the 'nerves' was effectively controlled by the lighting of a cigarette, which was serenely puffed while keeping a watchful eye for an enemy." But second, and more concretely, the war concentrated marketing on the younger population. Cigar production increased right through 1917; the exploding sales of cigarettes at that time therefore represented largely new customers. Within a few months after the armistice, the Reynolds company ran a puzzle picture in newspapers for about a week. When the main clue turned out to be Camels, "all the kids in town," as one reporter put it, came rushing into tobacco merchants for their "Humps," i.e., Camel cigarettes. The power of advertising to reach the young was clearly established before the 1920s began.[18]

The new advertising engendered a reaction from those who wanted to clean up American society. This alarm that advertising set off helped renew and reinforce the cigarette-prohibition movement so that it peaked just after World War I. Although advertising increased almost every year through the 1920s, cigarette makers took care not to offend until about 1926. After that, ads became so offensive that friends of the industry wondered if the cigarette-prohibition movement would not come back to life in protest.[19] In fact, it did not—a dramatic sign of the social changes that were taking place.

Because the anti-tobacco forces after World War I concentrated on the cigarette, and because respectable tobacco people considered them extremists, it was easy to write the anti's off as a joke or, at the least, misguided. When the time came, they fitted into the campaign of ridicule conducted by the champions of alcoholic beverages against repressive "Puritans." As one industry editorialist wrote of WCTU anti-tobacco efforts, "Isn't it rather too bad that an organization which undoubtedly did so much good in the fight against the saloon should . . . fly off on such a tangent? . . . The liquor and tobacco problems are as different as the sun and the moon. . . ." Unlike the case of alcohol consumption, undesirable effects of tobacco use were hard to dramatize, as wise industry leaders observed. Nevertheless, those leaders watched carefully all legislation affecting the industry and did not hesitate to represent their interests.[20]

In addition to the pro-alcohol forces who were popularizing the idea of personal liberty, the tobacco people had another set of allies whom they could mobilize in favor of cigarettes. These allies were male and organized: war veterans who were overwhelmingly, now, smokers. American Legion posts embodied a rebellious masculinity and in fact worked effectively to counteract anti-cigarette legislation.[21]

Within the space of just a few years, then, the traditional tobacco men saw one part of their business transformed by advertising. They continued their traditional respectable business as before, but the large sums of money suddenly involved in cigarette sales and the logic of the new kind of marketing pushed cigarette manufacturers (and to a very much lesser extent distributors) into campaigns to break taboos, to make cigarette smoking acceptable for men, for women, and for the young. What started out as simple marketing therefore ended up as social change.

Breaking Taboos

Cigarette advertisers actively challenged the taboo against young people's and women's smoking. World War I had had devastating effects on efforts to protect young people from the habit of smoking. All witnesses agreed that in the army, even nice middle-class "boys"—from WCTU homes—indulged in the cigarette custom. After the war, tobacco merchandisers were smart enough to cultivate young people, advertising in college newspapers, for example, and comparing Chesterfields to outstanding sports heroes. By the late 1920s, cigarette ads pictured explicitly modern young people, liberated from tradition, reaching for a cigarette.[22]

But the symbolic issue of the 1920s became women's smoking, and it raised troubling questions. One set of questions had to do with advertising that showed women's smoking and appealed to women to smoke and even to smoke publicly. The other set of questions developed around the right of women to smoke as men's equals. The most conspicuous arena in which the battle over women's smoking was fought was in the women's colleges, which involved trend-setting upper- and upper-middle-class people.[23]

The issue of women's smoking was the most acute symptom of changing standards in the 1920s. The fact that people at the time reacted so strongly, on either side, indicates that they understood the symbolism: that women did set American social standards, and if those standards gave way in the area of smoking, they would give way in other areas. A small percentage of American women had always smoked. But by the turn of the century, only a few deviant females at either end of the social scale did—lower-class country women, with their traditional corncob pipes, and daring upper-class eccentrics. In 1899, for example, an ad for Benedict Little Cigars featured a stylish woman smoking one—but no trend came of such campaigns. Indeed, many women's colleges did not have rules against smoking before World War I because such an unladylike activity was not an issue. In the culture, then, it was women's smoking—along with children's—that tied tobacco to deviant unrespectability. A writer of the 1930s could still spell out the danger: "Before the war, smoking among young women had, in this country, always been restricted to the underworld. It was, then, for respectable young women, a long hard step from the smokeless decorum of polite and decent society to the formerly despised smoking habits of the harlots, and once this step had been taken, it was not so hard to go one step farther and mingle with them at the bar of the speakeasy."[24]

Mass-media writers of the 1920s therefore connected smoking to rebelliousness and, implicitly, lifestyle. Historian Robert Sobel contends that tobacco merchandisers were delighted when extremists denounced cigarettes, because condemnation would cause young people to react in adolescent fashion and light up. In one important incident, the new media celebrity and hero Charles Lindbergh, within a few weeks of his famous flight in 1927, deliberately lit up a cigarette in public because he was indignant that a women's group had urged youngsters not to smoke because "Lucky Lindy" did not. "I won't be played for a tin saint," asserted the defiant new idol. And, indeed, commentators at the time paralleled the rebellious "smartness" of women's smoking with that of "the smoking boy who is just taking on the manly indulgence." Women, according to the wisdom of that day, were attempting to participate as equals in the new smoking standards for men that had been popularized by advertising and by the war—for the issue was cigarettes, not cigars.[25]

One horrified observer in 1929 wrote:

> First the woman appears in the advertisement—merely a pretty girl who becomes part of the picture; then she is offering the man a fag [slang term for cigarette]; next she asks him to blow the smoke her way; finally she lights hers by his. The one encouraging thing about this development is that the grade of women pictured in the posters has distinctly deteriorated in the process, until now we see at the turn of the road the most voluptuous, greasy-haired Medusa that was ever used to advertise anything."[26]

By 1930 or so, the smoking woman and all that she stood for had won, in the ads and elsewhere. Again, people at the time understood the importance of the ads as well as their symbolic value. But of course the ads were only the last straw. Journalists and advertisers had long pictured fashionable young women with cigarettes. "Advertisements of stockings and lingerie preceded the tobacconists with illustrations of women smoking," noted one observer, adding, besides, "Magazine artists had pictured flappers and their mothers with cigarettes long before"—as might have been illustrated by a cartoon of 1920 depicting an aunt saying of a sleeping boy, "The idea of that little imp having cigarettes in his pocket!" and the sophisticated young mother commenting, "It's lucky I found them; I haven't a single one left."[27]

Advertising therefore embodied only part of the triumph of smoking at the end of the 1920s. Other mass media contributed powerfully to the cigarette fad that helped establish new norms. Most motion pictures, for example, showed smoking, overwhelmingly now cigarette smoking (and one investigator found that in a sample of typical movies, heroines were depicted smoking more often even than were villainous male characters). But even in that entertainment medium, the cigarette advertisers, who knew what they were doing, saw to it that producers had leading actors and actresses smoke on the screen.[28]

Advertising as a Cultural Force

As the 1920s gave way to the 1930s, the cigarette companies were particularly quick to add radio as a new medium with which to advertise. Cigarette commercials soon became part of ordinary American life. Americans to whom rapidly developing commercial radio assumed great importance tended to associate cigarettes with popular music and other shared experiences of the culture. The ads in fact became major nostalgia items for those who lived through the era. And more even than drinking, actual cigarette smoking became a common American experience in the 1930s. Moreover, in the mass media, the heroes and heroines and the whole entertainment world continued to provide what were in effect lessons in how to smoke, along with pro-smoking propaganda to which young people would be exposed repeatedly—just as the 1880s tobacco utopian suggested might happen in schoolrooms. One satirical writer noted that by the 1940s smoking was so important in the movies that a whole school of acting could be founded on the way one used a cigarette to show all kinds of standard stereotyped reactions such as anger ("crush out a half-smoked cigarette—or cigar—impetuously") or disbelief ("exhale long puff of smoke slowly").[29] Generations of Americans viewed 1920s-to-1940s films that were filled with smoke.

That advertising came to dominate the role of tobacco in American life signified the changes that were taking place as national marketing of cigarettes generated huge profits, even in Depression times. Radio commercials increasingly replaced the old-time tobacco-company salesman. The sums that the major cigarette companies spent for advertising were stupendous: in 1934, R. J. Reynolds invested an amount equal to more than four-fifths of the net income of the company, which was still, in the Depression, at a level of two-thirds the income of 1928. The effectiveness of the advertising in spreading the habit of smoking meant that the tobacco business became increasingly important in the economy as well as in the culture. By 1929, cigar and cigarette firms had moved into the top ten among American industries in value added by manufacture. By 1933, the cigarette industry alone was in eleventh place. At the end of the 1920s, about 4 per cent of the money income of the country went for tobacco. In the Depression period, an average family spent as much 6.9 per cent of their income for tobacco.[30]

The cultural significance of smoking in the interwar period involved several forces simultaneously. One was the persisting positive self-image of most people in the tobacco business. Unlike the alcoholic-beverage vendors, tobacco people did not come from a background of deliberate criminality. "Disorder, crime and poverty do not grow out of consumption of tobacco," noted a tobacco-area editor in 1925; "The argument which was effective as to liquors, and as to habit drugs against which laws have been passed, cannot be made."[31] The number of people involved in bootlegging cigarettes in areas where they were forbidden was minuscule; for the most part, retailers not associated with the industry were the actual criminals.

Rather than identifying with rebellious antisocial elements, then, tobacco-business people tended to see themselves as producers of a luxury item. Indeed, spending for tobacco increased as family income increased. Smoking was appropriate for an affluent consumer society in which self-gratification was both socially acceptable and economically desirable. Opposition to tobacco, industry spokespersons noted, was akin to opposition to any pleasant luxury. "A strict vegetarian," noted one tobacco journalist, "could denounce sirloin steak as a vicious luxury." Throughout the 1920s, therefore, when the anti-tobacco crusade came into the news, American journalists tended to lump tobacco with coffee or sweets or some other source of innocent pleasure. In 1923, an industry editor defended the place of the weed in American life. Along with tobacco, he noted, "There are a vast number of things and customs the uses of which do not contribute . . . the slightest addition to mental, moral or physical advancement, and which serve only as a diversion, a relaxation, an amusement, or a consolation. But why destroy them?" he asked, a true reflector of the rapidly developing consumer ethic. As an Illinois newspaper editor concluded in 1929, "America is a nation of smokers. It has the money to spend at the court of Lady Nicotine and it spends it." It was no wonder that the tobacco industry could be compared to the automobile industry that also boomed in the post-World War I consumer era.[32]

Smoking therefore became an integral part of the consumer culture that characterized the United States particularly strongly in the 1920s and after. Smoking was a part of the lifestyle that advertisers sold with depictions of stylish women in luxurious surroundings to which members of the public in general aspired. And it was a lifestyle that included the cabaret-night

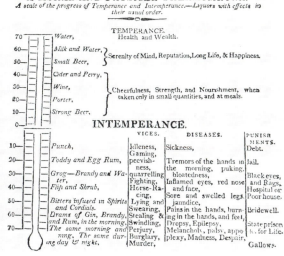

1.1 A Moral and Physical Thermometer. From Benjamin Rush, *An Inquiry into the Effects of Ardent Spirits upon the Human Body and Mind: With an Account of the Means of Preventing and of the Remedies for Curing Them* (1814).

1.2 Gambling at Pikes Peak, 1864, showing a desperate customer offering his watch in the foreground and a bar and fighting in the background, with a picture of boxers on the wall. *Frank Leslie's Illustrated Newspaper*, 1864. Courtesy, Colorado Historical Society.

1.3   Inside Harry Hill's dance house, a notorious institution in nineteenth-century New York. Matthew Hale Smith, *Sunshine and Shadow in New York,* 1868. Courtesy, Ohio State University Libraries.
1.4   The cover of James Dabney McCabe, *Secrets of the Great City,* 1868, showing the progression of vices. 1. Leaving home for New York. 2. In a fashionable saloon amongst the waiter girls—the road to ruin. 3. Drinking with "the fancy"—in the hands of gamblers. 4. Murdered and robbed by his "fancy" companions. 5. His body found by the harbor police. Courtesy, Ohio State University Libraries.

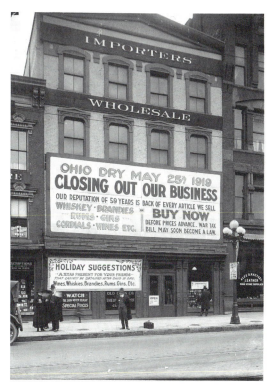

1.5 Smokers in their new role as deviants: 1988 satire. Boston *Herald.* Reproduced with the generous permission of the Boston *Herald.*
1.6 Liquor store going out of business, Columbus, Ohio, 1918. With permission, Ohio Historical Society/Columbus *Dispatch.*

1.7 Use of satire to discredit opponents of drinking and other bad habits, using the images of the intrusive Puritan and the self-righteous, disapproving old aunty. Cartoon from *Life*, 1921.

1.8 Miss Elizabeth Thompson of Chicago, a socialite crusading for the repeal of Prohibition, December 1930. Courtesy, Prints and Photographs Division, Library of Congress.

1.9 Pierre Du Pont (*left*) and his chief lieutenant in the Association Against the Prohibition Amendment, John Raskob, shortly after the repeal of Prohibition. With permission, Ohio Historical Society/Columbus *Dispatch.*

1.10 One of the first post-repeal national beer ads, including a depiction (in a mirror) of a young woman drinking; young women constituted an important new market for alcoholic beverages. *The Delineator,* 1933.

To good health and good cheer

Let Pabst Blue Ribbon Beer grace the festive board, it's hearty and healthy, sociable and sensible. Its amber glow and billowy foam lends charm to the table. Its satisfying taste lends zest to the meal.

Order it, and after you order it once, it will become your standing order — for holidays and other days as well.

PABST
BLUE RIBBON

THEY
FOUND
FOIE GRAS

⋯AND
COOLER SMOKE

These charming people!
Always so casually, yet so successfully
pioneering in the realm of enjoyment.
In smoking, they were first to discover
Spud and Spud's 16° cooler smoke.
Their trained senses were first to find
that cooler smoke transforms tobacco
enjoyment into enjoyment unburdened
by limitation, or even moderation . . .
that cooler smoke keeps their tobacco
appetite constantly alive to the full flavor of Spud's choice blend and leaf . . .
no matter how long or how gay the
evening. Thus, these charming people
lead the way again...this time to Spud,
the great modern freedom in old-
fashioned tobacco enjoyment. At better stands, 20 for 20c. The Axton-Fisher
Tobacco Company, Inc., Louisville, Ky.

MENTHOL-COOLED **SPUD** CIGARETTES

1.11   Pre-repeal ad for Spud cigarettes, embodying and glamorizing the new
standards based on cabaret night life, "unburdened by limitation, or even moderation." *Vanity Fair*, 1930.

1.12 Barroom in California in the 1850s. Frank Marryat, *Mountains and Molehills*, 1855.

1.13 Late-nineteenth-century ethnic promotion of lager beer. Courtesy, Prints and Photographs Division, Library of Congress.

1.14 The bar of the fashionable Hoffman House in New York, including a well-known, daring mural. Courtesy, Prints and Photographs Division, Library of Congress.

1.15 Hole-in-wall bar, typical of the first flush of profit seeking after repeal: the Ammer Saloon, on James Street in St. Paul, Minnesota, 1933–1934. *St. Paul Dispatch-Pioneer Press* photo, Minnesota Historical Society, by courtesy.

1.16 Post-repeal ad for the cocktail hour at the glamorous Biltmore Hotel. *New Yorker,* 1934.

1.17   Cartoon showing the conversion of the saloon into a cocktail lounge with women patrons in the 1930s. *New Yorker,* 1935. Drawing by Galbraith; c. 1935, 1963 The New Yorker Magazine, Inc.

1.18   Tavern in Chicago, 1941. U.S. Farm Security Administration Collection, Prints and Photographs Division, Library of Congress, by courtesy.

Left: 1.19   Beer Belongs: advertising in the campaign to normalize beer drinking. *Collier's,* 1950. Reproduced with the generous permission of the Beer Institute. *Right:* 1.20   Red Satin Whiskey ad from *Life,* 1965, using sexual suggestiveness to market alcoholic beverages. Reproduced with the generous permission of Schenley Industries, Inc.

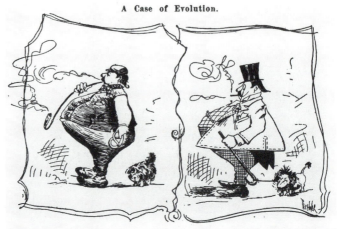

A Case of Evolution.

AS WE HAVE KNOWN HIM AND SEE
HIM TO-DAY.

AS WE WILL KNOW HIM IF HE ADOPTS
THE CIGARETTE HABIT.

1.21   A late-nineteenth-century cartoon disparaging cigarette smokers: the respectable, pipe-smoking man is turned into a ridiculous dandy (understood at the time as an affected sissy). *Tobacco Leaf,* 1898. Courtesy, Library of Congress.
1.22   Ad for Murad cigarettes, appealing to the new World War I stereotype of the masculine male smoking a cigarette. Washington *Post,* 1918.

Aunt: THE IDEA OF THAT LITTLE IMP HAVING CIGARETTES IN HIS POCKET!
Mother: IT'S LUCKY I FOUND THEM; I HAVEN'T A SINGLE ONE LEFT.

1.23   Cartoon showing an "advanced" young woman sharing the role of daring cigarette smoker with a rebellious boy. *Life,* 1920.
1.24   Learning to smoke from the movies; a lesson enacted in a Paramount picture, *Bill Henry,* released in 1920. *Tobacco,* 1919. Courtesy, Library of Congress.

1.25 Little Bruce Bidlack, of Bel Aire, California, in 1957, learning that cigarette smoking was a normal part of life in the United States in the mid twentieth century. He was being taught safety rules by using a lighter properly as he lit his father's cigarette. *Look*, 1957.

1.26 Cartoon from a late-twentieth-century consumers' group criticizing cigarette machine vending. *Tobacco and Youth Reporter*, 1989. Reproduced with the generous permission of the publisher, Stop Teenage Addiction to Tobacco, and of the artist, Vern Herschberger.

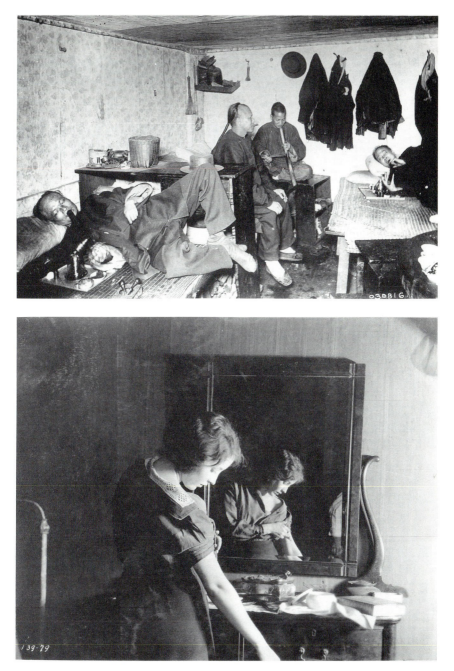

1.27 Opium den, 1890–1910. Courtesy, Prints and Photographs Division, Library of Congress.

1.28 Scene from *Human Wreckage,* a 1924 film. Courtesy, Stills Archive, Museum of Modern Art, New York.

1.29   Ad from a youth-oriented magazine for Acapulco Gold cigarette rolling papers and a drug advocacy organization, Amorphia. *Rolling Stone, 1973.*

1.30   Allen Ginsberg at the first Be-In. San Francisco, 14 January 1967. From David E. Smith and John Luce, *Love Needs Care,* 1971. Reproduced with the generous permission of David E. Smith.

club-night life stereotype in which both smoking and drinking were conspicuous. As in the movies, in the ads, also, people in evening clothes smoked cigarettes, and upper-class women endorsed the act that at an earlier time was more characteristic of lower-class boys. In the world of ads, smoking was so much the norm that it became a standard. In 1940, for example, A. B. Dick was advertising mimeograph machines with the opening line, "By the time you've smoked a cigarette. . . ."—the presumption being that "you" would include any American.[33]

The cigarette therefore took on a number of roles and through advertising played an extremely conspicuous part in American culture and society. The initial stage came when cigarettes took on the rebelliousness of lower-order men and boys who could not afford cigars, on the one hand, and, on the other, bohemians and then women. During World War I, middle-class men added another major element as the masculine ideal increasingly included the new convention, cigarette smoking. The models in the media and advertising thus utilized both upper-class consumption and lower-order masculinity and rebelliousness to establish lighting up as part of the new lifestyle of sophistication, self-indulgence, and spending. The content of the ads was designed to emphasize pleasure and comfort.[34] This set of associations, established in the 1920s and 1930s, lasted for many decades and, in advertising, almost to the end of the century.

Midcentury: The High Point of Smoking

The extent to which the culture accepted and reinforced the custom of smoking is astonishing. When World War II came, among service personnel the social pressure to smoke was overwhelming, and not only were cigarettes given out free and included in survival [*sic*] rations for soldiers but tobacco farmers were also exempted from the draft because they were "essential" workers. Likewise the pressure on women to smoke increased even more as many of them took over traditionally male jobs. Rosie, the Riveter, appeared with a cigarette in her hand or between her lips. Between 1935, when advertising urging women to smoke was well established, and the end of World War II, the percentage of American women who smoked doubled.[35]

By 1948, the tobacco utopia conceived in the 1880s was ever closer to realization. Lucky Strike and Camel each sold over 100 billion cigarettes.[36] The advertising that was so much a part of American life, chiefly in magazines and on the radio, was about to move into the new medium of television. The redistribution of income to lower-class groups had given almost everyone a chance to participate in tobacco use at a very high rate (from 1939 to 1947 the percentage of the U.S. disposable income spent on tobacco products varied only slightly from 2.5 per cent—even though that income rose dramatically). A few hygiene teachers and religiously motivated Americans spoke out against the habit—but even they could not help but be familiar with the advertising slogans of the major brands of cigarettes. At the middle of the twentieth century, 80 per cent of American men aged 18 to 64 used tobacco. About two-thirds of the tobacco users between ages 18 and 44 were given to cigarette smoking, and about half of those over 44.[37] It was in such a world that advertising now dominated, indeed, represented the tobacco industry and grew fat on the profits.

As the economic importance of the industry grew, other elements in American society deferred to tobacco-industry interests. Both in the local economy and as a major means by which governments at state and federal levels raised revenue, tobacco carried much weight in society and biased governmental officials just as alcoholic-beverage taxes did. By the 1960s, over three billion dollars in taxes on tobacco were collected each year. And the stake that other industries had in tobacco, from farming to publishing and advertising, was notorious. In 1964, for example, after the Surgeon General condemned cigarette smoking, the tobacco industry in opposing any warnings in cigarette ads lined up support from the American Newspaper Publishers Association, the Advertising Federation of America, the Association of National Advertisers, the Radio Advertising Bureau, and the National Association of Broadcasters. As was the case with alcoholic beverages, Americans with many different viewpoints over the years developed and maintained a substantial interest in furthering the consumption of tobacco products.[38] This interest was greatly complicated as tobacco firms diversified and acquired many unrelated businesses in the last part of the century.

Business Persistence and Cultural Impact

After the postwar high point, the industry underwent jarring changes. New products, including "king size" and filter-tipped cigarettes, were introduced, and no longer did a very few brands dominate the market, which was now split by many types and brands of goods that succeeded one another at an alarming pace. Grocery stores, especially chains of super-markets, became decisively the major outlets for cigarettes, with drug stores a poor second, and the profits constituted so great a percentage for the chain grocers as to affect the outlook of responsible leaders in the retail business. With the advent of television, local promotion of tobacco goods with increasing frequency took the form of selling programs and materials furnished and coordinated by the manufacturers, making national adver-tising more important than ever. The distributors, for their parts, took on other products, as retailers tended to include tobacco products among a number of "sundries," and tobacco journals contained ads not only for candy but also for watches that retailers might market alongside cigarettes and pipes.[39]

Cigarette advertising continued through the 1950s to be a remarkable component of American culture, a part of the media and consumer-culture fantasy, an undefinable American something that was even an aspect of what servicemen in World War II were fighting for. The place of tobacco in the culture did not diminish as it moved onto television. Virtually every-one had some awareness that the advertising was not true, at least in so far as any substantive assertions appeared in the copy. Yet that advertising became, if anything, more prominent in the common culture than before. As the tobacco market changed in the second half of the twentieth century, the advertising continued to reinforce or shape other cultural trends. After all, because (as researchers discovered) smokers could not distinguish one cigarette from another, the ads were just suggesting what the smoker thought he or she was experiencing—mildness, pleasure, or pleasant as-sociations customary in consumption.[40]

The first challenge to the world of cigarette advertising showed up around 1953, when the media reported the idea that smoking could con-stitute a serious threat to health. Beginning in the 1950s, the various com-panies attempted to use public relations, advertising, and political tactics to protect their businesses in the face of a serious attack in the name of both personal and public health. The companies even attempted to change products, which was a large part of the reason that they started emphasizing king-size and filter-tipped cigarettes, particularly.[41] In the late 1960s and 1970s, producers also touted low-tar and low-nicotine cigarettes presumably for health reasons. Fortunately for the companies, the new products turned out to be substantially cheaper to produce and sold more units, because users had to smoke more to get the same level of "kick" as from regular cigarettes. But except as veracity suffered, the tobacco marketers' efforts, to counter and meet the anti-smoking health crusade, did not directly contribute in a major way to their effectiveness as part of the constellation of minor vices.

After the health issue surfaced, the issue of individual responsibility became confused with reformers' concerns that young Americans tended to respond to advertising. In so far as tobacco purveyors pushed into the teen and preteen market, they finally took on an antisocial identity that clearly contrasted with that of an earlier day. The traditional attempts to get young people started in smoking had of course continued after World War II, in both subtle and obvious ways, not unlike those employed in promoting alcohol use, such as having tobacco-company representatives on campuses, giving out free samples there, and advertising relatively heavily in college newspapers and on student radio stations. Market research found that young smokers in colleges and the armed services often changed brands, and so they, along with those who had not yet started smoking, were very important targets of firm marketing. At midcentury, the near saturation of the market pushed marketers to pay special attention to this largest group of potential smokers, the young. Industry observers were particularly aware of the importance of girls as potential lifetime customers. From the point of view of advertisers and the media, cigarettes were just part of all consumption and should be treated like any commodity that could attract discretionary spending for pleasure or self-indulgence. *Life* magazine, for example, attempted to attract advertisers in 1953 by announcing that the magazine was as effective with cigarette as with chewing-gum consumers: "In the tobacco and confection business—where *everyone* is a potential customer—sheer size of audience is the most important dimension of an advertising medium." The ad was accompanied by drawings of both teenage and young-adult consumers.[42]

Tobacco merchandisers were particularly sensitive about the lucrative vending-machine sales, which permitted people of any age to purchase cigarettes. Targeted overtly at impulsive adults, the machines were notorious because in practice they enabled youngsters to evade laws against children's purchasing of cigarettes. By midcentury, in the wake of dramatic mechanical improvements, the 364,000 machines accounted for almost 20 per cent of cigarette sales.[43]

The advent of television introduced still another dimension to targeting young people. Even beyond the ability of *Life*, television could reach all age groups indiscriminately, rather like the billboards that had carried the first Camels ads. Moreover, television was a particularly effective tool in teaching young people exactly how to smoke. Journalist Thomas Whiteside told of his experience interviewing Jack Denove, a Lucky Strike advertising executive in 1950:

> I remarked to Denove that the cigarette advertisements in print I could remember seeing showed people not smoking but merely holding lighted cigarettes, but that this principle didn't seem to apply to cigarette commercials on television. "No, it doesn't at all," he said. "They actually *smoke* them on television. You don't show people smoking in still ads because the cigarette would hide the face. See what I mean?" Denove held one hand up to his mouth. "It doesn't look good, but smoking looks wonderful on television." Denove lit a Lucky, leaned back, and demonstrated the routine. "Look. You put your cigarette up to your face. You take your puff in the normal manner—watch me—and you blow out the smoke. It takes a couple of seconds. Then you see the person's face again. What could be more natural? . . . We like everybody to both inhale and exhale on our commercials.[44]

Particularly in television but more generally, too, advertising presumably aimed at adults was more or less detectably also aimed at the youth market. An early (1954) and extremely successful example was the use of an ungrammatical slogan, "Winstons taste good—like a cigarette should." This calculated violation of canons of language appealed to the rebellious, and particularly to young people in school who heard and saw an authority alternative to teachers.[45]

Eventually, the furor around youth-oriented advertising—and some well-publicized Federal Trade Commission hearings—caused a new advertising code to compel marketers to avoid material aimed especially at the young. Cigarette companies after 1963 were supposed no longer to advertise in college newspapers or use models who appeared to be under 25. Two things happened. First, the codes were violated. One study showed that children perceived the models to be mostly under 26, for example, although of course the companies denied the intention. ("What do they want us to use for a model," asked tobacco spokesperson Anne Browder a few years later, "a hobo wearing a torn raincoat and standing in front of a porno store? We have a product to sell.") But it also turned out that the more the ads pretended to target adults, the more they appealed to youngsters who desperately wanted to be "responsible adults." Lucky Strike illustrated the principle immediately in 1963 with a motto, "Lucky Strike separates the men from the boys . . . but not from the girls." Observers believed that the way in which youngsters would want to feel grown up made the appeal obvious. And this instance was followed by decades of similar appeals. Advertising with the text, "Smoking is a custom for adults," depicted young adults (whom youngsters would perceive as close to their own ages) in happy outdoor activities such as horseback riding and sailplane flying. Moreover, after television advertising was banned in 1965, the cigarette companies continued to appeal to young people in other ways. Marketers sponsored sports events so that young people watching them on television could not help but see the promotional material. The tactics followed those of the alcoholic-beverage industry and were immediately obvious: "In following the race the television cameras will pass fence advertisements while the crews and winners will be smoking with the cigarette pack prominently displayed," predicted a tobacco journalist, and so it came to pass. Moreover, print advertising appeared in journals patronized by younger audiences— again just as in alcoholic-beverage advertising.[46]

The issue in appealing to young people to be grown up and smoke or to enjoy sports and smoke was of course from one point of view a public-health issue. But another important and long-range issue was the assumption that good things like sports and adult behavior were somehow connected with smoking. That such messages appealed especially to youngsters did not diminish the way in which they affected cultural beliefs as a whole, those of adults as well as children.

Using the Appeal of Naughtiness to Sell Tobacco Products

Aside from the public-health debates, tobacco advertising in the closing decades of the twentieth century continued to contribute to the new world of inverted values. As did alcoholic-beverage promoters, advertisers, in the hope of increasing or at least maintaining tobacco sales, and in collusion with the entertainment media, continued to undermine any remaining beliefs and attitudes resistant to the constellation of minor vices. Critics for years complained about suggestiveness in pictorial and then television advertising and, after the television ban, in pictorial advertising again. In 1983, for example, a Barclay cigarette ad touting "pleasure" depicted a man lighting a cigarette and looking at a woman in a suggestive way although only her hand, holding a cocktail, showed in the illustration—a combination not unlike the 1928 Spud ad noted above but with a more direct appeal to sensuality.[47]

It should have been obvious what the tobacco marketers were doing. Witness memoranda exchanged between cigarette makers Brown and Williamson and the Ted Bates and Company ad agency:

In the young smoker's mind, a cigarette falls into the same category with wine, beer, shaving, wearing a bra (or purposely not wearing one), declaration of independence and striving for self-identity. . . . Thus, an attempt to reach young smokers, starters, should be based, among others, on the following major parameters:

Present the cigarette as one of the few initiations into the adult world.

Present the cigarette as part of the illicit pleasure category of products and activities.

In your ads create a situation taken from the day-to-day life of the young smoker but in an elegant manner have this situation touch on the basic symbols of the growing-up, maturity process.

To the best of your ability, (considering some legal constraints), relate the cigarette to pot, wine, beer, sex, etc.[48]

It turned out that there was good reason for advertisers to try to tie cigarettes and other tobacco products to the other presumably "adult" minor vices and to antisocial stereotypes in general. As early as the 1950s, motivational research had shown that the typical smoker not only believed that smoking was not good for a person but that it was "contrary to a puritanical attitude toward life. As a consequence the majority of the consumers have an abiding guilt about smoking cigarettes," one study concluded. To sell individual brands, then, advertisers could try to alleviate the guilt feelings, by making cigarette smoking appear acceptable—the technique used with heroes and social leaders and other devices to establish respectability from the 1920s on. Or the advertisers could, and of course in the late twentieth century did, exploit the enjoyment of wickedness. As another set of psychological researchers put it, using ambiguous terms such as "liberated" to communicate defiance,

Americans smoke to prove that they are virile, to demonstrate their vigor, energy and potency. This is a psychological satisfaction sufficient to overcome health fears, to withstand moral censure, ridicule or even the paradoxical attitude of enslavement to a habit. Smoking is a daring act; it shows one is liberated; it is a sign of poise and sophistication; it is exhibitionistic.[49]

Associating cigarette smoking with the other minor vices, then, made it a desirable and daring, if rebellious, habit—even when smoking was conforming, for the new conforming was to imagine oneself in rebellion against what was formerly decency and propriety. One indignant observer reported what he saw in 1974:

Recently in San Francisco, I noticed a handsome, fully mustachioed young man staring intently at me from a billboard. He was puffing perfect smoke rings, and the message said something like "No excuses. The Turk smokes because he likes it." The unspoken message was loud and clear: "and he doesn't give a damn what anybody says!" . . . Later I found a full page ad in a local newspaper. Languid Lee Bryant is poured sensuously over a rattan rocker, cigarette (of course) dangling casually from her delicate fingers. Her message: "I smoke. And I am not going to apologize for it. Sure I have heard it all. I light up at a cocktail party. And somebody would remind me what they have read about smoking in the papers. Well, I read the papers too. . . ." Tough, cool talk.[50]

This antisocial and antirational strategy interacted with "market need" to move marketers to reinforce the smoking proclivities of lower-class men. To a substantial extent, both rebelliousness and masculinity appeals seemed to make the biggest impression. The most notable new symbol was the Marlboro man, a figure of independence and macho manliness so conspicuous as to generate substantial social commentary about the symbolism, which was clearly designed to stimulate emulation of a heroic figure (and of course particularly appealing to people just coming of age who were unsure of their independence). The Marlboro man just happened also to be the epitome of a person's vigorously taking individual responsibility for his/her own actions. One extreme in this macho type of cigarette advertising, in which ties to the underworld style became explicit, appeared in commercials for Silva Thins in which a physically powerful male figure mistreated an attractive-looking woman in a more or less openly sadistic way, sometimes hitting as well as abandoning her.[51]

This rebelliousness against former respectability also appeared in advertising that targeted women. One cigarette had a notorious ad that tied smoking to being "liberated" ("You've come a long way, baby . . ."). Other industry media campaigns connected reacting against sexism with rebelling, far more than in the 1920s, in such a way as to advocate women's smoking and indulging in the customary constellation of misbehaviors. A cigarette ad in *Ms.* magazine in 1972 showed a woman lying back between a man's spread legs, with her hair hanging down on his stomach; both were smoking and acting playful and neither was wearing a wedding band. The title on the ad was "Temptation," and the large print said, "How good it is," and then continued in much smaller type, "with Winston's finer flavor."[52]

Other findings of motivation researchers of the middle to late twentieth century confirmed the importance of smoking as a defiantly rebellious and deliberately naughty action as well as one involving subjective pleasurable feelings. "We all have very definite ideas about cigarettes," reported one researcher, "but the most central meaning is that cigarettes are an evil. It is necessary to emphasize this in some detail in order to make clear later how important are the reasons for smoking, and the consequences for advertising. The idea of badness is demonstrated in a variety of ways," he reported. Children are not allowed to smoke, he continued, and everyone knew that it was "unhealthy—wasteful—a fire hazard—a filthy habit—and habit forming." He made fun of the idea that smoking relieved tension and calmed people. Did a smoker meet twenty crises a day that required tension reduction? he asked. No, that was a rationalization, he confirmed. Rather, people smoked because it was a highly personal act, having to do even with one's identity, so that there were, for example, extremely masculine cigarettes, like Camels. And many people even took pleasure in an activity that was dangerous, if not self-defeating—the ultimate perversity.[53] Altogether, good testimony from throughout the late twentieth century emphasized how smokers defied that which they knew to be good—which was not a new idea, but now smokers tended not to have just an indulged bad habit, as had been typical in the nineteenth century, but rather on the basis of that one bad habit to take on broadly negative cultural identities.

Cigarette advertising did not have to be effective in terms of the overt plea to smoke a particular brand for a particular reason. Indeed, there was evidence that even if people did not like an advertisement, they still would smoke the cigarette.[54] Much of the message of the ads, intended or not, was instead basically implicit and generally cultural. Advertisers helped tie a style of life and consumer-culture values to smoking and other bad habits and rebellious attitudes. Along with the media, they emphasized the world of illusion. Smoking turned out to be essentially visual, an image. "What we're selling is illusion," a brand manager told Thomas Whiteside in the 1960s. But the world of illusion involved both contemplating purchases in people's fantasy consumer worlds and buying in the real world. That kept the merchandising going. In the days when there were cigarette television commercials, one pictured a carefree and happy young couple bouncing over sand dunes in a jeep:

THEY LAUGH AS THEY SMOKE, CUT TO HER REACTING: LAUGHS AS SHE TAKES IN DEEP, DELICIOUS DRAG ON CIGA-RETTE. STAY ON HER AS SHE REMOVES CIG ... LOOKS AT FIL-TER WITH QUIET APPROVAL. CUT TO HIM FAST. HE BLOWS OUT SMOKE SO YOU KNOW HE THINKS PARLIAMENTS ARE GREAT.[55]

Such repeated imagining of pleasure and buying brought tobacco products into the consumer culture of postindustrial America in a fundamental way.

Tobacco-company owners, too, almost symbolically took the traditional tobacco industry into the larger areas of consumption, including, conspicuously, other bad habits in the traditional constellation of minor vices. With their huge cash flows, tobacco manufacturers were able to diversify so that their corporate profits became much less dependent upon a product that, after the 1950s health revelations, had an uncertain future. Within two or three decades, the number of acquisitions of the various corporations had brought them into possession of any number of major American companies, mostly in the consumer line. The most successful were alcoholic-beverage and related companies. Liggett, for example, started out by acquiring the company that made Alpo dog food and then, in 1966, the makers of J & B Scotch and the importers of Grand Marnier liqueur. Other acquisitions followed, including Wild Turkey bourbon. Altogether the companies that had originally been tobacco companies brought new life to alcoholic-beverage marketing, as Philip Morris did with Miller Brewing in the 1970s. The economic power of these companies and their economic interests intensified the problematic ways in which they and tobacco affected American culture.[56]

Indeed, the turning of tobacco marketers to other elements in the constellation of minor vices may have been symbolic of the willingness of businesspeople to make a change that the more general culture was slow to come to in the late twentieth century, namely, excluding smoking from the lifestyle of the age of commercialized bad habits.[57] A suggestion of the extent to which the age of narcissism, feelings, and body cult could do without smoking was the publication of a book in 1976, *How to Stop Smoking Through Meditation*.[58] The publisher was—Playboy Press! *Playboy* magazine, nevertheless, continued to carry numerous full-page tobacco ads.

Smoking had once been a widely indulged minor vice. Early in the twentieth century, through advertising, tobacco marketers brought cigarettes, particularly, into the new consumer lifestyle that made not indulging the bad habits a deviant act. After midcentury, it took twenty years for a health scare to make smoking unacceptable among a majority of middle-class Americans—and the shift came not on moral or even public health grounds but because of the concern of individuals for their own bodies. And in the meantime, smoking continued as a symbolic, often defiant, act among many young and non-middle-class and female population elements as seductive advertising, often suggesting dangerous, independent actions, continued to appear alongside health warnings. This same kind of cultural ambivalence, as will appear in the next chapters, underlay the acceptance of other kinds of addictive pleasures out of the underworld.

Taking Drugs

Taking "drugs" for pleasure rather than health has been a standard category of behavior for a number of generations. Moreover, American culture provided a special category for this kind of activity, different from the special categories provided for the use of the two other important substances with psychological effects, alcohol and tobacco. Indeed, it was only in the 1960s and 1970s that the highly deviant status of drug taking softened in the United States. Yet drug taking had developed traditional associations with the other elements in the constellation of minor vices—particularly with smoking, as when nineteenth-century drug "fiends" often used tobacco smoke to carry opium.

In the standard social conceptualization of the past, the taking of drugs for nonmedical purposes referred specifically to substances such as opium that were in some sense addictive and to substances that changed the ways in which people felt and perceived the world ("mood altering," in a recent phrasing). The nature of the vice consisted, in the first place, of becoming dependent on the substance—addicted so as to lose one's independence—and habituation, perhaps the extreme of the tendency to repetition, that is, ritual, in traditional vice. A second aspect of taking drugs was that they presumably provided escape from reality, a flagrant escape that made users defy the work ethic and also become socially irresponsible.

Traditionally, then, using drugs for pleasure or imagined pleasure had connotations that smoking and drinking did not necessarily have. The practice was clearly considered deviant by most Americans because it came to involve exotic and stigmatized groups, notably, at first, people whom dominant groups labeled "foreigners," such as Chinese and Mexican populations, as well as gamblers and prostitutes and, later, jazz musicians and hippies. Until the 1960s, only a very tiny fraction of the population, so small as to be insignificant, engaged in the seemingly exotic and extreme practice of ingesting unusual chemicals.[1]

The Origins of Deviant Status

The use of mood-altering or addictive drugs went through four stages. At first, such experiences were largely experimental. Then in the late nineteenth century, a large number of Americans—frequently of the middle or upper class—developed addictions, primarily through the intervention of well-meaning physicians. Just around the turn of the twentieth century, drugs became markedly lower order and deviant, even distinctly criminal. Finally, in the last half of the twentieth century, certain middle-class constituencies joined the deviant groups in advocating the use of drugs of various kinds, and some public-spirited citizens urged at least removing legal penalties for drug use and distribution.[2]

Up until the 1840s, Americans did not perceive drug taking to be a problem. It took half a century before many people, including physicians, became fully aware of the phenomenon of addiction. Although Americans in the China trade profited from dealing in opium, the nonmedical use of such materials took place far away and outside of the awareness of people in the United States. A writer in the *North American Review* in 1824 believed that "very few persons, if any, in this country, abandon themselves to the use of opium as a luxury, nor does there appear to be any great danger of the introduction of this species of intemperance." As late as 1837, a physician asserted that opiates were used to alleviate pain, but "of those who take opium for purposes of unnatural excitement and inebriation, we have no knowledge."[3] Although the model of alcohol inebriation was therefore already present, and the deviant use of drugs known to exist, Americans did not in their own communities detect any such practices that might be of social significance.

In the middle decades of the nineteenth century, a number of developments, along with European examples—well-read Americans knew, for example, of Thomas De Quincey's famous *Confessions of an English Opium Eater* (1824)—introduced the idea and practice of drug taking into the United States. European chemists sought the active principles in opium and produced morphine and, at the end of the century, a related new chemical, heroin. Meanwhile, after midcentury, the hypodermic needle came in, making the injection of mood-altering substances possible (theretofore they had been smoked or eaten). Finally, in the last half of the nineteenth century, the chemists also were furnishing a number of additional new substances for medical use, including chloral hydrate and cocaine, that at times were diverted for nonmedical purposes. By 1895, an ex-addict could describe an acquaintance who had been "actually an abject and complete slave of opium in six forms (morphine by mouth and syringe; gum and powdered opium, laudanum and paragoric [*sic*]), chloral, cocaine, cannabis Indica, stramonium, and belladonna, all of which he took in large quantities, and was, besides, an inveterate smoker of cigarettes impregnated with opium."[4] This picture of multiple drug use provides a convenient inventory of possibilities that had by that time become available for someone devoted to nonmedical drug use. But the obvious substances of most importance were opium and opium derivatives.

Medical Addiction

In the late nineteenth century, approximately 200,000 Americans were addicted to opium in one form or another. Most became addicted after they started using an opiate for medical purposes and then found that they could not give up the practice. Typically, a physician prescribed or administered a drug in order to relieve pain, or provide sleep, or calm a bad case of nerves, and the patient then became dependent upon the drug. In many cases, however, the addict did not even need the intervention of a physician to get started. In those days, one could buy any substance at a drug store or from any other legitimate dealer. People who could not afford a physician, or did not trust physicians, simply dosed themselves. Moreover, many over-the-counter proprietary medicines—including soothing syrups for babies—contained large amounts of opium, and the country was full of people who could not get along without a drugged "patent medicine" any more than could a paregoric "fiend" surrender his or her daily doses.[5]

The typical addict of the late nineteenth century, then, was a woman, often older, who had been introduced to the practice by medical prescription or self-dosing. For whatever cultural reasons, a disproportionate number of the consumers of opium lived in the South. The habit was relatively more frequent in towns and small cities than in the big cities where one might have expected to find vices concentrated. But what was most notable about the addicts was their social class. These were, again, the middle and upper classes, respectable people, those who could, among other things, afford regular doses of drugs. There were also two particularly important groups of men who were conspicuous among drug users. One was the professional class. Among them, the outstanding group was physicians themselves who had come to use opiates or cocaine freely and had become addicted. The other group was Civil War veterans who had been treated with opiates, most commonly to relieve the pain of their wounds.[6]

This high rate of addiction among respectable Americans had two sources beyond the quest for an easy escape from pain and the unpleasantnesses of reality: ignorance and the profit motive. By the 1870s, warnings about addiction began to appear frequently in medical journals. Textbooks of medicine, however, did not carry such warnings until the 1890s, when the general public, too, began reading in the press alarming stories about addiction. In the meantime, large numbers of unwary and ignorant physicians addicted their patients and themselves. Other members of the public, those who dosed themselves, were also entrapped without warning. Under these circumstances, the badge of unrespectability was slow to arrive. A dealer in medical instruments (all available, like drugs, to anyone with the money) reported in 1882, "People have discovered that [morphine injections] are not only of great service in the alleviation of extreme pain but that they afford a convenient sort of respectable intoxication.... There are one hundred hypodermic syringes sold now for each one that found a purchaser a few years ago."[7]

Clearly the potential for profit encouraged the trade in drugs as well as in hypodermic needles. Pharmaceutical firms advertised cocaine and heroin and made good profits from importing opiates and processing them. The interests of local druggists, especially those who protected the secret habits of their customers, were obvious to all observers. One late-nineteenth-century pharmacist noted that he was dependent economically on sales of opium: "If it were not for this stuff and my soda-water I might as well shut up shop." Moreover, many physicians found that opiates provided quick relief of symptoms in many types of ailments. Patients in fact often demanded such treatment. Particularly unscrupulous practitioners in what was then a highly competitive profession knew of course that once addicted, the patient then also needed expensive cures for his or her habit—and if carried out by someone else, typically with a kickback to the referring physician.[8]

Stages in the Deviant Identity

Enough people with economic motives therefore existed to encourage the use of opiates and other drugs among respectable Americans before World War I. Elsewhere, however, beginning in the 1870s, another group of consumers materialized in American society, and they were largely deviant in identification: the opium smokers. Opium smoking began among Chinese immigrants and spread to other members of the community—primarily in West Coast cities. From the very beginning, opium smoking took place in unrespectable surroundings—the notorious opium dens known from melodramatic fiction and sensationalistic journalism. Smoking dens were located almost invariably in, or adjacent to, the segregated district, that is, the red-light district, which in almost every city overlapped Chinatown and provided an area for illicit activities of all kinds in urban areas. It was easy, therefore, for opium smoking to become a part of stereotypical vice. In fact, eyewitnesses reported that prostitutes, criminals, and young men up to no good frequented the dens. As a late-nineteenth-century writer reported, "The first white man who smoked opium in America is said to have been a sporting character named Clendenyn. This was in California, in 1868. . . . The practice spread rapidly and quietly among this class of gamblers and prostitutes."[9]

The innocent or accidental victims of opiate addiction felt that they had nothing in common with opium smokers. As one of the accidentally addicted, William Rosser Cobbe, explained, such addicts as he "never form the habit by deliberate purpose." By contrast, "The smoker of opium becomes such through wantonness of desire. He is not in delirium of fever or made helpless by suffering. . . . This distinction alone, the fact of independent action on the one hand, and irresponsible subjection on the other, must forever divide the smokers from the eaters of the drug." Cobbe also spelled out the fact that opium smokers deliberately chose a deviant identity when they took a pipe: "They take it to gratify an appetite. Their eyes are open; and if they were not morally depraved, they could not remain long enough to smoke a single pipe. Only the facile pencil of the imaginative newspaper reporter could give fascination and [an] air of sensuousness to the opium joints of the United States, which are, without exception, dark, gloomy, vile places that can only excite disgust and loathing."[10] The fact remains that this deviant practice existed in vice districts in the cities and came to be a part of the constellation of minor vices and eventually gave the deviant identity to nonmedical drug taking in general.

After about 1900, the upper-class opiate addicts gradually became less numerous. Civil War veterans died out. Physicians became very conservative in prescribing addictive substances. Members of the public in general, fed on decades of scare literature, tended to try to avoid narcotics. Independence, not dependence, was the prized value, promoted all the more by the temperance and prohibition propaganda about enslavement to another habit, the whiskey habit.[11]

Indeed, except among those who deliberately chose a deviant identity, nonmedical narcotics lost any important constituency. Even the pharmacists and pharmaceutical interests surrendered and collaborated in various legislative attempts on every level of government to control narcotics distribution. By 1914, opiates and narcotics in general were outlawed by federal statute. When vendors found that they probably could not stop the anti-drug campaigns, they attempted to control the market and to reduce to a minimum any reporting procedures under the new laws. For most of the business firms, there was enough profit from legal pharmaceuticals, a substantial amount of which could still be prescribed or diverted (it turned out, for example, that for years under state laws, many addicts had made wholesale purchases that were exempt from the many restrictions that had come to be applied to retail sales). And it was some time, also, before the makers of proprietary medicines and Coca-Cola, which until 1903 contained cocaine, had to eliminate narcotic substances from their products.[12]

Drugs took on a criminal/deviant identity prior to the federal Harrison Act (1914) and other, similar state and local legislation—legislation that in fact only ratified the shift away from middle-class use. Public statements of that time confirmed the deviant status. A New York prison physician, for example, reported in 1914 that drug dealers had found the business very profitable. "Janitors, bartenders, and cabmen have ... been employed to help spread the habit. The plan has worked so well that there is scarcely a poolroom in New York that may not be called a meeting place of drug fiends." As early as 1909, respectable people were joking about deviant drug use:

She—The plumber who was here today acted dopey.
He—Probably he had been hitting the pipe.

Cocaine illustrates this transformation to deviancy. It had had some fashionable upper-class use at the end of the nineteenth century but then moved into the city underworlds in which users tended to be young and criminal. It thereby became absorbed into the changing pattern of deviancy.[13]

Many cocaine users switched to heroin after that substance was introduced at the beginning of the twentieth century, and laws and media publicity further reduced cocaine use. Meanwhile, the heroin habit—at that time mostly sniffing—in turn became associated also with gangs of delinquent boys, at least in New York City, where ample supplies in drug houses could be diverted. As the status of drugs changed, most addicts elsewhere moved over to morphine injection. After 1915, opium smokers in general shifted to heroin, and in the 1920s and 1930s heroin—now in the form of injections—spread widely and replaced other narcotics. Illegal dealers were particularly happy with heroin because it could be adulterated so easily. After a new group of gangsters came to dominate the trade in the 1930s, they adulterated their goods so much that addicts had to inject in order to get enough kick.[14]

During the 1920s and 1930s, the goals of American government policy were to stop the supply and to force addicts to seek treatment. By at least 1929, those who were medically addicted had shrunk in numbers to insignificance, and illegal supplies of drugs provisioned those who were nonmedically addicted. Throughout the interwar period, almost the whole of the public believed that all users were either deviant or criminal or both. As a writer in 1920 noted, "Heroin addiction is a public menace, as it increases the rebellious attitude of antisocial youth, and obliterates all controlling influences of the herd instinct. Heroin, under these circumstances, is naturally the drug of choice of the criminal class." In fact the number of addicts probably was relatively constant. The typical addicts were poor, urban men. Some young men of the working class in nonurban areas who were not standard devotees still sometimes, for example, made use of morphine to help sober up after alcoholic sprees or might try a mood-altering substance obtained from a city center. People continued to joke comfortably about the forbidden substances, as in the 1940s song parody,

"Who Put the Benzedrine in Mrs. Murphy's Ovaltine?" During World War II, drug use declined in the face of the draft, which eliminated some of the usual clientele, and transportation and trade restrictions, which cut off supplies. Some persistent substance abusers tried barbiturates, which were widely used anyway, and by the late 1940s ingesting that family of chemicals had become another standard form of deliberate, nonmedical, deviant drug taking.[15]

Drug addiction before the mid twentieth century was therefore not based on powerful economic or cultural interests. Pharmaceutical manufacturers and wholesalers from time to time tried to preserve profitable sales, but their interests were marginal or episodic. Over a period of time, except for changing details in regulatory law, they did not stand out from the community in general. Smugglers and dealers were isolated in the deviant community, except in so far as any criminal activity in American society overlapped respectable activities. The one important area in which drug use did overlap was in rebellious and sometimes self-consciously avant-garde groups who enjoyed slumming. User groups therefore often included not only the customary prostitutes, sporting figures, and criminals but also people from the arts and theater and "fast" society groups who had money and wanted to be trendsetters—the continuing reality behind the traditional stereotype of the degeneracy of the very lowest classes united with the decadence of parts of the upper classes. "Fast" elements continued in the interwar period to smoke opium in the old way as well as to use other drugs in the more contemporary underworld fashion.[16]

For generations after 1920, surveys showed that deviant or criminal activity preceded drug use—contrary to the stereotype that people crazed with one drug or another subsequently committed crimes. That addicts committed robberies for money to feed their habits was well known, but learning to take drugs was subsequent to the development of criminal patterns. By the interwar years, using drugs was a symbol of a deviant status. Deviants knew that drugs accompanied that status and therefore conformed to the expected role by taking drugs. A (typically) young person would therefore already have committed crimes and have a criminal identity *before* he or she began the use of drugs.[17] The secret habits of middle-class southern widows no longer existed in the social convention that created a trade in narcotics. So well established was the new identity as lower order and criminal, more like that of the cigarette-smoking boy, that it was a notable achievement for this persistent lower-order/criminal group later to move the practice of drug taking into parts of the middle classes.

In the interwar period, the mass media continued the confession and scare literature of an earlier period and depicted drug addiction as a sign of the most degraded condition into which people could fall. As a literary and media device, this portrayal of the misuse of drugs played a powerful role in endowing drug taking with its special deviant status. For instance, in the novels of Sax Rohmer (Arthur Sarsfield Ward)—and the Hollywood movies that came from them—a very large part of the population learned about the notorious Fu Manchu, an ideally villainous figure who wanted to enslave the world with drugs. Tabooing of mind-altering substances in all the media was extremely effective in signaling the deviant and forbidden nature of drug use. Most people were fearful and curious.[18]

Developing Kinship and Empathy with Drug Users

Beginning in the 1950s, the place of drugs in American culture began to change again. Actual users tended to come from a much younger population, although still concentrated in stigmatized groups. Typically they were criminal, urban, and, with new population patterns in the cities, black. But now those who tried drugs came more frequently to include also other kinds of young people who, though not slum dwellers, were conforming to the deviant standards. One factor in motivating this new clientele was their belief (shared by many Americans) that "jazz musicians" frequently used drugs, especially—and significantly for the immediate future—marijuana. Fats Waller, the famous musician, for example, during World War II had recorded a prewar underground song, "If You're a Viper," which begins, "Dreamed about a reefer five foot long. . . ." Eventually journalists picked up this change. Just at the beginning of the 1960s, especially, in addition to the usual criminal and scare stories about narcotics, a new kind of story began to show up here and there in the media. Playing on the juvenile-delinquency scare, media writers began to talk not about drug use in deviant populations but about "our kids."[19]

This portrayal was the first step in the process of developing what Jerome Lionel Himmelstein calls "kinship" to the drug problem and hence in transforming it into a new kind of middle-class concern. In an article in the *Saturday Evening Post* in 1960, for example, a father told how "My Son Was Caught Using Narcotics." The incident occurred when a large number of young people were apprehended in wealthy Westchester County, New York. They came, as the father said, from "families which have given their children everything that money can buy, every opportunity that schools, churches, and social welfare can provide." For middle-class people, such close-to-home depictions in the media made drugs less alien and of more immediate concern to many opinion makers.[20]

In fact, any attention in the mass media that did not evoke strong feelings of distance and deviance fostered the use of drugs. Even years later, this same phenomenon continued to operate, as a youngster from Philadelphia showed vividly in an interview from the beginnings of the 1970s:

A little while ago, there was an article about drug use among younger kids in some magazine. The article had a photograph of a bunch of fifth or sixth graders sitting around smoking dope. . . . the effect of that picture was that sixth graders all around the country looked at that article and said, "Gosh, I'm really getting behind. Here I am turning twelve years old and I haven't even smoked *dope* yet!" And so of course he smokes dope a lot sooner than if he'd never seen that picture. I know personally two seventh graders who started doing dope just because they had seen that article. Of course the article said in words, "Isn't this terrible" . . . but on another level it was saying, "Hey, kid, this is where it's at."

The interviewer continued: "I heard relatively few accounts like this in 1968, but I cannot count the number that I have heard in 1970 and 1971; drug users are increasingly aware of the catalytic effect of the media on the growth of their subculture"—and he and other observers credited media attention for the explosive number of recruits to the drug culture at that time.[21]

Developing Empathy

In addition to the occasional media stories pulling middle-class people to a kinship with drug problems, in the early 1960s, two further developments contributed to the embourgeoisement of drug taking. Psychedelic drug use began, and, at the same time, increasing numbers of non-lower-order young people turned to marijuana, which had to date not been an important stigmatized substance except, as I have noted, for some very minor use in Hispanic, jazz, and other subcultures. Numbers of middle-class young people were arrested for marijuana violations, and at almost exactly the same time, the mid-1960s, the media began suddenly to give much greater attention to drug use. Now journalists did not always use the same scary tone that was typical earlier. Indeed, at the time, the coverage could appear to be "balanced"—that is, explaining a little how a person could have become hooked. Moreover, in the media, at least, the site of the pot problem in particular moved to "the campus," so that it became decidedly a middle-class problem. Beginning in 1964–1965, middle-class people could for the first time identify with members of what was becoming known as the drug culture, for at that time the mass media introduced the element of empathy into portrayals of drug users—a process that Himmelstein designates the second stage in moving drug use into social toleration.[22]

Empathy grew particularly out of the severe punishments that a number of middle-class young people were receiving for their drug activities. The third of Himmelstein's stages, "normality" or normalization of drug use, followed, in so far as it did come, chronologically close on the heels of empathy. Drug use did not, in fact, completely reach a stage of normalization in American society. Rather, normalization was part of the hopeful propaganda to introduce drug taking into society just as repealers labeled alcoholic-beverage drinking "normal"—because everybody, supposedly, did it. Indeed, part of the argument, as will be noted below, was that illegal marijuana was more innocuous than legal booze. The media, at least, took up the cause of marijuana (though not, immediately, of all other substances) with vigor. In 1967, one hippie who enjoyed the idea that his pot was illegal came to believe that there must have been a conspiracy to deprive him of his pleasure in rebelling against the law—a conspiracy to have marijuana legalized. In July alone, writers in *Life*, *Look*, and *Newsweek* all questioned the penalties for marijuana use. Indeed, proponents of various drugs won so much media attention that a bandwagon campaign began, and Americans learned from the media that many respectable people believed that decriminalization and legalization were inevitable if not desirable.[23]

Media Saturation and an Expanding Drug Culture

So pervasive was the media coverage from 1968 to 1974 that hardly anyone could have failed to become aware of drug taking in the United States. But the media were describing a variety of different drugs, practices, and consumers. One practice was using marijuana. In the very late 1960s, taking cocaine became the modish way of experimenting. And then trying heroin also caused much concern in the press, especially as the old idea persisted and grew that "soft" drugs are the inevitable road to "hard" drugs. The

most important new element, however, was the publicity given the connection between crime and drugs, what H. Wayne Morgan calls "the
junkie-burglar-mugger" and "mobster-supplier" images. The ideas were
not new, but for some time public concern about them had been at a low
level. In 1969, President Richard Nixon called for a war on drugs and drug-
related crime. Not until 1970, however, did public-opinion polls show that
the media blitz to raise Americans' concern about drugs was paying off.
At that time, polls showed that public opinion was just beginning to rank
drugs a major national problem and a major cause of crime. Nevertheless,
the customary form of public reaction did not develop as it had in the
past, for the deviant image included another type of drug user—the perhaps
acceptable rebel. And so, taking drugs became only one of a host of other
political and cultural polarizations of the time that were symbolized by the
civil-rights movement and the Vietnam War.[24]

One sign that drug taking was often a symbolic deviant act was that,
as many writers in the media of the 'sixties and 'seventies lumped all drugs
together into one category, so also did the actual practice of drug taking
tend to shift to using any mood-altering substances, in any form. The older
addict, of another day, was devoted to one particular substance at a time
and was not inclined to accept substitutes. Even the 1960s hippies had only
contempt for such drugs as opiates and speed that did not enhance consciousness. This pattern of use gave way to that of young people who
were indiscriminate in what they took—standard opiates in whatever form,
cocaine, marijuana, LSD, barbiturates, amphetamines, and whatever anyone
had heard of or would sell. The idea was to alter mood, not to "abuse" a
particular substance. In one case, a rumor set off the smoking of banana
peels. In another, a substance with mood-altering potential made from kitty
litter was reported in an informal printed handout circulated on Long
Island. Within two weeks, credulous people had so depleted the supply
of litter that the local cat population suffered a crisis—the unintended
victims of a practical joke. "Polypharmacy" was therefore the face of drug
abuse by the 1970s—a symbol of both the quest for any change in mood or
experience out of the ordinary and at the same time the definition of a
category of behavior that had a deviant status.[25]

Polypharmacy had the advantage that by substituting one substance,
including alcohol, for another, any addiction problems (what people at the
time came to characterize as an admitted helplessness) were easily masked.
When, later in the 1970s and in the 1980s, cocaine replaced marijuana as
the drug of choice and as heroin or some new variation of an old substance

came in or went out of fashion, the changes began to appear more and more to be—just changes in fashion. New trends, as one veteran expert observed, generally depended upon whatever fads got started among certain groups of young people in California.[26]

Economic Interests

The foregoing summary delineates how drug use moved into the Victorian and post-Victorian underworld and evolved as a stereotypical deviant activity right through the 1950s, and, further, how it passed through stages after about 1960 to affect—at least by empathy—many respectable people and even the culture as a whole. The contribution of the mass media to these changes was both symptom and cause. But all these changes took place in a much larger context, in which any number of specific factors were operating. The shifts in the place of drugs in American society were clearly in part cultural—or, properly speaking, subcultural, as the population ultimately fragmented in the mid twentieth century. It would be foolish, however, to ignore the fact that real economic interests also developed and reinforced the changes and pushed them further and faster—even beyond the sensationalizing and publicizing carried out by the media. Both economic and cultural interests expressed themselves through the advocates of drug use who were conspicuous in the last half of the twentieth century.

Foremost among the obviously interested groups were the pharmaceutical manufacturers. At least one American house developed in part in the nineteenth century on the basis of morphine profits.[27] People sympathetic to drug taking chuckle to this day about the way in which the German pharmaceutical firm Bayer was advertising the virtues of not only aspirin but also heroin in the United States before World War I.

From the early nineteenth century to the late twentieth, merchandisers of drugs sold as much as possible of any substance as their lawyers would allow. In the 1960s, some time after it was clear that LSD was problematic but before state regulatory laws came into force, "all one had to do was send a little note to Sandoz Pharmaceuticals and tell them you would like some LSD, or did they have any extra mescaline around, and they would send it wholesale, perhaps with warm letters on how they hoped you would use it a lot." As late as the 1980s, makers of "poppers," doses of a chemical that underground sources believed enhanced sexual experiences, publicly defended manufacturing and marketing them and tried to push responsibility for possible abuse off onto the "responsible adult user." In the course of defending their actions, the makers managed to advertise the supposed safety of these obviously profitable products.[28]

Whenever it became inevitable that one substance or another would come under legal restrictions, manufacturers and merchants continued throughout the century to want to have as much monopoly as possible but to enjoy their protected status within a set of laws and rules that would keep enforcement to a minimum. In the early 1970s, when everyone saw that restrictions on amphetamines and barbiturates could no longer be avoided, industry representatives cynically persuaded legislators to water down the provisions of the laws so that diversion of the substances to nonmedical customers would continue to be relatively easy.[29]

As the trade in drugs became increasingly illegal, few ancillary industries appeared that could publicly advocate and pressure for drug taking—in contrast to the sellers and advertisers who profited from alcoholic-beverage and cigarette use and who did openly support the trade in tobacco and alcohol. But there were lively economic interests. In the early 1970s, one experienced newspaperman commented that "the fencing business in Baltimore is quite lucrative, quite busy. It's another product of the drug culture or subculture. It's created a whole new economic system. It's created jobs. It's created the profit." One of his colleagues pointed out that many of the fences paid off directly in drugs—a real, not imaginary, "linkage between crime and drugs."[30]

There were legal businesses with a stake in drug use. Beginning in the 1960s, the paraphernalia industry came to represent a significant economic interest, with trade mounting possibly into the billions of dollars each year by the late 1970s. The publishers of *High Times*, the magazine of marijuana use, at one point had to limit the amount of advertising they could accept, so great was the eagerness of paraphernalia merchants to sell their goods. Eventually the publishers also had to ask advertisers to stop using copy openly advocating the use of illegal substances. By 1976, a special paraphernalia trade publication had appeared. The manufacturers formed a formal trade association in 1978, and retailers also organized regionally. The interest of this industry was transparent, even when not shown openly.[31]

With relatively large-scale marijuana use in the 1960s, manufacturers of cigarette rolling paper became the largest interested industrial group (one of the largest tobacco companies, for example, distributed Zig-Zag papers). The sales of rolling papers doubled between 1971 and 1973 alone. In 1978, an ad for a wide paper made especially for marijuana won a national Cleo Award, on the basis of a radio plug that the manufacturers were running— clearly showing the interest of advertising and media people in the para- phernalia industry. This same cigarette-paper firm sponsored cars in var- ious auto races and thus in sports reporting garnered a large amount of free publicity for the rolling papers by doing so. In 1973, the makers of Acapulco Gold rolling papers—named after a marijuana—were advertising in *Rolling Stone* magazine for the end of marijuana prohibition and soliciting for membership in a pro-pot organization that was supported in part by sales of the rolling papers. In general, the extent to which legal businesses that had an interest in various illegal drugs took a role in overt pro-drug agitation is not in the public record, but members of the paraphernalia industry nevertheless left substantial evidence of their existence in Amer- ican society. Not only did head shops specializing in drug accessories appear, beginning in 1965, but even record stores took advantage of the perhaps 300 per cent markup over cost on accessories and carried, at the least, copies of *High Times* and other pro-drug magazines. That para- phernalia retailers were involved in linking the drug culture with other items—records, T-shirts, boutique goods, and even political items—was a cultural and economic phenomenon well recognized at the time. In the late 1970s, Burt Rubin, who made a fortune marketing marijuana cigarette paper, mused about the economic ramifications of his business:

> I've read quotes from the stereo music business attributing the growth of that industry to a great extent to marijuana. That was one of the first things people told you when you were gonna smoke. You're gonna get thirsty, you're gonna get hungry, and you're gonna really love music. I'd say *Sergeant Pepper* did more for the increase in smoking than anything around. You know how much money ITT Baking sells in Twinkies a year? Twinkies. Seventy million dollars' worth of Twinkies. Go to any 7-11 store, they'll tell you people buy a pack of E-Z Wider [marijuana cigarette papers], they buy a can of cherry soda, two Yodels and a Twinkie, and a few minutes later they're back for more Twinkies.[32]

The economic possibilities of drugs clearly were being realized in many surprising as well as obvious ways.

The Illegal-Drug Business Per Se

The economic system that sprang up to help addicts supply their habits was subterranean, but it did encourage sales, especially just by enhancing availability—one of the important factors in encouraging drug use. Over the years, any number of detailed exposés of the illegal opium and other drug trades appeared. Accounts of small-time traders in the slums were numerous as well, so commonplace as to present a consistent picture of marketers' shortsighted opportunism. When middle-class people came to be involved additionally as consumers and often dealers in the 1960s, the basic patterns did not change. A relatively few entrepreneurs controlled the sources of supply and many times were not themselves users. Often they operated in syndicates—following the decentralized pattern of other organized crime—in order to manage the capital, corruption, and expertise needed for any particular set of deals. Unlike in other businesses, fear of legal detection made consolidation undesirable and so fostered the development of many hierarchies of "middlemen," who carried out multiple levels of transactions before finally serving the relatively very large number of retailers who did the ultimate dealing. Only a remarkably high markup could justify such an inefficient market apparatus. The lower levels of the apparatus almost always included people deeply involved in drug use themselves. Indeed, as will be reiterated, because they were so often selling to friends, personal relationships sometimes obscured business connections. Most petty dealers, in fact, got their start by friendly distribution of goods and imperceptibly moved into dealing. The business represented some sort of perfection in the consumer culture—the goods brought prestige to both seller and buyer in a social setting in which the consumption was ideally appreciated.[33]

Dealers at various levels of the hierarchy tended to spend their money on immediate gratifications or to funnel it into enterprises that either were fronts for illegal activity or represented an attempt to leave the occupation. Accounts from the late twentieth century indicate that most traders saw their work as only temporary; very few indeed were dedicated, lifetime Fu Manchus. Although dealers at all levels lived in as comfortable a style as possible, law-enforcement efforts and the consequent inconveniences and stress were in fact successful in moving them to try to end their dealing. Altogether, few dealers at any level were motivated to invest in any long-term attempts to extend the use of drugs, although of course they recruited users as the impulse moved them, which was often. Moreover, many contributed to formal and informal drug-advocacy efforts in a sporadic way, and some did so to an important extent. The friendly relationship that was involved in most illegal transactions gave substance to the idea that dealers would hand out free samples—obviously to acquaintances who were trustworthy—to try to hook customers. How could one tell the difference between comradeship and marketing under such circumstances? Motives were mixed, and any user-dealer also wanted to have his or her friends become part of the drug culture to which he or she belonged—not least so that "everybody" would "do it."[34]

While the retailers tended to be the heart and soul of the drug culture and represented the power of small-scale as well as large-scale business to influence the culture, upper-level figures had significant legitimate social and business contacts. Through those contacts also, the dealers did influence the society—but only indirectly if the contacts were unaware of the illegal nature of the dealers' work. Dealers often obtained help and capital from legitimate figures who laundered illegal money and worked with front businesses. Indeed, a significant number of middle-level traders came into the business not as a result of personal use but through their "normal" transactions with dealers—for example, working real estate deals to cover illegal profits. Moreover, dealers corrupted bankers and others who served or cooperated with them. In this way, a number of wealthy or powerful respectables developed motives for seeing the trade protected, perpetuated, and expanded. Drugs in the end did not differ from gambling or other illegal activities that commanded a fair amount of covert support in any community—including that of government officials who took bribes or political contributions.[35]

Drugs therefore in many ways influenced legitimate businesses, including some parts of the media that notoriously were tied to criminal capitalists—or, like areas of the entertainment business, even more than in the 1920s and 1930s, to the drug culture. One obvious sign was the advertising that record companies—including major companies such as RCA and Capitol—placed, with friendly contents, in pro-drug publications, including *High Times*. In 1968, for example, a Columbia Records ad in *Rolling Stone* pictured a group of young people smoking what was obviously a marijuana cigarette.[36]

Rebellious Networks and a Drug Culture

The drug culture also embodied a very important force in drug taking: rebelliousness of both lower-order and bohemian varieties. The use by children of forbidden substances like cigarettes and alcohol, in secret and forbidden ways was not new. But at midcentury, grouping together with other rebels so as to connect into economic as well as larger social networks had practical effects even beyond those enjoyed by gangs of another era. Becoming a hippie meant taking drugs, and (in contrast to the late nineteenth century) taking drugs came to mean entering a drug culture. Beginning in the late 1960s, the fact that many middle-class young people participated with others in substance use underlined the rebellious factor.[37]

Over many decades, drug taking continued to be overwhelmingly a social act, even if only two people were involved. After midcentury, drug taking developed a special meaning and impact as networks of users and dealers formed the drug culture—a definite culture that spread into many aspects of society. As one group of researchers from the mid-1960s noted, "In the jails and prisons, they have transmitted the mystique of 'coolness' and romance attached to the unique experience of the addict. In the free and closed communities, they have served to foster addiction among those who were originally only criminal offenders." As these more formally criminal rebels against society came into contact with already rebellious young people, the culture spread from the criminal population to both working-class and middle-class groups, most conspicuously college students. One lower-order heroin user told how she began: "Both those chicks at the massage parlor had already been strung out and I really loved both them chicks. . . . They couldn't do no wrong by me. Everything they did was right to me so I just went ahead and went right along with them." Middle-class students told very similar stories—a friend or a group of friends started them. The vulnerability of young people to peer pressure was of course a constant and familiar phenomenon—just as in alcohol and tobacco use.[38]

Peer pressure therefore moved ordinary rebelliousness into networks that involved both criminality and systematic, reinforced dissent from society. As investigators at the time found, the more frequently a person used drugs, the more he or she tended to drop old friends and to move more completely into the drug-culture networks. In the group, one had to prove oneself as a deviant from the larger society—ideally, on one level, by going to jail, an action that addict opinion leaders tended to admire. Drugs came to represent not only a way of life but a whole outlook on life—often shared to some extent even by those who were only very casual in their use of mind- and mood-altering substances.[39]

Taking drugs during and after the 1960s therefore generated a number of unique attributes among the minor vices. One was recruiting intensely, person by person. Another was the ambiguous role of the retail dealer with his or her customer. The old-fashioned saloon keeper, for example, functioned in much the same way but never developed the close personal ties that existed between drug dealer and user and seldom commanded such overwhelming cultural loyalty. Saloons anyway generated business dependencies upward, toward suppliers, not downward, as into the personal-customer networks of the drug culture.

What was unique about the drug culture was the central role of the retail dealer. When one experienced investigator listed "myths of youthful drug use" that were obvious by the 1970s—such as "Adulterants and dilutants are generally harmless" and "Over-the-counter drugs are relatively safe"—the very first and most important common belief was "You can always trust your dealer." The importance of the personal networks in which dealers were involved was remarkable in a largely impersonal society. Truly, as they joked, they were involved in grass-roots capitalism. And they did explicitly identify themselves as the center of an alternative culture.[40]

Personal networks therefore established a powerful alternative cultural authority. In part, this authority represented the failure of credibility of social authority. Adults and media agents who had portrayed the dangers of various substances in dramatic ways made young people who tried them skeptical when nothing particularly negative happened—particularly with some marijuana and LSD use. Altogether, then, in many parts of American society, the absence of supposed immediate and obvious bad effects of some drug taking, just as in the case of tobacco use, made it relatively easy to credit the authority of drug advocates. Sociological investigators of members of the drug culture emphasized one question—how young people got involved. But a usually unspoken comment was amazement that the adolescent/peer-group patterns persisted among older members of the drug culture.[41]

Nor was the existence of an alternative authority a secret. A number of widely admired media celebrities and performers were known to use drugs, and news about them helped undermine the impact of anti-drug condemnations just as had happened in the heyday of the 1920s repealers. An actor, Robert Mitchum, for example, was arrested on marijuana charges as early as 1948. In one famous case, comedian Lenny Bruce died of a drug overdose, in 1966. When idolized members of The Beatles were arrested for marijuana offenses, their habits could not be kept secret from anyone. The entertainment media continually popularized the idea that taking drugs and participating in the drug culture were commonplace. A very popular "country-western" singer, Johnny Cash, in 1969 sang "Cocaine Blues." Well-known movies such as *Easy Rider* and *Superfly*, as one expert noted, "glamorized the free and easy coke dealer." Later chemical enthusiasts openly characterized two movie actors, "Cheech and Chong," as the stars of "the dope-smoking Seventies."[42]

"Better Living through Chemistry"

The content of news and entertainment media continued throughout the last half of the century to reflect as well as carry the impact of the drug merchants. The merchants expanded their trade and culture and developed a large number of cultural as well as economic allies in American society. Before the 1960s, drug dealing and drug use were not new and were not particularly important. What, then, caused drug trafficking suddenly to take on social significance? People at that time talked about factors operating in society at large, particularly the bad example set by large numbers of rebellious bohemians in an affluent culture and about the self-indulgence of a population who took pills for every ache or pain, imagined or real.

The coming of television and the so-called tranquilizer drugs in the 1950s did have a substantial impact on American life in general. Leaving aside the indignant criticisms of those who opposed an easy hedonism, many social commentators recognized that television commercials promised a cure for any discomfort or unhappiness, from hemorrhoids and headache to tension and unpopularity, if the viewer would only purchase one product or another. Pharmaceutical ads in particular showed people who became happy after taking some medication or another. As one critic noted in 1971, "Even from cursory television viewing, it is becoming apparent that drugs are filling in where cigarette advertising left off." Another critic of that era, Joel Fort, in 1969 made the obvious connection in this way:

We live in a *drug-ridden, drug saturated society*, in which from infancy onward we have been taught . . . "Better Living Through Chemistry." We are taught that there is a pill, a drink, or a cigarette for every real or imagined pain, trouble, or problem, and that the more of these substances we use, the better off we will be. Both the alcoholic-beverage industry and the tobacco industry spend between one and two million dollars every single day in the United States alone to promote and encourage the greatest possible use of their drugs by the largest possible number of people, and hopefully in large quantities. . . . Compoz . . . has been advertised in multimillion-dollar campaigns as the "little gentle blue pill" which makes women presidents of their clubs and men successful executives. . . . In addition to this fully legal advertising, there is a less explicit kind of advertising going on about the totally illegal drugs marijuana, heroin, and LSD. The advertising, propagandizing, and *glorification* are free, being done, if not systematically, quite thoroughly by drug policemen, certain politicians, and the mass media, who day after day . . . feature pot, acid, and "dope," exaggerating the properties of these drugs as well as their importance in the total context of our society, but very successfully arousing interest and curiosity, leading to ever-widening patterns of use.

Television itself, as many critics noted, changed and blurred perceptions. Why, then, they argued, should not marijuana or LSD provide a natural new way in which to see reality?[43]

When the media publicized the mood-altering qualities of such tranquilizers as Miltown and Valium, the new possibilities played further into Americans' pill-taking propensities. Tranquilizers became the most prescribed drugs in use. When a young person criticized for using marijuana could shoot back about the alcohol, cigarettes, caffeine, and tranquilizers utilized by the critic, the accusation was difficult to parry. Using drugs to ease imagined pain and to alter one's mood and perceptions was a common cultural behavior, especially in a culture in which pleasure was one of the values emphasized by both commercial and general media. In a well-known 1977 article in *Fortune* magazine, a pharmaceutical researcher's prediction for the immediate future was quoted: "We are on the edge of a choose-your-mood society."[44] Readers of *Fortune* presumably were interested in the business possibilities.

Finally, virtually all observers agreed that the drug culture was intimately associated with the ingress of rock-and-roll music, culturally as well as economically (a subject to which I return in succeeding chapters). Indeed, one variety of pop music, acid rock, was named after LSD. Although the extent to which rock music itself, any more than jazz earlier, caused people—presumably young people—to use drugs is conjectural, the fact was that the lyrics supported at least part of the drug culture directly, and the indirect support was generally affirmed by all observers. In 1967, a vice president at CBS was quoted as saying that Bob Dylan, the singer, was "the leading cultural force among young people today. . . . 'The Times Are Changin'' made questioning the American concept of standards the 'in' thing to do, and 'Rainy Day Woman' (which any junkie knows is a marijuana cigarette)," another Dylan piece, he concluded, was a very profitable composition. Dylan's "Mr. Tambourine Man" was "an exquisite hymn to drugs," according to writer Patrick Anderson. Four of the songs in the Beatles' famous album *Sgt. Pepper's Lonely Hearts Club Band* alluded to drug taking ("I get high with a little help from my friends"). The editor of the rock-related publication *Cheetah*, founded in 1967, made it a deliberate policy to include at least one drug allusion on every page. The first national rock-and-roll magazine, *Rolling Stone* (also founded in 1967), was understood at the time to be also a drug magazine. In 1974, a *High Times* editor believed that his publication filled "a gap left by *Rolling Stone* when they became a big publication." Stories in the early years of *Rolling Stone* not only told how to avoid getting arrested for drug taking but also publicized the drug culture. A good example featured a New York rock group with an unprintable name who in 1968 claimed to represent "dope dealers, hustlers, and 'street people.' "[45] From the very beginning, *Rolling Stone* advertised openly for high-school distributors of the publication. It would be difficult to epitomize better the combination of commercial and cultural drive to spread the drug culture.

Putting Drugs in the Bohemian Tradition

Both proponents and opponents of drugs tied the drug culture not only to the American mainstream but also to the deep cultural divisions that the so-called beat generation of the 1950s and hippies of the late 1960s symbolized and inflamed. The stereotypical bohemian of an earlier generation was rebellious against society, and perhaps drunk a part of the time, but the rebellion of that older time was notoriously in the sexual and political spheres—above and beyond the artistic. Narcotics and other drugs were not commonly a part of the stereotype. Except for some advanced experimentation and slumming, most traditional bohemians were not prophets of the drug culture. When the beat generation showed up in San Francisco in the 1950s, drug use was either a personal aberration or a part of traditional romantic self destructiveness. Sex was the big issue then—and a version of the old art for art's sake. The place of drugs in Jack Kerouac's description of the rebellious beatniks, *On the Road*, for example, is by later standards remarkably minor and ambivalent.[46]

With the coming of the hippie stereotype in the late 1960s, however, drugs did become an integral part of the new bohemianism; indeed, marijuana (and at one point, LSD) became a symbol around which the hippie element would rally. Mass media publicized the existence of a new deviant and pictured both males and females with long hair and wearing colorful costumes. According to the media, they were devoted to "sex, drugs, and rock and roll." Well-publicized hippie leaders spoke out strongly against the established order and tried, with considerable success, to embarrass and annoy authorities and expose hypocrisy. The rebels also endorsed alternative value systems that particularly included drug taking. A former writer for the *East Village Other*, for example, reported that when he worked there in 1967, "It was a condition of employment that you had to smoke pot." In particular, the rebels drew on the traditional interest that bohemians had in Eastern religious meditation and passivity, which they connected with drugs, particularly LSD and marijuana, substances that were supposed to have "consciousness expanding" qualities. The media particularly publicized "happenings"—starting with the Be-In—and the supposed hippie utopia in the Haight-Ashbury district of San Francisco was soon called "Hashbury" (hash was a term for cannabis).[47]

Two characteristics of hippies and others who were on the cultural left at midcentury made them especially attractive to drug advocates. First was their obvious rebelliousness and broad-gauge attack on previously conventional social standards. The other was the fact that they and many other people, including members of the mass media, believed that they were the new avant garde and that the behavior and attitudes that they pioneered would soon become standard for all of society. According to this agenda, in the new age, in the world that would be made by those on the younger side of the generation gap, drug taking would play a prominent part. It was, in short, a bold play by drug advocates to coopt love, peace, civil rights, and tolerance for the drug culture.[48]

Drug Advocates

As general economic and cultural forces continued to operate, even before the drug culture had started to expand out of the underworld in a major way, a number of Americans began in public to take the side of drug takers (if not directly of the sellers). The first advocates who showed up in the late 1950s were physicians and lawyers who disagreed with the punitive methods then employed to control narcotic use. Following the lead of alcoholism experts, many medical and other professional personnel spread the idea that people took drugs because they were already ill and that the way to prevent drug abuse was to provide each user with appropriate individual treatment. As the leading spokesperson for this point of view, Alfred R. Lindesmith, put it in 1958, "People ought not to be punished for disease or for actions which arise from it." Lawyers also were concerned because enforcement of drug laws was often exceptional as well as expensive. In 1955, the American Bar Association persuaded the American Medical Association to join in a study of narcotic drug control, and the critical report issued in 1961 questioned enforcement policies of that period. Significantly, a subsequent book by one of the lawyer advocates characterized the long-standing policies as "the American Experiment in Narcotic Drug Control"—once again suggesting that a social policy of prohibition, in this case drugs rather than alcohol, was only temporary and could be reversed.[49]

As the 1960s went on, the advocates of an individualized medical approach increasingly gained a hearing. They emphasized that the drug problem was one of individuals who would need treatment—not of people who were devoted to deviant behavior and groups. This approach became particularly significant because those people who came under treatment more frequently were middle-class young people with whom arbiters of public opinion could feel kinship and, eventually, empathy. The pioneer treatment group, Synanon, and other therapeutic efforts provided concrete alternatives to the criminal sanctions that in that era were more appropriate for minority and lower-order people. At the same time, a number of commentators and researchers blamed unfortunate social conditions for spawning drug use among the lower orders of society, suggesting, too, that, in the absence of major social changes, individual treatment was the most hopeful course to follow. Indeed, parallel to alcoholism, and in close imitation, a whole constituency of drug-abuse therapists began to appear. They had an interest not in prevention or social action but in individual treatment. Because many of them were former drug users, they represented an ultimate in empathy and claimed to be the experts in dealing with all substance problems.[50]

These essentially humanitarian efforts were congenial to proponents of drugs. They concentrated attention on the individual, as opposed to the substance—just as in the case of alcohol—and suggested that use might be normal and that only abuse was a problem.[51] And as more and more people felt empathy for the young middle-class users who were receiving harsh prison sentences, the alternative of individual psychotherapy—already generally popular in the culture—appeared to be more and more attractive as a solution to a dilemma. This line of thinking then led directly to the idea of decriminalization, that is, removing legal penalties from the act of using a forbidden substance and, in practice, punishing drug pushers mildly, if at all. In this way, what might have been a liberal and sensible stance quickly produced two further positions.

The first was an attack on the law and law-enforcement agencies, particularly in cases in which administrators had become advocates of particular laws and procedures. Indeed, in the case of anti-marijuana efforts, the attacks were aimed at undermining confidence in the laws themselves, on the basis that the chief federal narcotics enforcement officer, Harry J. Anslinger (to whom was attributed a variety of motives) had distorted facts in getting Congress to outlaw marijuana in the first place. One writer, for example, in 1972 condemned the "stupidity and savagery" of the whole law-enforcement and legislative effort of previous years. This attitude led to a general approval of law breaking. One of the ads in *High Times*, for example, was titled "Learn How to Pick Locks!"—which was not inconsistent with the many other ads and advice in the magazine about evading and breaking other laws.[52]

The cooptation of the therapists was more subtle. Therapy, argued drug advocates and their allies, should be voluntary, that is, freed of the threat of prosecution and wholly in the medical mode. "We believe that addicts, like most citizens, should have the right to choose their form of effective medical treatment," stated one group of researchers, plausibly enough, going on to add the addicts' right also "to discontinue it when they believe it to be inappropriate, and to seek treatment elsewhere without the threat of imprisonment."[53] If the drug taker, in short, became the judge of whether or not to continue treatment, or, implicitly, not even stop taking drugs, then treatment simply became a mask for social policy, namely, decriminalizing drug use.

The Advent of LSD

Just as this legal-medical debate was developing at the beginning of the 1960s, a new factor entered: a previously unknown substance with powerful mind-altering capabilities, LSD. It appeared, not as a secret criminal substance, but at first legally under the open advocacy of articulate and dedicated leaders, the most notable of whom was Timothy Leary. Leary, a

Harvard psychologist, experimented with psilocybin mushrooms and then pure chemical LSD and came to believe that he had found a technological facilitator for exploring the inner self in the manner of Eastern mystics. Leary or LSD had a substantial underground following as early as 1962. By 1962–1963, he was encouraging groups dedicated to the use of the drugs and was speaking to various audiences, chiefly in the bohemian/campus communities, extolling the effects of the drugs. This campaign came just as other types of unconventional agitation were developing. A 1965 observer, for example, described the connection between drugs and the new romantic idealism in this advocacy:

> Jazz, Hip, the Beat Movement, the Underground Cinema, the Happenings, the Marijuana Culture, the Folk Music movement, the Radical Left, Buddhism, Esoteric Christianity, the Indian worship of the Sun, the IFIF movement of Alpert and Leary, Existentialism, are no more than a handful of the many avenues that are finding a contemporary confluence and a contemporary agreement in the United States.

It was a group of LSD devotees who in 1966 held the first "Be-Ins," attempting to celebrate life with music, love, drugs, and what immediately came to be recognized as the hippie way of life and protest in general. In these and other "happenings," advocates were clever in manipulating the press to give drug taking publicity. Leary in particular became a media celebrity, and large numbers of Americans were exposed to his persuasive powers. In a famous interview published in *Playboy* magazine in 1966, Leary advocated using marijuana once a day and LSD once a week, and he repeated his famous motto directed to young people, "Turn on, tune in, drop out." Mustering all the standard arguments, Leary gave special emphasis to two of them. One was the aphrodisiac qualities that he attributed to LSD. The other was his claim that the best young people, those who would soon inherit the leadership of the country, had a special affinity for the new drug experiences. The hippies of that time joined Leary in arguing that, as Timothy Miller summarizes it, "dope is fun . . . revolutionary . . . and good for body and soul."[54]

In the cultural politics of the Vietnam War era, Leary's advocacy was confused with many other issues. Drug taking became a symbolic as well as a personal activity. Moreover, Leary also was recommending the use of marijuana just at the time that many other media figures were championing it as well, albeit less openly. Significant numbers of them often employed the double entendre based on drug slang to reinforce the shared cultural secret of those who used and talked about marijuana and other chemicals—whether an Armed Forces Radio Network announcer in Vietnam alluding ambiguously to someone who was "flying" or rock groups singing with the Beatles "I need a fix." Increasingly during the 1960s, double entendre changed to open advocacy, first in one place and then in another. Because the low point of marijuana arrests had come as recently as 1960, the extent of the change within a very few years was startling.[55]

The Pro-Marijuana Campaign

As early as 1961, beatnik poet Allen Ginsberg, known earlier for outrageous advocacy of many things out of the slumming/jazz-bohemian tradition, had publicly touted the virtues of marijuana on a television interview show. By 1964, Ginsberg had joined with other bohemians to agitate for legalization of marijuana and had even announced the formation of a group called LEMAR (Legalize Marijuana), although it was not clear how organized the group was.[56]

By 1970–1971, marijuana was sufficiently established to spawn formal advocacy groups, the most successful of which was NORML, National Organization for the Reform of Marijuana Laws. Three elements supported such groups. One element was marijuana users and their sympathizers, who were constantly telling each other—and anyone else who would listen—that society had no business interfering in a personal action that was innocuous. Users contributed some support and funds, and an occasional millionaire did give large amounts after a while (one wealthy hippie financed a pro-marijuana ad in *Time* magazine in 1974). Most of the energy and money, however, came from those with financial motives—not just the paraphernalia trade noted above but also actual wealthy drug merchants. One such major dealer, for example, Tom Forcade, who also became publisher of *High Times*, was very important in bankrolling NORML. The third element consisted of indirect allies, and in the case of NORML, there was a symbolic event: the initial, and main, financing for the organization came from *Playboy*.[57]

The Public Pro-Drug Argument

Drug advocates, whatever their intentions, in their rebelliousness supported the use of any and all drugs (whether or not they themselves practiced polypharmacy). Arguments for marijuana in particular were absolutely unoriginal and traditional, that is, they came out of the Prohibition repeal movement: personal liberty, cost, crime, forbidden fruit, the failure of legal restrictions, and everybody does it. Regardless of disclaimers, people on both sides of the debate recognized, as in the 1920s, that advocating one substance amounted to also advocating the others—light beer led to whiskey, marijuana led to heroin. The basic arguments were the same in each case. Moreover, everyone also knew that any step toward partial legalization was just a step on the road to full repeal. Du Pont recognized this fact in the 1920s. In the 1970s, the founder of NORML had to be persuaded by his supporters to disguise his purpose by labeling his group "for *Reform* of Marijuana Laws." He had wanted to be open and use the word *Repeal*—the acronym was the same. The ultimate purpose was still no secret.[58]

Having open advocates such as Ginsberg and Leary permitted workers in the mass media routinely to publicize pro-drug arguments and in so doing to transform the deviant status of drug users and drug merchandisers. In the emerging pluralism of American society, the drug spokespersons could act like just another—and legitimate—constituency. The gatekeepers of the media did not have to give attention to drug advocates. In fact, for years, only one side appeared in the press: law-enforcement officials dominated news about the subject. In the 1960s and 1970s, however, the controllers of the media had been affected by kinship and empathy, particularly as far as marijuana and LSD were concerned, and, moreover, were affected by the appeal of rebelliousness. By the 1970s, the idea of a conspiracy among the media to favor drug taking was no longer laughable. Whatever the precise cause, for some years, major stories from researchers who identified real physical dangers in marijuana use, for example, simply did not appear in the same American newspapers that earlier had carried scare stories. NORML press releases did.[59]

During the 1960s, following the lead of the *Los Angeles Free Press* and a national magazine, the *Realist*, the bohemian rebellious elements in the United States developed their own alternative—underground—press. These journalists soon found themselves proponents of the drug culture. Although the underground press was for the most part largely noncommercial, in 1967, drug dealer Forcade became the organizing force in the Underground Press Syndicate, an exchange service among the rebellious organs. The underground press eventually developed great influence on the mainstream media (some writers reported for major dailies or magazines by day and for the underground press by night). Underground editors favored sexual freedom and political radicalism and tended automatically to take the side of anyone who was persecuted—blacks, homosexuals, agitators, and—eventually—drug users and drug dealers. These alternative publications had a growing impact because they often were correct in their contentions about the corruption of those in power—the ultimate symbols were civil rights, Vietnam, the FBI, and Watergate—and they helped shame the mainstream press into a more balanced coverage of American society. They also attracted a hostile attention of law-enforcement and intelligence agencies potent enough to curtail their direct effectiveness.[60]

The underground press was nevertheless a major factor in promoting drugs, both because the editors spoke for and to rebellious forces and because of the influence this small group ultimately had on the mass media. How did drug advocates coopt the underground press? The answer is of special interest because prior to 1966 or so, in the few underground publications then in existence such as the *Realist*, drugs played no significant part at all, any more than among cultural rebels in general. The underground press in fact reacted to the mass media. Editors of the *Los Angeles Free Press*, for example, did not interest themselves in drugs until LSD advocate Richard Alpert came lecturing in Southern California and *Esquire* magazine published an article on the drug culture in 1965.[61]

Ultimately, kinship, empathy, and concern for the victims of the criminal-justice system operated on all of the media. But the appeal of the avant-garde arguments of Leary and others was even more dramatically effective with underground journalists. First was the subjective perception that the intoxicating effects of LSD and marijuana initially appeared, contrary to "authority," to be innocuous. In 1967, a woman of twenty-seven told an interviewer: "I recommend grass on all occasions. . . . it really doesn't hang me up . . . And, grass feels like the next door neighbor or your friend, yeah." And then Leary and others turned the use of drugs into positive idealism—if everyone were high on marijuana or finding new aspects of personal existence with LSD, they argued, the world would be very peaceful. The drug advocates therefore furnished a positive program for rebelliousness. As poet John Sinclair wrote in the *Marijuana Review* in 1971, marijuana "promotes communalism, sharing, ego-loss, increased sensitivity to the needs of other people, creativeness, heightened awareness of natural possibilities, and other related character traits of post-scarcity abundance."[62] In such a point of view, one could, then, have both personal gratification and social usefulness. The drug peddler became an agent of social advancement, truly an ideal combination of progress, rebelliousness, and profit.

The underground press also developed a whole style that greatly influenced mass media and more general styles. Psychedelic art and psychedelic language came into not only the press but television. Sexual and drug and criminal slang were widely used, now increasingly without the double entendre but more with just loosened meaning. "Turn on," for example, was surely one of the most ambiguous expressions ever coined. Quite innocent people spoke of getting the "munchies," an impulsive desire for food—usually junk food such as Twinkies—which was originally a term used for this common symptom of cannabis intoxication.[63]

Making Drugs Respectable

Dealers, users, rebels, and their allies enjoyed great success in the era of hippies and the Vietnam War. In 1970, for example, *Life* published a dramatic illustrated account of heroin in the high schools. In 1972, the Presidential Commission on Marihuana and Drug Abuse recommended decriminalization of marijuana use. In 1977, the Carter administration endorsed decriminalization of small amounts for personal use. In 1973, the state of Oregon actually did decriminalize marijuana use. By 1978, eleven states, containing about one-third of the population, had followed suit. In army barracks of the late Cold War period, drugs shared a fundamental place with alcohol in the bonding of the young males there, and again users often became dealers. One group of researchers determined that also on college campuses the status of marijuana changed between 1969 and 1976 to the point that those who *abstained* from the use of marijuana had become deviant within the college-student culture. The well educated, just as Leary had foreseen, had been coopted by the forces advocating drugs. Drug advocates resurrected the old anti-marijuana propaganda movie, *Reefer Madness*, as hilarious unintentional satire and used showings to raise funds for NORML. Of great significance, the now-traditional night life began frequently to include drug use, both in the media and among at least some subgroups, especially when the high price of cocaine made it fashionable. A prostitute of the 1970s, for example, recalled how "you wanted to go out to the discotheque and dance, the whole night life . . . coke is a part of that. It is. If you want to be cool and everything."[64]

By the late 1970s, then, drug advocates looked forward confidently to steady progress in decriminalization laws and in more informal social acceptance of the use of mood-altering substances. But then the momentum stopped. In 1969, a Gallup poll showed that 12 per cent of the citizens favored full legalization, and by 1977, the proportion had risen to 28 per cent; but in 1982, it had fallen to only 20 per cent.[65] Moreover, actual rates of use among young middle-class Americans declined through the 1980s. What happened?

To some extent, the pro-drug movement lost moral leadership. It turned out that only a tiny percentage of users truly were attempting to expand their minds. Most were seeking thrills and escape, not uplift in any sense, but quite the opposite. As a correspondent wrote to *High Times*, idealism was out, and hedonism was in: "This is the '80s and not the psychedelic era of the late '60s, early '70s. People are no longer looking to get high to understand each other. People just want to get 'high,' period. This is the era of looking out for *number one*," he concluded, refering to a book advocating selfish strategies in life. Vietnam War veterans, large numbers of whom had used drugs very extensively overseas, did not continue to do so at home and so diminished the appeal to righteousness that such a presumably normal, and to many, heroic, clientele had at first provided. Finally, after a very long delay, medical warnings about the effects of LSD and marijuana began once again to filter into the media. Even liberals became alarmed about addicts who were not victims and about the crimes associated with drug taking, regardless of decriminalization. Altogether, especially for a health-conscious generation, drugs lost some of the positive image that they had developed in the late 1960s media.[66]

Moreover, a counterattack against drugs developed by the late 1970s. Federal drug officials became more adaptive but still hostile. Public-health officials contested therapists for the authority to define drug-addiction problems. Cultural political elements, from the Moral Majority to militant black groups, attacked drugs in general as part of an immoral hedonism and set up rival ideals that were effective in some areas of society. To some extent, anti-drug forces won back parts of the media, particularly after a series of celebrity user deaths and health scares crowned by the news that hepatitis B and, in the 1980s, AIDS were being communicated by contaminated needles. In 1986, the media began publicizing a new fad, crack cocaine. It soon developed, however, that using crack was a largely non-middle-class practice, and media stories labeled crack users deviant. Finally, in many areas, from the 1970s on, angry parents organized effectively.[67] For a number of years, then, the momentum of the pro-drug forces, as measured by institutional change such as decriminalization, seemed lost.

Resurgence of Drug Advocacy

Yet open drug advocacy was still possible in the 1980s and into the 1990s. Within many important social constituencies, drug advocates could still maintain that abstaining from drugs was aberrant. Such demographic units tended to be urban, where they could flourish among large aggregations of people. Because drug taking had diminished dramatically among middle-class young people, empathy, too, had diminished. The media treated pro-drug statements as not "newsworthy" (after 1983, NORML, for example, appeared only once in the *New York Times* index and not at all in that of the *Washington Post*). When it was politically safe and already under way, still another president, later in the 1980s, proclaimed a public war against drugs.[68]

Then in May 1988, the editors of the *New York Times* ran a front-page story featuring a statement by the mayor of Baltimore and quoted others who advocated decriminalizing drugs. The report followed pro-legalization statements in a few highbrow policy journals. Immediately, all the media began to carry pro-drug statements as a number of prominent Americans began to speak out in favor of letting drug users take and even sell drugs, restricting sanctions for deviance to informal social disapproval—if that. Said one drug researcher who was astonished by the sudden interest, "It has been 10 years since anyone has been talking about legalization."[69]

The new advocacy had two main foci—still, however, utilizing arguments pioneered in the campaign to repeal Prohibition. Toleration proponents talked about economics and crime and connected the two. One theory was that if drug users had cheap drugs available, they would no longer terrorize the cities trying to get money to sustain their habits. That was the only new twist to the old idea that law enforcement of prohibitory measures bred violence as in Al Capone's days. The economics argument of the late 1980s and early 1990s likewise brought merely a newly sophisticated version of the 1920s repealers' contention that enforcement was too costly and filled the prisons and legal system with unnecessary bootlegging (1920s)/drug (1980s) cases. At the end of the 1980s, serious thinkers talked about "fiscal reality" and suggested that demand, not supply, was the problem. They also spoke in then-fashionable terms of free enterprise—let the buyer of drugs beware. Because by that time the demand was centered on the growing "underclass" of the cities, such views constituted a method of placing responsibility on the unfortunate for their own plight.[70]

What was not spelled out in the new advocacy and even the throw-everyone-in-jail opposition was the fact that the debate as presented in the media still recognized a place in American society for the recreational drug takers and their suppliers. With the initial embourgeoisement of the clientele and the coopting of radicals and bohemians, criminal and deviant drug forces, allied with rebelliousness, had won a place as an alternative in a pluralistic society. In the 1960s, poet Ginsberg was quoted in the *Oracle*, a pioneer journal in advocating drugs: "I am in effect setting up moral codes and standards which include drugs, orgy, music and primitive magic as worship rituals—educational tools which are supposedly contrary to our cultural morals. . . ."[71] More than twenty years later, asking a halt to the war against drugs, public figures with economic motives (not least wealthy taxpayers) had moved a substantial distance toward learning to live with Ginsberg's standards.

The success of the Americans who served rebelliousness and the drug trade in extending and legitimating drug taking therefore depended upon otherwise respectable people who accepted a number of previously deviant viewpoints. One was that the theretofore commonplace category of disturbing, uncivil, or extreme behavior was no longer valid—in mental illness or in drug taking. People in the 1960s and 1970s connected drug taking with idiosyncratic dressing, with nudity and ceremonial touching and "groping" as well as with nightmarish or formless psychedelic art. Closely related was the idea that the work ethic was invalid, that a person could and should "drop out." In such a view, drug taking up to the point that health was badly impaired was both "normal" and rational. Why, after all, should anyone be denied the possibility of experiences that are out of the ordinary? Here, in its most naked form, unrestricted hedonism was cultivated in the context of consumer choice. Over the years, researchers continually found that people who used drugs justified them as others justified tobacco use: because it was fun—with the presumption that no other reason was necessary. Such a view, emphasizing subjective sensation, feeling, and mood, was absolutely compatible both with the earlier alcohol-repeal arguments and with later television advertising. Leary compared selling psychedelic consciousness to young Americans of the 1960s with selling Pepsi-Cola to "the Pepsi Generation." Finally, drug advocates and their economic allies managed to convince large numbers of people that the addict was the last truly free person in American society—the ultimate outlaw status. This romantic outlaw rejected the older standards of society in favor of what the person imagined to be his or her own standards and institutions—but which historically came from the campaigns of Americans who, with media allies, were selling drugs, drug-related goods, and re-belliousness.[72]

Gambling

An ancient and very widely practiced human activity, wagering is known in most human cultures. But in America, gambling has traditionally been considered a bad habit. Like drug taking, gambling undermined the work ethic and embodied the danger of addiction. And, also traditionally, betting of one kind or another was connected to games and sports.

By the time the English colonies were founded, the problems of gambling in a commercial society were already well known. The colonists and their descendants therefore had continuously to cope with New World versions of wagering. As in the Old World, Americans found the practice a vice in two aspects. First, the gambling activity itself had direct effects on individuals and society. Second, the activity of gambling seemed to undermine good character—even beyond getting people to keep bad company, as in the McGuffey story of Tom Smith (see Chapter 2). As many sad magazine and newspaper crime stories—particularly those of the late nineteenth century—emphasized, people who lost money wagering were subject to overwhelming temptation to steal from their employers as well as to gamble away money that their families needed.

Many problems also grew out of the seemingly inevitable attempts of gamblers to cheat. As a critic of gambling noted in 1892, "Of course the social gambler always asserts that he plays with gentlemen, but the easiness of cheating offers a constant temptation on the part of gentlemen, who are pressed in money matters, to resort to this method of relieving themselves of their financial embarrassments." From early times on, commercial devices were available to assist cheating, from simple marked decks of cards to "sleeve machines," which helped a card player substitute cards noiselessly, and magnetic belts that affected loaded dice.[1] Implicit in both the betting habit and cheating was the practical consequence that gambling victimized people, whether in legendary informal wagering with untrustworthy strangers or in the misleading publicity that encouraged the credulous to buy lottery tickets. Over many generations, then, Americans continued to connect betting with bad character.

Colonial Traditions and Attitudes

Colonists who came from England knew a variety of types of gambling. Public lotteries financed both government undertakings and private ventures, including, from 1612 to 1624, the first Virginia settlement, at Jamestown. English aristocrats gambled notoriously, as part of their conspicuous consumption. Their specialty was horse racing ("the sport of kings"), but they also participated in various other games and sports, from card playing to cock fighting, in which people from every class joined them in wagering. Colonists of diverse backgrounds shared this heritage and brought with them customs of placing bets on all games and sports. In the South, at least, aristocrats, imitating those in England, were particularly obvious in utilizing bets as conspicuous consumption and status markers. Other groups, including enslaved people, also gambled freely, although in Virginia, at least, the law at one point forbade nonaristocrats from actually participating in the races. Southern culture in particular had a strong tradition of bloody sporting contests such as gander pulling (attempting to yank a live greased gander's head off) in which competing and fighting often mixed with betting.[2]

Calvinists who populated some of the shores of North America, and knew the customs, for theological reasons condemned card playing and similar gaming activities as morally wrong. One of the traditional ways of meting out justice in those days was to draw lots, with the understanding that the Lord would show His will through the results of the drawing. Such a drawing was a serious business, done prayerfully. To trifle with the will of God by putting down cards—much less betting on how the cards would come out—was an impiety among those who believed that the Almighty's will was involved in the fall of a feather from the least sparrow. This same thinking later helped fuel nineteenth-century evangelicals' condemnations of wagering.

Beyond social climbers who were attempting to imitate English aristocrats, many early Americans did indeed gamble as part of playful or adventurous diversions. Practical citizens who observed wagering therefore had more than a theological rationale for proscribing the activities of gamblers: those activities attracted and characterized idlers who were unproductive and who got into other mischief as well.

Therefore, from early on, most Americans in one way or another tended to connect gambling not only with undesirable and criminal behaviors but with antisocial elements in society. Yet, at the same time, a large number of ordinary citizens also continued to hold divided opinions on the subject.[3]

For generations, then, many Americans, especially in male groups, bet. George Washington was said to have won or lost in a single evening as much as nine pounds playing cards. Around the turn of the nineteenth century, many forms of gambling were public, such as those at cock fights and horse races where onlookers placed bets on the animals. Public lotteries, at first held to raise money for good purposes, also flourished. Benjamin Franklin at one point led such a scheme to finance building the defenses of Philadelphia. As the century progressed, journalists writing in newspapers reported that large numbers of upper-class people attended horse races or won and lost large amounts of money in card games. Proprietors of gambling establishments were known not only to "sporting men" but "in the fashionable circles" in various urban areas. Betting activity expanded with faro and with the "shell game," supposedly introduced by a "Dr. Bennett" who was later famous as a riverboat gambler. Yet many upholders of the public good, especially those who were middle-class respectables, continued to denounce card games and other types of wagering.[4]

Gambling as a Business

Gambling ultimately developed two distinctive aspects in the United States. It became especially prominent on the frontier, and it developed into a business. The new figure of the "professional" gambler was central to both developments. On the frontier, he (almost always "he") was the notorious riverboat "sharper" or the keeper of a gambling saloon in the mining and cattle towns. At the middle of the century, about 2,000 professional gamblers worked just the riverboats. In the growing cities, the professional frequented social groups both high and low. As early as the 1850s, a group of New York City gamblers took bets from the poor, sometimes within sight of gaming establishments for the rich. Pre-Civil War Americans in general classed professional gamblers as a subcategory of the more general "confidence man" and believed, for good reason, that sharpers would easily switch over to confidence "games" to follow the main chance. But the emphasis was changing. As early as the California gold rush, professionals had come to depend less upon cheating and more upon steady percentages— as behooved regular businesspeople.[5]

To many Americans, placing bets in connection with sport and games was in fact much like, if not identical to, other businesses. Many respectable people tried to make a killing not only at the card table but by investing in commodities, stocks, and real estate. Indeed, speculation was traditional in American society. Journalists of the late nineteenth century reported that commercial speculation could be another form of gambling, and gamblers often used this commonplace observation to justify themselves. John Philip Quinn in 1892, for example, described how "The 'operator' on the exchange, whose days are spent in watching the rise and fall of commodities purely speculative, finds the ordinary paths of life too quiet, too monotonous, to elicit more than a passing thought. From the moment when he leaves 'the floor' until he returns to it next day, his brain is in a mad whirl of excitement. What more natural than that he should seek relief for an overtaxed mind through exchanging one avenue of activity for another"— the commodities for cards?[6] Despite the obvious similarities, the speculator of course did not bear the stigma of those who took chances for recreational, as opposed to occupational, purposes.

Other commentators of that century singled out an additional aspect of wagering, one that went even beyond responsible business dealing and into assertive individuality or reckless machismo. In 1870, in his standard book on gambling, the English writer Andrew Steinmetz commented on the United States:

> It is not surprising that a people so intensely speculative, excitable, and eager as the Americans, should be desperately addicted to gambling. Indeed, the

spirit of gambling has incessantly pervaded all their operations, political, commercial, and social. It is but one of the manifestations of that thorough license arrogated to itself by the nation, finding its true expression in the American maxim . . . "Every man has a right to do what he *damned* pleases."[7]

Or, in fact, to defy convention and, possibly, respectability.

Yet the businesspeople who in the mid and late nineteenth century set American social standards hewed increasingly to another standard in the face of the process of industrialization: bourgeois thriftiness. As a moralistic writer put it in 1865,

> Let every man avoid all sorts of gambling as he would poison. A poor man or boy should not allow himself even to toss up for a halfpenny, for this is often the beginning of a habit of gambling; and this ruinous crime comes on by slow degrees. Whilst a man is minding his work, he is playing the best game, and he is sure to win. A gambler never makes good use of his money, even if he should win.

Such folk wisdom from the Puritans and their evangelical descendants embodied the work ethic as well as experience. Victorian-era Americans were in fact well acquainted with gambling fever, which could ruin families as well as individuals. As early as the 1830s and 1840s, for example, legal lotteries were already largely abandoned and outlawed as public nuisances. But that was in part because the lotteries had fallen into the hands of contractors who often rendered them fraudulent and promoted them so that they were not at all innocuous, although reformers all along denounced the way in which, by their nature, lotteries defrauded the poor. Until the twentieth century, however, gambling businesses, particularly policy syndicates and bookmaking on horse races, were widely and openly tolerated in American communities.[8]

The Connection of Gambling with Other Minor Vices

Like earlier settlers, nineteenth-century people never doubted that gambling was invariably associated with the other minor vices, and particularly with alcohol consumption. The stereotype of fast living was already well established, connecting gambling with smoking, drinking, and wenching. Mason Long, a former betting man writing in 1883, observed that "the gambler is almost invariably a drinker and the drinker very frequently a gambler. A man who is addicted to drinking is almost certain to get to

playing, and he who gambles will, sooner or later, become a drunkard"—
a judgment confirmed by other contemporary observers of the gambling
fraternity, who often also tossed in further presumptions that tied gambling
to smoking and sexual misbehavior.[9]

In the more-or-less public commercial institutions in which gambling
increasingly came to be carried out, such associations with the other minor
vices were geographical and financial as well as commonplace. Whether
in the West or the East, alcoholic-beverage sales and prostitution flourished
as adjuncts to card games and gaming tables. In the late nineteenth century,
the poolroom operated as a place where young men—largely those below
the middle class—spent their idle hours in activities that centered around
betting, betting on pool games but also other kinds of wagering. There,
along with gambling and drinking, were also found all the other bad habits.
As late as 1915, one witness described the activities: "Women not being
present and there being no restraint of any kind, often the lowest and
foulest expressions are heard. Obscene stories are related by small groups
who do not engage in the game, but congregate in the corners and smoke
cigarettes."[10]

As gambling centers became institutionalized in spite of sporadic enforcement of laws against gambling, both "dens" and "palaces" added a
connection to still another commonplace social problem: political corruption, through which the police and other officials allowed keepers to stay
in business. Along with prostitution and opium dens, gambling was often
segregated in special areas in the growing urban centers, a monument to
a society in which people knew the ties that existed between the activities
and yet were unable to eradicate the business enterprises. An 1876 description typically located the socially vulnerable and undesirable together in
gambling areas: "Some of the policy offices yesterday were crowded with
sailors, longshoremen, and others who were studying dream-books and
making out policy slips. In one place young boys were purchasing policy
slips."[11]

Despite the necessary payoffs, and despite competition from informal
social betting, investors in gambling establishments did well and gave the
activity a glamourous atmosphere that reinforced the image of carefree,
conspicuous consumption and at the same time prefigured other institutions
of the later consumer culture. In 1851, a hostile observer described the
leading San Francisco establishments:

> The hells are fitted up with superb furniture and appointments. On the gilded
> walls, often painted in fresco, are grouped copies of the most beautiful of

modern and ancient art.... The couches, lounges, divans, etc., scattered along the sides of these temples of chance ... are of every graceful and lovely shape.... Upon the marble tables are scattered flower-shaped vases of alabaster or Bohemian glass....[12]

Clearly, the gambling business was profitable. The big bettors set a rigorous standard for financial risk taking, a standard that guided numerous more modest wagerers—but they, too, contributed to someone's profits. Perhaps the most pitiful imitative development was the appearance at the end of the century of wretched "bucket shops," where poor people with only a little money could unlawfully place wagers on changes in stock and commodity prices on which the wealthy made and lost large sums legally. (By the early twentieth century, bucket shops went out of existence because they were replaced by the policy games, and, later, the numbers rackets that functioned as poor people's impersonal gambling of choice.)[13]

From Retreat to the Growth of a New Tolerance

Around the turn of the twentieth century, reformers often succeeded in systematically outlawing gambling, in large part because so many citizens witnessed not only the ruinous effects of their neighbors' losing money but also because of the inexorable connection of wagering with other vices. Barton Wood Currie, a reformer partisan, in 1908 only repeated a customary observation when he described what happened when, as he put it, the territories of Arizona and New Mexico finally

outlawed the gambler and [threw] off the heavy yoke of his presence, with all its attendant evils.... we have got rid of this insidious influence; we are sleeping better for it; we are kinder to our wives and children; we have more money to spend on the home; we have fewer worries to forget in drink; and our little towns and cities have become much more free of loafers and renegades, professional rogues and blackguards.

Currie went on to quote a longtime resident of one Arizona town: "Honest, I don't see how the saloons stand it, for nobody drinks any more since they cut out the games." In other towns, Currie went on, not only did people keep more regular hours but merchants also prospered because they were selling a large volume of regular consumer goods—pork and beans and, more importantly, pork and beans that now, as one storekeeper remarked, were paid for.[14]

In those early years of the twentieth century, when theological and personal moral rationales no longer sufficed for every reformer, those bent on improving the world tried, like the prohibitionists, to discover and root out the causes of evil, rather than just confront the symptoms. In that context, gambling presented special problems. It was easy enough to see that betting led not only to ruined lives but also to dishonesty when the inevitable victims tried to cover their losses. It was in itself, then, a potent social liability. Abolish gambling, went the argument, and so abolish an important direct cause of crime. But what was it about gambling that turned the honest employee into a thief or the official into a crook—or degraded a proud person in other ways? Reformers of that period focused on the essence of the activity. Jacob Riis, the defender of the poor and observer of police courts, summed it up by saying "Gambling is by instinct and nature brutal, because it is selfishness in its coldest form."[15] He wrote in a period when selfishness was a characteristic with a highly negative social value. In ensuing decades, as values changed and selfishness became more acceptable, so did gambling. Or perhaps it was the other way around.

Even beyond the extreme selfishness of devotees, which reminded people of the addictions of drug taking, gambling had distinctive attributes. More than drinking and sexual adventuring, gambling appeared in a context in which the activity could often take on a certain air of respectability. Beginning in the mid nineteenth century, the professional gambler always pretended to be a gentleman, attempting to capture the tradition of upper-class gaming. And in fact many very respectable men continued to act as if wagering were a gentleman's prerogative. For almost half a century, beginning in the 1890s, Edward Bradley ran a gambling house in Palm Beach that attracted numerous prominent and wealthy Americans who were vacationing in Florida. The luxury and exclusiveness of such places, just as on the mining frontier, kept the idea of evil associations to a minimum—or at least hid them.

Bradley himself owned two local newspapers and was lavish in his support of local churches, especially St. Edwards, the one that he built nearby and which he attended. As in this case, social leaders continued to patronize gambling establishments. Clearly a great deal of ambivalence was involved, just as was the case half a century earlier. Such behavior was contemporary with the double standard of sexual morality and fitted right into a familiar pattern of social sanctions and tolerances, including bad examples set by fashionable socialites. A popular song told that

> She bets on the horses. . . .
> She glories in poker,
> At billiards she's a corker,
> This up-to-date girl of mine. . . .[16]

The Profitability of Gambling

The other distinctive aspect of gambling was its relentless profitability—even without trickery, as the new commercial gamblers discovered. The well-known gambling-house owner Richard A. Canfield, of New York, Newport, and Saratoga, observed that it was quite unnecessary to use dishonest means, for "the percentage in favor of a gambling house is sufficient to guarantee the profits of the house. All any gambler wants is to have play enough for a long enough time and he'll get all the money any player has."[17]

Many gambling entrepreneurs were not successful. But those who were skillful found that the large amounts of money to be made in gambling overshadowed even the profits from the other minor vices. Just as in business generally, it was not long before such colorful captains of the betting industry as Canfield gave way to syndicates and, ultimately, corporations. The history of gambling in the twentieth century, therefore, involved two trends: 1) gangster groups and then legal corporate investors came to dominate institutional and organized wagering; and 2) opinion makers' tolerance for gambling and gambling profits grew.

The first major sign of a new tolerance came after World War I, which had familiarized many American men with gambling, particularly with craps, a dice game popular in the barracks. In the 1920s and especially the 1930s, a number of states permitted racetrack betting under at least some government supervision to help guarantee income to states, particularly, after 1929, states hard hit by the Great Depression. Throughout the 1920s, in Maryland and Kentucky, members of the legislatures attempted unsuccessfully to repeal the pioneer laws authorizing parimutuel betting in those states. But at the same time, in other state legislatures across the country, bills to legalize parimutuel racetrack betting under various arrangments kept coming closer and closer to success. In 1927, Illinois legalizers succeeded. With the advent of the Depression, and beginning in North Carolina and Florida in 1931, opposition gave way all over the country. In California, parimutuel betting came by referendum in 1933. That same year, New Hampshire actually made the parimutuel machine a part of the state al apparatus. By 1935, 16 states were collecting taxes from racetrack betting.[18]

Another sign of tolerance was the establishment of legalized casino gambling in Nevada in 1931 and the growth of charity bingo in the Depression years. Within a few decades, state governments were leading the way by establishing and then expanding public lotteries. From 1964 to 1974 alone, 13 state-operated lotteries opened. By 1989, three-fourths of the population lived in areas in which legal lotteries were operated by the state. The average annual household expenditure on lottery chances was $240 in those states, and in the mid-1980s, lottery advertising budgets had reached more than a tenth of the immense sums spent on beer ads nationally.[19]

ere were, then, two periods when major shifts occurred in the direction of reversing opinion and sanctions against gambling: the 1930s (with some harbingers in the 1920s) and the 1970s. In both cases, economic motives contributed substantially toward bringing otherwise-respectable people to support betting.[20] In particular, just as many wealthy people supported repeal of Prohibition in the 1930s as a way of raising tax revenues, so in that same period and also in the 1960s and after, influential wealthy citizens saw in taxes on gambling activities an easy method to shift the tax burden off of themselves and onto wagerers at the racetrack, the casino, or the state lottery.

Gambling, Sports, and the Victorian Underworld

The story of gambling in the mid and late twentieth century, however, is not as simple as the foregoing two paragraphs may suggest. Casinos, bingo, and lotteries in particular contributed in special ways to both the profitability and partial respectability of betting and gaming. But among a number of complications, the most important was the connection between gambling and what came to be classified as "sports." In colonial times, the South Carolina legislature, for example, lumped together with dice and card games not only playing for money but also skill games like shuffleboard and billiards and, in addition, contests that included both humans and animals. A visitor to Virginia in 1773 described the local "young men of fortune; they were gamblers and cock-fighters, hound breeders, and horse-jockies."[21]

The word *sport* itself originally was a verb, with connotations, as Noah Webster noted in 1832, of "to wanton, to frolic, to play." But that same definition observed a distinction for the sportsman who pursued "the sports of the field," such as hunting and fishing. Upper-class field pastimes set the positive connotation of sport. But as all active games of whatever kind increasingly came under the heading of sport, the category continued to carry other connotations, many of them ambiguous.[22]

In the United States, the sporting man or sport was often understood to be a bettor. George H. Devol, in his account of his years as a Mississippi gambler, repeatedly used the term "sport" and "professional sport" as synonyms for gambling men, members of the betting fraternity who might for example say "Gentlemen, are you going to sport a little?" meaning play cards for money. Indeed the connotation could be very negative, as was reported in 1861: " 'Sportsman' in America means sharper, gambler, swindler, gallows-bird."[23] The very language, then, suggested intricate social relationships between gambling and what became institutionalized as sports in the late nineteenth and early twentieth centuries.[24]

From earliest times, as in the English tradition, large parts of the population placed bets on sports events. Along with racing and competitive games, gambling on bull baiting and cock fights fell into a category that differed from activities dependent entirely on chance, such as throwing dice. Nevertheless, the association of wagering with both kinds of activities tended to bring competitive sports into the arena of the Victorian underworld. Moreover, traditions of male-only groups among Irish ethnic communities, in which masculine competition, particularly fighting, predominated, helped set the standard of this macho underworld. The larger "sporting fraternity" flourished among institutions that were male and that contributed to the rest of the underground: saloons, questionable hotels, gambling places, and even barbershops and fraternal halls. In such places, arguments arose around who could fight best or who could win a race, and betting naturally followed.

> 'T was on the famous trotting-ground
> The betting men were gathered round
> From far and near . . .

wrote Oliver Wendell Holmes in the 1870s. In the 1890s, social critic Thorstein Veblen tied sports and gambling to the conspicuous consumption of the leisure class and simultaneously to "lower-class delinquents."[25]

As urbanization proceeded in the middle and late nineteenth century, sports became entertainment and even spectacle. Sports also provided some social identities for males with few other social ties. Under these circumstances, commercial gamblers in fact moved in on any sport, no matter how innocent. A writer in 1876 in the *New York Tribune* complained that "they have attended upon the college boat-races until men are declaring that the evils accompanying such contests over-balance the benefits of the athletic training; they have popularized gambling under the guise of fair dealing, and they have got their toils about the rising generation." Another writer, in 1894, claimed that gambling interests had distorted horse racing by displacing long races with short sprints that were "arranged entirely to stimulate gambling" and were "on the programmes wholly in the interest of bookmakers."[26]

Horse racing was the sport most dependent upon gambling. In the late nineteenth century, bookmakers on the track were essential to the financial operation of the races, which had become national in scope by becoming the subject of major coverage in the newspapers and magazines. Horse racing actually went into a deep decline early in the twentieth century because, in most states, legislation discouraged racetrack betting. By contrast, baseball, which did not depend upon gambling but upon gate receipts alone, flourished—even though, as the famous "Black Sox" scandal of 1919–1921 showed, people did bet on the game surreptitiously.

Typically, members of the sporting fraternity shared with the criminal and marginal figures who made up the heart of the underworld a dissent from the cautious bourgeois standards of "respectable" Victorian Americans. Everyone knew that the underworld was not only the source of the mobs who directly confronted reformers and harassed temperance workers but would also furnish support for sporting activities on which one could wager. Evangelicals who tried to suppress at least cruel betting sports like bull baiting and cock fighting knew that devotion to such pastimes went with other vices and with coarse language. One wealthy patron of Tommy Norris's Livery Stable in New York suggested the coming entertainment standard that betting sports fostered when he described one night's bill as starting with a dog fight and then having "a cock fight, then rat baiting, next a prize fight, then a battle of billy goats, and then a boxing match between two ladies, with nothing but trunks on. . . ."[27]

At a time when the fighting and betting Irish constituted the bulk of the non-middle-class migrants crowding the cities, the saloon keepers and other members of the underworld with whom the poor were thrown stood for standard lower-order behavior: impulsive, undisciplined, and reckless actions subversive of most institutions in that bourgeois society. And it was just such non-middle-class behavior that marked many successful sports figures, such as John L. Sullivan, the boxer whose aggressive misbehavior was played up in the sensationalistic *Police Gazette* as he became arguably the first national sports hero.[28]

Boxing, to which gloves came to cover bare knuckles definitively only in 1892, represented the ultimate sport that gambling corrupted consistently. Offensive to the Victorians because of both its brutality and crookedness, boxing nevertheless involved so much money from spectator admissions, and especially from betting, that this essentially underworld activity rose in the most classic way to become a standard, socially approved sport. Enthusiasts from Theodore Roosevelt down wanted the manly art to become respectable, complete with Marquis of Queensberry rules. Journalists regularly played up the bouts—again, as spectacles—and played down the troubled contexts in which they took place, all the while publishing betting odds. But no measures seemed capable of cleansing the sport of the greed that corrupted the fights and led to serious injury.[29]

Boxing presented only the most notorious instance of the efforts that exponents of the strenuous life made to civilize the activities of the sporting fraternity and to make sport a part of American life after the model of Tom Brown's school days, so that young gentlemen would engage in manly competition and good sportsmanship for personal development, not for winning bets. But in fact, early in the twentieth century, the quest for vigorous and militant manliness turned into a ruthless desire to win at all costs, which of course suited the betting crowd best.[30]

At the same time, a whole school of journalism sprang up to display sports as mere entertainment, if not national regenerating rituals—although these same journalists continued to include betting odds conspicuously in news and feature stories. Indeed, the control of sports news became very important to illegal gambling in the twentieth century. Under this guise of innocent play and public amusement, sports betting grew and flourished over the decades as a fundamental activity of the underworld. By the 1970s, sports betting was a substantial factor in the national economy—somewhere between $17 billion and $67 billion a year, according to different authoritative estimates.[31]

Spectator sports were already big business by the early 1920s, and the coming of electronic media initiated still other changes. Beginning in mid-century, televised events came to involve much heavier betting than other kinds of sports. In the 1960s, the broadcasters in their quest for profits transformed sports competitions further. The new sports ideal came no longer from civility, team play, and good sportsmanship, such as reformers had attempted to impose for generations and which appeared in physical-education textbooks as well as printed rationales written by defenders of athletic competition. With television, the new standards of model sports figures gave way to (in Benjamin Rader's words) self-dramatization, "incivility, self-indulgence, and the blatant enlistment of the games on behalf of monetary interests"—not least the beer merchandisers who enrolled players in entertainment capacities in ads more captivating than many of the games. Uncivil and violent behavior drew audiences, and sports figures promoted bad behavior for commercial purposes just as did other television productions. Whereas once the media had tried to suppress the misbehavior and unadmirable actions of Babe Ruth and other sports heroes, in the age of television, the media moguls and advertisers made an open play for "the blue-collar crowd," traditionally those who wanted to make their betting more interesting. "We glamorize hoodlums," complained ex-football coach Darrell Royal in the 1970s; "The worst offenders of sportsmanship become our heroes." The underworld and gambling background of sports, in short, came out in the open and set the tone for much of American society in the last half of the twentieth century in emphasizing compulsive winning, brutality, and irrational betting, as opposed to careful bourgeois living and rational planning.[32]

Acts of Gambling and Acts of Consumption

The connection between sports and gambling became fixed in the twentieth century. Part of the reason for the interrelationship was the historical development of business interests in both sports and gambling. But events also suggested that the connection was innate in the social functioning of gambling. Even under conditions of organization, from the point of view of the ordinary American bettor, it made little difference whether the wagering involved boxers, cocks, horses, boats, whole teams of players, or cards, abstract numbers, and mechanical contrivances. The act of wagering in itself became paramount. Again and again, in accounts of well-known bettors, those who won at cards would religiously drop their winnings at the racetrack—or, sometimes, the stock market. Writers in a magazine for bettors in the 1970s actually gave tips on speculating in "collectibles," such as Oriental rugs. Operators of racetracks initially opposed lotteries for fear of losing patronage to other forms of gambling, but when the tracks lost on lottery issues in the legislature, they immediately applied for licenses to sell lottery tickets. Conventional wisdom for generations recognized this phenomenon of the interchangeability of types of wagering, in part by the custom of lumping all gambling into one category.[33]

Gamblers and high rollers had long represented an extreme of conspicuous consumption. Because it was the *act* of gambling, rather than any product, that was crucial, gambling fitted perfectly into the consumer culture that was developing in the United States in the late nineteenth and early twentieth centuries. Gambling also represented an extreme in the game of fooling the buyer that made wagering a special part of consumerism.[34]

Unlike other acts of consumption, however, gambling continued to have explicit associations with the underworld. Not just gambling men and women dropped their winnings at cards or the racetrack or whatever. The newly famous racketeers and gangsters of the twentieth century, with their conspicuous criminal profits, were notorious adventurers in sports betting and casino gambling. This widely acknowledged community of gangsters reinforced the traditional association of gambling with other crime from the days of the gambling-saloon muggers and the Mississippi sharper with his three-card monte. In the twentieth century, many bettors found that the danger that they might be arrested, cheated, and mugged actually in a perverse way increased the attractiveness of the activity, which already had antisocial associations.[35]

The Rise of Casinos and Lotteries

In Nevada in the 1930s, legalization transformed casino gambling from the status of speakeasy with a very limited clientele to a public institution. Meanwhile, all over North America in the early 1930s, a substantial amount of profits from certain local alcoholic-beverage enterprises and other lawless activities of the 1920s and after had begun to go into legal racetracks and illegal casinos. And it was just such gangster investors, able to furnish business-management experience and experienced gambling personnel, as well as capital, who successfully organized the new legalized casino gambling. Indeed, only extremely venturous people, people used to participating in risky deals—and who had ties to the entertainment industry—could have or would have attempted such an enterprise. One model for the Nevada casinos was the gambling ships that had operated outside the three-mile limit furnishing drinking and gambling during the Prohibition years. Such ships, sailing out of Los Angeles in particular, had a profound effect on motion-picture notables and appeared repeatedly in fiction and film in the 1930s. At the same time, all over the country, mechanical casino devices, denoted generically as slot machines but encompassing a variety of games, attracted many people into petty betting that continually passed over the border into illegality. After the gambling ships shut down, the Southern California patrons (as well as sponsors) of casino gambling tended to shift to a Nevada division point on the Union Pacific railroad, Las Vegas, where slot machines as well as the usual games proliferated. Beginning just before World War II, but especially after 1945, luxurious casinos, modeled in part on the gambling ships, appeared there and set the pattern for future legalized casino gambling—including continuous ties to the most powerful and dangerous criminal elements. With laws passed in 1967 and 1969, the Nevada legislature opened the way for publicly held business corporations to receive gambling licenses. Thereafter, the line between criminal and ordinary business became hard to draw as one corporation after another, including various major hotel chains, went into the casino business in Nevada and, after 1976, in New Jersey, often in implicit if not explicit partnership with criminal capital and management.[36]

Like casino gambling, betting in a lottery-type style also gained substantial impetus during the 1930s. Illegally playing the numbers attracted many humble patrons during the Great Depression, but other parts of the population came under the spell of bingo. Most people, if they knew bingo at all earlier in the century, recognized it as a game that was played at carnivals for prizes. Somehow it spread to church socials and in the 1930s became a very important fund-raising device for many churches hard-pressed by the Depression. Because the fad usually spread under the sponsorship of clerics, political opposition generally was stymied. Observers were nonplussed by such announcements as "Bingo Every Night in the Holy Spirit Room." Raffles and drawings, too, began to flourish in the 1930s, under both charitable and commercial sponsorship. "Bank Night" at the movies became an important social institution. All this activity increased and reflected public acceptance of getting rich quickly by gambling. By the 1950s, bingo was a hot political issue, and politicians who cracked down on abuses could find themselves unemployed because they appeared to be opposing organized religion or charity.[37]

Another impersonal method of taking a chance, large public lotteries, ultimately came to be the most acceptable form of gambling in the United States. There were long-established forms of lottery that did not qualify as gambling under most laws. In the late nineteenth century, Anthony

Comstock complained about advertising schemes in which making a purchase gave the customer a chance to win a prize (in one case, the soap marketers who had advertised the scheme denied that they ever intended to be honest enough to hold a drawing, thus evading the law that would have classified their activity a lottery!). This type of marketing promotion continued throughout the twentieth century, also.[38]

Over the years, many charitable fund-raising drives similarly utilized a form of lottery in which a person made a donation and in return received a chance to win a prize in a drawing. Then beginning in 1963, after years of agitation in various states with legislators frantic to produce income without additional taxation, New Hampshire organized a state-sponsored lottery, followed in 1967 by New York and in 1970 by New Jersey. In 1971, New Jersey's computer-based fifty-cent game created "action" that gave special impetus to the movement, first in the Northeast and then in other industrialized states. The trend became commonplace, and almost every year some electorate or other voted in a state lottery to raise money. In 1974 and 1976, Congress exempted state lotteries from most federal restrictions against gambling. From 1970 to 1988, the annual average sales growth of the lotteries was 31 per cent as they spread from state to state—an amazing figure and one that caught the attention of many people searching for high profits. The lotteries moved into second place, behind only education, as the largest service provided by states. After 1976, when lotteries were permitted finally on television, the subject became one of common conversation. There was even a successful television show, *Lottery!*[39]

Losing Deviant Status

By the 1960s and especially the 1970s, barriers to gambling of all kinds were being breached continuously. In addition to private ventures like church bingo, a large number of publicly regulated gambling enterprises were flourishing. Beyond horse racing, lotteries, and casinos, various states authorized (and taxed) dog racing, off-track betting establishments, and card rooms. By the 1980s, many social commentators believed that gambling no longer represented a deviant activity, that it had at last achieved the respectability that participants and exploiters had so long sought. One group of researchers of the mid-1980s maintained that "taking refuge in the myth of gambling as deviance and relegating commercial gambling to the status of a pariah industry" was no longer a reasonable position. These researchers emphasized the economic power of the gambling industry, with a 1983 income of $135 billion that made it "one of the largest leisure industries in the United States," bigger than the giant of that time, U.S. Steel.[40]

The economic power of legalized gambling soon translated into major political impact. In both economic and political arenas, gambling proponents worked single-mindedly to extend the advantages of businesspeople who made money from other people's betting. Moreover, economic power also generated an increasing ability to manipulate the media—even beyond the sports pages of the newspapers. The huge advertising budgets of state lottery officials were only a beginning. In modern journalism, big winners in any gambling scheme were of course big news. Suckers who lost were not news at all. But the entertainment ties of gambling and just the power of the well-financed acquisitiveness of the industry entrepreneurs led to more direct manipulation of the media. They were particularly effective in publicizing economic lures to win over legislators and voters alike, many of whom for various reasons (see below) were either not opposed to gambling or were actively promoting it. And on top of that, fiction and the electronic media over the years familiarized Americans of all ages with betting customs. A television hero of midcentury (not unlike the Marlboro man) had the theme song, as one viewer recalled it:

> Who is the tall dark stranger there?
> Maverick is the name.
> Riding the trail to who knows where,
> Luck is his companion,
> Gambling is his game.[41]

As the status of gambling was shifting into the nondeviant category in the mid twentieth century, individual gamblers as such developed some signs of a large-scale identity as members of a distinct group—beyond the traditional intense relationships that bound certain types of card players or racetrack habitués together. Mass magazines for bettors appeared in the 1970s. *Gamblers World*, "For the Individual Who Enjoys Action," carried numerous stories about celebrities who also enjoyed "action," referring to the entire spectrum of taking a chance with hope of gain. Through the 1930s to the 1980s, betting people as a group increasingly took on aspects of a community and a constituency that furthered gamblng activity.[42]

The individual bettors also had cultural ties, many of which directly or indirectly supported betting activities. Gaming and wagering, as I have noted, were a traditional part of life for many Americans from the beginning of the culture. Lower-order population elements, those who had no sense that betting was a social liability and those who hoped to make money in an easy way, patronized gambling institutions, legal or illegal. So did other types of people who shared part or all of their values. By the end of the nineteenth century and the beginning of the twentieth, the growth in the proportion of the population of the new immigrants and their children had greatly increased the numbers of people who grew up accepting at least some kinds of betting. They included particularly people from both the working and middle classes who followed Roman Catholic church doctrine. Official doctrine did not condemn gambling per se as immoral but denounced it only when, in individual cases, abuse of a harmless recreation brought bad effects—the familiar personal-responsibility approach. But many people, both of that faith and not, had the impression, especially after the rise of bingo in the 1930s, that the institutionalized Church somehow favored or at least tolerated any gambling.[43]

The Profits from Gambling

People who had something to gain from gambling worked most actively to spread it and, formally or informally, mobilized others. There were those who directly organized gambling activities for profit, indeed, for very great profit—usually criminals, both petty and major—although, again, many also failed. But those who were successful, even temporarily, stimulated the ambitions and the advocacy of others. Whether operating legally or illegally, gambling proponents showed great financial, political, and cultural influence—influence reflected, not least, in their repeatedly winning elections legalizing their activities and in gaining media support and patronage for betting institutions.[44]

What is most striking about gambling was the way in which large numbers of people supported it hoping to benefit indirectly. The most obvious group was no doubt the suppliers of gambling equipment. At first there were covert operators who furnished crooked dice or regular slot machines, enterprises that many people believed to be controlled in the twentieth century by criminal elements. But then the gambling-equipment industry blossomed, especially as technology developed. All the equipment used in casino activities, animal racing, and even card playing brought in substantial sums of money. Makers of bingo cards and cages, for example, made large amounts of money in the 1930s. Later, the contracts for servicing state lotteries involved enormous amounts of income for some of the leading corporations of the United States, such as General Electric. In the late twentieth century, when about 5 per cent of the huge amounts wagered went to retailers of lottery tickets, and another 5 per cent mostly to contractors for operations, the stakes were very large. In fact, in the Virginia lottery vote in 1987, 45 per cent of the pro-lottery funds came from Scientific Games, a big lottery contractor, and 22 per cent from the owners of the 7-Eleven convenience stores. Any business might develop a profitable tie to gambling, the most profitable minor vice. One advertiser in *Gaming Business Magazine*, for example, was the Gasser Chair Company, interested in casino furnishings. Many less-obvious business elements made money from servicing gambling activities. The list is almost endless. As early as 1903, the Western Union Telegraph Company was notoriously involved in illegal betting in "pool rooms," to which special wires for race results were attached. At one point, the company offered "to send an operator who was an expert at jumping out of windows" if the place was raided. In the late twentieth century, among those who ultimately profited most from gambling were large accounting firms that had intimate ties to the management of every major business in the United States.[45]

Other indirect gainers included those who were in the entertainment business, broadly speaking, as opposed to more regular merchants who wanted to sell pork and beans that were paid for. One 1930s survey found that when Santa Anita racetrack was operating, the sales of many lines of merchandise such as dry goods dropped dramatically in the area. In Beverly Hills, sales in stores dropped by 39.1 per cent. People in the hotel and associated tourist businesses, by contrast, often hoped to gain by having gambling operations open near them. Indeed, as I have suggested, "hospitality" firms often entered the gambling business as such. One motel chain, Holiday Inns, counted $1 million in "gaming" earnings in 1979. By 1983, the figure was $116 million—40 per cent of the total operating income of the chain.[46]

The most notorious examples of businesspeople who used gambling to increase their wealth were real estate and other entrepreneurs of Nevada, and particularly Las Vegas. Divided and at first unable to establish big-time gambling, the citizens who began in the 1940s to receive help from criminals found them spectacularly effective in civic promotion. Las Vegas gambling promoters were most conspicuously successful in establishing the "entertainment package"—gambling, alcohol, and prostitution—as a new standard for "recreation" in midcentury America and a significant supplement to the cabaret ideal.[47]

In the last part of the twentieth century, advertising revealed clearly the pervasive symbiosis between gambling and many other kinds of ventures. Gambling enterprises not only influenced the media directly and indirectly but also affected many other kinds of businesses. Convenience stores, for example, ran promotions for chances in many states where they marketed government lottery tickets. Various kinds of special events also led to targeted advertising that aided betting promoters. Horse-race celebrations drew sponsorship from corn-chip makers and General Motors. At one point, Caesars Palace, a casino, persuaded a copy-machine company as well as an automobile maker and a brewery to sponsor a special event that generated gambling activity. Casinos in general brought in large numbers of sporting events, especially boxing matches, to which myriad companies (otherwise apparently respectable) attached their names. Through such tie-ins, not to mention listings on the stock exchange and affiliations with charitable drives, exploiters of gambling confirmed and expanded their mainstream status.[48]

As parts of the gambling business became legal in more and more areas, entrepreneurs talked about how to market wagering behavior. In 1984, the "parimutuel industry," for example, faced with an aging clientele, was advised by an editorial writer in a trade paper to find "younger players who could become loyal and frequent patrons." A certified public accountant gave similar advice: racing-business people should work on "devising and experimenting with ways to attract youthful audiences." In the late twentieth century, an important new cultural element entered with the appearance of state lottery advertising. The lotteries, unlike traditional regressive sin taxes, worked to increase, not decrease, the taxed activity, engaging in powerful and manipulative advertising campaigns that were periodically denounced by consumer groups. An official policy of the Ohio lottery in the mid-1960s, for example, was "Schedule heavier media weight during those times of the month where consumer disposable income peaks." And all the ads were both seductive and misleading, emphasizing winning rather than real cost.[49]

The Public Face of Gambling Advocacy

The gambling marketers did well with their campaign to persuade more and more of the population to spend money on wagers. In 1939, 29 per cent of the population placed a bet during the year. By 1974, the percentage had more than doubled and was still rising. As opportunities for gambling increased, so did the amount bet, both legal and illegal. The idea that legalized gambling would drive out illegal activities was no more than a public-relations myth of gambling promoters; in fact, the more that people became used to the idea of betting, the more they bet under all circumstances. Those who became accustomed to legal gambling also found illegal bets—that were outside the tax system and provided better odds—very attractive.[50]

Arguments of gambling interests did not change substantially over the years. Gambling people contended that betting was manly, that taking a chance was courageous. As one ambivalent writer in the 1890s noted, "A genuine gambler is a great man gone wrong, and gambling is a misdirection of courage and energy and enterprise—of all those attitudes that make [a] man most manly." Like promoters of the other minor vices, gambling entrepreneurs insisted that wagering was not only a common behavior but that everybody did it. In the 1930s, some church officials maintained that "if wealthy churches can raise money by bridge, why should not the smaller ones play beano [bingo]?" And as in the campaign to repeal Prohibition, gambling interests enjoyed the alliance of writers in the cabaret crowd who utilized ridicule to undermine opposition. One such writer, Heywood Broun, for example, once observed, "The urge to gamble is so universal and its practice so pleasurable that I assume that it must be evil."[51]

Betting promoters also claimed that the larger the gambling enterprise, and the better organized and the more supported by government it was, the more the enterprise would be fair and honest and would discourage crime, or at least other kinds of crime. One of the important functions of organizing gambling, whether in criminal syndicates or in legal institutions, so the argument went, was to protect the consumer, to deliver an honest chance for the person who was a sucker anyway. Further, this line of reasoning went, the more public the institution, the better still the protection against cheating was—and also the less the particular gambling could be connected to criminals. Appearing to protect consumers was therefore one of the dynamics of Americans' growing acceptance of legalized betting in the middle and late twentieth century.

And always partisans of gambling talked about economic benefits, appealing to the monetary interests of businesspeople and taxpayers, just as in Nevada and the parimutuel states from the 1920s and 1930s on. In 1976, after losing an earlier vote in New Jersey in part because of publicity about their criminal ties, casino interests brought gambling to Atlantic City by arguing that gambling would help finance state services to old people, that the unemployed in a depressed area would benefit by the creation of jobs, and that legal betting and strict state supervision would reduce crime. Virtually none of these benefits materialized—indeed, quite the opposite—but in that case, gambling proponents showed that economic arguments that distracted discussion from the social costs of gambling proved an effective tactic. Elsewhere, similar wagering interests used the same strategy—stressing economic potential—to win changes in the laws.[52]

The combination of machismo, appeal to a glamorous lifestyle, and greed was effective only when proponents could persuade a large number of people that wagering of whatever kind was "a harmless leisure-time experience." At one time, critics of gambling had argued that individual actions had social consequences. "The gambling mania is at war with industry, and therefore destructive of prosperity and thrift. . . . Once possessed of the passion, an individual is lost to every sense of duty as husband, father, citizen, and man of business," wrote ex-gambler John Quinn in a conventional formulation in 1892. By the late twentieth century, such ideas were being swamped by modern versions of the strategy of ignoring net social costs and the vulnerability of various groups and, instead, continuing to place all responsibility for any untoward effects upon individual, independent, responsible adult wagerers. In Illinois in 1986, the state itself had a billboard ad in a poor black neighborhood that read: "How to go from Washington Blvd. [in the slums] to Easy Street—Play the Illinois State Lottery."[53]

Gambling proponents had a double argument based on the individual responsibility of the bettor who presumably hurt only himself or herself. Betting gave otherwise helpless people the power to make decisions of at least some consequence in their own lives, and the possibility of real harm to the bettor was an essential aspect of a wager. One philosopher, at least, noted that in existential terms, gambling might have real justification for an individual.[54] It was such a spirit of narrow self-centeredness that facilitated betting in the age of narcissism when merchandisers often appealed openly to the anti-bourgeois urge to take risks.

The other part of the individualistic argument was, as I have noted, that only the individual wagerer was responsible for any undesirable consequences of a bet (a view widely shared by many theologians—aside from sponsors of bingo). Following the lead of alcoholic-beverage marketers, members of the gambling business endorsed the idea that compulsive gambling was an individual illness unrelated to any gambling institution or law.

The business therefore came to support therapy programs for such unfortunate individuals who presumably suffered not from the attractions of gambling but also from primitive types of thinking, compulsive fixations, and defective "affect relations with their parents." Gambling proponents and therapists alike conceptualized the addictive element in some people's betting as a strictly idiosyncratic matter. Again, as with drinking and drug problems, a significant and articulate part of the public-health apparatus was drawn into emphasizing individual, not social, responsibility—and specifically the compulsive person, not the act and not the profit taker.[55] Despite a wide spectrum of critics and opponents who continued to work against legalization and social legitimation in the 1980s and after, both gambling and gambling businesspeople had managed to achieve substantial respectability.

Betting had started as an activity that repudiated the dedication to thrift characteristic of a population largely concerned with producing and saving. Betting ended up becoming an adventure for bored Americans who wanted to believe that they could get rich quickly and who found wagering congenial with the fantasies of a society dominated by consumption. From legendary riverboat confidence men of the nineteenth century to members of crime syndicates of the twentieth, many businesspeople made large illegal profits from the betting public. Many more gained by supplying and servicing gambling enterprises or furnishing what passed for sports and sporting news. Contrary to the promises of proponents of betting, illegal gambling did not decrease as various legal forms of gambling became more prominent in the United States during and after the 1930s and the 1970s. And total profits increased even more as both state governments and questionable corporations joined the outright criminals in gratifying citizens who just wanted a little "action," by itself or as part of an "entertainment" package. In moving so close to respectability, gambling in fact implicitly set a model for proponents of all the bad habits.

Sexual Misbehavior

Regardless of what they may have done privately, most Americans from colonial days to the late twentieth century believed that sexual activity outside of conventional monogamous marriage constituted misbehavior on some level. At all times, a variety of citizens nevertheless questioned the standards at least implicitly. But anyone who advocated alternative sexual standards operated within a very complicated and constantly shifting social context.

In the nineteenth century, despite local differences in behavior, standards tended to be general and conventional. By the first half of the twentieth century, implicit standards tended to diverge by social class. And by the last half of the twentieth century, the advocates of the minor vices, along with the cultural environment, were propelling alterations in standards across a society fragmented into many subcultural units among which opinions about sexual matters were often an important differentiating factor. Yet Americans' persistence in maintaining conventions of sexual conduct over many generations is striking.

In the histories of the bad habits, the theme recurs consistently that in some way traditional sexual misbehavior, or at least the idea of sexual misbehavior, was attached to the other minor vices. The glamour of even gambling, for example, would have been much diminished without its associations with prostitution and other sexual activity in dens, palaces, and Las Vegas casinos—not to mention the implications of the adventuresome machismo of the betting man. The connection was reciprocal, too, in the constellation of minor vices. Nineteenth-century bordellos served alcoholic beverages and often supported other activities. From the late 1970s on, pornography retail outlets offered not only dirty books and movies but, very frequently, prostitution, assignation, drug dealing, gambling, fencing of stolen goods, the laundering of gambling and drug money, and other criminal activities. These supermarkets of vice, organized around a symbol of sexual misbehavior, even accepted major credit cards (in one typical case, conveniently using on the charge slip the name of the affiliated bar/restaurant next door to protect customers who hired prostitutes).[1] All evidence, over many generations, then, is that sexual misbehavior, however symbolized at any time, was an integral as well as active element in the constellation.

Despite the traditional relationship to the other bad habits, sexual misbehavior as such in fact moved only slowly beyond local, commonplace events into the world of commerce. Eventually the mass media found it profitable in a number of ways to exploit ideas about misbehaving sexually, nudging American attitudes and standards toward a model that had origins in stereotyped small-time pornography and prostitution—a model that, in the twentieth century, reformers sometimes endorsed.

The earliest American settlers were well aware that sexual drives often broke through customary restraints and caused behavior that they deemed socially unacceptable. In records of community sanctions against deviant behavior in early New England, numerous scholars have found abundant proof of the universal presence of the temptations of sexual passion, even among members of these highly regulated social groups. The Puritans knew about adultery and rape, and, as befitted a rural community, on at least one occasion, bestiality. They also coped with ordinary nonmarital love making and, eventually, the custom of bundling, in which a young man and a young woman slept in the same bed (whether or not sexual activity took place was never clear). As Edmund Morgan observes, early New Englanders were not unduly ruffled by evidence of ordinary passions, and he quotes Governor William Bradford: "It may be in this case as it is with waters when their streams are stopped or damned up, when they gett passage they flow with more violence, and make more noise and disturbance, than when they are suffered to rune quietly in their owne channels. So wickednes being here more stopped by strict laws . . . at last breaks out wher it getts vente."[2]

Those early Americans, however, mostly lived in communities in which neighbors knew pretty well what everyone did, and the most private behavior could become part of group concern. Illegitimate births in particular sooner or later became common knowledge. When female servants entertained men secretly, or when a swain used a ladder to gain entrance to a maid's quarters, or when young men and women employed on farms did more than work together, such activities often did not escape watchful eyes. In April 1668, for example, two neighbors saw Sarah Largin and Thomas Jones "on a bed together at Theophilus Marches . . . ," as later church court testimony recorded it.[3]

The New England settlements represented only one type of community, however. In the middle colonies and the South and on the frontier, substantially different kinds of communities developed. Although the abstract standards were the same all over, outside of New England, the laws and sanctions were in general less stringent. One eighteenth-century clergyman, for instance, complained that "the manners of the North Carolinians in general are vile and corrupt and the whole country is a stage of debauchery dissoluteness and corruption, and how can it be otherwise? . . . poligamy is very common . . .—bastardy no disrepute, concubinage general." North Carolina had a particularly bad reputation among the colonists, but all observers suggested that in settlements both north and south of that colony, misbehavior was common and not heavily sanctioned. In many communities, women suffered for bearing an illegitimate child, but predatory males were generally indulged and sometimes admired.[4]

Concrete testimony about actual conduct or misconduct is relatively rare, and when it does exist, it usually takes the form of gossip or biased observation. Outside of the legal and church records of New England and occasional court actions elsewhere, virtually no specific evidence exists. One can hardly know what to make, for example, of the Church of England clergyman who in 1676 reported that in Maryland "all notorious vices are committed; so that it is become a Sodom of uncleanness, and a pesthouse of iniquity."[5] Clearly many early Americans did not confine their sexual activities to those within the bonds of marriage, but preachers whose sermons denounced fornication may have been serving areas in which either much or little actual misbehavior occurred. The sermons may in fact have been merely theoretical exercises or a response to one or two notorious cases rather than a reflection of a New World Sodom or Gomorrah. And although sexual misbehavior might have been part of bad character in general, it was not organized or institutionalized.

One conclusion that the written evidence does permit is that colonial Americans maintained a fairly uniform set of standards (however well or ill enforced). For all communities, these standards were unremarkable and traditional: sexual behavior outside of monogamous marriage was inappropriate. Moreover, although early Americans understood and tolerated a great deal of passion and even pleasure, the ultimate rationale for sexual activity was reproduction. The Puritans and many other Americans viewed marriage as an effective antidote for fornication and adultery. It was, for example, not uncommon for young fornicators who were detected to be whipped but at the same time enjoined to marry.[6] What ultimately varied from community to community was the amount of toleration that residents showed, in practice, for irregular and merely pleasurable sexual behavior.

Community Differences

Moreover, beginning in the eighteenth century and particularly in the early nineteenth century, two factors that have appeared in other connections complicated sexual misbehavior. One factor was the continuing development of towns. The other was the force of the religious evangelical movement that led most social leaders to emphasize personal moral behavior and to place a very high value on purity of conduct and language.[7] Each of these general factors, however, worked differently through local communities.

Indeed, the critical question is, what caused the variation between communities? One element in the answer was isolation. Robert Wiebe has used the metaphor of islands to describe the insularity of life in the many communities spread across nineteenth-century America. Each geographical population center was to a surprising extent a world unto itself. Moreover, sanctions for deviations from standards of sexual behavior and actual behavior itself also varied—and changed—according to events in the local community. Even among communities of enslaved people in the pre-Civil War South, for example, particular local circumstances caused wide diversities in standards and conduct.[8]

By chance an account has survived describing differences in sexual events in separate island communities in those days: the reminiscences of G. Stanley Hall, later president of Clark University. He was born in 1846 and grew up in the 1850s and 1860s in New England, an area that was by then generally greatly affected by evangelical repressiveness in public attitudes toward sexuality. At different times, young Hall attended different schools, each representing a community. In one, he encountered complete corruption among the youngsters; in others, he found innocence consonant with the repressive standards of his own home:

> The morals of my first Worthington school were, without exception, the "rottenest" I have ever heard of.... Homosexuality, exhibitionism, *fellatio*, onanism, relations with animals, and almost every form of perversion described by Tarnowski, Krafft-Ebing or Havelock Ellis, existed in this school. Once an older girl, when we chanced to be under a bridge by the brook, exposed herself to me. It was common for the older boys to catch us younger ones, unless we were fleet enough to outrun them, and to strip and exhibit us to older boys and even girls. Several couples were caught *in flagranti*. There was every kind of obscene word, tale, and cut, and things utterly indescribable—and I hope and believe incredible—were done for two or three years at this school. There were so-called French cards, apparently innocent but transparent when held up to the light, with obscenities, and various indecent pamphlets and leaflets were surreptitiously circulated.... The *fons et origo* of it all was one of the older and also mentally brilliant boys whose grandfather seems to have initiated him into every manner of lewdness.... In none of the other six schools that I attended was there anything whatever of this kind. . . .[9]

This account requires some commentary. The stereotypical types of forbidden sexual behavior were well known firsthand to the youngsters in Worthington—but, as Hall confirmed, little understood or acted upon by identical youngsters in other communities. Obviously, too, youthful corruption did not necessarily prevent a person's developing into a normal and useful citizen. As Hall noted as he continued his narrative, exactly that pattern of adult propriety and upstanding action marked childhood malefactors in the Worthington community. Clearly, lower-order patterns of behavior (what Hall naively conceived as hereditary degeneracy) could persist in the nineteenth century as much as later without serious damage to ideas of what the community in general held to be proper and normative.[10]

Finally, Hall shrewdly identified the source of corruption, namely, an adult (the grandfather). Some later scholars have tried to read back into the past the idea that a youthful counterculture at some point in history changed conduct and standards. As Hall's experience showed concretely, the potential for youthful misbehavior was always present, but the source for actual change was not the young people per se, who could develop in various ways and in fact as adults were not necessarily corrupt even when they had been exposed to misbehavior. Martin Duberman has found another example, from even earlier in the century, of two young men who had engaged in apparently high-spirited sex play with each other and who nonetheless rose to become pillars of South Carolina society—confirming, Duberman suggests, contemporaries' beliefs that, in many areas, young southern gentlemen took a completely amoral approach to indulging animal appetites. But there was, again, no evidence of an organized counterculture or interest, and whatever the hypocrisies, the conventional standards were not challenged.[11]

Industrialization, Urbanization, and Commercialization

Some scholars have attempted to connect restrictive changes in sexual behavior and standards with the rise of industry and capitalism in general, on the not-unreasonable grounds that there were correlations between the need for self-control and the factory system, leading to parsimony in sexuality as well as finances. Although the adaptive nature of lifestyles is not to be denied, the determiners of what happened in various communities were more complicated than mere responses to industrial work patterns. It was true that petit bourgeoisie in England and America led the evangelical moral crusade, but they, too, responded to much more than capitalism. Moreover, the issue was not new standards, but simply taking more seriously traditional aspirations to anti-sexual purity. In the United States, "purity" came to mean public demeanor and involved the high valuation that romantic love could bring. In fact, it turned out that sexual activity within marriage or even within a premarital love liaison did not, among most middle-class people, necessarily impair a woman's purity.[12] Regardless of behavior, standards, again, were never in question.

What confuses the industrialization issue is the fact that factories caused the growth of towns and cities, and urban centers were indeed centers of sexual misbehavior—to the point that everyone at the time recognized that when towns and cities grew, so did sexual misbehavior. It was common knowledge that the lure of the city included access to forbidden sexual items: prostitutes, loose women, and men-about-town, not to mention suggestive theater and pornography, which were decidedly not native to the farm. Above all, the larger the urban center, the more toleration there was for sexual nonconformity, ranging from enjoying indecency to premarital adventures to more deviant conduct such as prostitution and "perversions," to use an early-twentieth-century term. Indeed, the correlation of town size with relative toleration of misbehavior persisted into the twentieth century.[13]

It was true that life in larger urban areas became increasingly impersonal so that strangers could come and go unnoticed and that residents could be strangers to one another. But the most significant fact about towns and cities was that in them sexual misbehavior could, and often did, become commercialized, just as it had been and was in Europe. And of course such activity—and support for it—was centered in the geographical districts and associated population groups of what became the Victorian underworld.[14]

Although various elements of commercialized sexuality shaded into one another—as well as into drinking, gambling, and crime—two major varieties emerged in American urban centers: prostitution and media. In the nineteenth century, media included publications and pictures and entertainment. In the 1850s, William W. Sanger reported that in New York "boys and young men may be found loitering at all hours round hotels, steamboat docks, rail-road depots, and other public places, ostensibly selling newspapers or pamphlets, but secretly offering vile, lecherous publications to those who are likely to be customers."[15]

The smut peddlers tended to become tied into sexual goods of all kinds, in a way that was confusing to later generations who thought of "rubber goods" as birth-control devices rather than congeries of fraudulent and offensive items that went together with an at-best ambiguous condom that could have been used for disease prevention as well as contraception. The famous enemy of obscenity, Anthony Comstock, after whom public prudishness and sexual censorship is named (comstockery), in his first raid in 1876 arrested one Morris Sickel, who sold not only condoms but rubber penises and quack remedies. In the nineteenth century, obscenity was a substantial and profitable business and included much more than just imported French picture cards. Comstock found that at the beginning of the 1870s, of 165 objectionable books, unmistakably designed to be at least titillating, 163 had been issued by just three publishers in New York. And as soon as Comstock began to publicize his work in those years, he was flooded with information about the trade in obscenity. The size and organization of the business is confirmed by other evidence. In the 1860s, for example, Joseph L. Clayton of Georgetown, Ohio, offered men (including apparently Civil War soldiers) sexual goods by mail-order catalog, shipped in plain packages. Available were condoms, French ticklers ("During its use no female can remain passively still, so great and thrilling is the titillation"), books (with "spicy Illustrations"), posters, postcards, and other equipment and depictions common at the time. These goods were clearly not produced in Georgetown (population 1,012), and some were "of Paris."[16]

Prostitution

Prostitution was another kind of business, with other origins, but in the nineteenth century, it tended to converge with the commerce in obscenity. Prostitution was in fact not illegal, although lewd conduct in public and "night walking" could be both common-law and statutory offenses. From the seventeenth century on, port cities, at least, harbored women who were recognized by custom as prostitutes, functioning exactly as had those long known in European urban centers.

By the nineteenth century, Americans treated prostitution as an undesirable but inevitable social phenomenon and casually compared conditions from one city to another—again assuming that prostitution was a part of town life. Local newspapers carried stories about prostitutes and the local red-light district. All citizens were presumed to know where it was. Indeed, by the late nineteenth century, the "segregated district" served as a geographical boundary marker for society in general to indicate an area, not only in which deviant activity took place, but in which people specially labeled, particularly prostitutes, could congregate. Respectable people tended to tolerate the red-light district in part because the presence of the area and the labeling of the people there helped shore up understanding of what was good and proper elsewhere in society. In his unique, detailed account of prostitution in mid-nineteenth-century New York, Sanger ascribed much of the trade in women's bodies to the transient population of the city. "If by any miracle," he wrote, "all seamen and strangers visiting New York could be transformed into moral men, at least from one half to two thirds of the houses of ill fame would be absolutely bankrupt."[17]

Sanger calculated the economic forces involved in prostitution in New York City alone and found the sum very large indeed—in 1858, about six million dollars, not including hospital and police expenses, a total amount approximately equal to the entire city-government budget. Moreover, he found that the amount spent on alcoholic beverages directly in connection with prostitution constituted one-third or more of the cost. Others observed that in every city prostitution attracted saloons, tobacco stores, dance halls, and theaters, all of which, along with the robbing of customers, revolved around prostitution. "The dancing-saloons . . . are, in fact," reported Sanger, "so many accessories to prostitution, and many scenes there witnessed will not permit description." The dance hall indeed continued into the twentieth century as a source of sexual misbehavior in the cities.[18]

The well-established system of prostitution reached into many social institutions in urban communities. "Vice in the Metropolis," wrote reformer Samuel Paynter Wilson of Chicago, "is fostered by a class of disreputable real estate men," who rented to madams, pimps, and prostitutes. The business aspects of prostitution also intertwined with municipal politics from at least the mid nineteenth century on and were involved in police corruption as soon as there were police. For a century before the 1880s, the theater was intimately connected with prostitution, for prostitutes showed themselves and solicited in a special gallery—the third tier—reserved in every theater for prostitutes and their customers. Managers believed that the presence of this trade was an economic necessity if the theater was to survive: "In some instances in Eastern cities," reported an observer in 1866, "in addition to free admissions, messengers have been sent to the haunts of vile women, to invite their attendance as the necessary attraction of a large and indispensable portion of the patrons of the stage." People at the time testified that the theater had a powerful corrupting influence. Robert Turnbull in 1837, for example, told the story of a dying young man who said, "It would tire you to relate how I was first enticed to go up stairs into the splendid saloon, then to the third tier where the prostitutes are allotted a place. . . ."[19]

Observing that prostitution appeared along with the concentration of population—especially a transient population—and that all aspects of immorality and corruption interacted with one another gives only one dimension of the phenomenon. In the West, which provided an excellent comparison, independent solicitors of sexual activity existed, but whenever a substantial number of people gathered, any prostitutes present tended to become tied into other business and political institutions at least as much as in the East. Just as in older parts of the country, prostitutes gathered in houses; they associated themselves with saloons and other entertainment establishments; and they paid protection money or nominal fines to law-enforcement officials and judges.[20]

The Double Standard and Its Obsolescence

Prostitution functioned as an essential element in the double standard of morality that lasted into the twentieth century: women were supposed to be pure, or at least virgins, until married, and men, who were still constrained to uphold conventional standards verbally in public, were presumed in actual behavior to be beasts who could not resist sexual temptation, who sowed wild oats when young and whose passions would impel them to tend to commit adultery with any available woman on any occasion—with tacit community approval. As a YWCA spokesperson noted in 1899, ". . . society excuses the sin in men; in the women never." This double standard pervaded society without mitigation. At the end of the nineteenth century, for example, the lowbrow Peck's Bad Boy series (presumably family entertainment) repeatedly portrayed a preadolescent or barely pubescent son playing practical jokes on his father in connection with that unfortunate man's at least attempted infidelities to his wife (the boy's mother).[21] Yet, at the same time, public standards of this society emphasized morality and respectability, and people usually identified themselves with those public standards, not with shameful male "necessities" or anything else that was in some sense private.

The class of "fallen women" available for the uncontrollable passions of men worked into the double-standard system particularly well because in the nineteenth century many human relationships were based on a cash nexus. Marriage itself was in important ways an economic institution. As late as 1895, reformer B. O. Flower, for example, spoke about matrimony, as then practiced, as being so businesslike an arrangement as to make the marriage bond virtually a prostitution. A large part of the population, in short, viewed sexual behavior as a commodity for sale or trade so that prostitution was compatible with the whole society in style as well as substance.[22] Only later did economic and social events move commercial sexual exchanges beyond a functional level into other cultural and social streams.

It was in this context, then, that the institutional ties of prostitutes and the parasites who lived off them took on special significance because of their economic connections to the business community and politics, on the one hand, and, on the other hand, their special relationships with entertainment, alcoholic-beverage sales, and other kinds of vice.[23] Under special circumstances, in some cities the procurers could even tap into the international market in women: on the mining frontier in Virginia City, women were shipped in from all over the world to meet the sudden demand. But mostly the commerce and the corruption were local. To a large extent prostitution remained but an adjunct to other community social structures.[24]

Late in the nineteenth century, the urban population began to change, with an influx of migrants in whose cultures prostitution was far more acceptable and established than in the United States. But these newcomers also often mixed into the lower orders of society, and the double standard took on additional meanings. People, especially young people, among the lower orders of society, however much they praised virginity, nevertheless within their parochial groups had no use for purity. In urban areas, it was their pursuits of pleasure and money that especially scandalized and tempted the upholders of respectability.[25]

Early in the twentieth century, other social transformations began to affect the two aspects of sexual misbehavior that involved commercial interests, prostitution and obscene publications and artifacts. When many middle-class Americans learned of the newly discovered grave dangers of venereal diseases, which were spread primarily through tolerated prostitution and the double standard of morality, large numbers of citizens joined with the purity forces to try to wipe out prostitution—and simultaneously to persuade the purity forces in turn to join them in programs of sex education aimed at preventing disease and limiting sexual activity to monogamous marriage. At the same time, strong legal repression caused pornography to become economically unimportant.[26]

In the course of this campaign to end the double standard, standards of acceptable sexual behavior changed, particularly for practices within marriage. Although during the nineteenth century, most people had not admitted in public that love making was proper for any purpose other than procreation, in private, many couples indulged in the pleasures of the marriage bed even when not intending to beget children. Now, in the twentieth century, social leaders demanded publicly that modern marriage produce not just children but fulfillment. Indeed, they insisted that inducing mutual orgasm made married people unselfish rather than animal. With the support of a century of literary propaganda for romantic love, even religious people, by slowly spiritualizing marriage and removing guilt from sexual feelings, began to approve of self-indulgence—under the guise of true love ("permissiveness with affection" is the descriptive phrase of James Reed). By the 1920s, prostitution had changed into an activity restricted very largely to the lower orders and therefore had become far more marginal than a generation earlier—a major reversal of standards at the expense of the interests of the underworld. Middle-class Americans were acting on their beliefs in permissive behavior by making love—clearly now more frequently outside of marriage but, as far as surviving information goes, not necessarily outside of monogamy. That is, the increase in coupling came in premarital, not extramarital, activity. But, altogether, both attitude and activity changed for many parts of the population. And, moreover, among middle-class young people—the supposedly "flaming youth" of the 1920s—changes in the erotic quality, not the institutional setting, of the activity, was the most important modernization that was going on. Moreover, accepting the value of eroticism led young opinion leaders to question what they saw as the old repressiveness in a number of areas of life besides sex, all as a part of the changes in standards associated with the 1920s. But the changes before World War II among opinion makers were still far from an adoption of non-middle-class standards.[27]

Social-Class Differences

What had happened in the area of love making, in particular, was that social-class differences in patterns of sexual behavior became much more sharply differentiated with social leaders' rejection of the double standard early in the twentieth century. Everyone had, of course, always believed that the lower elements in society—however defined at the time—were immoral and loose, and probably degenerate, in their sexual behavior. Such beliefs, over many generations, often represented romantic primitivism in which middle-class people imagined that folks in other social groups were lusty wenches and studs easily seduced. What may not have been obvious was that by at least the mid nineteenth century, American men of the middle and upper classes were remarkably more chaste in attitude and behavior than even their counterparts in England.[28] Thus the transition away from the double standard to "pure" monogamous relationships that promoted guilt-free sexual satisfaction was not difficult for many middle-class people.

But there were other real cultural differences. Non-middle-class standards for the early twentieth century show up with great clarity in a number of materials. In the cities, social, work, and gender constraints led turn-of-the-century working girls to grant sexual favors to men whom they met in public places. "Don't yeh know," said one young woman, "there ain't no feller goin' t'spend coin on yeh fer nothin'? Yeh gotta be a good Indian, Kid—we all gotta!" The non-middle-class model continued for some time to emphasize both the double standard and a high theoretical value placed on female virginity, on the one hand, and, on the other, the cash nexus in the relationship and very high levels of tolerance for any misbehavior in practice. In early-twentieth-century Chicago, single women in the boardinghouse districts felt peer pressure—typically lower-order parochialism—to engage in sexual promiscuity and to exploit dates for presents just as the dates exploited the women for sexual favors.[29]

Beyond flagrant mistreatment of women under versions of the double standard, among the working class of many ethnic groups, serial monogamy—steady, usually live-in relationships, changing with more or less frequency—substituted for both glaring promiscuity and a commitment to marriage. One sociologist at the end of the 1930s reported that a group of young non-middle-class, street-wise males whom he was studying expected to be sexually active before and outside of marriage but classified girls as "virgins," "lays," and "prostitutes," with the clear implication that those in the second category did not suffer greatly in the boys' esteem.[30]

Within a few years, Alfred Kinsey and his associates confirmed in detail a number of other remarkable class differences reported by different investigators. Non-middle-class men and women were typically—and distinctly—very inhibited in what they did in love making, for example keeping as much clothing on as possible. Middle-class people, although not sexually active nearly as early or with as many partners as those in the lower orders and working class—and, indeed, often virginal until marriage—engaged in a much broader spectrum of activities and more extensive play with their (usually) monogamous partners.[31]

These early-twentieth-century differences in behavior among groups reflected attitudes that appeared substantially also in standards that were public, and the fact that different groups in the United States dissented from the dominant standards found in the media helped lay the foundation for a change in those standards. For their part, even reform-minded middle-class people deplored the dirty sex that children learned from lower-order companions—"the street," which was often in practice the Victorian underworld.[32]

By midcentury, sociologists had sorted out the complicated system whereby people of various class backgrounds deferred to the middle-class standard—monogamous but fulfilling marriage—even while pursuing and honoring sometimes quite different patterns of relationships and activities. As late as 1973, two investigators summarized the pattern:

> the lower class both envy and defer to middle-class values without necessarily embracing them. Members of the lower class frequently explain their position in terms of the vicissitudes of their daily lives which prevent them from following middle-class patterns. Middle-class values are dominant, both in the sense that middle-class patterns are upheld by the forces of the society as a whole whenever they conflict with the others, and in the sense that all classes pay symbolic deference to middle-class values while adhering to their own.

Two major changes, then, took place in the second half of the century. The first was the growing assertion by lower-order elements of the validity of their patterns, such as short-term serial monogamy and other varieties of nonmarital involvements. The second was the erosion of public deference to the symbols as well as the restraints of middle-class arrangements.[33]

In the first half of the twentieth century, then, the dominant middle-class population elements lived with high yet increasingly fulfilling standards. Yet even those standards were changing. In formal statements, such as those made by leaders in the sex-education movement, masturbation, once the focus of a great deal of fear, became not only harmless but an actual asset. Young people, as sex educator W. F. Robie pointed out explicitly as early as 1918, could use masturbation before marriage as a substitute for behavior that would spread disease and cause illegitimacy. Within marriage, all types and varieties of love making gained positive sanction. Indeed, authors of manuals suggested that hurried, missionary-position love making was thoughtless and possibly unrewarding (and, obviously, as it turned out, typically non-middle-class).[34]

Initially, reformers from the middle and upper classes drew upon romantic love and notions of spiritual union, women's rights, fear of disease, and uplift to emphasize personal sexual fulfillment. Elements pressuring for change emphasized the importance of both feelings and impulses, having in mind either the stereotypical artist or the lower-order person conscious of body and physical prowess—that is, both bohemianism and primitivism. Reformers and educators also talked often about spirituality in lovers. A long tradition of sexual reform operated under the guise of romantic love and drew upon such European reformers as Havelock Ellis (early in the century) and T. H. Van de Velde, whose work in translation was widely circulated and imitated beginning in 1930. Such writers emphasized and advocated extended and varied "love play" for "the couple," with demands on love making that brought the work ethic into sexual activity: people had to try conscientiously to carry love making off correctly. Eventually, especially after World War II, such advocates of play and feelings evolved into those who believed that mechanical mastery of techniques of love making could (if frequent enough) bring complete satisfaction and happiness—a stance not incompatible with the impulsive hedonism of lower-order standards (see below). Social leaders for a variety of reasons came to accept the idea that love making could be successful in and of itself and that it could involve "the couple" in many kinds of behavior (which might earlier have been considered perversions). Because each variant behavior nevertheless still emphasized the marriage partner, it thereby became legitimate—all this in large part because the standard makers believed that *any* factor that might strengthen marriage—including satisfying lust—was socially valuable and personally enhancing. Whereas once romantic love had served to help women control and restrain male sexuality, in the late twentieth century, love served to rationalize gratification, especially male gratification.[35]

For generations, then, the tension persisted between dominant middle-class sexual standards that emphasized fulfillment within marriage, on the one hand, and, on the other, lower-order standards that included the double standard, impulsive coupling, and various types of nonmarital serial monogamy. Eventually, a number of more general social forces galvanized marked shifts in sexual attitudes of both lower-order and middle-class groups, and they converged after World War II.

The Campaign for Unrestrained Behavior

One obvious influence on the change in middle-class standards was lower-order parochialism. Non-middle-class young people of many backgrounds, frequently allied with elements from the Victorian underworld, made amusement at Coney Island in New York (John F. Kasson's paradigmatic example) a symbolic behavioral alternative, legitimated by a public space devoted to non-genteel standards. As one commentator remarked in 1901, "Coney Island has a code of conduct which is all her own"—one markedly suggestive of sexual looseness as well as hedonism in general. Because of the superficial innocence of Coney Island, many respectables came to think of a visit there as harmless fun and missed the parochial agenda and commercialization embodied in mass amusements—such as activating hidden compressed-air jets that would blow female visitors' skirts revealingly high.[36] Such teasing was fun and might well pass for joking that reinforced, instead of weakening, the standards of the respectables. Only in the context of persistent patterns such as changes in the motion pictures did the significance move beyond what could be ignored as the defensive *tsk-tsking* of people too anxious to see sin everywhere.

Another influence was, again, World War I. Many young Americans from respectable homes encountered in their overseas experiences alien sexual standards and institutions, such as, in France, prostitutes sponsored by the government. Service personnel who were middle class also encountered in the service in general an atmosphere in which lower-order preoccupation with unrestrained sexuality set the tone, if not the standard, in the barracks. As in the case of cigarette smoking, no one doubted the impact of the service experience upon a whole generation of Americans, and everyone understood the implications of the popular song "How Ya Gonna Keep 'Em Down on the Farm After They've Seen Paree?" (1919).[37]

Finally, as middle-class reformers attempted to make sexuality more fulfilling, they introduced a negative campaign. They attacked repressive standards that they believed diminished the fulfilling nature of marriage. As in the anti-Prohibition campaigns of the 1920s, satire and ridicule were effective. By showing that those who hewed to the most restrictive standards of sexuality were in fact as bad as those who clearly were experimental if not deviant, reformers opened the door (often unwittingly) to almost any change—in part by using, once again, the everybody's-doing-it argument. In 1922, author Ben Hecht noted that among the hypocritical respectables were those "who find their secret obscenities mirrored in every careless phrase, who read self accusation into the word sex . . . who fornicate apologetically . . . who achieve involved orgasms denouncing the depravities of others . . . trying forever to drown their own obscene desires in ear-splitting prayers for their fellowman's welfare; who find relief for constipation in forbidding their neighbors the water closet. . . ."[38] As in repealers' satiric attacks on the drys in the same era, such critiques subverted the authority of standard setters and propagandized for a vague new program of nonrestraint.

The heavy emphasis that so many middle-class Americans came to put on fulfillment opened the door particularly to those who had special interests in particular kinds of sexual activity (typically homoerotic or fetishistic) and who could now work negatively against all sexual restrictions. The logic in this strategy was that if all restrictions were lifted, so would restrictions be lifted from the special practices on the agendas of those labeled deviant. By never explicitly challenging monogamous romantic love, proponents of a variety of sexual behaviors therefore found that they were able to advocate their particular tastes and styles of love making and living within a context of general indulgence and toleration for what "the couple" did. In the nineteenth century, as suggested above, Americans lumped all nonprocreative sexual activity together as disgusting and animal—whether masturbation or any of the so-called perversions. Indeed, one definition of perversion was any sexual activity not directed immediately toward procreation, thus including, specifically, prostitution. The many attacks of nineteenth-century writers on masturbation (attacks that later thinkers found extreme to the point of humor) when not physiological simply condemned all such self-gratifying, basely passionate acts.[39] In the twentieth century, defending passion as such often came to embrace defending a variety of types of sexual activity.

In addition, one important strategy for those who were breaking—or wanted to break—sexual taboos was to extend the numbers of persons who, for whatever reason, would feel vulnerable as taboo breakers. As in the case of drug taking, empathy with standard breakers was helpful, but identity was even better—again, the everybody-does-it excuse for one's own behavior. The everybody-does-it argument had two aspects. One was the suggestion that anyone who violated any taboo should identify and support anyone else who broke not only that taboo, but also any sexual taboo at all. The hope was that married people who varied their love making would therefore feel empathy, if not identity, with fetishists. The other aspect was the idea that a person could have the wish and intention of breaking a taboo and be unaware of it—but show it implicitly in his or her behavior. The agitators were particularly successful early in the twentieth century (with the help of coincidental scientific and medical developments) in extending the category of sexuality and sexual perversion to many previously innocent activities. Everyone, therefore, would be touched by at least some corruption (and it was such ideas to which Hecht, for example, was appealing). Consequently, the label of sexual deviancy would become diluted into meaninglessness. This was a time when Americans of all classes came to know about and to be conscious of everything from implied seduction in advertisements to overt homosexual activity. Sometimes literary people used symbolism (as in the notorious 1920s novel by James Branch

Cabell, *Jurgen*). Sometimes scientists used labels—so that even women who bonded together closely could be thought to be involved in sexual liaisons with each other.[40] Many American thinkers of the early and mid twentieth century, using concepts and ideas from Europe, including the systematic classification of the perversions, thus extended the conceptual realm of sexuality to the point that virtually no American who was aware of this sort of idea (such as signs of unconscious wishes to commit incest or bestiality) would have been eligible to cast the first stone at any other American at all, of whatever sexual proclivity. Hence, as these critics hoped, no one could articulate the condemnations that are necessary to uphold standards.

Enlisting Entertainment Sectors

In addition to the usual quota of rebels in American society, then, a number of forces attacked and undermined conventional standards: non-middle-class parochials; middle-class advocates of fulfillment who opposed repression; and the profit-hungry businesspeople working in prostitution, pornography, and sensational journalism. For decades, the respectables lost ground on every front except upholding (in the name of true love) monogamy that was fulfilling. But even there, their hold on public standards weakened in the face of rebellious attacks. And in one profoundly important part of American life, the rebels dared to attack restrictions openly: the theater and kindred entertainments.[41]

Most of the theater of the late nineteenth and early twentieth centuries had been cleansed of the prostitutes' balcony and of "indecent" subject matter. Authorities had no trouble, for example, in closing a showing of even George Bernard Shaw's moralistic play *Mrs. Warren's Profession* in 1905. Vaudeville was considered proper family entertainment. Yet the connection between theater people and deviant elements continued. Before World War I, the sex-education movement opened the door to sexual subjects on the stage by trying to use Eugène Brieux's *Damaged Goods* as propaganda to combat syphilis. Immediately, many managers began staging "vice plays" that were only superficially moralistic and were available particularly from the Continental repertoire. Thereafter, literary and theater people relentlessly attempted to introduce ever more candor of word and action in the name of art and realism—and in fact they did familiarize audiences with public recognition of nonmarital patterns of activity.[42]

As I have suggested, moviemakers, beginning as early as 1915, persistently compromised conventional respectability and played up unrespectable and implicitly erotic expressiveness in the ever more influential medium. By the 1930s, a significant new sexual ideal had emerged in the motion pictures: Mae West. Her public persona was not just that of the suggestively seductive vamp notorious in the 1920s. West made her intentions clear with her famous line "Come up and see me some time" and utilized flagrantly the conventional device of naughty theater, the double entendre. The provocative manner in which she delivered her lines was taken from the "drag queen"—a man dressed as an outrageously vulgar woman—of the male homoerotic community, with which West was well acquainted. And that exaggerated and openly seductive manner was in turn based upon the flamboyant prostitutes of an earlier era. In this way, the manner and attitude of the (male) ideal of unrestrained sexual activity, the self-conscious urban homosexuals and prostitutes, was repackaged and fostered by the mass media. The newspapers, it was reported in 1933, could not get enough copy on Mae West, who had just announced a new book, *How to Misbehave*. She was a genuine model and promoter—at least onstage—of the idea of unrestricted and unrestrained sexuality.[43]

World War II

In the 1930s, the mass media were also pushing the traditional clean-cut American boy and girl, but that ideal, despite superficial appearances, did not survive World War II. In 1941–1945, even more than during World War I, a generation of men were subjected to a lower-order environment in which casual, more-or-less exploitive sexual activity was an explicit norm. One case history published in 1940 illustrates the types of attitudes that draftees brought with them or encountered:

> Maurice was, from early childhood, brought into contact with sex in a way that constantly stimulated desires and passions. He lived in an industrial community and his early activities were unsupervised. He was associated with a group of young men who constantly jested about sex and used it as a means of sensual gratification. He was introduced to sex practices when very young, being induced to try intercourse at about eight years of age. Further, the gang with which he associated used to masturbate in groups and Maurice began the practice himself. . . . Masturbation was regarded as evidence of vitality and prowess, and the strongest individual was the one who

could masturbate most frequently. Lacking close supervision at home, Maurice took up intercourse as a continuous form of adjustment when about fifteen. He and a close companion abandoned themselves to a search for sensual pleasure. They were quite promiscuous and over the period of eight years, from age fifteen to twenty-three, Maurice estimated that he had intercourse with fifty or sixty different persons.

The counselor who recorded the case history noted that Maurice had no concern for the effects of his sexual activities on other people and also had taken to drink. The shock implicit in the counselor's account showed that he came from the world of respectability.[44] In the service during the war, however, it was the Maurices who set the standards and who in barracks society labeled as deviant such men as the relatively prudish—respectable—counselor.

In contrast to officers in World War I, when, regardless of what men talked about in the barracks, many leaders in the army worked hard to encourage continence among the troops, military leaders in World War II were indifferent to morals and instead concentrated on making sexual activity as free of the risk of disease as possible. They tended implicitly to accept the idea that young Americans were and should be sexually active and assumed that service personnel were. "If you can't say no, take a pro," was the motto (referring to prophylactic devices). At one point, fifty million condoms reached service personnel *each month*—often dispensed free or from machines.[45]

Because fear of disease rather than self-control was the primary motivation in official service V.D. programs, there was no effective force countering the standards that the Maurices of the world brought to the service experience. Any efforts to maintain higher standards also encountered the realities of what people at the time considered "sexually stimulating motion pictures," pinup girls, and suggestive advertising in the mass media. Moreover, expectations about women were by now radically different. The anti-venereal-disease campaigns revealed an official expectation that male troops would and could engage in sexual activity with any and all women, not particularly with prostitutes.[46]

Beyond official policy, the military experience had profound effects upon the American population. In addition to the constant barracks talk about sexual behavior on various crude levels, service personnel (if they had not already done so) had to learn to tolerate all kinds of animality openly expressed by close associates. Three-fourths or more of the army personnel were having nonmarital sexual experiences, often in foreign settings where, as in World War I, they saw various kinds of alien behaviors. "There is a new set of accepted rights and wrongs in this overseas situation," noted an authoritative military observer in the middle of the war. And upon returning, these men often tried to impose their new standards (and the ranges of their experiences) upon the folks at home; after all, why could not one's wife come up to the sensual performance of a paid companion encountered in the Orient? But the new standards were not new. They were simply those of many lower-order and non-middle-class populations, the numbers of which were now swamping the other population groups in the United States. In any event, the effects of actual experiences on the standards of both service personnel and those who were not in the service were profound and complex.[47]

Between barracks talk, service experience, and new expectations about female compliance, on the one hand, and movies and the mass media, on the other, prostitutes (in part through the mediation of Mae West) and lower-order people therefore increasingly set the standard for all Americans' sexual attitudes in the 1940s. But at that point, a series of events changed further the circumstances of sexuality and played into the hands of those who favored a standard of unrestrained sexual activity.

Penicillin, Kinsey, the Pill

The first transforming event was the advent of penicillin and other pharmaceutical measures in the middle of World War II. They destroyed much of the fear of venereal disease that had served as the main prop of the amoral military leaders in arguing against sexual activity. And then, after the war, came the Kinsey reports (1948 on men and 1953 on women) and, finally, the Pill (1960).[48]

Alfred Kinsey and his collaborators made two major contributions to standards in post-World War II America. First, their widely discussed research reports showed beyond much argument that, regardless of public standards, Americans in private engaged in a wide variety of sexual activities. Premarital and extramarital activities were widespread, masturbation almost universal, and homosexual experience not unusual, at least for men. Those who opposed restrictive standards immediately argued that "everybody's doing it." Those in favor of restrictive standards deplored the publicity that deviation had received and argued—correctly—that their opponents would justify misbehavior by appealing to the argument that numbers had rendered virtually no common behavior deviant in society.[49]

Kinsey's second contribution was to reinforce dramatically the efforts of others to focus attention on the orgasm. Kinsey set up as his basic units of sexual activity "outlets" measured by orgasms—equating experiences whether the orgasms were those of masturbators, "perverts" of any variety (provided they did have orgasms), or simply heterosexual couples. Edwin Schur later gave the 1960s sexual researchers William Masters and Virginia Johnson credit for following Kinsey up, to the point that "masturbation has attained a remarkable new image . . . now it has become salvation or treatment" in the quest for sexual gratification. The whole emphasis on orgasm as such was of course resoundingly nonprocreative, and it elicited critical comments from many points of view, including those of psychopathology and feminism. What was most remarkable, however, was the fact that such an approach was coincident with that of traditional lower-order macho sexual standards, stripped of their hypocrisies: any activity was expectable and excusable, and the more activity, measured by orgasms, the better. What Kinsey, the middle-class WASP did, in effect, was to offer a rationalization for acting on the code that parochial lower-order or underworld people—like "Maurice"—had been insisting must be universal and better—plus undermining any resistances to engaging in—and advocating as well as joking about—extended and diverse love play. Like mythical prostitutes, women in this cult of mutual orgasm were supposed to want sexual experiences just as men did. The large amount of media coverage in fact was seldom based on Kinsey's publications themselves but rather on the symbolic functions they served. Clearly other currents in the culture were preparing the way for Americans to justify new standards.[50]

The contraceptive pill that came along at the end of the 1950s facilitated nonprocreative love making, reinforcing the way in which penicillin had removed from love making some of the fear of consequences. Moreover, the Pill had a symbolic effect like that of the Kinsey reports, so that interested commentators could picture nonprocreative sexual activity as an inevitable future standard—a standard then explicitly both welcomed and deplored by many. The former of course argued that that which was inevitable was also desirable and right. They could further appeal to the contention that sexual fulfillment was personally gratifying as well as the traditional argument that, because it strengthened marriage, it was socially desirable.

Proclaiming a Sexual Revolution

The immediate tactic that the advocates of unrestricted sexual activity utilized to hasten change was to proclaim the existence of a sexual revolution. By the 1950s, many Americans believed that, regardless of the Kinsey reports, adult standards were changing, and that as long as no personal harm was done, private behavior was not a social issue.[51] Advocates of change enjoyed in particular the heartiest cooperation of journalists and even a number of professionals who remarked on the scientific and technical innovations surrounding sexual behavior and the ever more brazen content of the media. In addition to noticing personally the further breakdown of middle-class reticence in discussing sexual subjects, Americans of the last half of the century argued, often with considerable heat, about what people at the time were doing and whether or not that was good in terms of social and personal goals.[52]

Beginning in the 1950s, one important group working for change, promoters of the then-new rock music, built on the popular-music tradition, in which jazz had naughty sexual lyrics, and began to make sexual content public and increasingly explicit. In the case of rock, however, the movements of performers, now often visible on television as well as in live performances, were explicitly sexual—again, taken from the bump-and-grind routines of the unrespectable stage and other establishments. Everyone knew what Elvis Presley—"Elvis the Pelvis"—was doing when he moved his hips. But the lyrics, too, soon moved into the category of what had been shocking, first indirectly describing erotic experiences and then erupting into plain language and leaving the traditional suggestive double entendre far behind. For instance, using slang, vocalist Lou Reed in the 1970s described in "Walk on the Wild Side" sexual actions that he expected of his partner. Over the years, shrewd entrepreneurs in the music business pushed changing standards and showed that openly "dirty" songs and performances brought in large amounts of money.[53]

In 1961, David Boroff wrote in so many words about "The Quiet Revolution" in which younger people had come to speak barracks language and, he believed, to increase their coupling—at least quantitatively—in a dramatic way. Boroff found in literature and other types of publications evidence of great openness and of an approving attitude toward at least premarital activity.[54] By 1964, the editors of both *Time* and *Newsweek* had also "discovered" the sexual revolution. An incredible amount of commentary about standards and behavior began to appear in print. Of the observers whose comments were published, not a few noted correctly the place of the mass media in promoting sexual consciousness, if not activity. Material in the mass media and sometimes elsewhere convinced most writers, both mass and elite, that everybody was, in fact, doing it. They then implicitly furthered such activity by proclaiming the new standard. Conduct and institutions may have been slower to change than the proclamations, however. The daring underground paper, the *Berkeley Barb*, for example, began printing personal sex ads only at the end of 1966. And a correspondent writing from Los Angeles in April of that year had only just then discovered the apparently new dirty-movie arcades there.[55]

Such evidence reinforces common sense in suggesting that the media invented and promoted as much as described change. In fact, it took some years for the propaganda to have an effect and interact with other social changes. But in the 1960s and 1970s, both attitudes and behavior, at least among the young, did actually respond to public representations of standards. Women in particular reported becoming more consciously sexual in what one group of commentators characterized as "the battle for orgasm equity." Media emphasis on personal fulfillment fueled increases in premarital sexual activity and in divorce and even weakened the institution of dating, which had started out as daring earlier in the century but now had became associated with old-fashioned marriage-is-forever.[56]

Playboy

The chief symbol, if not instrument, of the so-called sexual revolution was a magazine first published in 1953, *Playboy*. As other magazines were dying in the age of television, *Playboy* grew spectacularly. Within six years, circulation had reached one million and in the early 1960s increased ever more rapidly to the point that a substantial fraction of the population— chiefly young, upwardly mobile males—read, or at least looked at, each issue. By the 1970s, about 20 per cent of American men were readers. In addition, the magazine spawned a host of close imitations (fourteen within the first three years alone). Finally, other magazines, even mainline magazines, also imitated *Playboy* and took up sex and advice and steamy sex. Sensational Peeping Tom publications like *Confidential* and a number of he-man pulps likewise flourished in the wake of the pioneering *Playboy*.[57] But *Playboy* directly gained the allegiance of the most influential part of generations of young Americans and had a cultural impact far beyond even the circulation figures. The impact came in part because the ideas in the magazine influenced an important group of young people. Even more consequentially, *Playboy* represented explicitly the standards and aspirations that proponents of sexual nonrestraint had already been working to further.

The magazine started out as the most conventional organ of lower-order-male—essentially World War II-barracks—ideas as translated by upwardly mobile lower-middle-class people. Sports, gambling, drinking, and smoking, along with anti-Puritan gibes and sex filled the pages between photos of partially clad or unclad women and naughty drawings. The tone was one of forced candor, but that candor was limited to the sexual realm. Where do dirty jokes come from? was a typical subject. It was essentially a magazine of fantasy for men. The fantasy was that women were eager to bed down with any man, for the sake of sexual gratification (exactly whose was sometimes ambiguous). As Benjamin De Mott described the message in 1962, women "are mad for it, have got to have it. . . ." The eyes and body of the nude in the centerfold, De Mott continued, say

> Oh please *please* give it to me now. And these eyes, these begging burning empty hands, are not to be dismissed as exotica. In a dozen canny ways the magazines undertake to establish that the nude in Nassau and the stenotypist in Schenectady—the sexbomb and the "ordinary girl"—are actually one creature: Essential Woman.

In this point of view, the essence was a single-minded desire and willingness to make love. This idea was pure fantasy, because most of the readers' experience had been that women were not always willing and eager, to say the least. But readers gorged themselves on the fantasy and allied themselves, probably often unwittingly, with people who wanted to turn the fantasy into a standard for the real world.[58]

Playboy, however, depended also on another fantasy—the same fantasy that underlay the consumer culture of midcentury America. This was the fantasy of wealth. The playboy implicit as well as explicit in the magazine had the ability to buy and consume as well as the time to fool around. The readers clearly had the ambition to become or imagine themselves stereotypically rich. The genius of publisher Hugh Hefner, remarked sex researcher Paul Gebhard in 1967, "is that he has linked sex with upward mobility." "Real sex" in *Playboy*, as one critic noted, "is something that goes with the best scotch, twenty-seven-dollar sun glasses, and platinum-tipped shoelaces."[59]

What *Playboy* in particular did was to conflate and short-circuit the glamour of advertising. For decades, advertising had emphasized glamour, particularly in the form of idealized seductive-looking women and night life. In *Playboy*, the sex that was implied in the ads became explicit and was given the trappings of an advertising lifestyle. All sex was connected to conventional material and commercial symbols of upward mobility—expensive clothes, cars, alcoholic beverages, and leisure activities. The editors published snobbish food and cocktail recipes and featured not only night life and tuxedos but theater and even, for a time, classical music. A cartoon in 1956, for example, showed a bordello in which both the women and the customers were dressed well—neckties for the men, not working or sports clothes, even in a sporting house.[60]

People of course could respond to *Playboy* because over so many years most Americans had learned through ads to associate glamour with both consumption and sex—and hence consumption with sex. Theologian Harvey Cox found that "*Playboy* is basically antisexual. Like the sports car, liquor and hi-fi, girls are just another *Playboy* accessory." The packaging included also an appeal to liberalism. The magazine took a stand (none too strong, especially early on) in favor of civil liberties and ethnic equality. And the editors crusaded against censorship. So did many imitators, who followed *Playboy*—for example in using four-letter words—but sometimes led *Playboy*—as in showing pubic hair in photographs. In 1961, a writer in the *Village Voice* referred to *Playboy* as "that self-styled swingingest of magazines with its liberal principles and broadminded policies." But the liberalism, albeit refreshing in a country still suffering from McCarthyism, did not include social justice or social responsibility. On the contrary, Hefner advocated individualistic free enterprise in the most strident and naive manner. Most of life, he held, was strictly a private matter, without community standards to dictate to individuals, whether in economics or sex. This line fitted in well with amoral, hedonistic, and superficial young men who had ambitions in an acquisitive society. It only occasionally embarrassed articulators who found themselves, for instance, unable to explain how "conscience" would condemn censorship or why playboys could do anything with consenting adults but not with animals or children. When later publications (most notably *Hustler*) carried the line of hedonism to a logical conclusion and spelled out what consenting adults could actually do, the playboys considered such advocacy "raunchy" and undignified and some of the actions unacceptable to "even dedicated swingers."[61]

Sometime around the beginning of the 1960s, *Playboy* changed from a fantasy magazine with soft photos and naughty jokes. Instead, it became a how-to-do-it manual, advocating that readers actually act out their fantasies. The shift was profound and had powerful social effects.[62]

Instructing readers how to act like playboys took two forms. The first appeared in the increase in the amount of instructional material in the magazine. Most notable was the advent of a Playboy Advisor column in 1960. The advisor not only advised on consumer matters—which beverage to buy, for instance—but also on sexual behavior. By 1965, for example, the advisor was enjoining a reader to participate in group sexual activity. Altogether, by the late 1960s, three-fourths of the articles were directly or indirectly instructional, whether dealing with behavior or consumption, categories that were, of course, confused.[63] The other aspect of how-to-do-it was that the magazine began to sell *Playboy* goods and services. The first *Playboy* club opened in 1958. By 1960, the magazine was advertising heavily for not only *Playboy* pins, garters, money clips (!), and ankle bracelets but also tours and record albums. Altogether, within a short time, the reinforcement of commercial advantage and what had formerly been sexual misbehavior became inextricably intertwined.

The editors of *Playboy* explicitly pretended to be purveying "taste," that is, expensive consumer behavior. Indeed, the editorial material featured consumer items substantially more expensive than those actually advertised in accompanying columns. Hefner, the publisher, publicized his living an expensive, night-life type of lifestyle in a ridiculously ostentatious mansion filled with sexually available "playmates"—consciously setting up role models that a surprising number of Americans took seriously. Again, economic factors attracted reinforcement. By January 1965, 51 out of 109 columns of external advertising were devoted to alcoholic beverages. Marketers of tobacco products constituted the next largest group of advertisers.[64]

What *Playboy* also did was to make pornography once again profitable, to the point that it had substantial social importance by functioning to set social standards for a large segment of Americans. After the magazine's mission changed to instruction, a new generation of imitators sprang up to take advantage of ever-increasing explicitness of content. In the so-called "pubic wars" of the 1970s, the circulation of *Playboy* actually declined as more crudely pornographic publications, such as *Penthouse*, intruded on that part of the *Playboy* market. The best-known of these publications, *Hustler*, made explicit what was often only implicit in *Playboy* but still

2.1   Arcadia Hall, a noted gambling establishment in pioneer Denver. *Harper's Weekly*, 1866. Courtesy, Colorado Historical Society.

2.2   A dogfight at Kit Burns's Sportsman Hall in New York, site of a bar and of rat and dog pits. From James Dabney McCabe, *Secrets of the Great City,* 1868. Courtesy, Ohio State University Libraries.

2.3   Gambling in a saloon in Pecos, Texas, in the 1880s. Generous courtesy of the Western History Collections, University of Oklahoma Library.

2.4   Boxers in the Bale of Hay Saloon, Virginia City, Montana,
about 1900. Photograph somewhat
blurred, but there is a spittoon in
the foreground and a child in the
background. Generous courtesy of
the Montana Historical Society.

2.5   Bagatelle gambling machine,
made by the Caille-Shiemer Co.,
1900–1910. It paid off in cigars.
Courtesy, Prints and Photographs
Division, Library of Congress.

2.6   Bank night featured at a movie theater in Farmington, New Mexico, in 1939. As in many other communities, a lottery was used to attract movie patrons. U.S. Farm Security Administration Collection, Prints and Photographs Division, Library of Congress, by courtesy.

2.7　Players at a roulette table enjoying the casino package at Tropworld, Atlantic City, 1991. Generous courtesy of Tropworld.

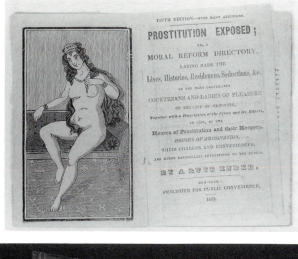

2.8   Book title page, 1839, *Prostitution Exposed*, which served as a guide to local commercial sexual activity in New York. Generous courtesy of Leo Hershkowitz, from his collection.

2.9   Patron leaving house of prostitution, Peoria, Illinois, May 1938. By this time, prostitution was a marginalized institution, no longer supported by the middle classes. U.S. Farm Security Administration Collection, Prints and Photographs Division, Library of Congress, by courtesy.

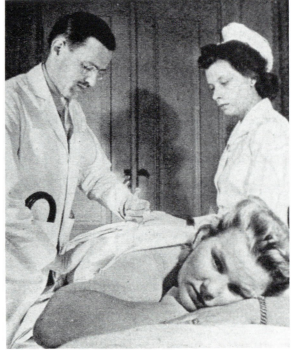

2.12 Pornography outlet, Times Square, New York City, 1969. *U. S. News and World Report* Collection, Prints and Photographs Division, Library of Congress, by courtesy.

2.13 Use of strong language sanctioned by World War I. Cartoon by W. A. Rogers, "Coming, Lloyd George, [in] spite of hell and politics." New York *Herald,* 1918. Courtesy, Prints and Photographs Division, Library of Congress.

Facing Page: 2.10 A collection of "8–pagers," cartoon pornography circulated surreptitiously in the 1930s. Photograph by Dellenback. Reproduced with permission of the Kinsey Institute for Research in Sex, Gender, and Reproduction, Inc., Indiana University.

2.11 Penicillin signals the imagined end of the danger of venereal disease. The new treatment was announced during World War II. The story included this photo in *Look* magazine, 1944.

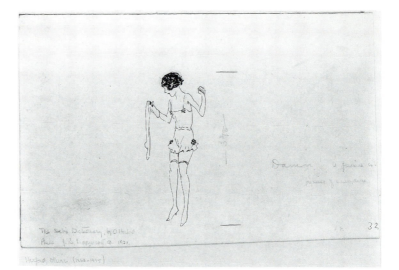

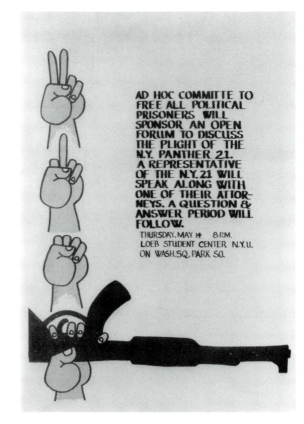

AD HOC COMMITTE TO
FREE ALL POLITICAL
PRISONERS WILL
SPONSOR AN OPEN
FORUM TO DISCUSS
THE PLIGHT OF THE
N.Y. PANTHER 21.
A REPRESENTATIVE
OF THE N.Y. 21 WILL
SPEAK ALONG WITH
ONE OF THEIR ATTOR-
NEYS. A QUESTION &
ANSWER PERIOD WILL
FOLLOW.
THURSDAY, MAY 14   8 P.M.
LOEB STUDENT CENTER N.Y.U.
ON WASH.SQ. PARK SO.

Left: 2.16   A glass-container company, pursuing economic gain by selling more bottles, urges the public to drink beer in the 1950s. Owens-Illinois ad from *Life*, 1957.

Right: 2.17   Beer ad, *The Delineator*, 1933, showing little girl and beer in a family setting.

Facing Page: 2.14   "DAMN!" defined as "A feminine expression of annoyance," from the caption for a drawing by Oliver Herford for *The Deb's Dictionary*, 1931. Courtesy, Prints and Photographs Division, Library of Congress.

2.15   Poster connecting obscene gesture with rebelliousness and social leveling. Ad Hoc Committee to Free All Political Prisoners, sponsored by the Black Panther Party, 1970. Artist unknown. Courtesy, Prints and Photographs Division, Library of Congress.

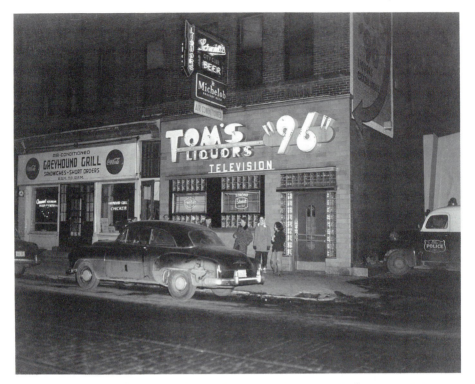

2.18   Tom's "96" Bar in St. Paul, Minnesota, advertising the fact that it had
the new medium, television, in 1953. Courtesy, Minnesota Historical Society.

2.19 *Hustler* magazine advertises its own cigarette rolling papers, 1978. Courtesy, Kinsey Institute for Research in Sex, Gender, and Reproduction, Inc., Indiana University. Reproduced with the generous permission of Larry Flynt Publishers.

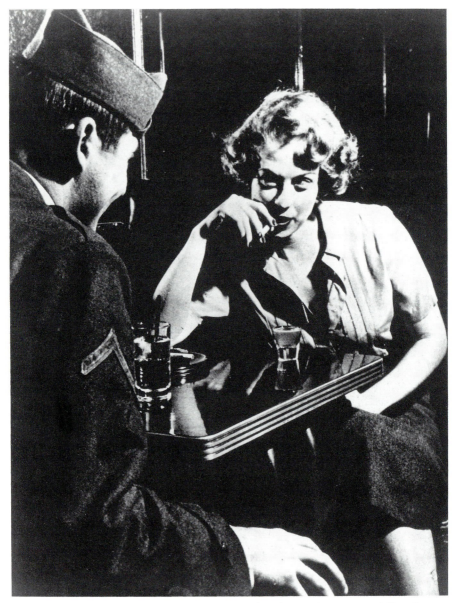

2.20   During the Korean War, the editors of *Look* magazine portrayed "lonely young servicemen" who became "fair game" for "organized vice" in American cities. The standard symbolic props included smoking and drinking. *Look*, 1952.

Welcome, brother,
if you're a Bourbon Man

To a Westerner, hospitality without Bourbon
is like a handshake without warmth.
Old Hickory shows you why.
Great Bourbon enriched by extra years.
The best friend ice ever had.
With it you rediscover Manhattans,
make Old Fashioneds new.

OBSERVED IN THE BEST CIRCLES

OLD HICKORY
Straight **BOURBON** *Whisky*
SIX YEARS OLD

86 PROOF · ALSO IN 100 PROOF BOTTLED IN BOND · OLD HICKORY DISTILLERS COMPANY · PHILA. PA.

2.21   The appeal to masculinity in marketing efforts: Old Hickory Bourbon ad,
Life, 1957.

2.22 Poster announcing National Marijuana Day, New York, 1973, promising a "20 foot joint & ten foot pack of rolling papers" and stipulating free marijuana for children, perhaps tongue-in-cheek, perhaps not. Artist unknown. Courtesy, Prints and Photographs Division, Library of Congress.

2.23 Toy car, carrying beer ad, 1980s. *Tobacco and Youth Reporter,* 1987. Reproduced with the generous permission of the publisher, Stop Teenage Addiction to Tobacco.

followed the basic idea that women as well as men were available for sexual activity and actively wanted it. And of course the instructional aspect was also imitated, so that editors and writers maintained clearly that anything sexual was desirable. In July 1975, for example, one in a series of articles in *Hustler* gave in quite plain language a set of favorable and detailed directions for anal intercourse.[65]

Hustler is particularly interesting because it acted as a vehicle not for superficial upward mobility but directly for lower-order attitudes. The most conspicuous was the marrying of advocating what was conventionally perversity with a high valuation of frequency of orgasm without restraint, that is, promiscuous and polymorphous but depersonalized sexual behavior. In short, even more than in *Playboy*, the reassurance was unmistakable that anything goes and that everybody's doing it. The publisher was entirely candid that the appeal was particularly to those who wanted pornography in order to enhance vicariousness and aid ordinary love making or masturbation. In an early pitch for advertisers, for example, the publishers ran an ad with a suggestive picture of a naked man and woman, tying the readers to pornography in general: "Want to reach men who are constantly in touch with themselves? You get their undivided erections in HUSTLER." Such unsubtle material and lack of pretense combined with resentment against power and authority figures and with fatalistic passivity typical of non-middle-class people. One of the endearing features for those who liked celebrity—and authority—bashing along with vulgar language was a graphic nomination in each issue of an "Asshole of the Month." Such tactics made explicit the generalization that pornography of all kinds functions at least in part as anti-Establishment rebelliousness.[66]

Pornography Reborn

Sometime in the early twentieth century, as noted earlier, pornography had diminished in economic importance, at the same time that prostitution did. Obscene books and pictures were not sufficiently profitable to make them considerable as a social force. Nor were motion pictures, even though they could be particularly arousing. "Stag" or "blue" movies were peddled by itinerant salesmen and rented to male social groups like college fraternities or American Legion posts for $50 for a late-night private showing. Similar distribution sources plus, apparently, some informal networks also furnished books and pictures (including totally obscene parodies of well-known comic strips—"8-pagers"). These materials were sold surreptitiously by various small-time entrepreneurs such as barbers and then circulated from hand to hand among friends—typically adolescent boys for whom viewing dirty pictures was part of male coming-of-age.[67]

Obscene and pornographic materials, subject to general social controls, did not present any special problems or have any special significance. If they socialized youngsters, it was to restrained and conventional love making that was at worst depersonalized. In the mass market, "girlie magazines" and romantic books and films of varying, relatively mild degrees of explicitness, exposure, and provocativeness pushed the limits of social tolerance, but not very hard. *Playboy* was at first mistaken for just another girlie magazine, until provocativeness and advocacy set it apart. Entrepreneurs then quickly caught on that they could make money from books and films as well as magazines. More and more, the profit potential contributed powerfully to motives to break down restrictions and standards that had theretofore restrained producers from describing or depicting indiscriminate, not to mention frantic, sexual activity. By the 1960s, almost 100 per cent of the pornographic movies depicted oral-genital contact, an activity that was unusual in the old stags, in which interest centered on ordinary intercourse.[68]

During the 1960s, the entrepreneurs of unmistakably pornographic material, located primarily in the New York City area and California, publicized the idea that their products that pushed or exceeded every limit were made for adults (so as to be both normal—adult—and to avoid the appearance that they corrupted children). Every urban area developed a "porn row" of adult bookstores where sales and rental of offensive material—as well as types of theaters and night clubs—were tolerated. Frequently, porn row was also headquarters for prostitutes, akin to the old segregated district, and, as noted above, they attracted other criminal activity, again as in the old days. Consumers who could not find material to suit them in local outlets could order by mail. Already at the end of the 1960s, there were 60 wholesale distributors of "adult" materials and 850 retail outlets devoted exclusively to them (with another 1,400 nonexclusive stores). Technology greatly increased the quality of illustrative material, and the possibility of viewing films or, later, video cassettes at home, in private, greatly expanded the market. Eventually the content of such materials left nothing to the imagination, at least in books. Fear of police action still prevented some motion picture/video portrayal of blood, children, animals, and excrement. The profits were mind boggling—a 600 per cent markup on some "sexual aids," for example. Indeed, the profits were sufficiently great to attract so-called organized crime, which moved in on such operations. *Deep Throat*, a 1972 film made notorious and chic by the media, netted $50 million for the "mob" distributors. By the late 1970s, major pornography merchants (using false names) met twice yearly in a convention. As late as 1981, the editor of the *Adult Business Report* was quoted as saying that "the sex business has the same potential for sales and profits as the food industry. It is a growth industry. . . ."[69]

Playboy and *Hustler* and other other big moneymakers in the mass market encouraged the porn merchants in developing a public market for pornography and in moving into more-and-more explicit materials, in part by encouraging toleration of extremes. As if running a consumer-protection service, *Hustler* in the 1970s reviewed hard core films—rating them chiefly on the basis of how stimulating they were. A writer in *Time* complained in 1975 that *Playboy* competitor *Penthouse* was "a veritable consumer guide to self-abuse, sadomasochism, bondage and other subjects that were once the province of hard-core pornography." The extremes of the pornographers thus served the mass marketers well by making the mass "sexploitation" look relatively mild. The mass marketers in turn argued that anything at all was acceptable in private and that lots of people did anything one could imagine. Therefore, they continued, it was not only acceptable but obligatory to respect the rights of those who wanted to expand the range of their "experiences" (arguments paralleling those of the advocates of drug "experiences" at exactly the same time). At each step in bringing increasingly explicit material into the public marketplace, commentators wondered how much further each type of exploitation could go. In 1974, journalist Edward W. Barrett speculated that having no restraint could, in the end, be healthy: "The trend may yet benefit society. It may ultimately so satiate juveniles of all ages with photos of breasts and genitals that they will occasionally need to think of other matters." But in fact the ability of the marketers to make money from such materials—and materials more extreme—continued. Moreover, extreme pornography crept into media that were not necessarily labeled pornography, particularly rock music and television based on it. One mid-1980s vocalist (although not a mainstream performer), for example, sang, "I'll either break her face/Or take down her legs,/Get my way at will . . . /Going in for the kill."[70]

What was most notable about the market in the 1970s and after was the new content. Whereas at the end of the 1960s only a fraction was aimed at fetishists, increasingly over the following years, more and more printed material, especially, openly involved the so-called perversions. Shoe-fetish material appeared in both *Playboy* and *Penthouse* magazines at about the same time as pubic hair, around 1975. But in particular the new content included sadomasochistic actions and coercion and violence and the dysfunctionally grotesque in general. Violence on television, particularly, tended to corrupt the commercial pornography. Like television producers and sponsors, the merchants of smut knew how to cultivate a market, and now they emphasized variety as much or more than frequency in sexual activity. Such material grew on itself and had notable social consequences, particularly reinforcing the ideas that everyone ought to do everything sexual that was possible and that the victims of sexual aggression derived pleasure from it. So was established a particular model ritual of sexual behavior. Pornographers depicted a regular (compulsive) progression consisting, as one student described it in 1976, of "a series of increasingly complex and perverse episodes of sexual activity:" typically, the pornographer would "begin with masturbation and proceed through normal heterosexual intercourse, followed by cunnilingus and anal intercourse to a grand climactic orgy involving several persons." The porn merchants helped spread throughout American society a version of sex that was therefore not only depersonalized but compulsive and, moreover, claimed a number of commentators, one that threatened respect for human beings. Persuading women to become consumers of pornography, particularly in the 1980s with "family viewing" on the VCR, was a notable commercial gain. It also helped pornographers blunt the arguments of feminist antipornographers.[71]

Pornotopia

Unlike purveyors of substances, advocates of more and varied sexual activities often made their ultimate goals explicit. Earlier advocates of sexual freedom, like Victoria Woodhull and Moses Harman in the nineteenth century, romanticized male-female relationships. These do-gooders' sexual platforms were part of a general social reform program (often equality for women). Such idealists, right down to the communitarians of the 1960s, were not part of the new advocacy and did not contribute to it. Advocates of sexual misbehavior per se had no sense of social context. Neither *Playboy* nor materials found in so-called adult book and movie/video outlets mentioned such grown-up subjects as childbirth (however connected to sexual activity) or social responsibility. Rather, the new aspirations were single-mindedly concerned with orgasmic gymnastics. In 1974, for example, *Hustler* magazine carried a "Sexplay Agreement" to be signed in contractual fashion by a male, Y, and a female, X, "for the mutual and simultaneous pursuit of satisfaction and/or pleasure, with the use of said parties' bodies and any other device—animal, vegetable, fruit, mechanical, or synthetic—that will aid and abet to either party's satisfaction, said pursuit. . . ." No commitment or payment was involved, and mutual agreement was all that was necessary to end the agreement.

> The purpose of this agreement shall be deemed to include, but shall not be limited to, traditional sexual intercourse. Any position, action, paraphernalia, costume, or setting conceived, imagined or fancied by either Y or X shall be given due consideration by the other and then incorporated into the experience with which this agreement concerns itself. Should any position, action, object, costume, or setting prove to be unpleasing to either party, it will be tried again and again. . . .[72]

Altogether such platforms involved much pressure to engage compulsively in a complete repertoire of behaviors with maximum frequency and hedonistic preoccupation—exactly the compulsiveness that characterized pornographic productions.

Literary historian Steven Marcus referred to such pursuits of sexual pleasure as a quest for pornotopia. An important feature of pornotopian statements was the negative quality in them—the same negativism that surfaced early in the century but now in a fully developed context. Allan Sherman, in a book published by Playboy Press, spelled out the platform of the supposed sexual revolution and displayed the negative nature of the program:

> Sexual Freedom
> Freedom of Nudity
> Freedom of the Toilet
> Freedom from Hang-Ups
> Freedom from Censorship
> Freedom of Pornography
> Freedom of Obscenity
> Freedom to Fool Around . . . .

Someday, we pipe-dreamed, there would be a generation of Dirty-Minded Americans strong enough to challenge the [American Puritan Ethic]. . . . That lucky generation would. . . . read dirty books, buy dirty novelties, think dirty, talk dirty. . . . They would experiment with new sex positions, new sex locations, new sex kicks. They would . . . give smut respectability by dressing it in the dignified cloak of science. They would shock, and shock again; they would *appall!*[73]

By clothing themselves in the mantle of freedom, science, and the inevitability of everyone's eventually doing it, such thinkers articulated goals that only a few years before had been strictly the domain of the most obsessive and ritualized—compulsive—pornography. One pornotopia, that which writer Bradley Smith projected from 1978 to the imaginary year of 2028, had a teacher instructing students about the way that society had freed itself from all the (obviously bad) inhibitions of an earlier time. Using the term "sexual pleasuring" to describe erotic activity, Smith gave permissive support to virtually anything that anyone might think of to do, including even to some extent incest. He strongly advocated bisexuality—evidently the most common preference in his pornotopia, where monogamy was necessarily a rarity. But compulsive completeness was the leading goal: "as you are all aware, total sexual pleasuring is available to everyone in our society. . . ." It turned out that Smith particularly meant that children were to be sexually active, with one another and with adults alike, and promiscuously. It also turned out that dirty words and drugs that enhanced sexual sensations were part of the pornotopia. Smith's pornotopia was, in short, both commonplace for social rebels and commercial pornographers and conformable to what most contemporaries would have identified as the most stereotypically degenerate versions of lower-order (and, once again, male) behavior patterns, those that violated older taboos and tended to be defined negatively in terms of those taboos.[74]

The Tortured Course of Sexual Liberation

In the late twentieth century, then, a portrait emerged of a resurgent pornography business in a society in which *Playboy* and advocates of pornotopia conditioned the outlook and standards of dominant population segments. This peculiar profile raises questions about what was actually occurring, and who was gaining what. Beyond the obvious growth of lower-order-male and traditional-prostitute viewpoints and images out of the Victorian underworld, customary conceptualizations do not adequately or fully explain the new developments.

The mass media followed the lead of the exploitation magazines during the last half of the twentieth century, just as the magazines followed pornography. In 1968, a maker of erotic films complained that his nudies were not selling anymore because big-studio movies had moved in on the territory. Consequently, he was moving toward more explicit eroticism—which everyone at the time expected, correctly, would also soon be taken over by the generality of Hollywood films. As television came in, it became possible actually to measure quantitatively the increasing explicitness of sexual references and then sexual actions on the electronic screen. Indirect or ambiguous references (to get by various restraining institutions) were underlined and decoded for naive viewers by the use of canned laughter. In addition to explicit behavior, producers depicted unmarried couples in sexual liaisons and other formerly questionable behavior such as homoeroticism in programs broadcast at all hours of the day and night. Altogether media personnel could quite reasonably at any point project for decades into the future a steady increase in the explicitness of language, suggestion, and portrayal.[75]

In both print and electronic media, the advantage of introducing sexual content and indeed provocative and even controversial and daring sexual material was that it drew audiences. Consensus on this point existed continuously. The pressure to portray as much sexual misbehavior as possible, for business advantage, pervaded both news and entertainment media. The large amount of ever-plainer sexual material in the television soap operas of the 1970s and after existed, as one contemporary expert noted, "mainly because the sponsors of these shows have discovered that sex sells." Moreover, to attract the largest amount of attention possible for their products, advertisers did not just finance changers of standards. The advertisers themselves introduced sexually daring content, such as "Does she . . . or doesn't she?" referring, it turned out, not to the willingness of a seductive-looking model but to whether or not she dyed her hair. Media experts could confirm once again that "sex sells."[76]

The Success of the Advocates of Misbehavior

Testimony was unanimous—except for those who wanted to deny the consequences of their profit seeking—that the sexual content in the media was effective in socializing young Americans. Sexually mature but cut off from marriage, and in a culture increasingly dedicated to indulgence, young Americans who could not deny themselves direct sexual expression could choose between masturbation and casual intercourse. Peer groups and the media provided instruction in sexual promiscuity and possibilities. From the media and ads, from rock-music lyrics, from *Playboy*, from the new cornucopias of pornography, many young people learned and tried to convince others that sexual slumming and compliance were the norm as well as the ideal. And, in fact, surveys after midcentury showed a strong generational difference in attitudes that reflected the multifarious socialization.[77]

The efforts of commercial interests to make sexual materials of all kinds available received important support in the culture from two special segments of the population: those with compulsive needs to act out sexually in whatever ways and those folks dedicated for whatever reason to many partners. Such people were often significant in numbers and also sometimes socially powerful, if personally complicated, individuals.[78] For ordinary citizens who were unable to meet the new standards, there even sprang up in the 1960s "sex therapy," so that people talked about the sex therapy "industry" and "the sex therapy market" in which counselors concentrated on "the couple" and of course measured success in terms of orgasms.[79]

Particularly striking was the way in which cultural and commercial forces together succeeded in converting middle-class women to what formerly had been essentially lower-order male and deviant standards—to the point that for many young people a singles' bar became a normative institution. In another index to attitudes, cheap romantic paperback books aimed at women changed in a startling way. At the beginning of the 1980s, euphemistic eroticism was replaced by works that portrayed very explicit love making, outside of marriage, with women in a new independent, personal, and equal or dominant role, in contrast to their former passive/subordinate role. Large numbers of customers—comparable to those of *Playboy* earlier—by buying tens of millions of the books gave commercial validation to the new standards. These standards supported romanticized sexual activity that was modeled on the old pornography, but the characters were cast in roles that came out of new gender relationships. The new video market paralleled that of the books. Creators of such materials worked on the presumption that institutions and attitudes that restrained one-on-one sexual behavior had to give way to personal expression and experience—assuming that stereotypes of techniques and behaviors from

the old underworld furnished appropriate models for the personal fulfillment of late-twentieth-century women.[80]

In the final decades of that century, the direction of change in the United
States was unmistakable. Advocates of much more frequent sexual activity,
for everyone, and those who wanted every variety of sexual activity to be
accepted and practiced, as in the new, extreme pornography, succeeded,
with the help of commercial interests, in making their point of view substantially normative. Early in the century, advocates of variety often masked
their interests in the form of advocating better marriages and stronger
families. Presumably the nuclear couple improved marriage and the family
by finding fulfillment in sexual virtuosity. By late in the century, advocates
of any kind of sexual variety could in addition appear as just additional
units to be tolerated in a pluralistic society. In 1967, for example, the Sexual
Freedom League formed a Visual Delights Circle for voyeurs. Only in the
single case of people who advocated many partners, in threesomes, four-
somes, and moresomes, did the change in standards appear to stop or
reverse. That retreat came even before the 1980s, when knowledge about
new permanent and fatal venereal diseases introduced a slight general modification in the direction of reducing the desirability of the number of
people's contacts. But by that time, the advocates of nonrestraint were able
to use the occasion to mobilize even more publicity for their point of view.
They enlisted public-spirited people and government agencies in a "safe
sex" campaign, pointing out to as much of the population as possible exactly
the practices that would permit people to avoid disease and still continue
to seek pornotopia. In the first flush of the AIDS scare, in 1984, *Time*
magazine proclaimed that "The Revolution Is Over." But the change boiled
down largely to a reduction of "one-night stands" among the middle
classes. When in 1991 a sports star, Magic Johnson, revealed that he had
acquired the HIV infection, presumably from one-night stands, the media
used the occasion to publicize "safe sex" rather than to boost monogamous
marriage.[81]

As the non-middle-class pattern of early and promiscuous activity became the norm, members of all classes also learned that variety in love-
making activities was not only acceptable but mandatory in the name of
extending hedonism. Mere personal taste tended to replace the older, conventional category of perversion. Indeed, as some 1980s advocates of sexual
enjoyment noted, "Gay men and lesbians held out a vision of sex utterly
freed from the old reproductive 'work ethic' that haunts heterosexuality."
In an age of self-awareness, the new standards pressured people to expand

their experiences and adventures. Recalled a woman of the 1960s, "What got me into the lesbian trip is I hung out with hippie types, smoked pot, . . . rebelled in every way I could think of."[82]

Through it all, the old-fashioned image of the totally dissolute prostitute exerted uncanny influence as a model for both men and women. Mass-media portrayals of attractiveness based on Mae West and *Playboy* fantasies came to dominate society. The singles' bar of the 1960s and after derived from the informal institution of sex-for-sale as well as from the traditional "gay" bar where people—often directly or indirectly imitating prostitutes—also met to initiate nonmarital sexual activity. The media glamorized "singles," but in fact innumerable commercial interests—most conspicuously merchandisers of alcoholic beverages and drugs—were exploiting these new public spaces in which the sexes attempted to meet each other.[83]

In the second half of the twentieth century, the profit motive therefore had a profound and increasing effect in shaping standards of sexual aspiration and activity. In some cases, the motive was direct, as in the reestablished pornography and sexual-paraphernalia industries. In the late 1970s, for example, a subsidiary of Time, Inc., distributed a weekly program for cable television in which couples, as the people of that time put it, "had sex." Much of the profiteering, however, was more indirect. The mass media and advertisers used erotic content and imaging for commercial purposes. To gain attention, they made the sexuality as extreme as possible—which turned out over a period of time to be extreme indeed. Most striking were the acute interests of the purveyors of other consumer goods who found that changes in sexual standards benefited sales.[84] The alcoholic-beverage interests were most obvious. Their advertising used sexual misbehavior blatantly to increase profits. Their retail outlets, especially bars in which people were encouraged to meet for sexual purposes, were, as already noted, of great cultural as well as commercial importance. But tobacco manufacturers and record and tape companies also advertised in *Penthouse* and *Hustler*, signaling their affinity with the pornography business.

Many reformers also assisted the changes in sexual standards and attitudes because they hoped to strengthen and inspire marriage. Other well-meaning people did also, in the name of not only innocent hedonism but also a quest for self-fulfillment, not only a righteous opposition to censorship, but creativity. In the realities of the twentieth century, the forces of commerce also carried many good people into alien cultural realms. As

Edward J. Mishan wrote in 1972, "Obscenity now struts openly in the market place. The latent demand, it could be argued, was always there. But . . . wealth, technology, and the acquiescence of the law were required before the latent demand could be made effective, before it could be stimulated and promoted."[85] Where once, especially under the old double standard, money had tended to buy people, such as prostitutes, a century later, "sex" itself was a commodity to be purchased. The Victorians had attempted to reduce the power of sexual animality. In the late twentieth century, innumerable business concerns had a stake in not only recognizing sexuality but also exaggerating its place in the culture.[86] The dynamics behind change were greed and self-justifying, lower-order culture. The instrument was a set of negative and rebellious rituals worked out by descendants of the Victorian underworld for sexual activity as well as the other minor vices in the constellation.

Swearing

S wearing provides a gauge with which to measure the extent to which the influence of the proponents of the minor vices penetrated American life and institutions in general. Yet swearing was different from the other elements in the constellation. The use of offensive language involved no overt behavior outside of verbal communication. "Words can never hurt me" was folk wisdom.[1] Nevertheless, some words, offensive words, evoked powerful effects.

Also, unlike the other bad habits, swearing seldom directly involved large commercial interests. Only entertainers and media executives who increased the size of audiences by using the power of shocking expressions to attract attention had much of an immediate financial stake in breaking language taboos. Why, then, attack those taboos?

One reason was the persistently strong association of swearing with the other elements in the constellation of the minor vices. The stereotyped deviant identity had always included the offensive, rebellious use of profane and obscene expressions. Swearing was, in fact, part of the ritual of antisocial behavior. In addition, swearing conveyed, symbolically and publicly, lower-order parochialism. Indeed, swearing was the purest example of the power of lower-order/underworld culture. Virtually all Americans over many generations understood the cultural meanings of swearing, whether or not any particular citizen might happen to agree with the viewpoint of a clergyperson who in 1889 attempted to express the distinctions he knew: ". . . it is the vice of the lowest classes, of the drunken classes, of the mean and vicious souls who swear best when they are dirtiest and most un-manlike. Of all the modes of asserting the equality of men it is the poorest when the better classes imitate 'the lewd fellows of the baser sort'. . . . with the euphemisms of the prize ring and the saloon."[2] Although swearing changed in content over time, the social-leveling function of offensive expressions did not.

The English who migrated to North America brought with them swearing customs that had already evolved over many centuries. Continental Europeans referred to English soldiers as "Goddams" because the men used the phrase so frequently as to make it characteristic. That expression and other profanities flourished as well in the New World as the Old, from the beginning. During the American Revolution when offensive language proliferated, George Washington, himself known to utter an occasional oath, issued a general order against "the wicked practise of profane cursing and swearing."[3]

Early allusions to swearing dealt with two kinds of verbal taboos: those against profanity (profaning things holy) and those against obscenity, which included the scatological along with the sexual in the sense of offensively obscene. Examples surviving from the prerevolutionary era include both types. The Puritans in New England prosecuted disorderly elements and other citizens for using the name of the Lord in vain, but one visitor noted that by 1699 they were "very *Prophane* in their common *Dialect*." In the South, reported Jonathan Boucher in the eighteenth century, "obscene Conceits and broad Expression" were commonplace, and "no sex, no Rank, no Conduct" was enough to protect one from hearing them.[4]

Although profanity and obscenity belonged together in the category of tabooed language, upholders of the taboo during the nineteenth century concentrated on profanity, which they understood to signify profaning religious ideas and symbols, especially by taking the name of the Lord in vain. As late as 1901, the University of Iowa philosopher G. T. W. Patrick listed seven classes of swearing, but only one involved "vulgar words. Words and phrases unusual or forbidden by polite usage." And only one other category of the seven was reserved for expletives. All of the rest in Patrick's almost unique sytematic consideration of the subject—names of gods, devils, holy persons; names of sacred things or places such as sacraments or "the holy grave"; and words connected with salvation and afterlife and expletives with a religious root—were essentially religious in nature.[5]

Particularly in the Victorian era, obscenity retreated out of the category of swearing into the area of sexual mores. Then in the twentieth century, much of the religious taboo became almost inoperative among most population groups. Swearing came again to involve the broader standard of sexual/scatological decency and propriety. The change involved not only the growing dominance of garden-variety secularism but also the uses that a number of social elements, particularly proponents of the other minor vices, came to make of swearing.

Swearing, Rebelliousness, and Deviancy Boundaries

Regardless of content, profane or obscene, swearing had one overwhelming social function: it shocked people. Patrick mentioned this function in 1901, and everyone understood it implicitly.[6] Swearing therefore represented more than the breaking of taboos, particularly more than what later secularists would characterize as *mere* religious taboos. Swearing was a direct assault on social institutions that could conceivably be involved in the taboos. Offensive religious and sexual language therefore threatened religious and sexual institutions.

Yet most Americans understood that people also swore in defiance of authority in general, not just the authority involved in religious and sexual institutions. Swearing was disorderly and disrespectful. Moreover, it partook of insult, and particularly of daring insult. Asking God to curse someone or something was certainly daring during most of American history and even later was not altogether without social consequences. But from the beginning, sexual insinuations and accusations, such as calling a woman a whore, were also presumptuous. Indeed, in seventeenth-century Virginia, most suits for slander concerned such sexual insinuations and accusations. And even more daring and effective was introducing sexual references into nonsexual situations, such as connecting a political act with personal incest or social status with a private anatomical part.[7]

All along, people recognized that swearing was an act of aggression, even beyond the bounds of personal insult. Both religious imprecations and sexual/scatological material in practice attracted attention and outraged the intended audiences of the swearers. Especially delightful through the ages was the inappropriate use of body parts and excremental products to describe people whom a swearer wished to insult or demean. Indeed, the demeaning could challenge the standard social hierarchy, as one ridiculed those higher on the social scale than oneself. Swearing often implied social leveling, typically dragging someone down to the level of the swearer. In addition, particularly with the emergence of tough-guy machismo in the twentieth century, tough guys could show that they fitted in with a lower social class by mastering the profane and obscene argot of members of that class. The use of argot was in fact an important badge of social belonging among the lower orders of society.[8]

The taboo against swearing further complicated the social role of offensive language. Because the taboo signaled boundaries of deviance, it functioned in many ways to help test those boundaries. Sometimes the language was itself a boundary marker, and it was customary to refer to vulgar language, from the commonest people, as unacceptable or at least borderline. Frequently Americans, aware of the slang and argot that marked the private language of exploited people's groups, attributed the very origin of unacceptable terms to deviant or devalued groups, as in the expression "gutter talk," referring to the expressions of lower-order people who congregated in the streets. In Kentucky in 1848, for example, a court decision suggested that a defendant "inadvertently used the Language undoughtedly which he learned from Negroes &c &c"—the same sort of pejorative attribution found in disapproved drug use or sexual behavior.[9]

Many times, breaking the language taboo involved humor—as with any taboo or shocking behavior in which boundaries are tested and then usually confirmed. Another product of the playful aspect of swearing was the large number of euphemisms that common folk thought up to use as expletives so as to swear without really swearing. Folklorists and linguists delight in such expressions and trace how they came into the language. "Heck," for example, was an Americanism first detected in 1865. Other common usages such as "doggone," "horse's caboose," "gee whiz," and "son-of-a-gun" had other origins over a long period of time.[10] Although humor and euphemism were good fun, in fact such playful usage transparently could and did reinforce strict social standards rather than function to defeat them. Saying "by golly" instead of "by God" seemed to most people a harmless compromise that left the taboo intact while keeping the format of a curse. Likewise, hypocrites who condemned swearing in principle could still uphold the taboo effectively as they themselves cursed vigorously. Altogether, long experience showed that language taboos were not simple.

Swearing in the Nineteenth Century

In the nineteenth century, at least some Americans were alarmed by the danger that swearing posed to the institutions of the day. To begin with, swearing went with other misbehavior. W. H. Luckenbach, a Lutheran clergyperson in Pennsylvania who wrote a whole book on swearing in 1884, cited the action of John Howard in England in the eighteenth century when the eminent reformer was in a crowd and "heard a man uttering a volley of oaths. 'Look to your pockets,' he cried aloud ... , 'always take care of your pockets when you find yourself among swearers. He who will take God's name in vain will think little of taking your purse or doing anything else what is evil.'" Luckenbach of course was also trying to make the point that anyone who did not take not just the name but the anger and grace of God seriously would probably misbehave in other ways. He went on to conclude that all the sins and vices "are so leagued together that [a person] cannot patronize one without encouraging *all* of them."[11]

On one level Luckenbach was merely exemplifying the common social assumption that all vices go together, especially in persons of bad character. But he and others were also emphasizing the way in which swearing threatened the social fabric and particularly the upgrading and civilizing process that restraint on speech as well as behavior involved—what in that day was described approvingly as self-control.

As early as 1815, in Ohio the Chillicothe Association for Promoting Morality and Good Order identified the main concerns that caused Americans to oppose swearing, above and beyond those that were strictly religious, and beyond the pragmatic worry that swearing undermined the use of oaths in legal proceedings. First, the upholders of Good Order argued, any breach of decorum (social deviation) was injurious to society: "The thief, the robber, the murderer, cannot be allowed to indulge that lawless liberty which they claim. Neither can the profane swearer, the Sabbath-breaker, or the drunkard. *These* overturn and bear away the very foundations of morality, order, and good government."[12]

The second element that the Chillicothe Association identified was the class distinction that was involved: only the vulgar, presumably, swore. Moreover, the writers of the association statement acknowledged the widespread belief that swearing was "an accomplishment"—with not only class but gender implications. The authors of the statement quoted a verse to bolster the courage of non-swearers:

> Maintain your rank, vulgarity despise;
> To swear, is neither brave, polite, nor wise.[13]

Finally, all witnesses, like those from Chillicothe, suggested that many Americans believed that swearing, even if deviant and characteristic of the lower orders, was, at the same time, manly.

Nineteenth-century Americans therefore believed that swearing embodied tendencies to overturn good order and level propriety, to substitute roughneck standards for civilized and restrained behavior. In the cities, members of the lower orders shocked visitors from abroad with rough language that they used to defy authority and consolidate comradeship among themselves. An Irish immigrant in 1863 described America as "the most wicked place I ever saw for Cursing Blasphemy." Upholders of an orderly society, for their part, in the American tradition codified their standards into laws. Innumerable efforts of legislatures to discourage profanity marked ordinances and codes across the country well into the twentieth century. (As late as 1935, a woman was convicted of breach of the peace when she shouted at a policeman "Mind your own God damn business.")[14]

Shocking Words in the Late Nineteenth Century

Beyond the law, Americans increasingly developed informal sanctions against breaking verbal taboos. The middle-class evangelicals were remarkably successful in establishing the "conspiracy of silence" against matters sexual. In the conspiracy of silence, no respectable person printed or uttered in public any word that carried any sexual content. So strong was the association between religiously disrespectful and sexual utterances that the conspiracy of silence came to include also the profane, particularly as impiety and ribaldry merged to constitute offensive speech and writing. By the late nineteenth century, social pressures of all kinds in fact succeeded in muting public use of offensive language. Swearing therefore took on even clearer class connotations—connected to antisocial behavior in general—or became private behavior—typically male, as in the double standard of sexual morality. Moreover, among street-gang boys of the lower orders, blasphemy and obscenity were of a piece with antisocial activity, such as gambling and vandalism. In their language, the boys were merely aping older males whom they observed practicing this ritual of swearing. Men, who presumably had to deal with the lower orders of society or learned crudity from male grouping or slumming, did know and use the tabooed vocabulary, but women were different. As D. W. Maurer recalled, "Even if women heard this vocabulary, especially as children, they were conditioned early to block it out and later professed ignorance of it." In the rural South, when rowdy, often drunken males crowded the small towns on Saturdays, women stayed away particularly to avoid hearing profanity and smutty talk.[15]

As early as 1885, one American witness, Edwin P. Whipple, believed that "in ordinary society blasphemy is banished from the polite tattle and prattle of good company," adding, "The conventional gentleman, though fifty or eighty years ago he might consider an oath as an occasional or frequent adornment of his conversation in all societies, now reserves it for 'gentlemen' alone, and is inclined to deem it slightly improper in the society of ladies." Whipple went on to observe, however, that

> a man of refinement cannot walk the streets of any city, or the lanes of any country village, without having his sense of decency shocked by senseless oaths and imprecations, whether coming from the lips of a hack-driver cursing his horses, or a farm laborer cursing his oxen. . . . In many cases the words express the real passion of coarse, hard, dull, envious, and malignant natures, indifferent to religious or moral restraints, finding a certain delight in outraging ordinary notions of decorum, flattering themselves with the conceit that in ribaldry and blasphemy they have some compensation for the miseries brought upon them by poverty or vice, and indulging in outward curses as a verbal relief to their inward "cussedness" of disposition and character.

In this way, then, middle-class Americans repeatedly confronted real people whose language embodied many of the cultural elements of the constellation of the minor vices that appeared in a lower-order and sometimes underworld setting: contrariness, amorality, and destructiveness.[16]

The power to shock with words therefore had more than a casual significance when people used swearing to challenge authority openly. Such implicit opposition to the powerful went beyond mere invective. The best evidence of the effect that swearing had on authority was the profound reaction of authority figures when a young person or a member of the lower orders of society swore in a defiant or impudent way. It was this type of confrontation that made swearing an act with real social meaning— and sanctions. Early in the twentieth century, a judge could proclaim openly that he had "no scruples about" removing children from a home in which he found "habitual indecent, vulgar and profane language."[17]

The success of refined people in setting up language taboos had progressed so by the late nineteenth century that sanctioned words came to include slang. The basis for the stigmatization was that slang gave status and recognition to expressions identified with the lower orders and indeed with lower-order and criminal behavior. Rightly or wrongly, people at that time did associate language with behavior. Nice children did not have anything to do with users of slang, who identified themselves by their words. A "slangy boy" was a dubious stereotype, at best quaint but still deviant and by implication probably a swearer. Slang, explained Ellen Burns Sherman in 1897, "being of emotional ancestry, is a first cousin to the oath. . . . It is so strong that it may be taken only very rarely with impunity." Both slang and swearing, in short, had shock value.[18]

Intellectual and Artistic Critics

All these high-Victorian standards of communication were vulnerable to critics. Around the turn of the century, well-educated people in substantial numbers for the first time began to undermine the taboos, albeit with good intentions. Many were confident that the standards were sufficiently secure as standards that they could be discussed without danger. Written defenses of swearing (not to mention realistic slang) began to appear in general and literary magazines. Defenders of swearing invoked the inexorable process of secularization. "Swearing is not generally a matter of morals," wrote critic Burges Johnson in 1916. It might offend propriety, he said, but swearing no longer profaned. "Seldom, in fact," he noted, "does one who utters an oath have the real meaning of the phrase in his thought."[19]

Such reasoned arguments for swearing as they were articulated in the early twentieth century involved much more than breaking the conspiracy of silence in matters sexual. Because the common people did in fact swear, so proponents argued, swearing ought to appear in fiction and drama. Why deny, they continued, that in spite of the successes of the civilizing process, even nice, admirable people occasionally let loose with a curse? Did not

Farragut damn the torpedoes? Moreover, the argument proceeded, everyone still knew that "strong language" was appropriately masculine. And, in an idea closely related, many commentators held that swearing was actually good, because the swearer got rid of bothersome or malignant emotions in a harmless way. "The human animal, like a locomotive," admitted Sherman, "seems to require escape-valves for occasions when there is too much steam in the boiler." The cathartic action of swearing, proponents argued, in an age when people sought a moral equivalent for war, was healthy and led to more constructive feelings.[20]

Intellectual advocates of swearing therefore tried to ignore the social implications of breaking the taboos and instead to argue that oaths and dirty words were *personally* important. Profanity, contended one writer at the turn of the century, is a valuable resource for a person: "The lifelong habit of self-control in speech is indeed an acquisition not lightly to be thrown aside; but is dumb rage in the presence of irremediable injustice, let us say, any better than honest Homeric oaths?" In such an atmosphere as these statements represented, essayists lamented "the lost art of swearing" and wished that if one were to use language of a profane and obscene sort, it might at least be artful, since politeness and secularism had robbed it of much of the traditional impact and left nothing but a cheap shock value. "What a humiliating spectacle is the word *damn!*" lamented Johnson, the critic: "Once a powerful invective, conveying all the righteous anger of the church, now a miserable subterfuge of the playwright if he needs a laugh...." Johnson longed instead for such expressions as "By the bones of Saint Michael! I will spit thee to thy cringing gizzard!" In the eyes of such commentators, colorful, personally expressive swearing did not threaten the institutions of civilization. More general popular opinion was not far behind the critics. In 1910, for example, a Morristown, New Jersey, jury found that a man who under provocation called a woman a "damn fool" was not guilty of violating the law against using profanity.[21]

War and the Inversion in Manners

Proponents and practitioners of swearing found in World War I a great opportunity for advocating such ideas and attitudes as well as simply using offensive language because it was personally gratifying. Wartime patriotism silenced most opponents of swearing. "One can hardly talk of the Kaiser," wrote one editor, without the word "damn." A generation of young men who aspired to respectability found that in the armed services swearing was not only masculine but another part of male bonding and of the essentially lower-order existence to which they were reduced. And so they swore. A YMCA secretary on the Western Front noted that "these kids all cuss whether they want to or not, or whether they have anything to cuss about." One day, he continued, an outfit came in, and of course

> they couldn't open their mouths without letting out curses. Cigarettes were blankety-blank cigarettes. Chocolate was blankety-blankety-blank chocolate. They were in a blankety-blank hurry. It was a blankety-blank long and blankety-blank hot, blankety-blank march to their blankety-blank destination. . . . I told them I was no preacher, but I said this war was going to be over pretty soon and they'd be going back home. "When you get back," I said, "you'll sit down at the family breakfast table and you'll be the whole show. . . . your mother will want to be filling up your coffee cup again, and your little brother will be crowding up against one side of you and your kid sister against the other, and you'll look across the table and say: "Goddamit, Ma, where in hell's the butter?"
> Those fellows stared at me when I got through, and didn't laugh, and one of them said, "Why, damittohell, you're right!"[22]

People commented at the time that even outside of the army, wartime enthusiasm served as an excuse for wholesale violation of the swearing taboo. Civilians not only shouted "Damn the Kaiser!" but also drove automobiles (still a badge of wealth) "with red labels on their windshields bearing the startling words, 'To hell with the Kaiser!' " Movies had "the same lurid title."[23] But what was most startling was that at the end of the war, the old standards did not come back to life. Swearing instead steadily gained ground.

In the postwar years, the "best people," and now women as well as men, used language that theretofore had served to mark lower-order status or at most the posturing of rebellious intellectuals. Frederick Lewis Allen suggested that the change grew out of a new social value, frankness. He cited writers who believed that as restrictions on public utterances gave way in the printed media, "honesty" was the winner. Despite the often-effective efforts of various kinds of official and unofficial censors who worried primarily about sexual impropriety in print and in public performances, the subject matter and language previously proscribed now came into common discourse. By the middle of the decade, even "nice" people knew that "S.A." stood for sex appeal. Because taboos in language were used continually to enforce taboos about subject matter, isolated uses of words were not just swearing in the early twentieth century but symbols of violations of public decency as well. Various books, for example, had been suppressed on the basis of using at first such a term as "breast," and later one of the four-letter words. But in the late 1920s and 1930s, those same books were often brought into circulation again on the basis that general content and context justified the language. As early as 1925, one editor commented that "it takes just as much courage to write a book dealing frankly with sex as it does to wave the American flag in a musical comedy." But many liberal people were still shy about using forbidden words as such.[24]

New customs in the postwar period also displayed the way in which language moved people into social change and particularly helped women enter a masculine world that had formerly been forbidden to them by the double standard—a move parallel to starting to smoke in those same years (and once again something that naughty boys had done traditionally). Because middle-class people had come to understand the phrasing and terms of the rough language that was used in the war, in addition to the ordinary "damn" and the like, close substitutes for stronger terms also came increasingly into use. "Nuts" got by simply by being ambiguous, but strong euphemisms increasingly showed up in public and in print, such as to "strut one's stuff" and to do "it"—as in the "It Girl," a public relations appellation for actress Clara Bow ("it" originally meaning sex appeal, in this case). The overseas experience of the troops in World War I increased the already-loaded significance of the word *French*, which was used in a variety of contexts and even as a verb. Terms from the jazz world also continued to come in. Swing music of the thirties was named after "swing your thing." All of this essentially sexual language functioned alongside the occasional "hell" that typically came to mark heavy drama on the stage.[25]

More Than Just Manners

But the fact that so many people now accepted the language and format of swearing meant more than just that the standards of playwrights and possibly brave soldiers were predominating in American society. Two processes were occurring simultaneously. The first was the increasing use of the language not of the perhaps colorful non-middle classes but of the criminal. This language contained criminals' traditional strong, if not degenerate, expressions. But it also now included their argot along with profanity and obscenity. Language use became a very tangible part of the general admiration for the gangster that developed in the 1920s as an aspect of the adulation of tough guys in general.[26]

The second post-World War I process was a gradual rejection of the institutions and social figures who opposed swearing and whom swearing defied, personified usually as do-gooders and ladies. The legitimation of some swearing was a part of the wholesale questioning of all taboos by "the best people," especially those people who in general sided with either refinement or uplift. Frankness in literature was especially important for trendsetters. Moreover, the new pillars of society (and converted old ones) could cite good reasons for their questioning and even violating taboos. In the case of swearing, they could make historical and anthropological comparisons that rendered verbal taboos—and often by implication other taboos—ridiculous. This was of course the same ridicule that knocked down the straw-man Puritan in all areas of standards. It was easy enough to make people who appeared to be afraid of a manly "hell," or of the very word *sex*, look silly. In 1929 in a skit at a rally against book censorship in Boston, the sale of a history of Middlesex County, Massachusetts, was satirically questioned because the title had the word *sex* in it.[27]

By the 1920s and 1930s, an important and powerful group had been added to those Americans who actively favored swearing: journalists. Journalists (and, later, media people of other varieties) enlisted under the banner of fighting censorship, which they generalized from politics to cover all areas of life. Following the lead of earlier intellectuals who had struggled for artistic freedom, media people, quite aware of their importance in setting standards, attempted to publish and broadcast any and all frequently used terms because they were authentic. In 1939, journalists congratulated moviegoers on being sophisticated when a character used "damn" at the climax of the motion-picture version of *Gone With the Wind*. Newspaper editors came to use the term "rape" after it had been introduced in a metaphoric sense in a nonsexual setting, the Sino-Japanese war in the 1930s. Book publishers financed court battles on behalf of authors to remove all restriction on language whatsoever. All in all, continual agitation led many Americans to view increasing latitude of expression as inevitable progress. "Banned in Boston"—referring to book censorship—became in news stories a term of ridicule of an outrageously outdated practice. By the late 1930s, journalists portrayed formal opponents of swearing as merely quaint eccentrics.[28]

Leading the journalists and popular media were many well-known literary people. By the 1930s and 1940s, a person could have learned from works published in the United States by such luminaries as William Faulkner, John Steinbeck, and Erskine Caldwell a great deal of common swearing, including all but the three or four most tabooed expressions.[29]

World War II and Accelerating Change

World War II greatly accelerated the process of breaking down barriers against profane and obscene language. Unconcerned with sexual purity, armed-services leadership was also at best indifferent to swearing if not actually favorable to the practice—unlike George Washington generations earlier. As a statement in the *Infantry Journal* in 1943 explained,

> The Army does not officially condone profanity; unofficially it knows it can do little to stop it. The society of soldiers is not polite. It is a society of men, frequently unwashed, who have been dedicated to the rugged task of killing other men, and whose training has emphasized that a certain reversion to the primitive is not undesirable.[30]

As in World War I, wartime service experience—and accompanying emulation by civilians—had a decisive effect. H. L. Mencken, writing at the time, noted that service language had shifted almost entirely to obscenity. He observed with regret, "It is all based upon one or two four-letter words and their derivatives, and there is little true profanity in it." Some of the (not necessarily new) terms that came home with the soldiers did not last, such as "Picadilly commando" (streetwalker), but others entered generally into at least covert use, such as "shack up." Many different types of people helped popularize code terms such as "snafu" (an acronym translated euphemistically as "situation normal, all 'fouled' up"), and everyone knew about the apocryphal returned GI who asked for the butter at his mother's table—only this time using not a profane oath but a grotesquely inappropriate adjective based on an obscene word for sexual intercourse.[31]

The key to the rapid acceptance of offensive language was large numbers of women's growing tolerance and use of proscribed monosyllables. Boys of whatever class had been using the language with bravado or otherwise, but even men from the lower orders, much less "gentlemen," avoided using dubious terms in front of most women. Such use would have constituted the public sign of acceptance. Now, however, after World War II, as Bernard DeVoto observed, the "educated or 'refined' women . . . who used to be the most censorious upholders of the taboo" tolerated or themselves used the offensively obscene expressions. During the war, DeVoto continued, "military life made most of the monosyllables automatic in the conversation of the soldiers and sailors whom millions of women knew." But there was even more to it, he continued, for now four-letter words had "come to signify frankness, sophistication, liberalism, companionability, and even smartness among a very great many educated and well-to-do metropolitan women," and women in other centers, he added, had followed this example. In short, major changes in values as well as customs were involved in what was becoming a common habit of speech—long recognized as a bad habit.[32]

Exactly when after World War II the keepers of public standards came to believe that all language was acceptable in public as well as private discourse is unclear. The trend, however, gained strength as the 1950s came to a close. In 1951, James Jones in his novel *From Here to Eternity* had to eliminate 240 uses of one four-letter word and 85 of another, but that still left 108 and 50, respectively. ". . . Towards the end of the fifties," recalled Walter Allen, "anyone like myself who habitually read American novels submitted to English publishers, usually in proof-form, could watch the forbidden word creeping into print and becoming, it seemed, almost obligatory in any novel that laid claims to realism." The phenomenon that Allen and others were observing in the most formal arena of communication, the published word, was accelerated greatly by a further series of court decisions in which works of art such as D. H. Lawrence's *Lady Chatterley's Lover* (legalized for circulation by a federal court in 1959) were distributed freely despite the fact that the authors used the commonplace but formerly very offensive four-letter words. By the end of the 1960s, the fight for total defiance of any remaining taboos had been won in some some public areas, such as literature and also the theater, where actions as well as language were an issue. Moreover, many people were making money by publishing and performing, outside of the realm of pornography, what had previously been forbidden matter.[33]

Journalism was probably the last public-communications arena in which virtually any expression—and the content that went with it—became acceptable (and the process was still far from complete at the beginning of the 1990s). Through the 1950s and 1960s, in newspapers and similar standard-setting publications, the amount of material on sexual matters increased, especially references to birth control and homosexuality, and the contexts in which the material appeared became more liberal, that is, accepting of sexual hedonism. But standards were still in a state of confusion in the late 1960s. In 1966, The New York *Herald-Tribune*, for instance, carried the word *penis* in a story about the Masters and Johnson research on love making, whereas the *New York Times* did not.[34]

Meanwhile, the appearance of the underground press greatly complicated the standards of journalism. It was 1962 before the *Village Voice* actually printed the principal four-letter word, but even then it was to mention the name of an iconoclastic magazine that, in an attempt to be offensive, contained the word in its official title. That same forbidden word did not appear in the *Berkeley Barb* until October 8, 1965, and then it was in quotation marks. The underground press did within a few years, however, set new standards in which total frankness of language as well as content was a distinctive characteristic. Underground publications pushed editors of regular magazines and newspapers to use terms and include material that *Playboy* and more openly pornographic publications had pioneered. As one observer concluded in 1968, "The story of the candid society is too big to be ignored. . . ." The changes in literature and in the self-styled liberation press were so rapid and followed one another so quickly that no one could tell who was most forward in publishing obscene language, which most commentators identified as part of the so-called sexual revolution. They believed that frankness was understood as furthering changes in behavior. In the 1920s, those advocating frankness were on the side of humanistic expression in literature. Later, the issue moved over into questions about material that went so far as to degrade human beings, especially women.[35]

Especially during the 1960s, when popular-music composers and performers pioneered drug advocacy and extreme candor in song lyrics, they helped validate the act of publicly using taboo expressions. Although, in the 1950s, lyrics of the most popular songs were often steamily suggestive ("Your lips excite me, let your arms invite me . . . my love won't wait," sung by Elvis Presley in 1960), the words still were not flagrantly offensive. By the late 1960s, however, there was often a show-off use of common language ("I laid a divorcée in New York City," for example, sang Mick Jagger in "Honky Tonk Women" by the Rolling Stones in 1969). In the 1970s, Frank Zappa was singing about "Titties 'n Beer." A decade later, with a proliferation of recordings, four-letter words and grotesque content were becoming commonplace. Some rock groups took obscene names. Advertising for rock albums with clearly obscene words and pictures provided another wedge for unacceptable material to penetrate into a variety of publications, not just those that were explicitly underground. In the mid-1980s, Congress held hearings on the "rock porn" issue. At the very least, as they repeated the language in simple songs, rock-and-roll fans were increasingly conditioned to the idea that shocking expressions were not deviant.[36]

Everybody Does It

Private discourse, too, grew cruder in the decades after World War II. One 1969 study of actual use of language, for example, showed that a group of adults in a leisure setting used *damn* and a four-letter word for excrement more frequently than they did *the* or *and*. Monitoring workplace talk and everyday college-student language yielded remarkably similar results. This process of vulgarization was speeded up by the continued experience of large numbers of men who passed in and out of the armed services during the Cold War. The crudest kinds of language, appropriate or inappropriate, still served to facilitate interpersonal relationships in the workplace and the barracks.[37]

Such were the practices that made it clear to everyone that the taboo that people broke so frequently was a taboo aimed almost entirely at proscribing the offensively obscene, not profane language. "In English," testified John Ciardi in 1966, "blasphemy has lost much of its shock value . . . , and English-speaking people have limited their emotional means by agreeing to reserve certain names for the parts, functions, and products of the endocrine and digestive systems as their shock language." Even late in the twentieth century, pornographic materials remained a category apart, with erotic goals. Swearing as such had other social functions, regardless of sexual content.[38]

For important segments of the population, including many underground-press producers and consumers, the issue in speaking and printing dirty and offensive words was not only art but free speech and censorship per se. These opponents of censorship wanted to be able to print or mouth in public any expressions whatsoever. The founder of Olympia Press, for example, a French publisher of "forbidden books" for the English-language market (and who actually moved his operations to the United States in 1967 after the climate had become friendlier than in France), declared that his motive, aside from making money as a publisher, was "to see how far I could go, single-handed, in a deliberate attempt to destroy censorship as a moral institution, as a tradition, as a method of government." Aside from his distaste for what he imagined were religious constraints, he was not interested in profaning. Rather, he wished to further eroticism. To liberate eroticism, then, was what he pictured as the point of destroying censorship of not only content but also words.[39]

Such "lewds" squared off against the "prudes" in the American public debates over censorship in the 1950s and 1960s. The advocates of complete candor in public continued their straightforward appeal to a combination of truth—facing up to utter realism—and freedom of expression. One way of making the argument was to use offensive words in public and show that nothing bad came of it. Such was the technique of a number of protagonists of shocking language, some in the underground press, some represented by public performers such as singers and comic monologuist Lenny Bruce, who operated chiefly in night clubs.[40]

For a brief time, in 1965, filthy language found formal, organizational leadership in the "Foul Speech Movement." In connection with the efforts of students at the University of California at Berkeley to gain unlimited rights of free speech on campus, some agitators used provocative language to stimulate the university and police forces to react. Eventually one agitator who displayed a sign bearing a four-letter word was arrested. Then others were arrested who similarly tested the limits of freedom of expression in public. Because public officials were at the same time licensing topless waitresses, the hypocrisy of curbing the use of language was obvious for anyone to see. The foul-speech agitators were not just the usual rebellious forces. They carried the burden of challenging the entire university and municipal power structure. The dirty word, in this case, was explicitly a tool of politics, and it lent itself to amusing confrontations, for example with signs varying the spelling of an offensive word (substituting a *ph* for an *f*) to see if the police would react.[41]

Two particular developments assisted the cause of swearing in the 1960s and 1970s. The first was unmistakable evidence in the media that leadership figures not only cursed on appropriate occasions but constantly used shocking language, that is, brought the previously distinctively lower-order or double-standard expressions into arenas of respectability. People listened politely when radical leaders of the Vietnam War era used the most offensive expressions. "Eldridge Cleaver, the underground's candidate for President," noted Ethel Grodzins Romm, "was the first politician to use the same language on the campaign platform as in the smoke-filled rooms." The revelations of Watergate included prominently the fact that a president of the United States who as a "prude" candidate had once attacked an opponent for using a mild expletive was himself consistently, unimaginatively, and degenerately foulmouthed.[42]

The second development was that the forces advocating no limits on expression, the "lewds," more openly argued from a high moral ground. They not only cited civil liberties of various kinds in opposition to censorship but also suggested that the truly obscene consisted not of body parts and functions but Dachau and degrading terms such as "nigger." Radical Bobby Seale of the Black Panthers shrugged off criticism of his penchant to use four-letter words with the comment that "the filthiest word I know is 'kill' and this is what other men have done to the Negro for years."[43]

The Goals of Advocates and Swearers

In the confrontational politics and public events that marked the end of the 1960s, the fundamental aim of the swearers finally emerged explicitly. They wished to shock. And they wished to shock in a destructive way. Shock, after all, can be used to touch people's sensibilities and call them to be aware of behavioral standards. Removing the ability to shock—as well as to be shocked—would remove one of the props of standards upholding institutions such as marital and power relationships. Commentators have often noted this naughty adolescent/rebellious lower-order quality in shocking language. As early as 1920, a critic wrote, "We live in an epoch when more is demanded in human speech in utterance of a high moral indignation than perhaps was ever known to man. . . . It is no time for cheap, ribald rottenness of vulgar profanity."[44]

In the 1960s and after, offensive language served any number of auxiliary destructive purposes. In confrontations, pillars of society were goaded into reacting in extreme and inappropriate ways when rebels used offensive language. And if the advocates of foul speech won, and everyone used silly obscenities commonly, speech practices destroyed social ranks and gender distinctions, not to mention sound standards of diction. Mark Rudd, one of the leaders of a confrontation at Columbia University in 1968, wrote somewhat optimistically about the self-styled radicals' use of the term most Americans considered the most offensive in the language:

We co-opted the word ... from the ghetto much as we adopted the struggle of blacks and the other oppressed as our own. When young people start calling those in power, the people whose places we're being trained to fill, "M----- ------[,]" you know the structure of authority is breaking down. ... The reaction to the style was stronger than the reaction to the content. All forms of authority, traditional "respect" (you show respect, obviously, by not using your own language), had broken down. The norms of repression and domination, maintaining the hierarchical structure of the classroom and the society, were swept aside. And at that time, shocking language had the advantage of selectively targeting established population elements: in addition to social-class differentials, younger people did not find crude language as offensive as did older ones.[45]

The proponents of filthy speech had a long tradition of appealing to lower-order standards by using expressions that were socially leveling. Rudd, by trying to make deviant speech ("your own language") standard, hoped to make other institutions of conventional respectability deviant, and alternative institutions therefore standard. Even if the achievements of foul speech fell short of such aspirations, the growth of public recognition of obscene expression had for rebels the desired goal of discrediting the opposition—as well as of getting attention.[46]

The intensity of feeling of both proponents of offensive language and opponents tended to obscure the social significance of leveling language while at the same time underlining it. Yippie leader Jerry Rubin wrote of the principal four-letter word:

But there's one word which Amerika hasn't destroyed.
One word which has maintained its emotional power and purity.
Amerika cannot destroy it because she dare not use it.
It's illegal!
It's the last word left in the English language. ...

As became increasingly clear in midcentury, language could threaten several kinds of social authority at once. Not only did words threaten overt social-political authority, but they also introduced personal levels of operation, even psychological conflict, into the public arena in a threatening way, as when accusations of incest or perversion were leveled. Indeed, political dissenters of the Vietnam War era used shock language to argue that the personal and political cannot be separated.[47]

Moreover, rebellious offensive language threatened the linguistic basis of consensual society, indeed, the rational basis of that society. As one author's scenario for changes in word use in the near future anticipated, soon when he had checked into a hotel he would "be able to slip a bell hop ten dollars to 'send up a prostitute,' and then answer a knock at . . . [the] door a half hour later to find *some hack writer with a scraggly beard, carrying a typewriter under his arm.*" In such use, the meaning of a powerful word lost precision if not significance. In short, all the positive bases for social authority were endangered and challenged by those who attempted to break the taboo on forbidden words.[48]

As was customary in midcentury America, a number of analysts devised psychological explanations for swearing, in large part to domesticate the use of bad language by reducing it to a purely personal phenomenon without social implications. Such theorists built upon the catharsis model that Patrick and others had described in the opening decades of the twentieth century. Anthropologist Ashley Montagu, for example, voiced the common belief that people who are frustrated develop aggressive reactions, which in his eyes explained why they used expletives. Psychologist Joyce Brothers, writing in a women's magazine in 1973, took up the same theme: "In a wildly frustrating situation, there's something healthy about the defiant outpouring of gutter language." She added that this type of masculine reaction is far superior to "helpless weeping." Women with responsibilities swore more than those without, she continued, and she believed that in general this taking on of masculine swearing was a part of female liberation. But Brothers also condemned obsessive swearing and recognized the hostile potential in it, at least as it might damage individual personal relationships.[49]

The confrontation of those upholding at least some parts of old standards with those advocating absolute leveling of expression in the 'sixties permitted many people to consider seriously for the first time what would happen if the principle of completely uninhibited speech should prevail. At that point pornography would join obscenity, for pornography is like science fiction in that both permit anything that can be imagined. The quest for complete lack of restraint, a totally negative goal, was where swearing led. The use of forbidden terms in *Playboy* and kindred magazines, for example, was rebellion in the direction of unrestrained actions as opposed to double entendres that were at best ambiguous in their social function.

Some Americans held back, as political scientist Harry M. Clor suggested in 1971: "In the total absence of restraints by organized society, this degeneration of ethical and aesthetic culture could conceivably be

carried to great lengths. Does the community have to put up with it?"
The force behind swearing was concerned also with unorganized society—anything, just so that "anything goes." And that same impulse had
no regard for the social usefulness of manners—which of course swearing
breached.[50] In the 1970s age of me-ism, the personal uses of swearing,
proponents indicated, were paramount to social considerations.

Advocates of the public use of offensive language therefore had a
number of agendas intermediate to achieving a society without restraint.
One was the destruction of certain traditions of deference and respect.
That involved social leveling, as seen, for example, in the late-twentieth-
century upper-class woman who acted tough and mouthed "redneck expletives" or a contemporary society matron playing "four-letter word
games" at a cocktail party, in each case implicitly connecting swearing
to another of the minor vices. These typical behaviors showed clearly
how not only age and gender authority but social-class authority was the
target of swearing.[51]

Whereas ordinary offensive language was part of the habitual expression and communication of various social groups, and particularly those
in the underworld, Victorian or later, making swearing standard behavior
for other class and authority figures, and especially for the respectables,
represented a major victory for lower-order rebellious parochialism. By
1990, when a very prominent professional football player twice on live
television used one of the two most offensive four-letter words, a commentator could observe, "He genuinely didn't seem to comprehend that
he wasn't supposed to say that on television." In fact, there was little
reaction.[52]

The traditional ties of swearing and offensive use of language to the
other minor vices and to deviant, criminal behavior continued in the
closing decades of the twentieth century. One of the standard mid-twentieth-century slang phrases for marijuana, for example, was a common
offensive word for excrement. For the proponents of the minor vices,
bringing offensive language into common use in the United States was a
symbolic victory, a signal that standards of all propriety had indeed been
turned upside down.

The campaign in favor of the ritual use of dirty words and oaths was,
like similar campaigns of the advocates of the minor vices, also negative,
a way of breaking standards. Moreover, in the late twentieth century, it
served a useful purpose, beyond assisting in the acceptance of profitable
pornography. The continuing ability to shock (as late as 1976 the Sex

Pistols caused a transatlantic sensation when they used a four-letter word on British television) showed that there were still repressive forces that could be offended and potentially might resist the still-urgent quest for an unrestrained society in which each and every bad habit could flourish.[53]

Swearing continued to provide an outlet for negative aggression on more than one level. Swearing provided a way of drawing deviance boundaries—only now to stigmatize the nonswearer, who still held back from lower-order customs. But the swearer also was able to strike out verbally against the stereotyped, repressive Puritan in general who many decades after the repeal of Prohibition still served proponents of the minor vices as a red herring, distracting the attention of well-meaning people away from the campaign of the champions of the minor vices to turn American culture into an affluent version of the Victorian underworld.

The Coopting Process

The foregoing chapters show that as economic and demographic changes took place, proponents of each of the commonplace misbehaviors of the nineteenth century turned into a powerful force, by the mid twentieth century influencing American culture as a whole. Each of the bad habits developed momentum independently. But in the end, each one converged with the others. Together they formed the dynamic, evolving minor vice-industrial complex that was based on culture as well as on an inordinate desire for profits. The next two chapters will recontextualize and highlight patterns and trends in the histories of drinking, smoking, drug taking, gambling, sexual misbehavior, and swearing.

The goal of the proponents of all the minor vices was to serve cultural and commercial population groups by freeing all behavior from restraint on impulses. The stance of the advocates of each of the bad habits was negative. Not a single one provided a positive program. All sought primarily to destroy restraints. When the Association Against the Prohibition Amendment suggested no concrete substitute for Prohibition, AAPA spokespersons could note vaguely that, after all, "many alternatives" to Prohibition existed. This vagueness masked the destructive nature of the repealers' critique.[1] Similarly, extremists in the areas of sex, drugs, and language had no restrictive platform or utopian prescription beyond unregulated freedom of indulgence for individuals, with tolerance for even extreme and disturbing behavior.

From Constellation to Cooptation

The advocates of the bad habits therefore had an implicit general program that grew with success. From the beginning, custom linked these misbehaviors into a constellation. They were, consequently, even in the nineteenth century, set potentially to reinforce one another and, in the Victorian underworld, they did. The connections among gambling, prostitution, drug and pornography dealing, and all other illegal activities contributed to the influence of the champions of the minor vices. Outright criminal activity shaded imperceptibly into legitimate business activity. Often the tie was on the retail level. Sexual goods and services led willing customers to numbers or drugs, and in the nineteenth and twentieth centuries alike, drinking establishments were the entryway to the rest.[2] Many writers have described how such activity, legal and illegal, lay at the heart of the underworld.

For a number of decades in the nineteenth century, however, in most parts of society, the minor vices remained under control, contained both in individuals by self-restraint and collectively in society. In the twentieth century, as economics worked on each one, the elements in the constellation continued to interact in American society and culture. This mutual reinforcement did not constitute a conspiracy, even though episodes such as Pierre Du Pont's organizing the repeal of Prohibition, *Playboy* magnate Hugh Hefner's bankrolling of NORML, or late-twentieth-century business consolidations and acquisitions between tobacco and alcohol marketers represented some level of collusion and might from time to time have given the appearance of conspiracy.

Instead of conspiracy, it is better to conceptualize the process by which proponents of the bad habits operated in terms of a series of concrete cooptations. Such a conceptualization is particularly useful because the cooptation process extended not only to alliances among the various badhabit supporters themselves but also to the process by which they pulled into their ranks agents of other cultural currents over many decades and, finally, even social elements who represented and led reform.

Economic Cooptation

The advocates of the minor vices initially coopted other elements in American society primarily in one of two ways—and, eventually, in both. As must be evident from the repeated patterns in the histories of each bad habit, the first type of cooptation operated by simple economic interest. The second was negative rebelliousness.

Beyond the wealthy who used taxes on drink, tobacco, and gambling to let someone else pay for government, the bad habits brought direct benefits to specific businesses. Some of the economic interest was obvious—not just that of the fences who paid for stolen property with drugs but the interest of the sugar and grain companies who supplied the alcoholic-beverage industry, or the newspaper owners who craved the revenues represented by cigarette advertisers and sensation-hungry readers—or even just the nineteenth-century drug store owners who sold opium and provided small amounts on credit to tide over regular customers who were short of cash at the moment. Sometimes the association was indirect. One never knew, for example, where special-event promotions would take a company. In 1975, the E-Z Wider cigarette paper racing car carried a Goodyear advertising sign on the side. In the histories of each of the minor vices, economic cooptation of various kinds took place over many decades, and at different rates. In the 1950s, for example, a full 7 per cent of all glass-container output in the United States went to the spirits-beverage companies. The Glass Container Manufacturers Institute, following an earlier campaign of one company, Owens-Illinois, began a series of ads in *Life* magazine urging readers to drink beer. The brewers of course constituted an even more important customer of the glass industry than the distillers.[3]

By the second half of the twentieth century, the proponents of the minor vices had succeeded in enlisting the interest of the bulk of larger American corporations, because so many had direct economic interests in supplying activities growing out of the traditional minor vices. In previous chapters there appeared the direct examples of Time, Inc.'s investment in sexually explicit movies for television and the sales of gambling equipment by General Electric, Control Data, General Instrument, and other high-tech companies. In addition, the great banking and investment houses—like the insurance companies who were underwriting loans to expand alcoholic-beverage marketing in the 1940s—had both direct and indirect economic interests in businesses that embodied all the bad habits, even items such as drug paraphernalia and unusual pornography. Virtually any enterprise could get a line of credit from a major financial house, including those houses that controlled the larger part of American economic activity. Once tied into one of the vices, a company became involved indirectly at least with the other parts of the constellation and contributed to the minor vice-industrial complex.

Throughout the twentieth century, any sizable business interest had great political and cultural power. Therefore the champions of the bad habits acquired formidable allies as the process of coopting businesses proceeded. Pierre Du Pont left in his papers a clear record of the way in which he enlisted the wealthy and powerful directly. Advertising provided another sign of economic interest, as record and high-fidelity sound equipment companies and the entertainment industry essentially subsidized pornographic and pro-drug publications. Later, as appeared most transparently in the alcoholic-beverage and tobacco businesses, the development of conglomerates and diversification after mid twentieth century intensified the process of cooptation.[4] By the 1970s, at least, and more likely the 1950s, virtually every large class of business had some financial interest in one or more of the elements in the constellation of minor vices. At one point, for example, beginning in 1976, the Sun Oil Company owned a major chain of convenience stores, the profits of which to an important extent involved sales of alcoholic beverages (in some local outlets to minors) as well as lottery tickets. In the 1910s, many transportation companies stigmatized alcoholic beverages and in the process antagonized the brewers. Half a century later, by contrast, transportation companies could not sell enough alcoholic beverages to passengers.

So it was that by the mid twentieth century, tracing the suppliers to racetracks, servicers of tobacco wholesalers, and, again, lenders for drug- and pornography-related commodities would lead back to the most powerful and "respectable" business elements in the country. Moreover, as the accounting firms and conglomerates illustrate, those entangled in the bad habits were not limited to simple industrial categories such as suppliers and financiers.

Economic cooptation was the major accomplishment of the proponents of the bad habits and the chief basis for their power and authority in American life. Merely totaling up the huge volume of business done by various enterprises providing the minor vices would not adequately suggest their impact, even if, for example, 1983 retail sales of hard-core video sales of $80 million were added to the figures on gambling and tobacco products and alcoholic beverages and drug paraphernalia used as illustrations in earlier chapters. Adding in such items as addiction costs (1 to 2 per cent of GNP by one estimate) and advertising and other indirect financial involvements would still not encompass the economic activity engendered by the bad habits.[5] But precise measurements are not necessary. The fact remains that the minor vice-industrial complex reached into the economy with an astonishing power of penetration.

Although the economic power of the minor vice-industrial complex through large-scale economic organizations was great indeed, the desire for gain had an additional enormous impact through small-business units engaged in commercializing leisure, most typically drug peddlers but also corner shops selling cigarettes to children or offering betting slips or *Penthouse*—in short, any retailer anywhere in a community who developed a financial stake in any or all of the bad habits. Driven by an often noteworthy interest in money, these individual units were direct agents of cultural influence and change—in the aggregate, remarkably effective emissaries of the minor vices.[6]

Cultural Cooptation

The second mode of cooptation came from the negative identity of deviants and rebels. Some deviants and rebels were of course born into an ethnic or other social group that dominant groups labeled deviant or alien. Many people among the lower orders received the deviant label from the respectables. And those so labeled typically learned many rebellious attitudes and forms of rebellious behavior from both the labelers and from people who consciously rebelled against the dominant groups—just as adults and peers alike influenced the young "newsies" of Hearst Alley, or respectable young women in boardinghouses learned from their neighbors.

Rebellious antisocial influences were extensive and pervasive. In an early-twentieth-century factory, for example, even respectable workers symbolically acquired criminal nicknames.[7] As part of their becoming coopted, low-status people often participated in, first, the Victorian underworld, and, later, other groupings around the fast life and illegal or semi-illegal activities. Most notable and obvious was the coopting of many immigrant groups, particularly members of Italian and Jewish families who by tradition used alcohol only very sparingly, into anti-Prohibition stances and heavy drinking in saloons. Second-generation Americans, in contrast to their parents, in particular tended to utilize all the commercial establishments of the minor vices as they took various kinds of rebellious and parochial stances.[8]

Rebellious folk were of course contrary. They deliberately separated themselves from the mainstream, as they perceived it. In 1959, a Greenwich Village observer claimed that many teenagers "have turned to homosexuality in the same way that others have taken up jazz, grown beards, or smoked pot; it represents rebellion against the established order."[9] Similar words could have been written about the bad habits of generations before and since. Such rebels chose a deviant identity, including that of the underworld—Victorian and later—within which an outsider could go "slumming." People for generations spoke meaningfully of "night life."

That was one way that rebelliousness served to define and test social standards. But in addition, when a humble person strayed into one of the bad habits, it was possible for that person to take on a general deviant identity. Such deviants learned—from labeling by "respectables" or, in the late twentieth century, from ads such as those of cigarette companies—that they were expected to drink, smoke, gamble, and generally indulge defiantly in the constellation of minor vices that everyone knew.

The familiar model for this traditional negative identity was the old-fashioned idea of the prostitute. Because she had lost her virginity, she might, as people traditionally believed, just as well go on and be entirely depraved—drink, smoke, swear, take drugs, and gamble along with the underworld "sports." In such cases, deviant status created the affinity among the bad habits. Other versions appeared at other times. In the late twentieth century, for example, the editor of a drug paper told how, in the 1960s, he had lived in a hippie commune financed, as he figured out afterward, by a drug dealer who used the inhabitants to run drugs. The residents played out the most stereotyped "anti-conventional" behavior, using drugs and alcohol and indulging in casual sexual activity—including acts with a resident Saint Bernard dog. "We were naked all the time and we were stoned all the time," he recalled. In that condition, it did not matter what they did, any more than it had for the old-time stereotyped prostitute. There was no condemnation as everyone, dog included, "did his own thing" without restraint.[10]

What is remarkable about this model is that in the twentieth century, the proponents of the minor vices took the deviant identity and turned it into an attractive style of life and a dominant mode. Repeated assertions that "everybody does it" helped change society so that everybody did do it—or aspire to do it. (Meanwhile, of course, many people—a growing segment of the population—continued to grow up in homes in which the deviant identity was primary anyway—either criminal or in some sense alienated from older "conventional" standards.) And they all believed that it—indulging in the bad habits—was still anti-conventional, even as they argued that everybody did it. A soldier interviewed during the Vietnam War indicated this confusion: "We talked about dope all the time. We were constantly stoned. It was a rebellious action. We knew that they wouldn't do anything about it because it was so big. There were lieutenants that were doing it. The Man knew that we knew...."[11]

The changes that came into the minor vices therefore operated on at least three levels, in each case in a complicated way:

1. At the lowest level, the minor vices, for a variety of reasons, provided one form in which the forces of economics and social-group parochialism and rebelliousness manifested themselves.
2. Because people persistently connected the minor vices into a constellation, invoking deviance as well as custom, that is, the supposedly natural affinity of bad habits for one another, each minor vice also from time to time coopted the other minor vices of the constellation into aggressive assaults upon restrictive social standards.
3. The proponents of the minor vices, singly and in concert, in turn coopted many other elements in American society—and this to the point that the values peculiar to champions of the bad habits became dominant. The most spectacular cooptations were those of the media and of the "good" people in society, the reformers.

The way in which commercialization and the pursuit of profit worked to enlist people in the service of the minor vices was relatively straightforward. The way in which many cultural elements interacted with the Americans working in support of the bad habits was more complex.

Lower-order parochialism was rebellious only as members of such groups perceived their status to be deviant. Many poor and exploited people, as pointed out above, still acted essentially as middle class and did not identify themselves as deviant. In terms of the bad habits, at least, lower-order deviance was therefore defined by lifestyles and values—namely, those of which the members of the originally dominant respectable elements in the United States disapproved. Moreover, lower order shaded over into criminal—in part in social status and in part in lifestyle and values.[12] Regardless of their social *status*, people who lived according to a lower-order *lifestyle* and set of values were parochial in that sense: their implicit goal was to impose on all Americans lower-order and underworld values and standards. The more explicit goal was to have everyone share a lifestyle.

The various minor vices had advantages for lower-order rebels. When anyone "respectable" indulged in a bad habit, the rebels could use such illustrative material to show that "everybody's doing it," that is, that "everybody" shared the lower-order lifestyle—not just the people in stigmatized groups. So the saloon owners at the turn of the century exposed sinning preachers when ministers were conspicuous among those who condemned saloon keepers. Showing that "everyone" indulged in a vice therefore provided an easy route to normalizing (rendering nondeviant) the lower-order lifestyle, as, typically, with the use of vulgar swearing.

Moreover, the bad habits represented impulsiveness, that particular attribute of non-middle-class people that respectable folks hated and feared. The fundamental style of impulsiveness showed up best, probably, in the drug culture and in gambling in which participants explicitly rejected the conventional work ethic.

Negativism among lower-order rebels was very powerful. It was such negativism as people in the 1890s projected onto naughty cigarette-smoking boys. But the other rebels, the cultural rebels, by contrast held an even more unremittingly negative and destructive attitude. Their goal was typically to destroy current standards as such, to obliterate all kinds of discriminations that labeled one type of individual behavior or another deviant. Like the Greenwich Village denizens of the early twentieth century or the hippies of a later period, cultural rebels typically came out of the classes and groups against whose standards they were rebelling, and so negating those standards took on a special urgency for such rebels, regardless of the fact that they usually favored art and perhaps intellectual snobbery. They could, and did, talk about "freedom."[13]

When, therefore, commercial interest began to galvanize the minor vices, two powerful preexisting forces were waiting to reinforce and push the new social impact of the bad habits: the resentful parochialism of lower-order people who wanted, understandably, to devalue respectables and show them to be corrupt and just like people in the criminal and semi-criminal classes; and the negativism of artistic and intellectual rebels who envisaged a society without personal constraints. With commercial stimulus, the subcultures turned into countercultures, members of which worked actively to overthrow existing arrangements, in the process furnishing recruits to the ranks of those advocating the minor vices.

The many faces of greed, parochialism, and rebelliousness in this way complicated the history of all the bad habits as their proponents helped shape the evolving culture. Each cooptation of a social element of course represented a special set of circumstances. The ultimate merging of smoking and drinking into the same or overlapping business corporations in the last half of the twentieth century was not the same in nature, timing, or motivation as the impact of lower-order sexual standards on many middle-class men and women as a result of World War I and, particularly, World War II. And neither resembled closely the gamblers' suborning of wealthy taxpayers who accepted parimutuel betting and then state lotteries as means of shifting the tax burden off of themselves.

What was remarkable was therefore not any specific change but the direction of all the changes. It was always the same, so that ultimately the multifarious cooptations moved American society as a whole into inverting values so as to accept and endorse the whole constellation. Regardless of the pace of the happenings in the history of each special bad habit, after mid twentieth century, as social determiners, they converged. That convergence was the final and striking end-point of the pattern discernible in them all.

Coopting One Another

As commercial interest developed in the various minor vices, the combinations that were at first mere custom or aspects of a deviant identity came to have practical business aspects. So, in the outstanding example, the pre-Prohibition saloon not only served alcohol but was an apparently necessary base for prostitution and gambling on the basis of commercial advantage. In 1914, for example, when Colorado went dry and the saloons closed, gambling activities also withered away, because they were not immediately profitable without the saloons.[14] Although tobacco products were usually also for sale in saloons, swearing (except in so far as pornography involved shocking language) was not yet a commercial element, however much it added to the atmosphere and bonding among workers and members of the underworld.

One of the remarkable aspects of this coopting process was the continuing primacy of alcoholic beverages. When Sanger in 1858 spoke of the way in which the public sexual evils of New York City coalesced around drinking places, he was recognizing one type of obvious affinity. People had another reason for thinking that drinking was the primary minor vice: they believed that alcohol could weaken a person's inhibitions so that it was much easier for him or her to give in to temptation and indulge in one or more of the other bad habits—that is, alcohol destroyed restraint on the individual level.

Altogether, then, each bad habit, either by the customary identity as a deviant practice or as a business interest, had affinities for the rest of the constellation of minor vices. In such a manner, still confused in the late twentieth century, did two leading advocates of sexual misbehavior, the publishers of *Playboy* and *Penthouse*, independently invest in Atlantic City casinos. Both in their magazines advocated drinking, swearing, gambling of various kinds, sports that were specially related to gambling, and night life in general. Others who were commercially interested in tobacco and alcoholic-beverage advertising united with cultural advocates of sexual license in denouncing "censorship." After midcentury, the editors of *High Times*, the marijuana magazine, admitted that their readers expected sex as well as drugs to be featured in the publication. One of the most remarkable cooptations was the belief, fostered by 1960s drug advocates, that drugs in some way provided sexual freedom and enhanced sexual enjoyment. Moreover, many conspicuous advocates of more-or-less stigmatized sexual activity embraced drug, tobacco, and alcohol use—not to mention offensive language—as expectable accompaniments of their distinctive outlooks.[15]

It is true that cultural trends were often almost impossible to separate from business interests. Nevertheless, both culture and profit seeking were important and valid determiners of historical developments. Moreover, as proponents of the minor vices coopted one another, they established a pattern that could be followed to bring other aspects of American culture and society into alliance with what was originally a deviant element. The appeal that 1920s anti-Prohibition campaigners had for tobacco manufacturers differed little from the capture of public officials who raised money through taxes on cigarettes, alcoholic beverages, and gambling. Both represented the process of cooptation. In each case, those who were coopted found themselves carried with the whole of the constellation of minor vices further than was their original intention in enlisting with just one part.

In coopting general cultural elements, the impact of the advocates of the bad habits was more far-reaching even than entangling businesses. In the case of lower-order parochialism and chronic rebelliousness, again, who coopted whom—from the time of the Victorian underworld on—is not always easy to discern. In general, like greed, cultural assertion helped galvanize the proponents of the minor vices into acting as historical forces. But in the end, only when significant monetary interest was present were deviant groups markedly successful in inverting more general social values.

Coopting the Media

Over many generations, the most crucial and influential cooptations occurred as the mass media developed and almost immediately came to serve the proponents of the bad habits. From the eighteenth century on, newspapers and magazines served increasingly as the voice of the community in complicated symbolic as well as direct ways. Writers in the press generally, with the owners and managers who ultimately controlled content, therefore played a crucial part in the evolution of the culture. For the most part, they spoke for established power groups and for whatever conformity consisted of at the time, and they largely defined what behavior was deviant and what was not.[16]

In the nineteenth century, long before television, the various advocates of the bad habits had already begun furtively and gradually to influence the press. The mass-circulation newspapers of the mid nineteenth century contained, in addition to conventional material, a great deal of material on crime and sex—material that served to define unacceptable behavior but at the same time to attack corruption in the upper classes, showing that social leaders misbehaved. Of course, such material sold newspapers and other publications. Because the attacks were on individual misbehaviors—for example a young sport from a leading family who murdered a prostitute—the social structure was not attacked, only particular people in it. The pioneer mass media also accepted advertising, much of it of an unrespectable kind—if not, for example, for lotteries, then at the very least, solicitations on behalf of medical quackery (not infrequently sexual in nature, aimed at those who needed cures for venereal disease or abortions).

From the new publishers' point of view, advertising from a variety of sources freed publications from political patronage and underwrote the independence of a newspaper or magazine. It fostered a relationship, however, that later would take an ironic turn as the publications became dependent upon the patronage of powerful advertisers.[17]

The journalists were therefore already appealing to the prejudices and interests of non-middle-class people and covertly the Victorian underworld. The new publishers themselves tended to have socially dubious backgrounds. So was established a convention in American journalism of sensationalism and social subversion. In emphasizing a storytelling style and giving close attention to details of crimes and the actions of miscreants, the sensationalist writers permitted the reader to empathize, to understand how a malefactor might have come to commit a crime. Formerly this empathic treatment had been reserved for the wealthy or for important officeholders. But gradually a new identification and model for the ordinary reader appeared, even if hemmed in by some explicit moralizing. In the meantime, other elements of information and entertainment, too, combined sensationalism with appeal to the lower-order parochialism that would make much stigmatized behavior private and free of social sanctions. The most notorious instance was the *Police Gazette*, which combined an interest in sports with sex and crime. The well-known series in that publication "The Lives of the Felons" already in the 1840s exemplified strong descriptions of deviance, individual responsibility (as opposed to the corrupting power of the social environment), and sensationalism—a sensationalism that had the potential for inducing empathy with wrongdoers. It was no wonder that "nice" parents at the time were alarmed when their children read this and similar material in "dime novels," from which anyone could learn authentic criminal slang and techniques and, presumably, attitudes.[18]

Such people as made up the Victorian underworld and the mobs who attacked anti-liquor and anti-prostitution crusaders did constitute an important market and constituency for the early mass media. When sensationalism grew in the press at the end of the nineteenth century, people of all classes came to enjoy it and accept it as "natural." Moreover, with the new sensational journalism came an explicit reaction against the moralism of the conservative press. The new journalists felt close to and in many ways admired the tough businesspeople and police and corrupt politicians and criminals and underworld characters about whom they chose to report. Theodore Dreiser, who also represented some of the artistic aspirations of realists and naturalists, spoke proudly of the writing profession: "One can always talk to a newspaper man, I think, with the full confidence that one is talking to a man who is at least free of moralistic mush."[19]

The reporters' and editors' and publishers' refusal to take a moralistic stand frustrated reformers at that time. Reformers were also alarmed by the explicit cynicism of those who controlled much of the voice of society. One reformer, for example, W. W. Ramsay, a clergyperson of Winchester, Ohio, in 1895 denounced not only the sins of omission of the newspaper people who refused to crusade but noted that the "press affords actual encouragement to the drink business by the repeated assertion that it cannot be suppressed, thus laying the foundation for its legalized existence for a money consideration." This observer quite correctly discerned how financial considerations reinforced cynicism: "There is no class of business that receives through advertising so much for its money as the liquor business." And, in fact, in the new cheap magazines of the turn-of-the-century era, advertising comprised as much as half of each issue. Finally, it was clear that advertising was something that people in the developing consumer culture liked to read.[20] So with the rise of modern journalism, sensationalism, cynicism, marketing, and business interest was the scenario set for a century.

By the beginning of the twentieth century, the combination of news and entertainment had broadened the concept of media to embrace not only print but theater and professional entertainment and sports. Although with separate roots, the print media and commercial entertainment evolved into the modern world of the media—bringing together, over many decades, newspapers, magazines, pulp magazines, and books, the theater, and then cabarets and night clubs, motion pictures, radio, music recordings, and television.[21]

The champions of the bad habits had two major direct avenues of approach to the developing information and entertainment media. One, obviously, was through business influence. Entertainment aspects of the media utilized shock and sex to gain audiences, up to the point that offensiveness or boycotts might cut down on patronage. Advertising, however, was the more pervasive means by which business considerations shaped media content. The other direct avenue to the media was through the writers and performers, an access that came chiefly, at least initially, through bohemian rebels and night life.[22] Once again, both culture and greed fostered the bad habits and an atmosphere tolerant if not friendly to them. Commercial interest through non-middle-class patronage was somewhat less direct but, as television rating wars showed, effective.

Advertising

Whereas, in the nineteenth century, advertising, to say nothing of news, concerning gambling was increasingly tabooed, by the late twentieth century, news media competed for gambling advertising, whether bingo, trips to casinos, or official state lotteries. Over many decades, news material included not only various kinds of sporting odds but much exposure of lottery chances and results. For both smoking and drinking, advertising exerted a powerful influence on the editorial content of the print media. The print media were in fact particularly vulnerable as technological change proceeded. As one editor from the 1930s reported,

> I recall a country editor who, 25 years ago, amazed his colleagues by cutting out all liquor and tobacco advertising. He didn't believe in the use of either of them, and he wasn't going to lend his newspaper to their propaganda. A few months ago he confided to me that he wanted to "change over" from a weekly to a tabloid daily—he figured the town had grown enough . . . , and besides, just look at all those fat cigarette advertising releases that went to the dailies.

No one could seriously doubt that editors of the Luce publications of midcentury were careful about what they printed, in view of the huge sums brought in by alcoholic-beverage advertising in Time, Inc. publications. In fact, studies show that those and other publications did trim their editorial sails in the face of tobacco and alcoholic-beverage advertising. In the 1980s, an official of the National Association of Broadcasters predicted that if all alcohol advertising were banned from the radio, a number of stations would go bankrupt. After all, 12 per cent of their revenue came from beer and wine ads. In addition to the advertising itself, other content was always affected.[23]

Although shaded editorial matter was often obvious, the most insidious form that advertising influence took was systematic "under-reporting" of the undesirable consequences of tolerating or patronizing the various bad habits.[24] This particular bias of the press (especially noticeable in the second half of the twentieth century) had the effect of making anyone who publicly discussed negative aspects of the bad habits appear to be deviant because such material was (with the exception of occasional flurries about drunk driving or drug use) itself unusual in normal public discourse. Suppression of bad news about bad habits therefore combined with other media presentations to prejudice even well-informed people against the idea that the bad habits might generate social liabilities.

Media interests were not different from any other important business interests. Where businesses representing any of the bad habits could, they influenced the press. One means was contributing ads to support a sympathetic organ. Alcoholic-beverage sellers worked on pre-Prohibition and post-repeal magazines alike. Members of the paraphernalia industry supported pro-drug publishers. The hunger of the media for advertising revenue not only made them vulnerable to pressure on nonadvertising content but also weakened efforts to control the content of ads themselves. As advertising merged into culture, this influence was also cultural—as well as simple business. The most obvious example was the openly nonmarital sexuality pioneered by the underground press of the late 1960s in advertising that showed up in the "straight" media in the guise of entertainment as well as suggestive copy—advertising that in the consumer culture constituted in fact an important form of entertainment.

Various population elements and pressure groups objected to the messages of the advertisers. In the late nineteenth century, the pressures of social responsibility were relatively effective in curbing advertisers. Then in the 1920s, the cigarette marketers confronted the traditional standards on the issue of advertising smoking for women. At that point, the advertisers faced the opposition down. Indeed, this was one of the turning points of the twentieth century, for it meant that proponents of the minor vices could utilize all aspects of the media to further the business interests of the bad habits without exciting really effective opposition. And so it worked out immediately, in alcoholic-beverage advertising and the advocacy of night life and other activities that twentieth-century "Puritans" supposedly disapproved of.

Indeed, the merchants of the minor vices then expanded greatly their indirect influences on the media. Whereas in the early decades of motion pictures, much of the smoking and drinking was cultural, by the television age, marketers were paying for subtle "exposure" of cigarettes and alcohol products in what still passed for entertainment vehicles (the cost for having Marlboro cigarettes featured in the 1981 movie *Superman II* was $42,500).[25] Similar exposure at sporting events was designed in part to appeal to the young, but of course people of all ages viewed the material as much as they would have billboards. And instances were recorded of similar promotions in popular-music events and materials.

There certainly was no evidence that any part of the advertising industry held out very long, or wanted to, any more than anyone else in the communications area. Smoking and drinking in particular showed up as incidental props in quite unrelated advertising, such as that for soap or telephone services. The goal, as in the overt smoking and drinking ads, not to mention those later for sexual rubber goods and drug paraphernalia, was to get away with whatever one could to move goods and services.[26]

Vulnerability of the Media

In short, the proponents of the minor vices over the long haul were able by commercial interest to coopt the media, which were both favorably inclined and vulnerable. The vulnerability centered particularly on two aspects of the media. The first was the way in which the mass media responded to manipulation, particularly manipulation by public-relations personnel who could create media events that the press would cover automatically. The news media in particular often invoked the fairness doctrine, whereby a second, counterbalancing point of view, however flawed, had to be presented if any material passed as news. So the media in the name of "fairness" publicized various cultural elements, including antisocial elements, even drug advocates and pedophiles. Indeed, in this way the media also gave the spokespersons for the bad habits a legitimate social status.[27]

The other vulnerability of the media lay in their automatic response, which has appeared repeatedly in previous chapters, to what might be construed as "censorship." Even advertising revenues were defended in the name of "freedom." In midcentury, the communications industry lined up openly with merchants of the minor vices to lobby for people and groups who were promoting any and all the bad habits.[28] People with the best of intentions invoked, first, artistic freedom and, then, freedom of expression on behalf of every single one of the bad habits and also made offensive language a symbol of those freedoms.

Advertising and public relations therefore shaded over into the cultural means by which, wittingly or unwittingly, the advocates of the bad habits coopted the media. But in the cultural realm, there was obviously still another weak link: the writers and those engaged in the creative aspects of entertainment.

Sometimes the cooptation of writers was direct. As in other industries, minor-vice businesses found any number of ways to reward friendly news coverage. Beginning in 1955, the Edgar Awards of the beer, wine, and liquor industry, for instance, went in many cases to journalists who supported the public relations of the industry. In 1961 alone, Harry Dole of *Life* magazine won the Friend of the Industry Award, and the *American Weekly* (a Sunday general newspaper supplement) won an award for Best Newspaper Article of Benefit to the Industry.[29]

Such straightforward business manipulation of the press was unremarkable in those decades and afterward. But over a long period of time, the writers and their editors showed themselves to be much more susceptible to the general influence of lower-order parochialism and rebellious/artistic bohemianism. Indeed, traditional newspaper people's affinity for the Victorian underworld carried over to the age of television. There was good reason why the anti-Prohibition Personal Liberty Association of the early 1920s was made up of veteran newspapermen. Remarkably consistent testimony showed that there was truth in the stereotype of the drinking journalist. "There is no great mystery about how newspapermen acquired the reputation of being heavy drinkers," wrote Stanley Walker in 1939. "They earned the reputation on honest and sometimes spectacular performance." An empirical study from a later period showed that outright alcoholism was in fact much more frequent among journalists than among other Americans.[30]

When not partaking of the stereotype of the hell-raising newspaper man or woman, writers participated conspicuously in two other twentieth-century institutions subversive of many conventional standards: cabaret and night-club society, and the overlapping avant-garde and bohemian society. Writers of various sorts (by the 1970s some of the leading journalists of the United States) also interacted with the drug culture in a most familiar way. Their presence at one famous party in 1977 led to the dismissal of Peter Bourne, the chief government drug official (but not the reporters who were also implicated).[31] When the proponents of the minor vices brought economic pressure to bear on the information and entertainment establishments, whether before or during the repeal era or half a century later, there already was in place a corps of writers, editors, producers, and other personnel who were inclined either out of rebelliousness or braggadocio to question older proprieties and to advocate the lifestyle that became so conspicuous in all the media in the second half of the twentieth century.

The New Popular Culture

But an additional institutional change pushed the media into siding against the respectable elements in society. In particular, the motion pictures of the early twentieth century created for the first time a truly formidable popular culture, alternative to high culture and uplift. Whereas yellow-journalism sensationalism and the publicizing of deviant behavior in dime novels and the *Police Gazette* had nourished cultural dissidents, the movies lent the underworld general recognition. Both audiences and producers of movies initially were overwhelmingly working class and immigrant. In New York, some early theaters had exits that went into saloons. Middle-class commentators from the beginning recognized that the movies were alien to uplift and also were a powerful cultural force—hence the brief pre-World War I attempt to control them. Clumsily, at first, the commercial motion pictures came to embody not only sensationalism but obvious—chiefly non-middle-class—social values. The ideal of night life as purveyed by the movies was of fundamental importance in the 1920s. In addition, everyone knew that matinee idols such as Fatty Arbuckle in their private lives set a very bad example that for many decades was widely publicized—and, by many, admired. Indeed, even aside from scandal, motion-picture profits were very important in financing the new parimutuel racetracks. Despite attempts to censor and introduce a superficial moralism into the films, both bohemian and lower-order rebelliousness continued for many decades to dominate the motion pictures and therefore the new genuinely popular culture. In movies, the moral earnestness of reformers became consistently a subject of satire.[32]

That same popular culture slowly came to dominate radio, beginning in the late 1920s. With the decisive intervention of extraneous commercial interest in this first electronic medium, a new standard was set for all the media. The affinity of radio and the movies created a world within which sensationalistic content combined with attitudes that promoted selling. The way was open therefore for both the cultural and the business influences of the proponents of bad habits—especially in the age of television. From smoking and drinking in the silent films of the 'twenties to the ingress of drugs and ambiguous aggression into the content of both print and electronic presentations of the 1970s, media embodying popular culture were willing—and usually lucrative—supporters. Indeed, when television impinged on the profitability of supposedly "family" movies, the motion-picture studios first modified and then in 1966 jettisoned the voluntary code that had restrained some of the content for thirty years.[33]

There were two remarkable aspects of the new popular culture that started with the early movies. First, it came to be taken for granted, as if it were natural and good. Critics—and there were innumerable critics over the years—acquired from both the industry and the media the negative labels of elitist or moralistic. Among the bulk of Americans, popular culture came to symbolize American culture. The night club and gangster along with automobiles and Coca-Cola and other consumer items were all served up together as Hollywood glamour.[34]

But the electronic media especially developed a relationship to individual Americans that had no precedent. When radio came into the home, it disrupted normal social relations and rendered the front porch, from which one could visit with neighbors, superfluous, as human relationships began to give way to those that came out of the air. The movies, too, intruded into previous social relationships, particularly among young people. A new peer-group pattern, decidedly alien to the home and even the community, grew up as youngsters attended the movies, almost always in groups, and their conversation came to concern what they had experienced as they did so. By the 1970s, sociologists could measure the extent to which intense relationships developed between individuals and the television world—beyond the way in which, for example, fictive characters and commercials provided one of the dominant topics of such conversations as still took place.[35]

Over a period of many decades, critics of the media and especially of the electronic media assembled a damning indictment of what was purveyed to the public. The most effective part of the indictment was the relatively transparent way in which popular-culture media exposed young people to bad examples and unhealthy influences. Critics traced tendencies toward antisocial behavior not only to the electronic media but even to the comic books in which cartoon characters reflected traditional dime-novel material in a graphic form. Ever more graphic television violence contributed substantially to both generating violent behavior and persuading people to tolerate it. Ironically, in a supposedly sophisticated age, both producers and consumers of this material denied the blatantly sadistic element in it (a point not lost on people two or three generations earlier who objected, for example, to boxing films and turned out not to be as naive as their descendants). A critic of post-World War II comic books cited a sequence in which a man shot in the stomach and grimacing in agony was ridiculed: "Any water he'd drink'd pour right out of his gut! It'd be MURDER!" (The publisher was "Tiny Tots Comics, Inc.")[36]

The way in which cooptation worked on the media was therefore relatively transparent. The depiction of smoking, drinking, gambling, swearing, misbehaving sexually, and even taking drugs attracted large audiences, which translated into advertising and sales. Gangster material—firmly fixed in popular culture by movies of the 1930s—and its equivalent also aided the proponents of the minor vices, not only by encouraging impulsive behavior but also by emphasizing personal, not social, standards. In 1948, seven of the ten most popular radio programs were comedies such as the slapstick and wisecracking *Fibber McGee and Molly*. Ten years later, seven of the top television programs were violent Westerns, such as *Gunsmoke*.[37] At the same time, of course, moral earnestness, with regard especially to the bad habits, continued to be depicted unfavorably, especially in "entertainment."

The impact of the media, and particularly the electronic media, went far beyond the relatively explicit messages. The major effect of the media was to cultivate a lifestyle—a term that had meaning only in a culture in which the major aspirations were acts and fantasies of consumption. Over the years, the media, and especially television, shaped character by setting models of behavior and by legitimating—both directly and indirectly—decisions to act in antisocial ways. In particular, as Richard Maltby points out, the great loosening of plot narrative and the emphasis on character in the 1970s "permitted stars to perform antisocial activities with impunity," and movie stars such as Paul Newman and Robert Redford "charmed their audiences into acquiescing in criminal activities. . . ." [38]

Popular Music

The proponents of the minor vices in the twentieth century enlisted particularly effectively the medium of popular music, both recorded and live. The impact of rock-and-roll music was so remarkable that it has already appeared in my narratives. The effectiveness grew out of the fact that listening to or producing musical material appeared for a long time to be an innocent activity. By the 1920s, objections to the "turkey trot" and other fad dancing and music were hooted down. Only late in the process, then, did both opponents and proponents make the "sex, drugs, and rock 'n roll" link, despite the fact that rock music was an unusually important social phenomenon. Even then it was still easy to ridicule people who took seriously the idea that rock had any serious social effects. Moreover, opposition was also labeled merely generational change in musical taste. Hence, champions of the bad habits were able to coopt young people further and use musical fashions to move many toward a lifestyle that carried in it tolerating, if not indulging in, the minor vices.

Parts of popular music, especially that popular among lower-order and working-class groups, had a long history of embodying and sometimes expressing social rebelliousness and subversion—jazz, rhythm and blues, country, and folk genres. Early in the twentieth century, when such music, and the dances that went with it, came to mainstream Americans' attention, many conservatives were alarmed. They particularly recognized the potentially subversive nature of one type of non-middle-class musical expression, jazz, in which—beyond the emotionalism of the music—apparently nonsense terms in the lyrics were in fact sexual slang, like the term "jazz" itself, originally a very offensive four-letter word.[39]

As was suggested in connection with the history of drugs, the jazz community comprised a usually "advanced" part of the American social groups who advocated rebelliousness. From early on, jazz appeared frequently and significantly in places in which upper-class or bohemian elements might go slumming. In their habits and in their lyrics, the jazz people were therefore already helping provide to intellectual rebels, theater folks, and other "advanced" people an idea of an alternative lifestyle. Critic Seymour Krim in 1958, for example, believed (and apparently hoped) that "jazz always existed in an atmosphere of drugs, marijuana, booze, and a general air of franticness" and that those uninhibited "new jazz-pleasure values . . . [had] finally crumbled the shaky house of U.S. puritanism . . . 'responsibility,' 'thrift,' 'thou shalt not. . . .' "[40]

As technological developments furthered the rise of nontraditional popular music, by the 1950s a number of middle-class groups "discovered" what was in effect a counterculture of non-middle-class musicians who had new markets based on post-World War II prosperity. In the middle of the 1950s, especially with Elvis Presley, the suggestive singer, rock and roll hit the mass media as a major part of popular culture. As noted in previous chapters, the overt messages of the lyrics grew bolder. In the

1950s, Presley sang "Love Me Tender," which, like some of the older jazz and blues songs, communicated sexual passion clearly. A decade later, an explicitly rebellious group, the Fugs, sang songs like "Boobs a Lot" and "Wet Dream Over You." By the 1980s, a significant stream of rock groups were scandalizing even parents who had themselves grown up with rock. The lyrics and publicity releases described and advocated violence and particularly the degradation of women in terms that were the most extreme available. Tipper Gore told how she was impelled to warn parents against rock when in 1984 she bought for her eleven-year-old daughter a record by a rock star, Prince, only to find lyrics on it about a woman masturbating with a magazine in a hotel lobby.[41]

Over several decades, young Americans all over the country learned with their peers to emulate the new musical style and defend the attitudes embedded in it. Clearly these generations learned to find in the music an intense, perhaps mystical experience. Commentators noted that rock and roll represented a new dimension of popular music. As a 1970 critic wrote about the Rolling Stones:

> All that counted was sound and the murderous mood it made. All din and mad atmosphere. Really it was nothing but beat, smashed and crunched and hammered home like some amazing stampede. The words were lost and the song was lost. You were only left with chaos, beautiful anarchy. You drowned in noise.[42]

Many middle-class American adolescents and young adults in the mid twentieth century identified with the delinquent teenagers so widely denounced in the press. Moreover, despite the large quantities of money that American young people had, many of them also identified at least for a time with oppressed groups so that black and working-class music held a special appeal. Hippie spokespersons as well as agents of lower-order parochialism claimed rock for the young and alienated of all classes. With the music, came lower-order values and attitudes, right out of the nineteenth-century underworld. Whereas fans earlier were primarily female, young males took over much of rockdom. In the lyrics, at least, the standards included heroes whom one analyst described as follows:

A. They are front-runners in socially unacceptable practices and illegal activities.
B. They are notoriously individualistic and egotistically arrogant about their personal reputations.

C. They rarely take time to "sing the blues," to rationalize their plight, or to philosophize about their actions—instead, they are invariably action-oriented and habituated to the practices of physical violence.

D. They may be black or white, rich or poor, young or old, married or single, or from rural or urban areas—but they are invariably prone to exhibitionism in a variety of activities including dress, dance, and sexual behavior.

E. They are accustomed to dealing in drugs (using and pushing), in alcohol (consuming, brewing, and distributing), and in various forms of gambling as keys to their physical well-being and economic existence.

F. They are hostile to all forms of authority, from dictatorial high school principals to nagging wives—but reserve a special loathing for police officers.

G. They reject all conventional forms of social courtesy, legal sanction, intimate relationships.[43]

It would be difficult to assemble a better list of the goals of the combined proponents of the minor vices than these abstracted from late-twentieth-century rock lyrics and performances.

Analysts of that period generally agreed that the music in and of itself was not as important as the way in which the presentations, electronic and live, direct and through the media, coopted young people into becoming advocates of a distinctive "youth" style. The contents of the youth style were set by commercial interest that was fueled at first by consumerism and then by a frantic search for self-indulgence—another side of which was rejecting traditional moral and achievement attitudes. As Dave Marsh, a rock critic who started out with a Detroit magazine, *Creem*, recalled, the music was incidental to "what went on at the edge of the music." He noted specifically, ". . . everyone I know got involved in all of this—rock and roll—to get laid, centrally. I really believe this, bet you could prove it scientifically." In fact, the number of sexually explicit songs in the so-called top ten, such as "Hot Child in the City," about juvenile prostitution, or "Let's Do It in the Road," increased dramatically between 1973 and 1983, parallel with explicit references to the minor vices in all the media.[44]

By advocating illegal drugs, participants in the rock-music experience helped confirm a group identity. They were in opposition. They were even embracing the marginality of rock and, based on implications of being possibly deviant, seeking to break loose and have an experience out of the ordinary. At the legendary rock concert at Woodstock, a slogan was "Keep America Beautiful—Stay Stoned." Many rock groups set out to see how outrageous—in a very ordinary sense—they could appear. Over the years, still following the heroic aspirations noted above, virtually every traditionally respectable standard was assailable by even broadly popular groups.[45]

The drive to coopt rock and roll for the various bad habits came not just from lower-order parochials overjoyed to see children of the "nicest" people mouthing offensive words and adhering to a "slum" standard. Important economic groups sprang up selling the electronic delivery of sound, merchants who had every reason to want to expand their sales by means of promotion and sensationalism. Record and sound-equipment advertisements were essential to keeping much of the underground press going—regardless, apparently, of the editorial or advertising content, no matter how extreme. Nor did these businesspeople have scruples about other audiences in their quest to reach likely users of their goods. After other nonsexual advertisers had dropped out, the last full-page ad to appear in the blatantly pornographic *Hustler*, in April 1978, was from a hi-fi maker (Audi). The softer competitor, *Penthouse*, as early as 1970 featured full-page ads from Columbia Records—right alongside alcoholic-beverage and, later, cigarette and condom ads. The advertising alone showed the power of rock and roll to move the promotion of the entire constellation of bad habits from marginal to central, and to do so even while targeting youngsters. Record sales passed a billion dollars as early as 1968, with teenagers buying 81 per cent of all records. At one point, 70 per cent of the readers of *Rolling Stone* owned at least one musical instrument.[46]

By using the superficial format of conventional mercantile practices, the advertisers and sellers undermined the critics of rock-and-roll music. Since the music was publicized as a novelty, most early commentators believed that it was a temporary fad no more serious than teenagers' wearing penny loafers. Safe in the identity of unremarkable profit-seekers, apparently respectable economic exploiters encouraged outrageous behavior because it could get attention and sales among affluent teen peer groups. By the late 1960s, music companies were hiring "company freaks" and "kept hippies" (colorful characters who used expressive and outrageous behavior to attract attention) to push their products. The exploiters covered their actions by explaining that the music and the musical acts were mere entertainment. In fact, both the positive aspirations of the constellation and the fundamental negativism of the combined minor vices found a superb vehicle in youth-oriented rock—the music/entertainment idols, the repeated messages of the lyrics, and above all the style. As Jim Morrison of the Doors asserted, "I'm interested in anything about revolt, disorder, chaos, especially activity that has no meaning. It seems to me to be the road to freedom." If rock no longer appeared to some people as subversive in the 1980s as it had earlier, it was either because the culture had changed to conform to the rock program or because conservative standard setters were still unaware of the content, style, and impact of "mere entertainment"— or both. "Punk," which flowered in the late 1970s, carried rock into a discernible destructiveness of form that was in the tradition of Dada and the Nazis, advocating the unthinkable, as in extreme pornography. By the 1980s, an important segment of rock musicians were imitating compulsive pornography explicitly.[47]

Coopting the "Good" People

As must by now be obvious, the proponents of the minor vices succeeded so well because they often masked greed and lower-order parochialism not only as innocuous business but as civic virtue. In so doing, advocates of the bad habits made their aspirations appear to belong on the side of the angels. The ultimate cooptation therefore was the cooptation of "good" people.

The standard tactic used in the campaigns of all the bad habits was established early, long before the repeal campaign. The editor of a saloon publication in 1907, for example, denounced the conventionally good people as themselves the sources of trouble:

> The greatest obstacle to sane, sound and safe government in America to-day is that small-headed, narrow-minded element which believes that human nature can be made good by law. It stands in the way of the sensible regulation of the social evil [prostitution]. It secured the abolition of the Army canteen and is consequently responsible for the spread of various evils among our private soldiers. At present it is trying to take the sport of horse-racing out of the hands of the gentlemen who have made it reputable and to hand it over to the keeping of crooked gamblers and black legs. It harrasses billposters who post burlesque or ballet posters, finds pruriency in works of art, fine statues and rare paintings, and even attempts to stop theatrical performances which are powerful sermons and suppress books that point great morals.[48]

The editor thus linked the minor vices together and asked for their acceptance as "sane, sound and safe," not to mention civilized—exactly the program of the alcoholic-beverage sellers and their allies for decades before and after. By sounding like reformers themselves, such partisans of the bad habits coopted many well-meaning Americans. And there was no evident limit, ultimately, to the ways in which proponents of the minor vices were able to use "good" elements in society to advance merchandising and parochialism.[49]

One of the traditional virtues that supporters of the bad habits embraced conspicuously was moderation. Opponents claimed that moderation opened floodgates. By the last half of the twentieth century, critics could point to excessive drinking, gambling, and other practices that bad-habit partisans still justified in the name of moderation. Moderation was particularly easy to invoke in a consumer culture in which extremes were often not deviant any longer. If individuals judged their own moderation, there was in fact no social restraint—obviously, again, the goal of the proponents of the bad habits—so they could advocate teaching children to drink—moderately—or smoke and take drugs moderately. Yet many "good" people over many generations joined forces with the proponents of the minor vices in the name of moderation.

Intellectuals and Bohemians

An especially prominent group of people who increasingly supported the minor vices were the traditional intellectuals and artists, particularly as they shaded into bohemians and social rebels.[50] They were vulnerable in two ways especially, above and beyond the elemental rebelliousness that appears throughout this book.

First, intellectuals and artists often tended to value hedonism, particularly in the context of art and music, in which subjective sensation was at least part of the act of appreciation if not of creativity. Proponents of sexual rebelliousness, drinking, and drugs all appealed to artistic or theoretical hedonism in one form or another. In the late twentieth century, supporters of drinking, smoking, taking drugs, gambling, sexual misbehavior, and even of uttering oaths argued explicitly and intellectually the justification that one or all of them made one feel good. Artistic quests for new subjective experiences led to the drug advocacy of Timothy Leary and Richard Alpert. A number of such thinkers argued sincerely that "expanding one's consciousness" could have effects that were both personally and socially desirable.[51]

Especially in the 1960s, advocates of the bad habits jumped in and used bohemians and would-be bohemians to mask business strategies and the advocates' determination to spread all the minor vices. The symbolic event was the 1967 San Francisco summer of love, founded chiefly on the essentially religious tactic of attempting to show that society could be changed by changing individuals' consciousnesses. The movement almost immediately fell into the hands of exploiters. Not only did hard-drug pushers take over in bohemian San Francisco, but also, as one eyewitness put it, ". . . the big-time Las Vegas act moved in, minus the slot machines and crap-tables, but the rest of the action was there. There is more money in tits, booze, neon, smack, and professional pussy than there is in poetry and pot."[52] But throughout the twentieth century, again and again, intellectuals and bohemians with the best of intentions focused on subjective experience to the point that they usually did not notice the ways in which they served such purposes as greed and parochialism.

Intellectuals and bohemians were also vulnerable to the proponents of the minor vices through their fears of censorship. In the history of all the bad habits, appeals to liberty and freedom repeatedly operated to cover the advance of the advocates of all elements in the constellation. If some attack on the vices threatened the profits of any businessperson, like the saloon editorialist of 1907 just quoted, the entrepreneur would trot out censorship and repressiveness to frighten anyone connected to the world of art and intellect. The romantic idea that art makes its own rules fitted well into the notion that no person should be inhibited, especially if the activity involved some advantage to a businessperson, whatever the business. People could actually, as William Philips noted in 1967, "make a principle of going out of bounds in every possible way—in morals, in sex, in art."[53]

Such a principle served the advocates of the bad habits well. They confused freedom of thought with freedom of commercial exploitation. They were particularly successful in confusing literature with pornography ("porno chic," as one 1970s commentator dubbed it), with the result that any criticism of the actions of an individual—or his/her commercial suppliers—could be tied to the issue of freedom of expression. As another critic of the 1970s noted, "A goodly portion of contemporary American fiction dedicated itself to the full-throated affirmation that surrender to instinct was somehow good for the soul, the supreme blessedness of existence."⁵⁴ Not just pornotopia but all the minor vices thrived on this type of emphasizing impulse.

It would be an error to underestimate the impact of the intellectual elite and avant garde, however few their numbers. Literary, artistic, and intellectual figures had profound influence in defying censorship, in setting new standards. Liberal highbrow magazines, for example, not book publishers, took the lead in the mid-1920s campaign against indecency censorship.⁵⁵ Particularly the media and entertainment worlds were conduits for rebelliousness. Just as Prohibition repealers utilized writers' and artists' works of satire to advance repeal interests, cabaret and artistic and underworld people all played into and reinforced one another's attempts to undermine traditional community standards and hypocrisies. In this context, intellectuals were fundamental, both directly and indirectly, in bringing the new standards to what Americans read, saw, and heard in both high and popular culture.

Reformers

One of the reasons that the proponents of the minor vices were so successful in arguing that they represented liberty and freedom was that many conscientious people were genuinely alarmed about repression of ideas and expression in the post-World War I Red Scare and in the McCarthy era of the 1950s. Dramatic defeats of inept censors in the 1920s and later were engineered by people who were genuine, public-spirited reformers. Many Americans came to think, with good evidence, that they had to support all attempts at free expression. "Free," however, came ultimately to include a wide variety of stances that were at the very least problematic. In the 1950s, for example, conspiracy-minded officials sometimes tied their Red baiting to the contemporary narcotics scare and even argued, as in a headline in the *Los Angeles Times* in 1951, "Dope's Flow Said to Have Red Backing."⁵⁶ Such material led civil libertarians to confuse repression of ideas with repression of drug taking.

It was under these circumstances that, for example, the National Student Association came out for legalization of marijuana in 1967. The sentiments could be understood to be liberal, but the resolution was in fact drafted in part by LEMAR, the marijuana advocacy group then supported substantially by dealers. Freedom of the press was an especially consistent theme used to justify the unfettered flow of advertising dollars. Obnoxious patent-medicine vendors and media owners had used the same slogan for generations, as did the merchants of the minor vices when there was any chance that their advertising might be curtailed.[57]

Playing the censorship and repression themes, the Prohibition repeal forces of the 1920s scared not only liberals but even public-health organizations away from any attempt to criticize alcoholic-beverage merchandising. By midcentury, any charitable organization that could get funding from undesirable sources was expected to do so, just as businesspeople were expected to service any trade—or bad habit. When in 1976 the Chicago Lung Association as a remarkable exception to cooptation declined to accept an offer of some free publicity in *Hustler* magazine, the editor dubbed the well-meaning organization "Asshole of the Month."[58]

During much of the twentieth century, the most useful citizens who should have stood up for reform in fact collapsed in the face of ridicule and other forms of social and financial pressure that the proponents of the minor vices increasingly had at their command. Some collaborators were formally connected to the component bad habits, such as the Drug Abuse Council or various state liquor "control" boards. Others were simply good people caught up in naive attempts at a very limited and ostensibly irrelevant charitable or civic purpose, such as the program in the early 1980s of Ketchikan, Alaska, to enhance tourism and urban renewal by restoring—and hence romanticizing—the Creek Street red-light district.[59] These random examples can be only suggestive of the pervasive movement over most of the twentieth century. The supporters of the bad habits never relented. They moved in on every reform or charity to coopt whenever possible the cultural as well as economic and political leaders of all parts of the United States.

Religious Bodies

At the beginning of the twentieth century, merchandisers of alcoholic beverages understood that religious bodies represented the major force against alcoholic beverages. By the mid twentieth century, socially active Protestant churches had been intimidated by the ridicule of the repeal era, and they turned to other issues. In the age of *Playboy*, representatives of most major churches did not stand up to powerful business interests, and reformers in the churches tended to focus on politico-economic social problems. In the World War I era, Protestant leaders came to believe that attempting, for example, to hold to extremes of purity in the public arena was not profitable. In the name of sex education and highbrow literature, the leadership retreated. Especially after World War II, the Methodists shifted their attention from temperance to helping individual alcoholics. Roman Catholics had always been at least divided on the issues of drinking and gambling. Their increasingly ethnic base often discouraged the leadership from opposing lower-order parochialism. Conservative Catholics' attempts to work for sexual purity were very often inept and received unfavorable treatment in the media. Even on the applied level, church influence was often frustrated if not coopted. For example, in Nevada in the 1960s and 1970s, Mormons whose rectitude and citizenship were beyond question found themselves in the gambling and alcoholic-beverage businesses.[60]

Proponents of the minor vices took full advantage of every weakness and division in the churches. But the most curious cooptation, and the most subtle, came under the heading of true love, which captured profoundly pious church people for sexual hedonism. Peter Gardella has shown how first liberal religionists tried to remove sinful implications from sexual pleasure, in the early twentieth century, and then, in the 1960s and 1970s, fundamentalists, who were rejecting much of modern America, came to praise sexual pleasure, even to identify religious experience with sexual excitement. The end result was to place a very high value on the sexual experience, much as were contemporary advertisers and pornotopians. They all played into the efforts of the proponents of "the family" who had various sexual activities as a hidden agenda in their advocacy (the best example: the organized sex-in-a-group movement was resoundingly pro-family).[61]

The Split among Reformers

Early in the twentieth century, and especially after the end of the Progressive era, the prosocial forces of American society split. As early as 1907, social critic Edward A. Ross attacked the "old Puritans" and praised American leaders who "see in graft and monopoly and foul politics worse enemies than beer, Sunday baseball, and the army canteen."[62] Over the years, the "good" people who were concerned with morals and social and community standards tended to ignore the issue of social justice for workers and ethnic minorities. The rest of the "good" people, liberals who tended to work for social justice, left themselves open to cooptation by the advocates of the bad habits because of a tendency to indulge minority groups of all kinds, including behavior groups. This cooptation was most notably embodied in the *Playboy* program in the 1950s and 1960s that included not only anti-censorship "liberty" but, within a few years, some civil rights. Over the years, urban liberals additionally reacted against the politics of the political and religious right that often invoked formulations of "traditional morality." It was such stimuli that pushed well-intentioned advocates of a pluralistic society to accept the idea that sexual misbehavior, gambling, and the like should enjoy equal status and recognition with ethnic and religious and class peculiarities. In the 1960s, leaders of the Sexual Freedom League (dedicated to unimpeded, guilt-free "sexual expression with other consenting persons") described themselves as "persons of a minority persuasion" and their status and stance comparable to that of other American minorities.[63]

One of the great victories of the proponents of the bad habits was to be able to ally themselves with people in the mid twentieth century who spoke up about social wrongs and stupidities. In this way, what was "bad" came to look to many Americans to be a "good" thing. Particularly in midcentury, powerful artists influenced a whole generation into such a confusion. As Richard Fantina wrote of the revolutionary rock group the Fugs in 1966–1967, "To be young and innocent and to see this band proved that your instincts were right. Sex wasn't bad. War was cruel and wasteful. And drugs were fun."[64]

Once again, the processes of social deviance played into the hands of those who were turning values upside down. One important set of groups, the homophiles, illustrates strikingly the way in which the underworld coopted otherwise irrelevant social elements into advocating the whole constellation of minor vices.

Most accounts of American homophiles (those whose private sexual preferences were directed toward people of the same gender) have focused on those who became politically active and attempted to win public respect and recognition. In addition, implicitly or explicitly hostile accounts have emphasized a small but sometimes conspicuous group who imitated seductive prostitutes and who fulfilled social expectations of a deviant stereotype. In fact, there were large numbers of homophiles who lived quiet lives and often held positions of great social influence, most particularly in the potent fields of the arts and entertainment. Moreover, many homophiles, at least in the twentieth century, were important citizens and leaders of reform.[65] For the proponents of the minor vices, this group of social uplifters was a prime—and vulnerable—target.

As labeled deviants, homophiles had for generations often been driven into the underworld and, in the case of middle-class people, cabaret life. There other minor-vice elements attempted to attach to them all the then-deviant behaviors. As early as Mae West's drama *The Drag* (1927), for example, homophiles were associated with drug abuse. One public space that was sometimes available for such citizens was the drinking place, and so the "gay bar" developed. But most members of this heterogeneous population continued to split their lives: they aspired to be respectable publicly while they had a subterranean existence under private circumstances. The first homophile organizations were elaborately and strikingly prosocial in identity, not antisocial.[66]

When the media took up gay liberation in the 1960s and 1970s, the "perversions" of stereotyped homophiles' sexual activities served to legitimate lack of restraint in everyone's sexual performance—a plank in the platform of both the sexual underground and those who hoped to improve the world through fulfillment. Since no-restraint in general was the central goal of the advocates of the bad habits, the homophiles thus found that their desire to break taboos in one limited area of behavior carried them into alliance with extremes and lack of restraint in other areas. So, for example, when gay liberation became public, spokespersons often advocated the use of offensive language and drugs. A Boston woman who went public in the 1960s recalled, "Learning to drink played a big role. The whole culture revolved around the bars." A new machismo fueled sadomasochistic activities and bisexuality (always a part of the underworld). In the media, homosexual prostitution came to compete successfully with more traditional streetwalking as a normal social institution. Altogether, the media influenced the young among the homophiles to ally with not only alcohol marketing and drug dealing but more general stereotyped misbehavior. As one columnist in a homophile publication wrote in 1969, "No snow-job will convince people we're all sexless saints. Why try?" Older members of homophile groups also absorbed new antisocial standards. Harassment by police had already, of course, prepared many of them to some degree to embrace dissenting and even antisocial attitudes.[67]

By the late twentieth century, then, many homophile Americans who had favored the best in society, had shifted to acting as another set of advocates for all the bad habits. Earlier in the century, many quiet, middle-class lesbians, in particular, had in individual capacities represented real bulwarks against underworld values. Now such people frequently found themselves pushed toward allying with alcoholic-beverage marketers, drug smugglers, prostitutes, pornographers, and other Americans who wanted to break down all restraints on behavior. Many of these former upholders of respectable society surrendered to macho lower-order parochialism or to any businessperson who wanted to service the hedonism of the conventional vices. In the late 1960s, for example, the *Advocate* began as an anti-censorship, consenting-adults publication. Within two years, it began carrying "beefcake" pictures and material about supporters among nightlife and bar personnel. To protect one limited, isolated kind of sometimes-stigmatized activity, all homophiles found themselves pressured toward supporting an inversion of an entire set of values.

Cooptation on the Individual Level

So far this chapter has summarized some of the cooptations described in the parallel narratives, adding a few additional concrete examples to try to show the pattern in which over many decades the proponents of the minor vices either actively enlisted other elements in society or at least subverted opposition. It is appropriate that historical movements, as such, affect large groups of people and have an impact on impersonal social institutions. But the patterns in the histories also suggest how the cooptation process operated at the individual level. The process of cooptation was not a mere generalized abstraction but affected, in their own lives, the attitudes and behaviors of, ultimately, the bulk of the individuals in the population.

One model for change in this type of behavior is that of an epidemic, in which infectious disease spreads from person to person. From the nineteenth century, G. Stanley Hall (quoted in Chapter 7) provided a graphic description of the way in which sexual misbehavior spread from one person to another, beginning with a single individual in the community. More than a century later, social-psychological researchers examining American society demonstrated that, regardless of gender, virgins did not seduce virgins. Almost invariably, a nonvirgin was still the source and occasion of new sexual behavior.[68] Other social scientists at about the same time made notorious the fact that drug taking spread from individual user to individual nonuser.

Clearly people from the underworld or from deviant groups could start the infection of many individuals by employing any, or all, of the minor vices. But modern studies suggest that other factors also operated. In addition to individual persuasion, peer groups determined behavior. Sociologists of midcentury and later particularly identified the army and college fraternities (not to mention the traditional street gangs of youths) as significant "deviant" influences leading young subjects into smoking and drinking and other "bad habits" and then reinforcing that behavior. From the experience of these limited subjects of academic investigation, it is easy to extrapolate the impact of similar groups. The universal pattern was: people developed from peer groups their susceptibility to the contagion of values and behavior. High-school students who became problem drinkers in the late twentieth century, for example, were markedly more "peer oriented" than fellow students. Finally, it should be spelled out that peer groups, especially of young people, were profoundly affected by the mass media, which implicitly coordinated individuals and groups alike and at times functioned in the place of peer groups. Either as individuals in an epidemic or as members of peer groups in which everybody was "doing it," by the late twentieth century, individuals had to be ready—culturally prepared—to take up any of the minor vices. The media functioned as the primary agency in that cultural preparation.[69]

How did individual cooptation work out in practical terms? In almost every case, it started with either a public space or some initially innocent social activity or, of course, a combination of the two. Friends—or strangers—of any age might have come together to play a game or make music or just socialize, or might, say, have participated in a more formal athletic organization such as flourished among some ethnic groups. There might have been an ethno-religious gathering for any purpose, or no purpose. Or someone may have gone slumming. In each case, some commercial interest imposed itself on the activity—some purveyor of alcoholic beverages, most commonly, but it could have been people who made money from gambling or pornographic materials. Often the commercial interest was represented by someone close to or familiar to the group, such as—prototypically—the drug user/seller. Or the commercial interest might have entered in impersonal ways, particularly as mass society and mass media became more pervasive in the lives of twentieth-century Americans. It might have come in the form of cigarette advertisements that found a ready set of children or adolescents or gatherings of young people. It might simply have come as part of the impact of sensationalizing mass media and advertising generally, especially as individuals developed intense relationships with media fantasies.

There were therefore a number of circumstances and combinations of circumstances in which the bad habits spread by an individual route. All this was taking place in a culture in which both deviant identities and an underworld existed. If one was not born into the underworld, it was possible for a person to choose, temporarily or permanently, some activity that was deviant—either on a private, possibly rebellious basis, typically on the inspiration of the media, or as a visitor or recruit to the underworld. In such cases, the behavior could be isolated so that the person was simply a temporary and garden-variety hypocrite and still prosocial in identification—do as I say, not as I do. Or the behavior could change the identity of the person so that that person became an advocate and recruiter for a single one of the bad habits—a deviancy—or all of them. This was the familiar attempt to make true the belief that everybody does it.

Commercial interest, in particular, operated through one of the most potent agencies aiding the individual advance of the minor vices, consumption communities. Mass consumer society began in the late nineteenth century to develop new impersonal social groupings—the consumption communities—in which people who bought one type of commodity or even brand of commodity or another found themselves linked to other consumers with whom they shared the identity of buying a particular item and identifying with that item. All major marketers exploited this new type of identity, which was spread primarily through advertising. At one time, the Packard Motor Car Company urged, "Ask the man who owns one." Later, a soft-drink merchandiser persuaded people to identify with "the Pepsi Generation." From the 1920s repeal propaganda attempting to set an upper-class and respectable image of the consumption community of drinkers, to all the advertising of the mid and late twentieth century, merchants who had something to gain created these abstract but effective groups in which people imagined themselves to be linked to—and reinforced by—shared acts of consumption. Shared consumptions involved not only pens and household cleansers but also cigarettes, alcoholic beverages, records, sexual products and publications, gambling and sports, and of course drugs. In addition to the group identified directly with a commodity, merchandisers claimed other consumer groups as well. In 1959, for example, beer producers began a campaign to convince customers of bowling alleys that bowling was traditionally tied to beer drinking. In the era of mass media, the consumer communities could and did function as peer groups for a majority and more of Americans. As various historians have emphasized, in the consumer culture of the mid-to-late twentieth century, the act of buying a product came to represent a form of social belonging. In order to participate in the culture fully, a person had to acquire or imagine acquiring publicized goods—and those came to include the products of the commercial side of the minor vices, including all the items involved in the bad habits—alcoholic beverages, cigarettes, lottery tickets, *Playboy*, and sometimes marijuana cigarette papers.[70]

Through such multifarious cooptations, the proponents of the bad habits enlisted innumerable supporters and penetrated into every aspect of American life, beginning in the late nineteenth century. The cooptations led to deceiving appearances. Fanatical defenders of personal liberty in the post-repeal repealers' groups served the alcoholic-beverage merchandisers by working to expose children to education in alcohol use. The undoubted good of the Police Athletic League in helping youngsters go straight, and even the national and personal benefits of physical education, could unwittingly contribute to a system that supported indiscriminate gambling. The histories of each bad habit and innumerable further examples all confirm the basic pattern of increasing numbers of cooptations in American society over a long period of time.

From the Victorian underworld, from expanding business corporations and aggressive marketers, from population groups in revolt against parts of the dominant social order, cultural and particularly pecuniary interest pushed the constellation of minor vices into the entire continuum of institutions that comprised American society, including those dominated by "good" people. Each small step appeared inconsequential at the time—an individual decision, some high jinks with a peer group, a new account in a business, a new style, some harmless entertainment. And a small step could be taken by someone otherwise not a collaborator with proponents of the minor vices. But in each case, the change represented a step in the process by which advocates of the bad habits managed to gain economic and cultural dominance as Americans moved into postindustrial prosperity.

Patterns of Convergence
in a Complex Society

The successes of the advocates of the minor vices were portentous. But in the secular world of nineteenth- and twentieth-century America, it must have seemed silly to take every little aspect of misbehavior seriously. Certainly there ought to have been a place for innocent fun and colorful style. And in a society in which impersonal social change operated, why should one person's single action have had any significance?

Yet it was precisely the openings created by such commonsense observations that permitted the Victorian underworld to expand so effectively. Through myriad individual actions and the inclinations of whole population groups, the often-unwitting proponents of the minor vices managed the transformation of a culture. The process ended in the convergence and social dominance of these proponents of the minor vices. What had begun so innocuously as indulgence in bad habits in early-nineteenth-century America ended as major historical change in the twentieth. Through a variety of cultural means, advocates of the minor vices came to set public discourse and shape the actions of even Americans who originally avoided and opposed the bad habits.

So far, the evidence has indicated the ways in which champions of the minor vices shaped common cultural patterns over many generations. Many of the witnesses cited were moralistic, the materials those of exposés or, recently, of enthusiasts in the modern consumers' movement. For many decades, cynical media and leadership figures have conditioned most Americans to reject or discount or ignore such evidence. Rehashing violations of decency or restraint can sound like breathless naïveté or tiresome muckraking. But now it is necessary to ask, why believe a witness with commercial interest or a witness defending questionable behavior more than a moralistic witness?

When all the evidence is aggregated and placed in the context of social change, the significance of the actions of the bad-habit partisans becomes evident. Patterns of cooptation described in the preceding chapter permit one set of generalizations about the operations of the advocates of the minor vices over many generations. The cooptations also provide background for other general ways of understanding Americans who tolerated or fostered the bad habits. Not only was there no conspiracy, but the forces were also not monolithic. Otherwise quite decent citizens from time to time acted as agents of greed and lower-order parochialism—and sometimes of the simple meanness of many antisocial people. But even the most temporary recruits to the bad-habit advocates played a historical role in the victories of partisans of the constellation of minor vices. In particular, it turns out, the development of the minor vice-industrial complex fits into other findings of modern American historians, particularly those working in the history of gender, underclasses, the consumer culture, and sociocultural relationships.

A Recapitulation of the Events

During most of the nineteenth century, socially effective advocacy of the constellation of bad habits existed in only an embryonic state. The alcoholic-beverage industry embodied the best developed of the partisans as distillers and brewers struggled to consolidate and to extend sales, primarily through the retail institution, the saloon. Gambling, which already had much potential, appeared where alcoholic beverages were served but also spread as sporting events flourished and became more commercialized. In metropolitan areas, prostitutes and sometimes pornographers gathered around the saloons. In segregated districts in cities, drinking, prostitution, gambling, and, later in the century, drug taking flourished together in a mutually stimulating setting. The practitioners and merchants of these bad habits formed the backbone of the Victorian underworld, which in turn had intricate ties with political corruption, crime, and sports.

As secularization, industrialization, and urbanization continued, the forces of reform and normal rebelliousness, along with the rise of the mass media, contributed powerfully to shifting the flow of events. The progress of the proponents of the minor vices was not inexorable, as occurrences in the early twentieth century show. Prostitution and pornography declined precipitously in American life as the goal of sexual reformers—marriages that were fulfilling to both partners—drew on rebelliousness as well as tradition to emphasize that both variety and frequency of sexual activity were desirable.

The temporary defeat of the alcoholic-beverage industry with the Eighteenth Amendment, however, energized merchandisers and personal-liberty advocates to try to overturn not just Prohibition but all restraints on both business and personal behavior. In the process, a new, covert folk hero emerged—the gangster, who was a model of personal freedom and unrestraint, not to mention entrepreneurship. The tobacco industry, stimulated by cigarette profits, became caught up in the repealers' campaign for a new style of life and joined in with additional advertising to get everyone to smoke and drink and enter the presumably high-status lifestyle of the cabaret crowd.

In the cabaret—later night club—theater and saloon styles joined together, along with implications of sexual misbehavior and even the practice of smoking, to set a new standard of recreation in the flowering consumer culture. This night life was a vital element in the ultimate success of the repealers' propaganda. Another essential contribution came from American participation in World War I, in which the army experience spread underworld standards in drinking, smoking, gambling, sexual misbehavior, and, most symbolically, much greater public acceptance of shocking swearing.

Throughout the early twentieth century, rebellious elements were pulled into the underworld as well as into commercial agendas. The rebels deeply influenced journalists who considered themselves avant-garde when slumming in the underworld and cabaret world. The aim of the journalists and the rebels—as well as the repealers—was to mold social standards according to their own pattern, which at the time was more or less deviant.

Advocates of the bad habits led the way in getting Prohibition repealed. Just as Prohibition was not a simple incident, repeal was no mere normalization of American social arrangements. Instead, it symbolized profound changes in American society and culture.

In the new mass media, "respectability" began to lose influence in the 1920s and 1930s. Thereafter, the commercial and cultural forces consolidated their gains by expanding markets and extending the cultural reversal. As the immediate commercial interest in changing standards grew, so did more general business interest, as firm after firm gained from the economic activities of purveyors of the various bad habits. So did wealthy taxpayers, as the Great Depression spawned tolerance of easily taxable gambling and drinking.

Victory and Convergence

The movies and the electronic media in particular worked with great success to make drinking, smoking, gambling, and at least a little swearing unambiguously the norm by the 1940s. In World War II, the armed services and the service experience undermined much of what remained of resistance to lower-order standards, and particularly sexual standards. Within a few years, with the dawning of the *Playboy* age, lower-order promiscuity and frequency combined with middle-class or bohemian variety in love making and gained vigorous open allies. They were able profoundly to change standards further in the direction of unrestrained indulgence and the fantasies that derived originally from ideas about the most flamboyant of old-fashioned prostitutes. The alliance was successful, to the point that a powerful pornography industry arose, allied, once again, with journalists and with cultural rebels who wanted to defy authority—typically now not only with sexual misbehavior but also with drug use and shocking language.

Both alcoholic-beverage and drug merchandisers used the promise of sexual adventure to push their products, building on the sex-encounter singles' bar as well as the theater and cabaret model of entertainment. At the same time, the long campaign to bring first the cocktail hour and then the six-pack into the home—the symbol of the otherwise-respectable family—helped make media models of drinking part of domestic practice. By the 1970s, Americans could project into the near future the full development of a society without restraints but with a great deal of consumption centered on the constellation of minor vices. The most powerful economic forces and largest companies were tied into the gambling enterprises of criminals and ex-criminals, not to mention the profit seeking of drug peddlers and pornographers. In those same years of the 1970s, momentum from the campaign to repeal the Eighteenth Amendment seemed destined to extend legalization to virtually all the bad habits that had ever been restricted by law, even drug taking.

Moreover, the mass media were gratuitously granting social sanction to an ever-greater range of activities, so that the authority of the descendants of the Victorian underworld was virtually complete in American society—especially when someone could go into business to make money from a traditional minor vice. So complete was the victory that at some point after 1920, the proponents of pornography, the advertisers of cigarettes, the advocates of drug taking, the merchandisers of night clubs and six-packs, the advocates of casinos, cardrooms, and state lotteries— all began to argue from high moral ground and even self-righteously, not only invoking "freedom" but particularly the family, as in "the family cocktail hour" or the rationales of couples' group sexual activities. In each case, traditional deviancy was turned upside down. Not only did the definition of acceptability change so that "nice people" could retain respectable social status despite indulging in one or more minor vices, but in the language itself in midcentury, the words *bad* and *evil* used as trendy slang also took on positive connotations, for example in describing a person as a "bad dude," meaning "cool" or admirable.

As the parallel histories show, each element in the constellation had a distinctive evolution—developing faster or slower and in particular directions as circumstances changed. Sometimes, as during early-twentieth-century Prohibition or in the case of smoking in the 1980s and 1990s, proponents of the bad habits suffered reverses. But what is striking about the histories in the aggregate is the way in which the forces appeared together consistently, and how they came to reinforce one another in a society with, increasingly, standards of personal unrestraint. One might, for example, have thought that marijuana smoking would cut into the sales of cigarettes. In fact, quite the opposite was the case; those who smoked pot also customarily used tobacco heavily.[1]

Delinquents' Arguments and Rituals of Pleasure

Acting separately or together, how—beyond cooptation—did the proponents of the bad habits reverse the deviant status with which they started in the nineteenth century? Gresham M. Sykes and David Matza note in a classic paper on delinquency that people who are socially deviant attempt in a number of ways to neutralize social pressure that they may feel as they engage in antisocial activities. These strategies counter any tendency to feel either shame or guilt. It is striking that proponents of the bad habits used exactly these same manipulative approaches whenever they attempted any public defenses of their activities and standards. What is even more striking is the extent to which more subtle cultural currents brought other Americans to accept and even second these arguments.

Delinquents deny their own responsibility—if they indeed admit that their actions are unacceptable. So merchants of the minor vices, for example, were just doing business, not committing moral acts. Delinquents also deny that their actions cause any injury—the traditional contention that actions do not have any important consequences (the bad habits were mere relaxation and entertainment). Then delinquents blame the victim, a tactic now well known by that name: those stupid enough to believe advertising should be cheated; anyone who married a drunk deserved it; people who were dumb enough to smoke should get addicted and even die; women who caught the attention of rapists asked for it—the list goes on and on. Ultimately, in addition, delinquents condemn the condemners, the people who have set and enforced the violated norm. It was not just in the 1920s that indulgers attempted to ridicule and discredit reformers. Finally, delinquents appeal to higher loyalties—loyalties to the deviant him/herself and his/her group, as opposed to the larger society. In short, as the advocates of the minor vices converged, they legitimated themselves and one another with these arguments. In the process, they established an authority alternative to that of "nice" people or the traditional respectables. This reinforcement initially established the basis for the community aspect of the then-deviant Victorian underworld as well as the later mass-media world that propagated the minor vices and the delinquents' strategies to uphold underworld standards.[2]

Even though advocates of the minor vices often invoked loyalty and other prosocial values of the culture, the manipulative techniques of the friends of the bad habits were fundamentally defensive, even negative. They were essentially anti-modern in that they denied anyone the ability to discern social causes that might lead to social control. So negative were the proponents of the constellation that they denied not only the validity of the the standard makers' authority but also the validity of any social standards at all except fad, fashion, and style, which they represented as spontaneous and perhaps natural but in any event uncontrollable.[3] In only one area did forces representing the minor vices pursue a superficially positive strategy.

What the proponents of the minor vices had to offer that was positive was hedonism. Indeed, it was possible, as did many people at the time, to view the inversion of values in the 1920s as the ratification of hedonistic goals. By their very definition, bad habits were intrinsically pleasurable. Merchandisers built upon various population groups' rituals of pleasure—working out ambivalently, as described throughout this book, as rituals of transgression: of drinking, of smoking and taking drugs, of betting, of swearing, and even, carefully spelled out in print and on the screen, rituals of sexual activity.[4]

The rituals, of course, lent social legitimation to the actions. From the ritual legitimation came another gain: the actions could be depicted as prosocial, not antisocial. In movies and television, that positive depiction was vital, because children, at least, learned to imitate prosocial models even faster than they did antisocial activity.[5]

Therefore if an admired figure in the media or entertainment world indulged in one of the ritualized vices, it was a major victory—as in the case of Lindbergh's cigarette or drug taking by a pop musician. Likewise television and movie (not to mention various print-media) audiences learned about the admirable drinker and about "nice" people whose sexual activities violated some people's norms. Those audiences also saw a figure still familiar from fiction and movies, the brave and attractive gangster.

So, as they coopted, the proponents of the minor vices also tried to change perceptions held by large parts of the population in general and by opinion makers in particular. And so deviant became nondeviant, and opponents of the minor vices, rather than advocates and practitioners, became deviant. But that reversal appeared in part not just because of the advocates, institutions, and processes that worked together but also because of general cultural changes that interacted with drinking, smoking, and the other bad habits. Two cultural shifts in particular, the growth of the consumer society and of the lower-order lifestyle, were notably important in making the convergence of the partisans of the minor vices effective in a complex culture.[6]

Consumer Culture

Consumption communities were involved in still another aspect of cooptation in the twentieth century. Acceptance was not enough for the merchants and advocates of the bad habits. Both groups acted as if they wanted all Americans to become practitioners and supporters. In the most public face of the bad habits, cigarette and alcoholic-beverage advertising, advertisers openly stated that they wanted not just initial adherence but also repeated sales and, moreover, increasingly frequent use of their products.[7] Lower-order parochials wanted to spread their own countercultures. So not only did the various proponents of the bad habits seek to draw people into the culture of the minor vices, they also wanted to strengthen and reinforce it. Moreover, the quest for commercial advantage added great intensity, indeed, extremism, to the campaigns of those who were working to change ideas of what behavior was deviant. It was, therefore, not only values but also money that was involved in this cultural clash. As late as 1988, for example, teams of teenagers found that clerks in three out of four stores, including big chain stores, would sell cigarettes to obviously underage consumers, and the rate remained high even after local pressure had been exerted on the merchants.[8]

There was more to the power of consumer communities in an otherwise-fragmented society in which goods gave social identities to rock-and-roll record buyers, beer drinkers, and drug users. People in the consumer society were dominated by the fantasy world of advertising and more broadly by a whole universe of symbol and imagination. It was particularly in that universe that the proponents of the bad habits succeeded in capturing the subtle determiners of standards such as style and symbol. As Lary May argues, the whole revolution in manners and morals was based on the popular "acceptance of a new economic order," consumer society. Beyond the literal content of the motion pictures, for example, was the dreamworld of Hollywood and the ads. Leisure and public space were transformed. Becoming part of a crowd, a member of an audience, a consumer of mass media, even a victim of advertising became a positive and desirable experience in which the imaginary world and the idea of style gave Americans meaning and satisfaction in their lives. As early as 1935, for example, a writer in a beer distributors' magazine advised merchandisers to use show-manship to sell beer; each retailer should "make the customer's stay as happy and pleasant as a theatrical manager plans for the entertainment of his guests."[9]

By the turn of the twentieth century, before the movies, such ordinary institutions as amusement parks and department stores were transforming public spaces and the aspirations of Americans of all classes. Emphasizing color, sensation, sensationalism, and style, the new consumer institutions also emphasized spending and quite anti-bourgeois indulgence and hedon-ism. All men, suggested one writer, should act like gigolos, pleasing and indulging the customer. But it was at the time of the movies and in the 1920s, especially, that the consumer culture expanded in the United States. In that culture, the goal was excitement and imaginary enrichment of life through purchasing. The commodity itself was necessary and even sym-bolic, but it was not the end in itself. The payoff came in the imagination.[10] The cabaret and then later the "party" style of life offered one version of excitement. Mechandisers devised others, for many decades, using both traditional and modernist symbols. It was in the context of traditional symbols, for example, that merchandisers tried to tie cigarettes and beer and cocktails to high-status women and the family.

After midcentury, vendors of tobacco, alcohol, and drugs appealed di-rectly to the supposed social effects of the goods. The ads confirmed and developed the idea that the substances made interaction with other people easier and more satisfying as well as providing or enhancing a subjective feeling of having "fun."[11] In that atmosphere, Americans came to identify hedonism and consumption with the minor vices to a striking extent. In the consumer culture, symbolism and imagination interacted with goods and services. With the new fad of "sex therapy," for example, one could presumably purchase not just objects or services but sexual pleasure—a subjective state—per se.[12]

The more money one spent, the better, according to standards of both the consumer culture and the world of the minor vices. The conspicuous spending of sports and gamblers of an earlier day provided a memorable antecedent for modern betting folk, but even portrayals of stereotyped homoerotism in the media of the late twentieth century involved assump-tions and fantasies of wealth and spending (as well as, in a very complicated way, libertinism).[13]

The merchandisers of goods associated directly with the minor vices therefore flourished in a society in which Americans spent money and time making symbolic purchases. Almost everyone believed that the minor vices represented sensuousness and excitement, the desiderata of consumer culture. What more could merchandisers hope for, than that their commodities should be the object of a new social conformity, the symbols of community aspiration—and nonusers considered deviant?

Commercialized Leisure and the Struggle over Public Space

Even as an act of consumption, indulging in one of the bad habits was essentially a leisure activity. When the sphere of leisure became distinct from the sphere of work in the towns and cities of the nineteenth century, the bad habits were set especially well to flourish in a commercialized form and mobilize numerous small as well as large businesses.[14]

Leisure therefore opened markets that involved drinking and gambling and sports, with sexual misbehavior, particularly prostitution and pornography, as an implied ancillary—in short, the institutions of the Victorian underworld. The notorious late-nineteenth-century poolrooms, which were reservoirs of opposition to respectability and encouraged every minor vice in addition to gambling, were a direct outgrowth of the new separation of work and play. The theater and ultimately the amusement park became involved, and the entire commercial leisure complex competed very successfully with the parks and libraries of the uplift forces and could undermine conscientious citizenship. As a Denver labor activist noted in 1886, "The Whiskey drinker and variety theatre-attending working man who reads the Police Gazette is also the one who says he has no use for socialism." Indeed, there was a whole mass movement that involved seeking sensational commercialized amusement during leisure time. The movement grew when the new immigrants crowded into the cities around the turn of the twentieth century. The respectables lost control of leisure. As a disapproving social scientist commented in 1912, the "Devil appears to be the only sociologist who, in modern times, has given his mind to the subject of recreation."[15]

In this evolution of leisure, the commercial success of the merchants of the minor vices was noteworthy. A survey at the end of the nineteenth century showed that better-paid workers, whose family earnings averaged $768.54 a year, spent $326.54 for food, $122.92 for rent, and $9.49 for religion but $17.44 for amusements (such as cheap theater and dance halls), $25.53 for alcoholic beverages, and $17.44 for tobacco. Even the poorest workers found time and money to frequent the less-uplifting commercialized public spaces such as saloons and amusement parks. The money that these consumers spent greatly reinforced the power of lower-order culture because businesspeople immediately had an interest in recognizing and protecting that culture.[16]

Just as reformers attempted to control what took place in public areas, non-middle-class and ethnic as well as underworld groups attempted also to control those areas. Earlier in the nineteenth century, the controversy often took the form of arguing over so-called blue laws that restricted activities that could be carried out on Sunday, including moving mail on the trains as well as drinking beer and holding sporting events wherever and whenever one pleased. By the end of the century, the issues were usually secularized and fought out directly, but the model continued to be the struggle to do business and play, on the one hand, versus, on the other hand, a variety of moral restraints and social devices to enhance intellectual and spiritual development. In 1906, for example, ethnic groups in Chicago demonstrated so effectively that the city government gave up trying to enforce saloon-closing laws.[17]

The struggle over public space was enlarged in the twentieth century, and merchandisers of the minor vices had great advantages. Lower-order male activities such as gambling, drinking, and braggadocio swearing all had to be carried out in public spaces such as poolrooms, saloons, and even the streets where gangs congregated. Eventually a large part of what was functionally public space became most importantly the media—as the movies and radio and television came to embody advertising and the cabaret ideal. As previous chapters have suggested, the cabaret ideal was first determined chiefly by the marketing of alcoholic beverages and, to a lesser extent, by sexual misbehavior. Female impersonators on the stage, for example, were not commonly identified as homosexual (with the implication of promiscuousness) until the night club developed in the 1930s.[18] In the late twentieth century, with the rise of Las Vegas and the Las Vegas package, gambling contributed heavily to forming ideas of what entertainment and leisure activities and aspirations ought to consist of in American society.

The Vulnerability of Non-Middle-Class People

At the onset of the twentieth century, lower-order influence found new avenues into society and culture and won a great advantage when middle-class as well as non-middle-class people began to yield to the sensationalism of the yellow press and to the attractions of lower-order public spaces, including the saloon. Then the movies came in, with profound effects on recreational patterns as well as the development of a popular culture noted above. The movies benefited from the diminished prominence of the saloons during Prohibition. Whereas non-middle-class people had once been active in shaping their amusements, as the importance of the movies grew, those same population groups became more passive, more shaped by the commercial interests of the mass media and advertising, interests that at the same time catered to what respectables considered the lowest tastes. The ways in which lower-order parochialism exerted its force therefore moved from the direct influence of local Victorian underworld groups who were struggling for control of public spaces to the more subtle interplay between commercial interests, on the one hand, and, on the other, consumers of various backgrounds who were indulging traditionally lower-order tastes. All this took place at the same time that across the country the underworld and the culture associated with it continued to operate and also to contribute to the cabaret ideal of the 1920s and 1930s, in part using the common belief that the drinking place was a public space devoted especially to the bad habits.[19]

The consumerism quest for sensational and sensual gratification flourished because the new immigrant groups who increasingly made up the workers, the non-middle classes, and the population in general were particularly susceptible to the new mass media. People early in the century, who were not shy about grouping their fellow citizens, commented repeatedly on the "low taste" of those not of the middle classes, particularly those people who came from cultures in which individuals were much more expressive, physically and emotionally, than were traditional respectables. At one time, for example, expressiveness had provided a basis for caricature of the Irish and others as "brutal and apelike." Many decades later, expressive people turned the tables and condemned their more bourgeois and controlled neighbors as "uptight." Basically, those who had few cultural aspirations beyond looking out for themselves and their immediate social groups—particularly the family—were not successful in resisting or opposing sensational media messages, whether of the yellow press and radio of the first half of the twentieth century or of the television of the second half. With the encouragement of the underworld, many such Americans were, however, successful in resisting the more demanding and restraining culture of the uplifters and responded instead to sensation and hedonism. "Only suckers work" was a motto that came continuously from the self-justifying criminal population. Even the most conscientious Americans, as pollster Daniel Yankelovich pointed out in the 1980s, ultimately came to feel a strong obligation to "do what you *want* to do"—making an ethical norm of imagined personal desire, as opposed to self-denial or social responsibility. Doing what one wanted to do, and definitely deemphasizing restraint, became a standard for a culture that revolved not around work but around consumption and leisure.[20]

The Resurgence of Stereotyped Masculinity

The development of a consumer society in a population that was increasingly unresponsive to old middle-class standards reflected in large part the ways in which that society set standards. After all, the audience for the mass media and advertising increasingly came from growing population groups that did not have extensive traditions or training in old-fashioned respectability. It is hardly surprising that the bulk (again, not all) of non-middle-class people often allied with non-middle-class standards. But what may not be obvious is the way in which lower-order attitudes played into and were identical with the traditional male stereotype, although the identity was well understood in the time of the Victorian underworld when saloon society was dominated by "a sneering *machismo*" that often produced mistreatment of women. In the late nineteenth century, the very large and consciously male "bachelor subculture" of the cities shaded over into the underworld that was attempting to counter Victorian domesticity and respectability. That attempt included a lot of clearly expressed attacks on "damnable feminization" and the introduction of pejorative anti-feminine terms such as "sissy."[21] Social-class factors in fact were profoundly confused with gender-stereotypical standards, in local peer groups and mass media alike.

Indeed, one of the great assets of the bad habits was their masculine identity, building especially upon the belief traditional in many cultures that alcoholic beverages provided masculine strength—both physical prowess and strength to handle anxieties. Gambling from the beginning involved macho risk taking. In late-nineteenth-century cities, lower-order boys came into manhood in all-male settings on the basis of ritualistic swearing, gambling, and drinking—and "male license" in general. The same was largely true in the rural South. To an adolescent boy, wrote a mid-twentieth-century researcher, "sure of neither his masculinity [n]or his adulthood, the assumption of adult masculine habits can be very reassuring, so reassuring" that a boy would, for example, endure much discomfort while learning to smoke. From the 'thirties through the 'sixties, alcoholic-beverage merchandisers overwhelmingly targeted masculine customers as did cigarette advertisers, who suggested that a nonsmoker, as one 1957 critic noted, was "a flip-top zombie" deprived of his manhood. Merchandisers used the male gender stereotype to identify commodities—and by so doing increased sales even, it turned out, among women.[22]

In the early twentieth century, social scientists discovered that regardless of people's biological gender, typically masculine interests—for example, in sports—correlated strongly with conventionally "lower-class" status. Feminine interests (including high culture) tended to increase as one went up the social scale. This finding only confirmed the often-misogynistic stereotypes from the late nineteenth century in which the underworld tough was fundamentally masculine. In that day, reformers used the idea of the strenuous life to try to recapture masculinity for the do-gooders who were characterized as females and effeminate ("long-haired") preachers and the like. "Tobacco is not wicked," wrote a Michigan journalist in 1925, "but it is taboo to two sexes—the female sex and that neuter sex to which teachers and preachers are supposed to belong." One of adman Bruce Barton's triumphs in the 1920s was turning Jesus from a feminine to a masculine character—incidentally by means of placing him in the context of a consumer society with vigorous, masculine supersalesmen. Later moviemakers, television moguls, and rock-music producers continued the confusion between masculine sexuality and violence familiar in the traditional underworld. The two usually boiled down to a romantic masculine willfulness—doing what one damn well pleases—as opposed to traditional bourgeois self-control and restraint.[23]

Making reform appear effeminate and misbehavior macho was an obvious and persistent tactic of the advocates of the bad habits, from the pro-saloon mobs of the nineteenth century to gangsters, *Playboy*, and sexist rockers in the twentieth. The exploitation of the masculine identity was not only cultural: war veterans were openly mobilized to exert political pressure on behalf of smoking and drinking. But the proponents of the minor vices also used another strategy in the twentieth century. They moved all American society to a macho standard that favored the marketing of goods connected with the bad habits. By the last half of the twentieth century, Americans of all classes, regardless of gender, were markedly more "masculine" in interest than their predecessors earlier in the century had been. The advertisers were therefore idealizing and targeting not necessarily male but specifically masculine audiences.[24]

Whether it was slumming or primitivism that moved social leaders decisively toward standards that were both lower order and masculine, the transformation was a major one. Many symbolic changes suggested the shift just within the consumer arena. Middle-class females came to wear what had been the distinctive uniform of non-middle-class male workers, Levi's. In recreational settings, upper-class people danced lower-order dances, and the macho female gambler became ubiquitous among betting folk. At all times, both men and women increasingly used words that were defined as those that would offend well-bred, middle-class women, certainly, and sometimes even men: "gutter language."

For Americans who were championing any part of the constellation of minor vices, setting a lower-order/masculine standard meant not just imposing a set of standards but also defeating reformers who were opposed to the bad habits. In the purity and kindred movements of the late nineteenth and early twentieth centuries, women had, in fact, spearheaded the campaigns to clean up American life. The millions of dollars that subsequently went to convert women to smoking and drinking—especially middle-class women—therefore had effects beyond just marketing, as Pierre Du Pont recognized in the repeal campaign of the 1920s. Commercialized, as opposed to uplifting, recreation won out decisively in the 1920s and 1930s when women moved into "masculine amusements" and took up "masculine vices"—particularly in the drinking culture. All across the country, one cultural force after another moved both men and women toward lower-order standards, whether the foolish machismo of the gangster and Marlboro man or the new hero of cultural rebels, the stereotyped ghetto black male who was presumed to set the standards for substance use, rock music, and aggressively offensive language.[25]

Over many decades, then, middle-class people of all groups were overwhelmed by the lower-order and masculine standards that appeared in the guise of both the cabaret/night-club ideal and a primitivism that romanticized anti-bourgeois and anti-feminine behavior alike. Moving women's sexual standards—often with the best of intentions—toward those of pornographers represented one of the most striking victories of the advocates of the minor vices. By the 1970s, sexually oriented material was openly available for middle-class women. *Playgirl*, a blatant imitation of *Playboy*, exploited male nudity and cast women buyers as sexual predators, following the example of men and many women in conventional male pornography.

Much resistance to underworld-male and prostitute ideas of sexual propriety continued, but late-twentieth-century standards still demonstrated the masculinization of both men and women in the United States in a striking way—and the direction of change was toward the traditionally underworld standards.[26]

The Meshing of Cultural Changes and Use of Lifestyle

Many observers of modern society have identified ways in which the massing of great numbers of people exerted a cultural leveling influence that José Ortega y Gasset characterized as the "revolt of the masses." So in the United States, as I have shown, there came a time when the usual process, in which the classes set standards for the masses, was reversed, when cultural lag between social leaders and those lower in the hierarchy was inverted. Over many decades, non-middle-class and particularly lower-order standards instead began to percolate up the social hierarchy in what Marvin E. Wolfgang calls reverse diffusion of culture.[27]

In so far as anti-bourgeois standards of impulsive and self-centered attitudes and behavior spread to middle-class groups, then, and even women became more masculine, the lower-order standards fostered by the proponents of the bad habits meshed with other tendencies in American society. Innumerable commentators have described the late-twentieth-century cultural trends of narcissism and the selfishness of the immediately bonded group (typically the nuclear or extended family)—the so-called "me generation" and the "we generation." Many perceptive observers also commented on the resurgent romanticism of that period, in which willfulness and expressiveness, or just plain impulsiveness, replaced control and enlightened self-interest as desirable social styles. That was the era in which Americans' heroes came to be those media celebrities and fictional characters who appeared to be self-consciously tough or fun or simply hedonistic.

The evidence shows that the power of lower-order parochialism in the United States was usually not sufficient in itself to achieve the great inversion of values of the twentieth century. Additional impetus from commercial forces was necessary, as appeared in the cultural clashes around the issue of repeal. A striking example makes the point. The custom of frequent bathing came in in the late nineteenth century. Body deodorants arrived in the interwar period. Both developments came parallel in time with the expansion of the underworld and with the new cabaret ideals. Not bathing was distinctly anti-bourgeois and nonmiddle class. But that non-middle-class tendency did not have commercial backing. On the contrary, the economic interest of the soap and cosmetic industries was enormous and made effective by advertising and even by propaganda in the schools. Smelling bad, therefore, did not (with the exception of a few late-twentieth-century supposedly super-masculine perfumes—commercially promoted!) percolate up to the middle classes as a desirable rebellious norm.

The advocates of the minor vices, however, succeeded because profit seeking operated in a society in which consumption and emotionality and impulsiveness and machismo all worked together to negate restraint, particularly in the area of recreation and leisure or just plain self-indulgence. In that society, how one *felt* was the primary desideratum. Moreover, hardheaded observers and social scientists alike could see that general cultural influences translated into consumer behavior with direct effects on business, including, for example, the drug-paraphernalia marketers who benefited from the way in which pharmaceutical firms promoted tranquilizers. And of course business interests involved in the minor vices in turn affected culture, particularly through advertising, almost invariably reinforcing impulsiveness and self-indulgence and lack of restraint.[28]

One way, already noted, to view these cultural changes is to consider that they embodied the negatives of conventional bourgeois values. Indeed, over several generations, rebels argued in favor of the new values precisely because they were the negatives of bourgeois values. But labeling late-twentieth-century values as merely the negatives of bourgeois virtues obscures the significance of the change; indeed, it represents using another nineteenth-century conceptualization, bourgeois values, that trivializes the minor vices and conceals the economic and cultural power of advocates of the bad habits.

There was another concept, however, that people of the second half of the twentieth century used that helps place events in a better perspective. That concept was lifestyle. Lifestyle is particularly useful because it suggests how the different proponents of the minor vices converged and caught up in their convergence all the coopted elements. In advertising and public-relations efforts of the late twentieth century, promoters of various of the bad habits spoke explicitly about "lifestyle marketing." It was not only drinking and smoking that set the lifestyle in which those commodities sold well; "Lotteries and horse racing can really make use of lifestyle marketing" also, explained Rick Reilly, the Illinois lottery director of special events, formerly associated with the Budweiser Million at Arlington Park.[29] Again and again, lifestyle ads promoted drinking, smoking, sexual misbehavior, and gambling, drug taking, and swearing, either directly or indirectly, because everyone knew that "party time" could or should involve them.

Lifestyle had two advantages for the proponents of the minor vices. First, it united them and confirmed the logic that made the constellation a social reality. The second was that lifestyle helped remove from the arena of values indulging in one or all the bad habits and instead rendered the actions trivial matters of merely personal whim. A mere style, which could change at any moment, involved neither principles nor social consequences. And besides, a pluralistic society obviously had room in it for many individual styles, understood as "doing your own thing." Over many years, toleration of extremes in conduct in general grew along with toleration of indulging in all the bad habits. Public displays of extreme or uncivil behavior made ordinary indulging in a minor vice appear to be mild—and prevented social reactions to the bad habits. Kenneth Auchincloss wrote in 1984, in connection with the actions of a media celebrity, that "it is impossible to be humiliated in contemporary America."[30]

It was not inappropriate for the minor vices to end up functioning under the label of lifestyle—first a high-class and bohemian lifestyle, then more frankly as just a lower-order but affluent lifestyle out of the macho and consumer society. After all, the bad habits had been at first, in the early nineteenth century, deviant behaviors, made or recognized deviant because of labeling. Lifestyles in the 1920s and 1930s and afterward were simply subjected to relabeling, in which those same minor vices were portrayed as matters of taste, and, it should be emphasized, individual taste.

Individual Responsibility

Through all of these strategies and arguments on behalf of the minor vices, then, ran a theme that provided a rational argument for partisans: behavior in the area of the attractive vices was strictly each individual's responsibility and therefore a matter of personal freedom, like any taste or style. The individual-responsibility/personal-freedom argument went far beyond just manipulating and coopting well-meaning people. It was, on the one hand, of course, a shibboleth of Marlboro Man machismo and irresponsible advertisers' self-justification and propaganda. But it was, on the other hand, also a very effective ideology and, on rare occasions, logical argument. When right-wing journalist James J. Kilpatrick took a stand in favor of decriminalizing cannabis in the 1970s, he declared, "I don't give a hoot about marijuana, but I care about freedom!"[31]

One striking rationalization for removing any social sanctions from individual minor vices—or other actions—was given a name late in the twentieth century: the victimless crime, when the argument gained currency far beyond the delinquency rationalization described above. This concept depended upon the idea that some person's action (1) had no effects on anyone else and (2) suffered from being arbitrarily labeled deviant by "society." The idea of a victimless crime was one of the most potent rational arguments used by the proponents of the minor vices as they coopted many good people. Reasonably conscientious citizens might well believe that if there is any harm at all in an action, the harm affects only the person taking the action (committing the crime or taking a risk of harm), not anyone else. Masturbation (not a crime, but a sometimes heavily condemned action) would be perhaps the most arguable example, and to a lesser extent nonpublic sexual misbehavior, but substance use of all kinds has also often been put into the category of "victimless crime." The victimless-crime argument often involved the idea that rules embodying moral standards were not appropriate for social action anyway—"enacting morals into laws"—because moral standards are subjective or at most cultural. Such was another version of denying that actions have consequences, that is, denying any action social cause and effect.[32]

For the most part, however, and excepting the idea of victimless crime, the individual-responsibility arguments did not change over time. From the 1840s, writers in the *National Police Gazette* and similar publications began a steady repetition of the already-traditional idea that evil was the result of individual moral choices. In 1886, the editor of *Bonfort's Wine and Spirit Circular* quoted a writer in the *Journal of Commerce* who opposed laws restricting the excessive use (and, obviously, sale) of alcoholic beverages: "They know very little of human nature who apply . . . this class of remedies. The source of the evil is inward, and external applications will not reach it." The repealers of the 1920s made particularly effective use of the argument, only now it was just choice, not moral choice. The same kind of thinking justified the repeal of the federal ban on shipping boxing films in 1940 as well as the continuing post-1933 efforts to deal with individual drunk drivers. "The government cannot make choices for its citizens"—words taken from the statement of a marijuana advocate of 1979 could just as well have been, and often were, used to justify the irresponsible actions of publishers in the 1940s, television advertisers of the 1960s, or in fact any of the advocates of any of the minor vices over a period of more than a century and a half.[33]

Across the years, the businesspeople profiting from the various bad habits recognized their stake in individual, as opposed to social, explanations of the possible bad effects of any of the minor vices.[34] Entrepreneurs arguing individual responsibility had an advantage because for so long so many people, particularly those with certain moralistic religious backgrounds, continued to view problems associated with the minor vices as the result of personal moral decisions of those who indulged. Particularly in the late twentieth century, a secular version of an individual moral outlook, the so-called therapeutic view, was also markedly serviceable for merchandisers. In such a view, notable especially in the cases of alcohol, gambling, and drug habits, any social problems were in fact individual problems, to be dealt with on an individual basis, usually by therapists or counselors. Socially disruptive behavior (typically alcoholism) became an individual illness or maladaptation (as well as possibly a crime, as in the case of sexual transgressions). At one consistent extreme, each of the minor vices, including sexual misbehavior, became an "addiction," suitable for individual treatment by an understanding and accepting therapist (who posed no danger to any business). So swearing was justified because it served a cathartic, "therapeutic" function for the swearer. Not only did alcoholic-beverage merchandisers contribute to alcoholism therapy movements and Mothers Against Drunk Driving, but one of the major supporters of the late-twentieth-century sex-therapy movement was—*Playboy*![35]

The individual-liberty/freedom argument had a number of aspects to it. One was the idea that choosing to indulge in any of the minor vices was a rational decision by a responsible person. Both consumers and providers of services, for example, reacted with indignation to the suggestion that gamblers were mindless victims. "Most drug use is not irrational," commented a moderate advocate of drug decriminalization in 1979, adding, "Should we incarcerate people who ski, or skydive or ride motorcycles? . . . They all take risks; but if they recognize and deal with them intelligently and not cavalierly, is that not all we can expect?"[36] The argument that taking a risk was rational was modern. But the rest of the reasoning was not. Earlier, as I have suggested, many people held that advocating hedonism was not an irrational stance. But the point is, that by making advocacy of one or all the minor vices rational, embracing the bad habits became not just acceptable as one tolerated viewpoint in a pluralistic society but actually modern and acceptable in a reasoned, planned universe.

Another aspect of liberty was that traditionally it was essentially negative—freedom from something. As such, the liberty argument fitted the negativism of the program of the proponents of the minor vices perfectly—even the negativism of the pornotopias. Rebels and many good people alike could, and did, rally when they heard the cry of personal liberty, much less censorship. In the 1980s, a conservative critic of a government report on obscenity wrote: "... I believe in individual responsibility and individual liberty. I don't think that any federally appointed sack of fatheads knows what's best for me. I voted for President Reagan to get government off my back, not into my pants."[37]

By the 1970s, when discussion of influencing people's drinking and smoking and so on had moved to the point that reformers spoke of "lifestyle modification," one commentator concerned about personal freedom warned against what he called the "new paternalism" of health advice and regulation. But the same negativism had been caught earlier and more directly by a 1920s anti-Sunday-law editor who quoted an anti-repeal publication: "What would happen to this country if all its citizens had no higher conception of liberty than freedom to get drunk?" Answered the libertarian editor: "THE BLUES [blue-nosed, repressive Puritans] WOULD GET IT."[38]

Finally, over the years, many people noticed the ideological affinity between business free enterprise and personal liberty. The Du Pont repealers moved back and forth between advocating the right of a person to drink and defending the right of a businessperson to make and sell anything to anyone. Early in the nineteenth century, Sunday-law advocates were explicitly anti-business. Reformers used the precedent of destroying the trade in lottery tickets to justify laws designed to destroy the alcoholic-beverage business—at which point merchandisers still tried to invoke the right to do business. From that day on, business interest—in these cases a euphemism for unusual pursuit of profits—continued to be a vital issue in arguments about the bad habits. Opponents of the minor vices in fact often launched direct attacks upon the various businesses involved and thereby threatened profits. The businesspeople responded with appeals to the liberties of both merchandiser and consumer. As late as the 1960s, tobacco sellers invoked not just freedom of enterprise but also the economic necessity of the tobacco producers: it was too important an industry to destroy. In 1978, the editors of the *Paraphernalia and Accessories Digest* included a foldout sign for merchants to hang in their stores, "Certain items will NOT BE SOLD TO CHILDREN," but in the accompanying editorial they noted that "you can still sell to whomever you damn well please."[39]

Critics of the personal-liberty argument wanted from the beginning to the late twentieth century to put individual actions into a social context. "God has given you somewhere a post of duty to occupy," wrote a moralist in the *Lady's Home Magazine* in 1858,

> and you cannot get above or below your obligations. . . . You cannot excuse yourself by saying, "I am nobody; I don't exert any influence," for there is nobody so mean or obscure that he has not some influence, and you have it whether you will or no, and you are responsible for the consequences of that influence, whatever it is. Take your stand before the world. . . .[40]

Such an attitude led to both modernist beliefs in the ability to control one's fate and to the sense of civic responsibility that animated American reform and troubled the proponents of the minor vices for so long. Spokespersons for the bad habits, by contrast, attempted to cast the world in personal terms, not only their own individual freedom but personal actions of other people. Typically, people in the drug world in the late twentieth century, for example, did not deal with abstract concepts like the system or even the institutions of justice and law; according to beliefs common among druggies, their struggle was with individual law-enforcement officers.[41]

Champions of the bad habits and their opponents therefore took divergent approaches to self and society. Those proponents of the minor vices who assumed the mantle of righteousness emphasized ethics, standards, and morals in terms of the individual. Their uplifting opponents, by contrast, argued the importance of community and social demands. Throughout the nineteenth and twentieth centuries, the proponents of the minor vices cited and praised anyone who argued individual liberty on either a popular or a more formal level or who simply reacted sympathetically, as in censorship controversies. At the end of the 1970s, boys who drank significantly more than the average showed marked tendencies to deny the idea of social responsibility and to assert a macho individuality. Whether the attitude contributed to the behavior or rationalized it does not matter. In practical terms, it was part of a general approach to living that was an essential element in the operation of the tacit alliance of those advocating the minor vices. Formal arguments in favor of individualism of this variety provided those advocates a rationale.[42]

Opponents of the individual-liberty/personal-freedom argument continued to raise the question of where it would end and what kind of world it would lead to. One thinker, concerned about the immoral influence of motion pictures in 1921, imagined that the end result might be "anti-Americanism, immorality, and disregard for law—a condition in which each individual is a law unto himself."[43] The idea of each individual's being a law unto himself or herself was indeed part of the implicit agenda of the proponents of the minor vices, part of the negativism that opposed social standards that got in the way of the bad habits. By the late twentieth century, it was no longer necessary to speak in speculative and vague terms (such as "anti-Americanism") to find out where the individual-liberty argument would lead. The successes of the proponents of the minor vices provided concrete evidence.

The Persistence of Proponents of the Minor Vices

However plausible the liberty/freedom arguments, in practice the advocates of the minor vices showed a remarkable persistence. In business, this dedication earned merchants the label of greedy as they pushed heavy users of tobacco, alcohol, drugs, and gambling to indulge even more. When Nevadans legalized prostitution in the mid twentieth century, in one community a brothel and a school occupied adjoining buildings. Partisans popularized the slogan "Don't move the brothel—move the school," and in the end it was indeed the school that had to move. In the same period, a pimp explained, "Pimping isn't a sex game. It's a skull game. . . . It's a brainwashing process. When you turn a chick out, you take away every set of values and morality that she previously had and create a different environment" with a wholly new set of friends.[44]

Increasingly, the proponents of the minor vices were not content with toleration or partial victories. There seemed to be no limit to their ambitions to set social standards. One articulate member of the drug culture described the drive:

> I really enjoy turning on somebody to dope for the first time. I guess it's partly a power trip thing. You know all about it and he doesn't. . . . Suddenly he understands a whole lot of things. And that gives me a really cool feeling, to know that there's one more person who knows, one more person who's begun to see through all the programming he's gotten since he was born.[45]

Constantly propelling the advocates, then, was not only greed, but group reinforcement, the quest of practitioners of the bad habits to be aware of like individuals—in person, as in the drug culture, or with symbolic presence, as in the consumer communities.

The most striking persistence of the proponents of the minor vices appeared in their attempts to win children over to the various bad habits—and often in the name of personal liberty so that the responsibility lay on the child, not the merchandiser. A mid-twentieth-century editor of objectionable comic books declared, "We are not selling books on the basis of bosoms and blood. We are business men who can't be expected to protect maladjusted children."[46]

In the last half of the twentieth century, advocates of the minor vices became major figures in the general cultural movement to destroy protections that society had traditionally provided children. In part, cultural change in the middle and late twentieth century removed earlier distinctions between childhood and adult status. Everyone, regardless of age, read the same comics, saw the same television, knew whatever there was to know about what formerly had been adult "secrets" and spheres of operation. And the proponents of the minor vices contributed powerfully to this blurring of child and adult identity. In the 1950s, for example, a comic strip appeared in the newspapers with the announcement "Philip Morris, the cigarette with the man's kind of mildness, presents 'Duke Handy,' " and it was unclear whether the audience that was being called on to buy cigarettes was adult or juvenile. In fact, in the developing dissolution of distinctions of that time, it was both. In a signal later parallel, a successful campaign, begun in 1988, to sell cigarettes with ambiguous child/adult cartoons of a "smooth" camel eventually evoked a storm of protest. An anti-censorship writer spoke for many in the minor-vice camp when he asserted, "The premise that mass publications must be edited for 'families' always seems to ignore the fact that families are growing up"—obviously with children who were now, like grown-ups, to be held fully responsible for their choices and to be exposed to any and all media. In this wholly adult world, the overwhelming importance of "the couple"—particularly in ever-present sexuality—left no place for a child's identity. Advertising in particular portrayed children as sexual beings, miniature adults.[47]

The proponents of the minor vices benefited from and of course encouraged still another cultural development to remove expectations as well as protection from childhood. The now-adultlike child was to be identified as a "youth" in the mass media. In the evaporation of distinctions, youth culture was to become the model for everyone. The idealization of a mythical youthful style of life had played an important role in the culture of the 1920s and the battle for repeal of Prohibition. It idealized irresponsibility and impulsiveness. Advocates then and later identified the bad habits with a desirable youthful style of life and depicted opponents as outdated as well as old and probably hypocritical. "There are, unfortunately," wrote one pro-smoking writer in 1926, "many elderly crabs who are making capital or seeking notoriety by deploring those habits of the younger generation which differ from their own habits, when they were young." In the mid and late twentieth century, the (presumably desirable) image of youth absorbed another element, the juvenile delinquent, that is, the lower-order youngster who acted on parochial antisocial standards.[48] By these standards, any child should have the freedom to choose "youth" culture—especially if urged to do so by television messages and peer groups.

By the last half of the twentieth century, the proponents of the bad habits were therefore taking advantage of all the movements in American culture that removed protection from children and made them responsible for their decisions. When some pedophiles, for example, had organized and were receiving a hearing as a legitimate advocacy group, their major reservation to adult-child sexual activity was that the child should have "full freedom of choice." One writer in an advocacy newsletter in 1982 advised a father asking about getting involved with his daughters, "I would urge you to find a teen or adult to take care of your orgasm needs, and involve the children only in an occasional romp in bed with mommy and daddy." A paraphernalia advertiser in 1979 offered a pipe, the "Pocket Size Power Hitter," noting that it "Fits Small Hands, Delivers a Big Hit." The similar appeals of cigarette and alcoholic-beverage advertisers over many years have already been noted.[49]

In this same time period, other traditionally protected groups, such as the mentally ill and developmentally handicapped, were similarly turned loose in an exploitative or, at best, indifferent society in the name of individual liberty. In the age of television, the appropriate ideal for children became an adult who in the media and media advertising was increasingly a consumer who "chose"—using individual liberty—to purchase the commodities of the minor vices and to behave in an unrestrained manner.

The Twentieth-Century Transformation of Deviancy

In a whole variety of ways, then, the proponents of the minor vices wittingly and unwittingly used twentieth-century mass media and consumerism to change standards of deviance by labeling it "normal" when an individual indulged—even to an extreme—in the pleasurable bad habits without shame or guilt. Some of the arguments of the advocates of the bad habits were at least superficially rational, such as appealing to the individual nature of the action or maintaining that rebellious or youthful misbehavior was natural and, hence, inevitable and irrepressible.

What Americans found most confusing over the years were some of the aspects of the process (of labeling actions deviant) and maintaining the boundaries between deviant and acceptable. As the repeal experience of the 1920s showed, the joking and daring with which people marked and tested boundaries indicated that standards, even traditional standards, could be tenuous. In the 1920s, what for some years had been playful testing became bitter and effective ridicule that undermined first one and then another in a whole set of standards.

The extent to which standards were changing appeared in the next stage, when advocacy that everyone took as kidding did not suffice, and advocates began to expect their audiences actually to carry out formerly forbidden activities. Then increasingly those who indulged in the minor vices found that they had changed their essential identities to those of people who defended their actions rather than taking the rueful hypocrite's role. The new identities were easy to acquire because audiences of the mass media and advertising were exposed to powerful favorable depictions of bad habits and new lifestyles, including endless models of misbehavior. The most dramatic change was the move in *Playboy* from teasing advocacy to serious how-to-do-it material. The alcoholic-beverage recipes in ads directed toward young people symbolized another aspect of this shift. Actual events as well as talk in the military experience of the two world wars and the Cold War provided still another aspect of mass movements from words to actions.[50]

By the late twentieth century, neither culture nor commerce was satisfied with mere talk or with joking about largely lower-order standards. Psychotherapists were finding not internal conflict in patients' symptoms that the culture was producing but rather (as, traditionally, in nonliterate and premodern cultures) "impulse-ridden" "acting out"—actual behavior, not fantasy, and behavior that was, moreover, directly antisocial.[51] In this context, continual pressure in the media to increase the toleration of disturbing and disruptive behavior was an important element in cultural changes that fostered the bad habits (most transparently pornographic and substance-taking behaviors).[52]

Proponents of the minor vices grouped together because they traditionally were connected to one another, but they converged and reinforced one another finally because all of them answered the inner logic of the standard of lack of restraint. Their program was a short-term program. The long-term goals implicit in their program were usually as hidden from the friends of the minor vices as from the more general public. Many proponents were marketers who wanted to sell and to create a favorable climate for further sales of their products. They wanted action and got action, unrestrained, impulsive, and interacting with a culture in which the norms increasingly tended to favor actually indulging in pleasurable vices. As the evidence shows, what made the difference and transformed the teasing about boundaries of respectability was the power generated by the profits to be made from bad habits.

The power of the minor vice-industrial complex in American life was comparable to that of the military-industrial complex, not only because of the great sums of money involved but also because of the social and cultural dominance that the advocates of the vices exercised. That dominance appeared particularly significantly in the continuing resistance of the media to any suggestion that indulging in a bad habit might have negative consequences or any consequences at all. The record, however, suggests that drinking, smoking, taking drugs, gambling, sexual misbehavior, and even swearing could no longer be written off as mere personal taste, as mere difference in lifestyle, as mere entertainment, or as *mere* anything.[53] In twentieth-century America, the minor vices of the nineteenth century had become in and of themselves major shapers of American society, culture, and history.

Epilogue

The victory of the advocates of the minor vices was not complete, even in the closing years of the twentieth century. Many Americans remained still to be recruited, and the quest for even more profits continued. Moreover, the natural history of the minor vices showed that proponents of the various parts of the constellation still had to contend with two threatening realities of American society. The first was that, in the face of obvious consequences of the various bad habits, spontaneous resistance often appeared, resistance that was not initially moralistic but was instead based on experience. And the second was the fact that, contrary to common wisdom and cynics' assertions, social-control measures worked.

Possibilities for the Bad Habits

In a population that increasingly became more complex and fragmented, many cultural subgroups continued actively to oppose some or all of the minor vices, for a variety of reasons. Moreover, many people were for one reason or another committed neither for nor against one or more or all the minor vices. Many citizens who still themselves held to the work ethic, for example, did not care if other people were foolish enough to gamble. The victory of proponents of the minor vices therefore had two aspects. In addition to gaining active supporters, simply winning toleration and noninterference constituted a major goal of the champions of the minor vices, and one they had largely achieved. It was in this context of toleration that the trend in the mass media to suppress discussions of undesirable effects of drinking, gambling, and other bad habits took on such significance. Finally, it was clear that much room remained for the attractive minor vices to expand, either singly or as a constellation, into populations who were indifferent as well as those who were hostile.

In the last decades of the twentieth century, one never knew when and how partisans favoring the bad habits might act in culture or in business. At the beginning of the 1980s, in a strikingly symbolic action, for example, Seagram distillery interests effectively took control of the Du Pont corporation. Or, to cite another instance, a mid-1980s reporter found that a mail-order fancy fruit company, Harry and David, had sent customers a survey form in which the questions included attitudes toward sexual swinging and legalization of marijuana. The survey was in fact conducted by the corporate owners of the gift-fruit outfit, none other than cigarette maker R. J. Reynolds. One commentator suggested that perhaps the company was compiling a list of "outrageous swingers who think that marijuana should be legalized."[1] It was difficult to know where the merchandisers of the minor vices might show up next and in what guise.

The meshing of the minor vice-industrial complex with demographic changes, with the consumer culture, and with media and advertising run amok in the age of narcissism made the advocates of the minor vices appear invulnerable. In their public-relations form, at least, they could fit into new virtues that flourished among well-meaning Americans. For example, emphasizing personal relationships and community—main points in a set of prevailing standards that Daniel Yankelovich found from his polling around 1980—was not incompatible with honoring the bad habits, supporters of which had long since coopted romantic love and pluralism as well as consumer communities.[2]

Troubling Times for Advocates of the Bad Habits

Yet the future of the bad habits was, still, by no means certain. The history of drinking, smoking, taking drugs, gambling, sexual misbehavior, and swearing showed that although they were always present in society, at one time they had, albeit with continual difficulty, been kept under control. The bad habits did not grow spontaneously. Expansion was not necessarily

their certain destiny. Nor was their progress steady. Pornography, prostitution, and even drinking had suffered major defeats early in the twentieth
century. Late in the century, other straws in the wind suggested that the
further progress of the minor vices might not continue uninterruptedly.
Not only was smoking becoming deviant, but drug legalization halted after
1978. In the 1980s, marijuana and cocaine, particularly, became less socially
acceptable. Health concerns—first about herpes, then AIDS—in the 1980s
and 1990s were modifying at least some Americans' sexual practices (besides
the group-sexual "swinging" that had an aborted development a few years
earlier). Even alcohol consumption was not flourishing to the extent that
marketers had reason to hope and expect. Stories about "a new temperance" appeared in the media as alcoholic-beverage makers introduced nonalcoholic beers to maintain their markets in the late 1980s.[3]

Experience showed that in general the minor vices built on themselves,
as legalizing betting led to more betting, for example, and toleration of
drugs generated more drug taking. But experience also showed that people
faced with the immediate consequences of the minor vices could eventually
react against them. In the early nineteenth century, excessive drinking gave
birth directly to the temperance movement. At the turn of the century,
disease and the double standard inspired purity reformers, and the saloon
begat the Anti-Saloon League. Late in the twentieth century, other critics
of the bad habits materialized, whether the parents of drug addicts, relatives
of people dying from lung cancer, dependents of gambling addicts, or
victims of drunk drivers—or even otherwise-tolerant neighbors of bars that
generated fighting, screaming, car noises, drug dealing, and indiscriminate
urination in and about the parking lots. Such critics indicated that there
were still limits to how much disturbing behavior people could and would
put up with. By that time, not only were there therapeutic programs in
response to the direct individual effects of the bad habits, particularly for
drinkers, smokers, gamblers, and sex offenders, but there were also actual
public-opposition groups, based largely at first on public-health considerations. Indeed, proponents of the minor vices derisively labeled some
health workers and consumers' advocates of the 1980s the "Neo-Prohi-
bitionists."[4]

Finally, the historical record showed that, contrary to the propaganda
of the proponents of the minor vices, the traditional ways of constraining
behavior in American society—namely, education and legislation—did indeed work. There was in this record no support for the propaganda of
the supporters of the bad habits that "you can't legislate morals." In fact,

not only Prohibition but also many other laws were effective in modifying people's behaviors, even that of drug dealers (the media of course continued to emphasize instances in which people defied the law, as in Prohibition times, not how discouraging even imperfect law enforcement can be to those trying to carry out a stigmatized activity). A certain amount of violation does not change a standard or invalidate a law (such as speeding laws or even laws against murder, which are very often violated successfully but the repeal of which would have remarkable consequences).[5]

Laws are symbolic as well as coercive—as the repeal of Prohibition showed dramatically. In the last half of the twentieth century, a number of sociologists reported that legal regulation did very much influence social habits. Hardheaded investigation showed consistently how rules frustrated the advocates and merchants of the pleasurable vices. At the very least, for example, local availability of substances (whether narcotics, alcohol, or tobacco) was a major factor determining how much people used them, a factor as effective in the slums as among the more general population.[6]

The decline of smoking serves as evidence that education worked just as laws worked. Merely changing people's perceptions by changing the labels in movie ratings had substantial effects on public acceptance of sexual portrayals in the 1980s, when the stigma of an X was restricted to films for "adult" theaters, not mainstream productions, which were no longer considered pornographic, regardless of content.[7] Over many decades, agents of the proponents of the minor vices tried by propaganda and advertising to counter education and by many means to prevent or reverse either educational or formally legal condemnations of everything from swearing to cigarette machines. Those merchants of the constellation certainly believed that opposition by education was effective. Indeed, some alcoholic-beverage merchandisers were distressed by the material effects of the "just say no" anti-drug campaign of the late 1980s, which they believed carried over into the realm of alcoholic beverages.

For all these reasons, then, the future of the proponents of the bad habits still retained a substantial element of uncertainty despite all their cultural power and their base in the minor vice-industrial complex. Champions of the minor vices were implicitly familiar with the repeal campaign of the 1920s, when the myth of failure of the law became self-fulfilling. Their actions at the end of the twentieth century showed that they were aware of the danger of admitting even the possibility that their victories could be limited, much less reversed.

For the time being, then, advocates of the minor vices argued that "everybody does it," and in fact they continued to enjoy an astonishing dominance[8] in both culture and society. One sign of that dominance was the fact that most Americans of the late twentieth century were unaware that the minor vices had and continued to have social and, moreover, historical, significance—or even that there were identifiable groups of people with cultural and economic motives to defend and expand the place of the constellation of those minor vices in the United States.

Notes

Preface

1. Genevieve Kupfer and Robin Room, "Abstainers in a Metropolitan Community," *Quarterly Journal of Studies on Alcohol* 31 (1970): 119.

O N E : *Introduction*

1. The witty and informative book by Judith N. Shklar, *Ordinary Vices* (Cambridge, Mass.: Harvard University Press, 1984), concerns vices of character: cruelty, hypocrisy, snobbery, betrayal, and misanthropy; I am concerned with other categories of behavior. I am using in particular, besides "bad habits," the term "minor vice," a conventional expression found for example in a relevant passage in Crane Brinton, *The Anatomy of Revolution*, 2d ed. (New York: Vintage Books, 1965), 180.
2. See particularly Richard Stivers, *Evil in Modern Myth and Ritual* (Athens: University of Georgia Press, 1982), who emphasizes the role of ritual. My work to some extent parallels that of Lionel Tiger, *The Manufacture of Evil: Ethics, Evolution, and the Industrial System* (New York: Harper and Row, 1987), who is concerned with changes in which apparently respectable activities came to have consequences that were dubious or even deplorable.
3. Frederick Wertham, *Seduction of the Innocent* (New York: Rinehart and Company, 1954), 256–57.
4. As will become obvious here and there, the traditional accounts, in so far as they exist, are to a substantial extent based upon propaganda and shaped by historicist interpretation as well as systematic exclusion of evidence. Even though still unrefined, a shifted view-

point should not be so hard to consider, simply because the original versions turn out to be so unsubstantial when examined closely. A particularly egregious error of conventional accounts has been that historians have excluded evidence on the basis of the rhetoric that accompanied the report. Simply because some behavior was described as wicked or vile or disgusting does not mean that the writer did not witness the behavior. Such testimony, along with other evidence, has contributed to my narrative.

5. I do not wish to dissemble that my work is not adding fresh material on each of the specific bad habits treated. In each of the narratives there is some, and, in some cases, a great deal, of innovative narrative and analytic material based on extensive use of primary sources, as the notes will indicate. The history of swearing in the United States, for example, has not, to my knowledge, been assembled before, nor are there good accounts of the taking of drugs after 1960. It is only fair to point out, to cite another example, that to some extent my history of sexual misbehavior differs from that of earlier scholars; the patterns that I describe are based not just on those secondary sources—as far as they go—but often on fresh materials from the past. For all the sections, I have in fact not only searched the secondary literature but also at least sampled the primary sources extensively.

6. See, for example, Warren I. Susman, *Culture as History: The Transformation of American Society in the Twentieth Century* (New York: Pantheon Books, 1984), 105; on xxii and 271-85, Susman characterizes a large part of the change as that from character to personality as the dominant cultural model. I am, on the other hand, focusing more directly on a set of historical currents, although the end result may have been somewhat similar. Elizabeth Douvan, quoted in Daniel Yankelovich, *New Rules: Searching for Self-Fulfillment in a World Turned Upside Down* (New York: Random House, 1981), 96. A typical specific summary of changed standards is in Robert Straus, "The Need to Drink 'Too Much,' " *Journal of Drug Issues* 14 (1984): 130-32. Compare Lawrence Veysey, "A Postmortem on Daniel Bell's Postindustrialism," *American Quarterly* 34 (1982): 64: "I remain disposed to argue that a real shift in attitudes did occur around the 1920s." The entire argument of Lary May, *Screening Out the Past: The Birth of Mass Culture and the Motion Picture Industry* (New York: Oxford University Press, 1980), is based on a major shift in standards that culminated in the 1920s.

7. Commentators who over the years called attention to the significance of the reversal in values have not been taken seriously, in part because most of them came from the social or religious right. (Those on the left, preoccupied with corporate capitalism and social justice, did not recognize the significance of the change.) Moreover, none of those who attended to the change in values, to my knowledge, utilized the perspectives that the concept of deviance can offer, and none of them attempted a systematic history of the change. The major exception—a work that involves both deviance theory and an attempt at developmental explanation—is Ronald J. Troyer and Gerald E. Markle, *Cigarettes: The Battle Over Smoking* (New Brunswick: Rutgers University Press, 1983). See below in this chapter and also Chapters 4 and 10. Paula Fass, *The Damned and the Beautiful: American Youth in the 1920's* (New York: Oxford University Press, 1977), 326, does speak of the way in which spokespersons for youth in the 1920s were "enforcing a deviant standard," and Norman H. Clark, *Deliver Us from Evil: An Interpretation of American Prohibition* (New York: W. W. Norton and Company, 1976), takes up the subject in his discussion of the cultural clash over drinking. See Chapter 2, below.

8. I am not attempting a historiographic discussion here but merely endeavoring to explain how my approach fits in with other writings. A recent examination of historians who in midcentury and after emphasized the ironic evil consequences of attempts to do good is David W. Noble, *The End of American History: Democracy, Capitalism, and the Metaphor of Two Worlds in Anglo-American Historical Writing, 1880-1980* (Minneapolis: University

of Minnesota Press, 1985). Richard M. Abrams, "American Anticommunism and Liberal Internationalism," *Reviews in American History* 10 (1982): 457, identified "The Failure Syndrome of the 1970s—the tendency of Americans across the partisan spectrum to see failure in every American reform and institution." As early as 1967, Robert Bremner, "Editor's Introduction," in Anthony Comstock, *Traps for the Young* (Cambridge, Mass.: Harvard University Press, 1967), vii, referred wittily to the possibility of "a national rogues' gallery of reformers." The professional historiographical background of this kind of history is described in Gene Wise, *American Historical Explanations: A Strategy for Grounded Inquiry* (Minneapolis: University of Minnesota Press, 1980); and Fred Matthews, "Hobbesian Populism: Interpretive Paradigms and Moral Vision in American Historiography," *Journal of American History* 72 (1985): 92–115. The symptom was more comprehensive even than the parochialism that Clark, *Deliver Us from Evil*, 10–11, identifies in the work of Richard Hofstadter.

9. The barrier cannot have been the difficulty of identifying proponents of unrespectability; scholars have talked about reformers even though they claim to have had the greatest difficulty in identifying who really was a reformer; it should have been similarly easy to identify advocates against whom the reformers pitted themselves. See, for example, the debates referred to in John D. Buenker, John C. Burnham, and Robert M. Crunden, *Progressivism* (Cambridge, Mass.: Schenkman Publishing Company, 1977). Social scientists of the early twentieth century tried to gain objectivity and naturalism by avoiding all moral and moralistic assumptions and just working with facts so as to remove the context and leave the particulars. In so doing they developed such an intellectual aversion to conventional moral standards that such standards were denied validity on any level as well as being excluded from analytic considerations—unless isolated in a group context, as in a backward culture. Social scientists, and the many historians influenced by them, we can now add, therefore missed the possibility that moral standards might have meaning in and of themselves without regard to whether they were right or wrong. The social-science study of values proceeded to another level of generalization, missing the possibility that the moral phenomena had obvious significance on a purely functional level. See Edward A. Purcell, Jr., *The Crisis of Democratic Theory: Scientific Naturalism & the Problem of Value* (Lexington: The University Press of Kentucky, 1973), 22 and passim. In passages in one of the classics, Robert H. Wiebe, *The Search for Order, 1877–1920* (New York: Hill and Wang, 1967), 9–10, 38–40, seemed to side with mobs and the underworld in a plausible way. Leo Hershkowitz, *Tweed's New York: Another Look* (Garden City, N.Y.: Anchor Press, 1977), maintains that Tweed was a victim, and that reformers used uplift—at least in politics—as a way of gaining power. As will be remarked below, Charles E. Rosenberg, "Sexuality, Class and Role in 19th-Century America," *American Quarterly* 25 (1973): 131–53, provides a glimpse of the functional importance of one set of morals in Victorian society.

10. See especially Paul Boyer, *Urban Masses and Moral Order in America, 1820–1920* (Cambridge, Mass.: Harvard University Press, 1978).

11. *Look*, quoted in John D'Emilio, *Sexual Politics, Sexual Communities: The Making of a Homosexual Minority in the United States, 1940–1970* (Chicago: University of Chicago Press, 1983), 179.

12. Tim Spencer, "Cigareetes, Whusky and Wild, Wild Women" (Unichappell Music Inc., 1947); title differs slightly from actual lyrics. William Waller Hening, *Statutes at Large: Being a Collection of All the Laws of Virginia, From the First Session of the Legislature in the Year 1619* (Richmond: Samuel Pleasants, 1812), 3: 71. See, for example, the list of bad habits in T. S. Arthur, *Advice to Young Men on Their Duties and Conduct in Life* (Boston: Phillips, Sampson, and Company, 1855), 144–45. An intermediate example is Deets Pickett and Charles C. Rarick, eds., *The Allied Reforms: A Handbook Dealing with Six Subjects*

(Washington: Board of Temperance, Prohibition, and Public Morals, n.d.). In my book, I have not attempted to explain why the elements in the constellation originally attracted one another; the traditional affiliation was very old; the English essayist, Charles Lamb, "A Farewell to Tobacco," in John Bain, Jr., *Tobacco in Song and Story* (New York: The New York Public Library, 1953 [1906]), 43, for example, referred to tobacco use as "Brother of Bacchus."

13. See, for example, *The Temperance Tales* (Boston: Whipple and Damrell, 1838), 1: 54; James Parton, *Smoking and Drinking* (Boston: Ticknor and Fields, 1868); William Jovanovich, "Sex, Crime, and, to a Lesser Extent, Sports," *Saturday Review*, 18 July 1964, 14–17. See, for example, David P. Thelen, *The New Citizenship: Origins of Progressivism in Wisconsin* (Columbia: University of Missouri Press, 1972), 146–47.

14. William Holmes McGuffey, *McGuffey's New Third Eclectic Reader: For Young Learners* (New York: Gordon Press, 1974 [c. 1853]), 118–20. Paragraph numbering omitted. Balls and suppers is a euphemism for unrespectable night life. A satirical counterpart, showing how much attitudes were changing after three-quarters of a century, appeared in Richard J. Walsh, *The Burning Shame of America: An Outline Against Nicotine* (Mount Vernon, N.Y.: Printing House of William Edwin Rudge, 1924), 12: "Every moralist knows full well that you must not let the camel's nose inside the tent. Let a boy smoke and his moral resistance breaks out and he soon gets other evil habits.... Immediately after starting to wantonly smoke, the next bad habit is spitting.... Next comes swearing. The braggadocio of smoking causes one to feel that he must also indulge in profanity. Then, alas!! follows rum! In nice homes smoking is not allowed to be done. So the smoker has to go where he can find boon companions. So he wends to the saloon (now the speakeasy) or to the club. There, while smoking, he is often urged to take his first sip of liquor. A sip leads to a swallow, a swallow to a bottoms-up, and soon he becomes a guzzler and ends in the gutters.... After that, all the horrors of the primrose path stare him in the face. Gambling and race-track touting, sleeping late in the morning like a sluggard, gadding about with wild women and other features of night life, marital quarreling and often hideous crimes of larceny, pilfering, embezzling and assault and battery, may be the outcome."

15. See, for example, Eric Single, Denise Kandel, and Richard Faust, "Patterns of Multiple Drug Use in High School," *Journal of Health and Social Behavior* 15 (1974): 344–57. A later version is in Phyllis L. Ellickson and Robert M. Bell, "Drug Prevention in Junior High: A Multi-Site Longitudinal Test," *Science* 247 (1990): 1299. Some of the cultural considerations are discussed in the anthropological literature, at least, which is referred to below in the notes to Chapter 3, but such discussions are by and large too ahistorical to be useful even in the face of the persistence of the constellation over many generations. In the 1950s, a researcher tried to determine if cancer was connected to alcohol as it seemed to be to cigarettes, but he was unable to find enough hard drinkers who did not smoke to constitute a statistical sample; "Cancer—The Progress," *Newsweek*, 11 November 1957, 112.

16. Neil Larry Shumsky, "Vice Responds to Reform: San Francisco, 1910–1914," *Journal of Urban History* 7 (1980): 31–47.

17. Roger Thompson, *Sex in Middlesex: Popular Mores in a Massachusetts County, 1649–1699* (Amherst: University of Massachusetts Press, 1986), 197. In that community, of course, some people saw the systematic work of the devil in all such misbehavior.

18. David W. Rose, "Prostitution and the Sporting Life Aspects of Working Class Culture and Sexuality in Nineteenth Century Wheeling," *Upper Ohio Valley Historical Review* 16 (1987): 7–31, provides a vivid, rich, and specific example of the evolution of a local underworld that illustrates the points to be made in the following paragraphs. In the late eighteenth and early nineteenth centuries, according to Ian McCalman, *Radical Under-*

world: Prophets, Revolutionaries and Pornographers in London, 1795–1840 (Cambridge: Cambridge University Press, 1988), especially chap. 10, the British underworld activities (most relevantly pornography and libertinism) contained sociopolitical and especially anti-clerical and populist motivations and overtones, but this element, particularly in rebellious and commercial naughtiness and pornography, largely disappeared by midcentury, and no serious counterparts appeared in the developing American underworld of the mid and late nineteenth centuries except, as will be noted, general resentment against Establishment respectables.

19. Brief accounts calling attention to the significance of this underworld in the United States in general are in Benjamin Rader, *American Sports from the Age of Folk Games to the Age of Spectators* (Englewood Cliffs, N.J.: Prentice-Hall, 1983), especially 88–89, 97–99, and an unpublished paper by Rader. I take the term "Victorian underworld" from his work. See, for example, "The Descent into the Abyss: Die literarische Entdeckung des social Untergrunds in der amerikanischen Fiktion des späten 19 Jahrhunderts," *Amerikastudien* 26 (1981): 260–69; and the casual brief description in Christopher Lasch, *The Culture of Narcissism: American Life in an Age of Diminishing Expectations* (New York: Warner Books, 1979), 198–99; and in Elliot J. Gorn, *The Manly Art: Bare-Knuckle Prize Fighting in America* (Ithaca: Cornell University Press, 1986), especially 182–83. A systematic account of the English counterpart is Kellow Chesney, *The Anti-Society: An Account of the Victorian Underworld* (Boston: Gambit Incorporated, 1970). Lynne M. Adrian, "Organizing the Rootless: American Hobo Subculture 1893–1932" (doctoral diss., University of Iowa, 1984). Elisha K. Kane, "The Jargon of the Underworld," *Dialect Notes* 5 (1927): 433. A classic early description was a series of articles by Edward Crapsey that ran under the title "The Nether Side of New York," in *The Galaxy* 11–12 (1871), and included all varieties of petty crime and destitution as well as gambling and dissipation.

20. See especially Mark Haller, "Urban Vice and Civic Reform: Chicago in the Early Twentieth Century," in *Cities in American History*, ed. Kenneth T. Jackson and Stanley K. Schultz, (New York: Alfred A. Knopf, 1972), 290–305; Mark Peel, "On the Margins: Lodgers and Boarders in Boston, 1860–1900," *Journal of American History* 72 (1986): 813–34; Richard B. Stott, *Workers in the Metropolis: Class, Ethnicity, and Youth in Antebellum New York City* (Ithaca: Cornell University Press, 1990); Joanne J. Meyerowitz, *Women Adrift: Independent Wage Earners in Chicago, 1880–1930* (Chicago: University of Chicago Press, 1988), chap. 5; Neil Larry Shumsky, "Tacit Acceptance: Respectable Americans and Segregated Prostitution, 1870–1910," *Journal of Social History* 19 (1986): 666–77. Marlou Belyea, "The Joy Ride and the Silver Screen: Commercialized Leisure, Delinquency and Play Reform in Los Angeles, 1900–1980" (doctoral diss., Boston University, 1983), provides a striking local history of the evolution of the cultural forces of the underworld; this outstanding work provides a powerful balance to accounts emphasizing eastern cities. The underworld was ultimately a cultural, not a geographical, unit, however much overlap there was in one time and place or another; see, for example, David Ward, *Poverty, Ethnicity, and the American City, 1840–1925; Changing Conceptions of the Slum and the Ghetto* (Cambridge: Cambridge University Press, 1989).

21. An outstanding description is in Mark H. Haller, "Policy Gambling, Entertainment, and the Emergence of Black Politics: Chicago from 1900 to 1940," *Journal of Social History* 24 (1991): 719–39. See, for example, Rachel Amelia Bernstein, "Boarding-House Keepers and Brothel Keepers in New York City, 1880–1910" (doctoral diss., Rutgers University, 1984), 119–21 and chap. 4 in general; and especially Haller, "Urban Vice and Civic Reform," 292. Jack-rolling meant robbing drunks.

22. Rose, "Prostitution and the Sporting Life," 16, uses the more descriptive term "anti-society." Susan G. Davis, " 'Making Night Hideous': Christmas Revelry and Public Order in Nineteenth-Century Philadelphia," *American Quarterly* 34 (1982): 185–99; this

has been expanded in Susan G. Davis, *Parades and Power: Street Theatre in Nineteenth-Century Philadelphia* (Philadelphia: Temple University Press, 1986). Ted Ownby, *Subduing Satan: Religion, Recreation, and Manhood in the Rural South, 1865-1920* (Chapel Hill: University of North Carolina Press, 1990), especially chap. 2.

23. See previous notes and especially Belyea, "The Joy Ride," and Haller, "Policy Gambling." Paul A. Gilje, *The Road to Mobocracy: Popular Disorder in New York City, 1763-1834* (Chapel Hill: University of North Carolina Press, 1987).

24. Adrienne Siegel, "Brothels, Bets and Bars: Popular Literature as Guidebook to the Urban Underground, 1840-1870," *North Dakota Quarterly*, Spring 1976, 5-22, especially 7.

25. John F. Kasson, *Amusing the Million: Coney Island at the Turn of the Century* (New York: Hill and Wang, 1978), 29. Adrian, "Organizing the Rootless," notes specifically that the underworld counterculture values were set in a larger set of values common to the whole culture, and in practice of course most underworld people as individuals followed a mixed set of standards.

26. There are a number of accounts of the origin of the dominant position of the respectables and respectability in northern communities in which religious institutions and beliefs were the key factors in a society faced with economic and social changes early in the nineteenth century; see, for example, Randolph A. Roth, *The Democratic Dilemma: Religion, Reform, and the Social Order in the Connecticut River Valley of Vermont, 1791-1850* (New York: Cambridge University Press, 1987), especially chaps. 7 and 8; and Paul E. Johnson, *A Shopkeeper's Millennium: Society and Revivals in Rochester, New York, 1815-1837* (New York: Hill and Wang, 1978). W. J. Rorabaugh, "Beer, Lemonade, and Propriety in the Gilded Age," in *Dining in America, 1850-1900*, ed. Kathryn Grover (Amherst: University of Massachusetts Press, 1987), 24-28, presents one discussion of the middle classes on whom respectability was based. Lewis Perry, *Intellectual Life in America: A History*, 2d ed. (Chicago: University of Chicago Press, 1989), 178-79. An anatomy of respectability and to some extent anti-respectability in England, which was in striking ways similar to that of the United States and in many ways differed from it, is F.M.L. Thompson, *The Rise of Respectable Society: A Social History of Victorian Britain, 1830-1900* (London: Fontana Press, 1988). Peter Dobkin Hall, *The Organization of American Culture, 1700-1900: Private Institutions, Elites, and the Origins of American Nationality* (New York: New York University Press, 1982), traces another source of respectability and points out, especially 182, how respectable nineteenth-century Americans became obsessed with the idea of "character."

27. The original exposition cited in the Oxford Dictionary and emphasizing group determinations of prosocial and antisocial is Robert R. Sears, "Relation of Early Socialization Experiences to Aggression in Middle Childhood," *Journal of Abnormal and Social Psychology* 63 (1961): 471.

28. A virtual handbook of ideal respectability is Samuel Fallows et al., *Hot Shot Fired at Fashion's Follies and Society's Abominations: Portrayed by Eminent Thinkers and Writers* (Chicago: Standard Publishing Co., 1889).

29. The clearest example utilizing historical materials is Kai T. Erikson, *Wayward Puritans: A Study in the Sociology of Deviance* (New York: John Wiley and Sons, 1966). Sociologists distinguish between deviant actions and deviant people; typically a person can commit one or many deviant actions without necessarily becoming deviant him/herself. See, for example, *The Substance of Social Deviance*, ed. Victoria Lynn Swigert and Ronald A. Farrell (Palo Alto: Mayfield Publishing Company, 1984).

30. I am well aware that sociologists differ about deviance in theory. The fact remains that in sociology or history, fine points of theory tend to disappear in empirical research. My use of the concept is not aimed at improving sociological theory but simply at helping make sense of historical events and the evolution of social structures. See David Downes

and Paul Rock, *Understanding Deviance: A Guide to the Sociology of Crime and Rule-Breaking* (Oxford: Clarendon Press, 1982), especially 253. See, for example, Robert L. Hampel, *Temperance and Prohibition in Massachusetts, 1813–1852* (Ann Arbor: UMI Research Press, 1982), 32–35. An insight into the operation of deviance in the nineteenth century is found in David Murray, "College Morals," *American Educational Monthly* 10 (1875): 29–31, describing how college students established a separate sovereignty of moral standards and affected even the surrounding community—until the students were integrated into the general society. Even being the relative of a deviant (a mental patient, for example) can confer a special, and not necessarily desirable, social status, as in the past many victims of vice and their families also found out. A particularly relevant modern discussion is Charles W. Lidz, Andrew L. Walker, and Leroy C. Gould, *Heroin, Deviance and Morality* (Beverly Hills: Sage Publications, 1980). The historical application and examples are from Benedict F. Giamo, "On the Bowery: Symbolic Action in American Culture and Subculture" (doctoral diss., Emory University, 1987), especially chap. 2 and 326–27; Giamo describes in detail the process of labeling in late-nineteenth-century America.

31. Troyer and Markle, *Cigarettes*.

32. I have used the term "greed" to indicate that people who were making money from the bad habits tended in a remarkable way to act with immoderate and unusually single-minded zeal to maximize their gross incomes (often, incidentally, not successfully). I have avoided the more precise term indicating unusual pursuit of gain, "avarice," to avoid theological overtones as much as possible. Greed was particularly out of place as, over many decades, especially in the twentieth century, American entrepreneurs—with many, many exceptions—tended to get away from crudities in the stereotype of the new rich and instead to pursue business aims with a mix of motives and in a broader social context. Money could of course also be made in ways other than by merchandising. My narratives below contain many instances, for example, in which the rich used their wealth and influence to defend various of the bad habits so as to shift taxes onto consumers and save the money of the privileged. It should also be noted that, contrary to many historical analyses, the evidence that I have found shows that the business interests that are described below ultimately were not devoted to shoring up bourgeois behavior but rather were undermining and opposing it; by the mid twentieth century, simplistic historical interpretations connecting capitalism and advocates of respectability will not stand up, and the opposite, rather, was the case. Moreover, Richard Butsch, "Introduction: Leisure and Hegemony in America" and "Home Video and Corporate Plans: Capital's Limited Power to Manipulate Leisure," in *For Fun and Profit: The Transformation of Leisure into Consumption*, ed. Richard Butsch (Philadelphia: Temple University Press, 1990), especially 18–19 and 220–23, 227, comments that economic interest in many ways proceeded through small as well as large businesses, a point to which I shall return.

33. One scholar who has recognized the importance of parochialism is David Hollinger, "Ethnic Diversity, Cosmopolitanism and the Emergence of the American Liberal Intelligentsia," *American Quarterly* 25 (1975): 133–51, and he saw progress in the way in which both bourgeois WASPs and lower-class groups escaped parochialism. For the nineteenth century, see Gregory H. Singleton, "Protestant Voluntary Organizations and the Shaping of Victorian America," *American Quarterly* 27 (1975): 549–60. Other scholars have resisted recognizing the real power of lower-order identity. Roy Rosenzweig, *Eight Hours for What We Will: Workers and Leisure in an Industrial City, 1870–1930* (Cambridge: Cambridge University Press, 1983). Francis G. Couvares, *The Remaking of Pittsburgh: Class and Culture in an Industrializing City, 1877–1919* (Albany: The State University of New York Press, 1984), especially 118–26. An early example is described in Paul Johnson, " 'Art' and the Language of Progress in Early-Industrial Paterson: Sam Patch at Clinton

Bridge," *American Quarterly* 40 (1988): 433–49. Characterizing lower-order parochialism as a quest for autonomy, as many scholars do, underlines the negative aspect of this parochialism, as I shall comment below. Obviously, those people were attempting to be autonomous from something, and that turned out to be the respectables. Butsch, *For Fun and Profit*, shows how lower-order parochialism was transformed by commercialization.

34. See previous note. Leonard Ellis, "Men Among Men: An Exploration of All-Male Relationships in Victorian America" (doctoral diss., Columbia University, 1982), chaps. 1–3, especially 50–54.

35. Because so many people have difficulty with the concept of lower class, despite the fact that generations of contemporary sources describe class phenomena clearly, I have tried to avoid that term although including parts of the idea in the more functional designation of lower orders of society. Even classical Marxism recognized the existence of large numbers of poor people who were not worthy of being included within the virtuous working class. The fact that the term "lower" (as in "lower orders") is generally understood and at the same time is prejudicial does not make me abandon it; indeed, it carries in it the deviant connotation of past times. Anyone should nowadays be able to consider either the unfortunate or the different worthy of respect. Even if one were to retain the term "lower class," as I shall remark again, especially in Chapter 10, lower-class *status* (imposed from the outside) is substantially different from lower-class *patterns of behavior*; I am concerned with people who manifested the latter. As I have noted, many people who were poor had middle-class standards; and many comfortably well-off folk conducted themselves according to slum standards. Stott, *Workers in the Metropolis*, 270–75, explicitly defines social class in cultural terms. Ellis, "Men Among Men," xvii; and see Ira M. Wasserman, "Prohibition and Ethnocultural Conflict: The Missouri Prohibition Referendum of 1918," *Social Science Quarterly* 70 (1989): 886–901, who suggests that ultimately not ethnicity but recency of immigration determined alliances with unrespectability. I shall be noting below, particularly in attitudes toward sexual behavior, the complexity of standards, in that many groups with persisting patterns contrary to middle-class standards nevertheless, and apparently quite sincerely, gave lip service to the conventions.

36. A recent partial history of one type of rebelliousness is Stanley Coben, *Rebellion Against Victorianism: The Impetus for Cultural Change in 1920s America* (New York: Oxford University Press, 1991), especially chaps. 2 and 3. Grady McWhiney, *Cracker Culture: Celtic Ways in the Old South* (Tuscaloosa: University of Alabama Press, 1988), has written dramatically of the origins and nature of regional cultural differences—in effect, anti-bourgeois attitudes and customs—that in the North translated often into social-class differences. This regional devotion to leisure and defiance of respectability McWhiney characterizes as primarily a cultural difference; it became rebellious only when northern respectables attempted to change the local customs. Stott, *Workers in the Metropolis*, 267–69. Meyerowitz, *Women Adrift*, 114–15.

37. Edward Abrahams, *The Lyrical Left: Randolph Bourne, Alfred Stieglitz, and the Origins of Cultural Radicalism in America* (Charlottesville: University Press of Virginia, 1986), especially 2–3, 10.

38. See especially Boyer, *Urban Masses and Moral Order*. Jed Dannenbaum, *Drink and Disorder: Temperance Reform in Cincinnati from the Washingtonian Revival to the WCTU* (Urbana: University of Illinois Press, 1984). Charles C. Cole, Jr., *The Social Ideas of the Northern Evangelists*, 1826–1860 (New York: Octagon Books, 1977 [c. 1954]), especially 98–99, 114–25. I am not in this book attempting to treat systematically the forces of good; some account of the secularization of morals and the evolution of do-gooding can be found in such works as William E. Nelson, *The Roots of American Bureaucracy* (Cambridge, Mass.: Harvard University Press, 1982), chap. 4; and Mark Fackler, "Moral Guardians of the Movies and Social Responsibility of the Press," in *Mass Media Between*

the Wars: Perceptions of Cultural Tension, 1918–1941, ed. Catherine L. Covert and John D. Stevens (Syracuse: Syracuse University Press, 1984), 181–97. See also note 9, above (Purcell).

T W O : *The Turning Point: Repealing Prohibition*

1. K. Austin Kerr, *Organized for Prohibition: A New History of the Anti-Saloon League* (New Haven: Yale University Press, 1985), chap. 7, stresses the power of the alcoholic-beverage businesses on those rare occasions before Prohibition when they did unite.

2. Daniel Yankelovich, *New Rules: Searching for Self-Fulfillment in a World Turned Upside Down* (New York: Random House, 1981), comments on the amount of change that did occur, given how slightly culture as a whole—using Middletown as a sample—changed over those decades.

3. Durant Drake, *The New Morality* (New York: Macmillan, 1928), vi. Walter Lippmann, *A Preface to Morals* (New York: Macmillan, 1929). Another well-known contemporary example was Freda Kirchwey, ed., *Our Changing Morality* (New York: Albert and Charles Boni, 1924).

4. See previous note and, for example, Robert Erwin, "What Happened to Respectability?" *American Scholar* 52 (1983): 354–62. Lary May, *Screening Out the Past: The Birth of Mass Culture and the Motion Picture Industry* (New York: Oxford University Press, 1980), xii. Stanley Coben, *Rebellion Against Victorianism: The Impetus for Cultural Change in 1920s America* (New York: Oxford University Press, 1991), gives a version of the shift emphasizing gender and ethnicity.

5. Frederick Lewis Allen, *Only Yesterday: An Informal History of the Nineteen-Twenties* (New York: Harper and Row, 1959 reprint [1931]), chap. 5. It is striking that a modern historian, May, *Screening Out the Past*, assumes and confirms the revolution of manners and morals that Allen described, with the same connection to a consumer culture. Ross L. Finney, "A Sociologist's Views on Character Education," *Religious Education* 25 (1930): 207. For more modern scholarship, see, for example, Gilman M. Ostrander, "The Revolution in Morals," in *Change and Continuity in Twentieth-Century America: The 1920's,* ed. John Braeman, Robert H. Bremner, and David Brody (Columbus: Ohio State University Press, 1968), 323–49. Another scholarly account is found in Paul S. Boyer, *Purity in Print: The Vice-Society Movement and Book Censorship in America* (New York: Charles Scribner's Sons, 1968), especially chap. 4. Paula Fass, *The Damned and the Beautiful: American Youth in the 1920's* (New York: Oxford University Press, 1977), confirms that crucial changes in standards took place in the 1920s; sometimes (20) she characterizes the change as a destruction of values, and in other places (260–62) she speaks of new standards, but she delineates clearly the timing and substantial nature of change and, true to her age, characterizes the new as "modern." Roderick Nash, *The Nervous Generation: American Thought, 1917–1930* (Chicago: Rand McNally and Company, 1970), writes in terms of conflicting standards. John Modell, *Into One's Own: From Youth to Adulthood in the United States, 1920–1975* (Berkeley: University of California Press, 1989), especially 39 and 70 and chap. 3 in general. Norman H. Clark, *Deliver Us from Evil: An Interpretation of American Prohibition* (New York: W. W. Norton, 1976), 210–14, sets the change specifically in the context of Prohibition.

6. Moreover, many of them read into the association a particularly contorted—but much repeated—piece of logic: misbehavior represented a revolt against Prohibition, and therefore Prohibition caused the misbehavior. There is more to be said about this line of reasoning in other connections, not least that the repeal of Prohibition was utilized later to justify the rightness of the misbehaviors.

7. See, for example, "A Cross Section of Veteran Sentiment," *Home Sector*, 17 April 1920, 7. This campaign may also have derived from the attempts of conservatives to manipulate veterans' groups for economic and political purposes. The strident writing in favor of drinking, smoking, and so on in addition had more than a slight flavor of hostility to what were perceived as female standards, in other words, expressed conventional lower-order misogyny as well as rebellion against the moral arbiters of respectable society; this subject will come up again, especially in chapter 10.

8. Kerr, *Organized for Prohibition*; Clark, *Deliver Us from Evil*, 4. The narrative and analysis that follow draw particularly upon Clark's work.

9. The relationship between law and morality is not relevant to my considerations here. Paul L. Murphy, "Societal Morality and Individual Freedom," in *Law, Alcohol, and Order: Perspectives on National Prohibition*, ed. David E. Kyvig (Westport, Ct.: Greenwood Press, 1985), 67–80, summarizes a changing relationship. See also chapter 10, below.

10. *Literary Digest*, quoted in Jo Ann Dotson, "News Coverage by Selected Publications of Prohibition from 16 January 1919 to 16 January 1920" (Master's thesis, Pennsylvania State University, 1964), 36.

11. See especially John R. Meers, "The California Wine and Grape Industry and Prohibition," *California Historical Society Quarterly* 46 (1967): 19–32. Thomas Pinney, *A History of Wine in America: From the Beginnings to Prohibition* (Berkeley: University of California Press, 1989), especially chap. 16, puts the wine industry in context. Home production of wines was based on an interpretation of Section 29 of the Volstead Act. Some states, such as Kansas, did outlaw possession of alcohol.

12. Ernest Gordon, *The Wrecking of the Eighteenth Amendment* (Francestown, N.H.: The Alcohol Information Press, 1943), 18–35, presents evidence that the federal official charged with supervising enforcement, Secretary of the Treasury Andrew Mellon, was involved both financially and politically in the alcoholic-beverage business; he was certainly not an effective enforcer of Prohibition. Cf. Harvey O'Connor, *Mellon's Millions: The Biography of a Fortune* (New York: The John Day Company, 1933), 236–37. Mark H. Haller, "Bootleggers as Businessmen: From City Slums to City Builders," in *Law, Alcohol, and Order*, ed. Kyvig, 139–42. Mark H. Haller, "Philadelphia Bootlegging and the Report of the Special August Grand Jury," *Pennsylvania Magazine of History and Biography* 109 (1985): 215–33.

13. The basic narrative of the foregoing paragraphs is best followed in Clark, *Deliver Us From Evil*, but special points appear in Kerr, *Organized for Prohibition*; J. C. Burnham, "New Perspectives on the Prohibition 'Experiment' of the 1920's," *Journal of Social History* 2 (1968): 51–68; and other works cited in the notes to this chapter.

14. David E. Kyvig, *Repealing National Prohibition* (Chicago: University of Chicago Press, 1979), 56–58. Some suggestion of the complexity of New York politics is found in Robert F. Wesser, "Women Suffrage, Prohibition, and the New York Experience in the Progressive Era," in *An American Historian: Essays to Honor Selig Adler*, ed. Milton Plesur (Buffalo: State University of New York, 1980), 140–48. The repeal, however symbolically it was interpreted then, ironically did not in fact diminish substantive participation on the part of New York State Police in enforcement because bootleggers were almost invariably involved in other criminal activity at the same time; see Allan S. Everest, *Rum Across the Border: The Prohibition Era in Northern New York* (Syracuse: Syracuse University Press, 1978), especially 61–62.

15. Boyer, *Purity in Print*, especially chap. 5, 151–54.

16. Details of the basic events of repeal are in a number of scholarly studies, chiefly Kyvig, *Repealing National Prohibition*, which emphasizes the legal and formally political events; Dayton E. Heckman, "Prohibition Passes: The Story of the Association Against the Prohibition Amendment" (doctoral diss., Ohio State University, 1939), in which the

propaganda campaign is the center of the account; and Andrew Sinclair, *Prohibition: The Era of Excess* (Boston: Little, Brown and Company, 1962). A recent perceptive historiographical discussion is Mark Edward Lender, "The Historian and Repeal: A Survey of the Literature and Research Opportunities," in *Law, Alcohol, and Order*, ed. Kyvig, 177–205. See also previous note.

17. Larry Engelmann, "Organized Thirst: The Story of Repeal in Michigan," in *Alcohol, Reform and Society: The Liquor Issue in Social Context*, ed. Jack S. Blocker, Jr. (Westport, Ct.: Greenwood Press, 1979), 174, raises the public-opinion issue pointedly. See especially Bartlett Campbell Jones, "The Debate Over National Prohibition, 1920–1933" (doctoral diss., Emory University, 1961); William P. Beazell, quoted in ibid., 261.

18. See in general and for the stages, Heckman, "Prohibition Passes," and Andrew Cyrus McLaughlin, "Satire as a Weapon Against Prohibition, 1920–1928: Expression of a Cultural Conflict" (doctoral diss., Stanford University, 1969). Particularly astute and revealing is Robert F. Burk, *The Corporate State and the Broker State: The Du Ponts and American National Politics, 1925–1940* (Cambridge, Mass.: Harvard University Press, 1990), chaps. 2–4.

19. Lavinia Larson, "An Inquiry into the Propaganda of Some Prominent Organizations for and Against Prohibition" (doctoral diss., Columbia University, 1927), 29–30. This point is made from another perspective in Burk, *The Corporate State*, especially chap. 3.

20. The high point of nominally dry election strength in Congress was 1928; most people were unaware of the shallowness of actual dry strength until very late. The wet strategy is described in Heckman, "Prohibition Passes." The dry disaster is explained in Kerr, *Organized for Prohibition*. And see in general, Kyvig, *Repealing National Prohibition*, especially 54; Fletcher Dobyns, *The Amazing Story of Repeal: An Exposé of the Power of Propaganda* (Chicago: Willett, Clark and Company, 1940). It would be an error to underestimate either the importance of the AAPA or the fact that other groups were extremely influential; the most obvious national organization with which journalists had contact was the United States Brewers' Association.

21. Kyvig, *Repealing National Prohibition*, especially 39–51, 72–97; Burk, *The Corporate State*, chaps. 2–5; Dobyns, *The Amazing Story*, chap. 1, presents additional details from a set of congressional hearings in 1930, which can be supplemented with the Papers of the Association Against the Prohibition Amendment and the Women's Organization for National Prohibition Reform (microfilm edition, Wilmington, Del.: Scholarly Resources, Inc., 1981).

22. See particularly Heckman, "Prohibition Passes," and, for example, "Newspaper Treatment of Prohibition News," *Christian Century* 48 (1931): 292.

23. See especially Heckman, "Prohibition Passes," and Burk, *The Corporate State*, chaps. 2–5.

24. Kyvig, *Repealing National Prohibition*, 58. See also Jones, "The Debate," 208.

25. See especially McLaughlin, "Satire as a Weapon," 3, 28, 38, and passim; this study is much broader than the title might indicate. Edward A. Martin, *H. L. Mencken and the Debunkers* (Athens: The University of Georgia Press, 1984), especially chap. 1, traces the roots of satirizing philistinism in the United States. James H. Billington, "Education and Culture: Beyond 'Lifestyles,'" in *Virtue—Public and Private*, ed. Richard John Neuhaus (Grand Rapids: William B. Eerdmans Publishing Co., 1986), 3, identifies the aesthetic as an opposite of moral in American life and specifically contends that the ultimate development of the aesthetic has been television with all its horrors.

26. New Orleans *Times-Democrat*, quoted in "The Impending Demise of John Barleycorn," *Current Opinion*, July 1919, 8. Heckman, "Prohibition Passes," especially 87. Dotson, "News Coverage," 38.

27. See Sinclair, *Prohibition*, 309–15; Heckman, "Prohibition Passes," chap. 4; and Burnham, "New Perspectives," 65. Details as to the way in which news was twisted are in Larson, "An Inquiry into the Propaganda," 59–61, 70. New York was still an issue in Freeman Tilden, "The New York Influence—America's Journalistic Poison," *Scribner's Commentator*, December 1941, 7–12, although the controversies were different. See below in this chapter for other events that helped determine the shift in the mass media.

28. Dobyns, *The Amazing Story*, 58. Papers of the Association Against the Prohibition Amendment, Reel 1, contains not only Du Pont's incriminating letter but also others indicating how the network of great wealth was used to try to show that leading businesspeople opposed Prohibition. The approach to the businesspeople was almost always in terms of respectability and couched in a context of defending business—if the alcohol makers could be held responsible for drunkenness, as one of Pierre Du Pont's chief arguments of the late 1920s went, so could the auto industry be held liable for auto accidents and be put out of business by law. Reels 1–2. Burk, *The Corporate State*, especially 46–47, provides details of the extent to which actual financing of the AAPA was centralized and concentrated in the Du Pont family.

29. Sinclair, *Prohibition*, 313, makes this point but only alludes to the increasing demographic and power base of the lower-class provincials ("semi-literate workers," as he calls them). As noted above, Ira M. Wasserman, "Prohibition and Ethnocultural Conflict: The Missouri Prohibition Referendum of 1918," *Social Science Quarterly* 70 (1989): 886–901, shows that neither urban nor religious factors influenced voting on Prohibition; the critical and decisive element was recent immigration. The role of Bernarr Macfadden's *Graphic* in New York in the 1920s was important in reorienting the press to the lower orders.

30. See especially Sinclair, *Prohibition*; Burnham, "New Perspectives on the Prohibition 'Experiment.' "; Larson, "An Inquiry into the Propaganda," 70. George L. Bird, "Newspaper Attitudes in Law Breaking," *Journalism Quarterly* 15 (1938): 150. Implicit in the crime news was the idea that any violations at all would represent a failure of the law, which was then and now not the usual standard for judging laws (for example traffic laws, or laws against mugging, as will be noted again below). Repealers never would say what a tolerable level of violation was any more than drug and gambling advocates later would.

31. See McLaughlin, "Satire as a Weapon," especially 78, 141–71. President's Research Committee on Social Trends, *Recent Social Trends in the United States*, 2 vols. (New York: McGraw-Hill Book Company, 1933), 1: 424–28.

32. See McLaughlin, "Satire as a Weapon," especially 39–40, 72, 80. H. L. Mencken, quoted in Jones, "The Debate," 189–90.

33. Thomas B. Gilmore, *Equivocal Spirits: Alcoholism and Drinking in Twentieth-Century Literature* (Chapel Hill: University of North Carolina Press, 1987), 16, 170–75, finds the modern alcoholic figure emerging just around the time of repeal and a negative reaction to alcohol only a half century later. Jack London, *John Barleycorn* (New York: The Century Co., 1913). Andrew L. Knauf, "Alcohol as Symbolic Buttress in Hemingway's Long Fiction" (doctoral diss., University of Detroit, 1979), 9n; the incidence in *A Farewell to Arms* was 36 per cent of the pages. The list of "wet" novels that were prominent in the Prohibition years is impressive and indicative, including also works by Gertrude Atherton, Sinclair Lewis, and William Faulkner; see Campbell, "The Debate," 208. Donald W. Goodwin, *Alcohol and the Writer* (Kansas City: Andrews and McMeel, 1988), documents the astonishing number of leading American writers who were actually alcoholics, including four or five out of the six U.S. Nobel Prize winners.

34. Sinclair, *Prohibition*, 319–24; Edgar Dale, *The Content of Motion Pictures* (New York: Macmillan, 1935), especially 167–70. Traders in alcoholic beverages were well aware that before Prohibition, movie makers had been very effective in generating dry sentiment

by portraying alcohol in an extremely unfavorable light and reinforcing dry propaganda so as to blame alcoholic beverages, as one trade journalist complained, for "all the crimes and carnality of which human beings are guilty." Joan L. Silverman, " 'I'll Never Touch Another Drop': Images of Alcoholism and Temperance in American Popular Culture, 1874–1919" (doctoral diss., New York University, 1979), 317–18, 336–37. The contrast in the 1920s was both extreme and significant.

35. May, *Screening Out the Past*. Robin Room, "The Movies and the Wettening of America: The Media as Amplifiers of Cultural Change," *British Journal of Addiction* 83 (1988): 11–18.

36. Dotson, "News Coverage," especially 17–21. See especially Lewis A. Erenberg, *Steppin' Out: New York Nightlife and the Transformation of American Culture, 1890–1930* (Westport, Ct.: Greenwood Press, 1981). Stanley Walker, *The Night Club Era* (New York: Frederick A. Stokes Company, 1933); the quote is from 52.

37. Erenberg, *Steppin' Out*; Walker, *The Night Club Era*. Harold Ross, as quoted in Mc-Laughlin, "Satire as a Weapon," 105. As will be noted in the next chapter, Perry Duis, *The Saloon: Public Drinking in Chicago and Boston, 1880–1920* (Urbana: University of Illinois Press, 1983), goes so far as to suggest that the saloon was actually on the decline before World War I as the cabaret began to coopt public drinking in the large cities. If the night club was the saloon of the rich, then once again, the issue in Prohibition was the saloon. The way in which the point of view of the rebellious sophisticate and the New York journalist was rapidly taken up by upper-middle-class groups attempting to appear up-to-date is demonstrated repeatedly in Fass, *The Damned and the Beautiful*, which is based largely on material from college newspapers.

38. See, for example, McLaughlin, "Satire as a Weapon," 106–17. Don Hausdorff, "Magazine Humor and Popular Morality, 1929–34," *Journalism Quarterly* 41 (1964): 510.

39. Richard Jensen, *The Winning of the Midwest: Social and Political Conflict, 1888–1896* (Chicago: University of Chicago Press, 1971), 185. Timberlake, *Prohibition and the Progressive Movement*, 55.

40. See especially Paul A. Carter, *Another Part of the Twenties* (New York: Columbia University Press, 1977), 96–100; Heckman, "Prohibition Passes," 207; and Papers of the Association Against the Prohibition Amendment.

41. Carter, *Another Part of the Twenties*, 94–95, calls attention to the implicit anti-clerical element in the wet propaganda.

42. See especially Jan C. Dawson, *The Unusable Past: America's Puritan Tradition, 1830–1930* (Chico, Calif.: Scholars Press, 1984); the quote is from 131; Frederick J. Hoffman, *The Twenties: American Writing in the Postwar Decade* (New York: Viking, 1955), 314–27. Early use of the stereotype can be found, for example, in *Puck* 19 (1886): 360–61, and *Life* 64 (1914): 272. Rollin Kirby, "The Death of a Puppet," *Vanity Fair*, December 1933, 56. Warren I. Susman, *Culture as History: The Transformation of American Society in the Twentieth Century* (New York: Pantheon Books, 1973), chap. 3. McLaughlin, "Satire as a Weapon," especially 78, 141–71.

43. Kyvig, *Repealing National Prohibition*, describes these AAPA campaigns in detail. Heckman, "Prohibition Passes," chap. 9, describes the inversion of symbols. Martin, *H. L. Mencken*, points out that the aesthetes were offended in large part by the inflated language of the forces of propriety—like Matthews's "fiendish, corrupt, and hell-soaked institution"—and wanted more precise expression. The satire therefore was tied to literary streams symbolized in part by realism.

44. Carter, *Another Part of the Twenties*, especially 90–91, explores some of the personal-liberty attitudes and arguments. See, for example, C. C. Vincent, "A Warning," *Libertarian*, Fourth Quarter 1923, 27, and other issues of this journal.

45. McLaughlin, "Satire as a Weapon," 91.

46. Kyvig, *Repealing National Prohibition*, especially 46–47, 49, 94–96; Heckman, "Prohibition Passes," especially chap. 12. Dobyns, *The Amazing Story*. Papers of the Association Against the Prohibition Amendment, passim.

47. Boyer, *Purity in Print*. McLaughlin, "Satire as a Weapon," especially 32, 81.

48. One account is Gordon L. Dillow, "Thank You for Not Smoking, The Hundred-Year War Against the Cigarette," *American Heritage*, February/March 1981, 94–107. See Chapter 3, below. See, for example, the anti-cigarette cartoon in *Tobacco Leaf*, 8 June 1898, 4. "Prohibition and the Trade," *Tobacco*, 15 October 1908, 1. "Candy in Cigar Stores," *Tobacco*, 15 May 1919, 6. "Dethroning King Tobacco," *Tobacco*, 21 April 1921, 6. "Shall Tobacco Follow Alcohol?" *Independent*, 12 April 1919, 50.

49. Examples include Joseph Mendelsohn, in *Tobacco*, 17 April 1919, 4; Leroy R. Eisenhower [president of the Personal Liberty Association], in *Tobacco Leaf*, 15 September 1923, 18. "Cigarette Magic," *Tobacco*, 1 March 1928, 8.

50. A. Bijur, quoted in "Attacks Explained," *Tobacco*, 22 May 1919, 4. I return to this subject in Chapter 10.

51. Roland Marchand, *Advertising the American Dream: Making Way for Modernity, 1920–1940* (Berkeley: University of California Press, 1985). Malcolm Cowley, *Exile's Return, A Literary Odyssey of the 1920's* (New York: Viking, 1956 [1951]), especially 60–65. The consumption ethic appears elsewhere, below, especially in chapter 10.

52. Eyewitness journalist Will Irwin, *Propaganda and the News, Or, What Makes You Think So?* (New York: McGraw-Hill Book Company, 1936), 270–72, comes to the same conclusions that I do about the relation of repeal and gangsters in the media. Images from the works of writer Damon Runyon and movies starring James Cagney in the 1930s are still-familiar examples.

53. See Paul Gregory Kooistra, "American Robin Hoods: The Criminal as Social Hero" (doctoral diss., University of Virginia, 1982), especially 20–21, 50, 294–95. *Judge*, cited in Hausdorff, "Magazine Humor," 510.

54. See especially Rupert Wilkinson, *American Tough, The Tough-Guy Tradition and American Character* (Westport, Ct.: Greenwood Press, 1984), especially 3–4, 106–7; and Richard A. Filloy, "Of Drink and Detectives: The Genesis and Function of a Literary Convention," *Contemporary Drug Problems* 13 (1986): 249–71. H. L. Mencken, quoted in McLaughlin, "Satire as a Weapon," 54. Instrumental alcohol consumption is use to achieve some secondary end, such as courage or social conviviality.

55. Dotson, "News Coverage," 28–31. "John Barleycorn's Hopes," *Literary Digest*, 8 March 1914, 14.

56. May, *Screening Out the Past*, 32–41, traces the revolution in morals directly to the new urban rich just after the turn of the century, and he also includes the lower orders as a force subversive of the old respectabililty. Samuel Walker, "Terence V. Powderly, the Knights of Labor, and the Temperance Issue," *Societas* 5 (1975): 279–93. At one point, saloon keepers who had been expelled from one fraternal organization, the Knights of Columbus, because their occupation was not respectable, sued to keep the benefits of the group; *Bar and Buffet*, January 1908, 3; and this same magazine reported many other instances of saloon keepers' being excluded in these years.

57. Copy of Pierre S. Du Pont, "Prohibition Plainly Put," radio address, 9 June 1932, furnished by Eleutherian Mills Historical Library from Longwood Manuscripts Group 10, Series A, File 1023–25.

58. Burk, *The Corporate State*, dissects Du Pont's motives in detail and places them in a broad context. The resentment of populist respectables was suggested by Elliott Rosen, a scholar who has been allowed access to the Du Pont papers, at "Prohibition Fifty Years Later: Implications for Law, Alcohol, and Order," meetings at the Eleutherian Mills Historical Library, April 1983. Kyvig, *Repealing National Prohibition*, especially 80–84,

discusses explicit motivations, which turned out to be mouthing of slogans commonly available in the wet press. When, later, John D. Rockefeller, Jr., went from the dry side to the wet side, a dry editorial writer in "Who Made Mr. Rockefeller Wet?" *Christian Century* 49 (1932): 757–58, noted from his statements that "his mind reflects the credulity induced by daily reading of the wet metropolitan press," a not-implausible inference of the impact of the press even had Rockefeller not been credulous.

59. *Washington Post*, 6 May 1908, 5. *Delineator*, December 1933, 44. *Vanity Fair*, December 1933, 4k. *Delineator*, November 1933, 93; November 1934, 72. Room, "The Movies and the Wettening."

60. So far scholars who have recognized that broad issues were involved in the repeal of Prohibition have talked in terms of the clash of cultures—usually formulated, following propagandists such as Mencken, as rural bigotry versus a tolerant urban pluralism. Joseph R. Gusfield, *Symbolic Crusade: Status Politics and the American Temperance Movement* (Urbana: University of Illinois Press, 1963), more precisely describes a status conflict between old middle-class evangelical temperance groups and the very rich/very poor who always had drunk. He shows, too, how urban working-class and lower-order groups were coming into power, and he concludes that the symbolic temperance crusade that brought Prohibition polarized cultural groups in the United States as much after 1933 as before. Sinclair, *Prohibition*, another shrewd scholar, comes to a similar conclusion and holds that both bone-dry Prohibition and the total repeal of Prohibition were extremist actions that only sharp social divisions can explain. Gusfield goes on, however, to point out specifically that the Prohibition struggles involved the social status of the cultural groups involved, so that the temperance forces lost out to lower-order and urban working-class standards, to the point that it was possible to talk about "abstinence as a deviant behavior." A general discussion of the 1920s clash is Paul A. Carter, *The Twenties in America*, 2d ed. (Arlington Heights, Ill.: Harlan Davidson, Inc., 1975), chap. 3. Clark, *Deliver Us from Evil*, also discusses these matters.

61. *Vanity Fair*, November 1930, 105.

62. Patricia Helsing, "Gambling—The Issues and Policy Decisions Involved in the Trend Toward Legalization—A Statement of the Current Anachronism of Benign Prohibition," in Commission on the Review of the National Policy Toward Gambling, *Gambling in America* (Washington: U. S. Government Printing Office, 1976), Appendix 1, 773. See, for example, in a relevant context, Charles W. Lidz, Andrew L. Walker, and Leroy C. Gould, *Heroin, Deviance and Morality* (Beverly Hills: Sage Publications, 1980), 29–30.

THREE: *Drinking*

1. Robert L. Hampel, *Temperance and Prohibition in Massachusetts 1813–1852* (Ann Arbor: UMI Research Press, 1987), 5. Some indication of the scholarship that does exist is found in the notes to this chapter and the preceding one. An incisive history of temperance efforts is Jack S. Blocker, Jr., *American Temperance Movements: Cycles of Reform* (Boston: Twayne Publishers, 1989). David Weir Conroy, "The Culture and Politics of Drink in Colonial and Revolutionary Massachusetts, 1681–1790" (doctoral diss., University of Connecticut, 1987), describes the conditions that made tavern keepers a special political but not necessarily cultural opposition group.

2. This paragraph and the following paragraphs are based upon the excellent and recent secondary literature, which includes: a fine standard history of the use of alcohol, Mark Edward Lender and James Kirby Martin, *Drinking in America: A History*, 2d ed. (New York: The Free Press, 1987); Ian Tyrrell, *Sobering Up: From Temperance to Prohibition in Antebellum America, 1800–1860* (Westport, Ct.: Greenwood Press, 1979); William J.

Rorabaugh, *The Alcoholic Republic: An American Tradition* (New York: Oxford University Press, 1979); Paul Aaron and David Musto, "Temperance and Prohibition in America: A Historical Overview," in *Alcohol and Public Policy: Beyond the Shadow of Prohibition*, ed. Mark H. Moore and Dean R. Gerstein (Washington: National Academy Press, 1981), 127–81; and a particularly incisive synthesis in Jed Dannenbaum, *Drink and Disorder: Temperance Reform in Cincinnati from the Washingtonian Revival to the WCTU* (Urbana: University of Illinois Press, 1984). I cite these works further only where special points are made. Sarah E. Williams, "The Use of Beverage Alcohol as Medicine, 1790–1860," *Journal of Studies on Alcohol* 41 (1980): 543–66. C. C. Pearson and J. Edwin Hendricks, *Liquor and Anti-Liquor in Virginia 1619–1919* (Durham: Duke University Press, 1967), 4–7. Conroy, "The Culture and Politics."

3. *The Virginia Gazette*, quoted in Paton Yoder, "Tavern Regulation in Virginia," *Virginia Magazine of History and Biography* 87 (1979): 275. Jack Larkin, *The Reshaping of Everyday Life* (New York: Harper and Row, 1988), 281–82, summarizes the place of the tavern in the community. Conroy, "The Culture and Politics," suggests that in Massachusetts a greatly increased number of public houses provided the basis for organized opposition to authority and particularly to the authority of the Crown in the second half of the eighteenth century, when large numbers of the Sons of Liberty, for example, were tavern keepers (especially 250–51). Conroy also takes up the special conditions of public drinking in Massachusetts, which included the use of tavern licenses as a way of enabling poor people, such as widows, to stay off public support; so far other scholars have not found such political and social complications in other colonies as permits Conroy to depict the early public drinking space as so major a source of political power.

4. See especially Rorabaugh, *The Alcoholic Republic*, 1–7, 46; Lender and Martin, *Drinking in America*, chap. 1; James H. Cassedy, "An Early American Hangover: The Medical Profession and Intemperance 1800–1860," *Bulletin of the History of Medicine* 50 (1976): 405–13. Darius Lyman, quoted in Marc L. Harris, "The Process of Voluntary Association: Organizing the Ravenna Temperance Society, 1830," *Ohio History* 94 (1985): 169; opposition to Lyman's temperance efforts clearly included community leaders who were able, for example, to deny him the use of public buildings.

5. Roy Rosenzweig, *Eight Hours for What We Will: Workers and Leisure in an Industrial City, 1870–1920* (Cambridge: Cambridge University Press, 1983), especially chap. 2. Richard B. Stott, *Workers in the Metropolis: Class, Ethnicity, and Youth in Antebellum New York City* (Ithaca: Cornell University Press, 1990), especially 180–81, 216–17. See also Chapter 10, below. Tyrrell, *Sobering Up*, sets these matters in an even broader context.

6. Rorabaugh, *The Alcoholic Republic*, chaps. 3 and 4, especially 76.

7. See especially Hampel, *Temperance and Prohibition*, 3–4, 80.

8. Tyrrell, *Sobering Up*, especially 11–12, 269–78. Dannenbaum, *Drink and Disorder*, especially 123. Ruth M. Alexander, " 'We Are Engaged as a Band of Sisters': Class and Domesticity in the Washingtonian Temperance Movement, 1840–1860," *Journal of American History* 75 (1988): 763–85. Hampel, *Temperance and Prohibition*, especially 181. Lender and Martin, *Drinking in America*, 58–63.

9. Rorabaugh, *The Alcoholic Republic*, especially 134, 227.

10. Rosenzweig, *Eight Hours*, especially chap. 2, emphasizes the influence of Irish customs in setting nineteenth-century public drinking patterns. Victor A. Walsh, " 'Drowning the Shamrock': Drink, Teetotalism, and the Irish Catholics of Gilded-Age Pittsburgh," *Journal of American Ethnic History* 10 (1990–1991): 60–79, explores not only the complex variety of patterns of Irish-American attitudes toward drink but also the powerful Irish-Catholic temperance movement that was aimed at reforming individuals (but not, like many other temperance efforts, institutions); although it was only a minority within the ethnic group, the drinking Irish bachelor subculture was indeed of great importance. As

will appear repeatedly below, the fact that many producers and retailers were also immigrants added to the cultural clashes over alcoholic beverages.

11. See especially K. Austin Kerr, *Organized for Prohibition: A New History of the Anti-Saloon League* (New Haven: Yale University Press, 1985), chap. 1; Stanley Baron, *Brewed in America: A History of Beer and Ale in the United States* (Boston: Little, Brown and Company, 1962); Amy Mittelman, "The Politics of Alcohol Production: The Liquor Industry and the Federal Government 1862–1900" (doctoral diss., Columbia University, 1986), who, on 115–16, points out that northern banks owned most of the whiskey in Kentucky producers' warehouses; the quotation is from 186; Pearson and Hendricks, *Liquor and Anti-Liquor*, especially 156, 165–66. In Atlanta in 1885, the local saloons did $2,000,000 worth of business, but the wholesalers in the city took in $4,500,000; John Hammond Moore, "The Negro and Prohibition in Atlanta, 1885–1887," *South Atlantic Quarterly* 69 (1970): 39. W. J. Rorabaugh, "Beer, Lemonade, and Propriety in the Gilded Age," in *Dining in America, 1850–1900*, ed. Kathryn Grover (Amherst: The University of Massachusetts Press, 1987), 34–36, points out that alcohol merchandisers also had to meet the competition of new soft drinks, particularly those made from newly available tropical fruits, such as lemonade.

12. Ruth Bordin, *Woman and Temperance: The Quest for Power and Liberty*, 1873–1900 (Philadelphia: Temple University Press, 1981), 24. Rorabaugh, "Beer, Lemonade, and Propriety," 34.

13. Hermann B. Scharmann, in United States Brewers' Association, *Twenty-fourth Annual Brewers' Convention*, 1884, 11–12. "The U. S. Brewers Assn.," *Bar and Buffet*, September 1906, 6. "The American Saloon-Keeper," *The Liquor Dealer*, 20 April 1912, 1.

14. For example, Pearson and Hendricks, *Liquor and Anti-Liquor*, 8. Kerr, *Organized for Prohibition*, chap. 1. James H. Timberlake, *Prohibition and the Progressive Movement, 1900–1920* (Cambridge, Mass.: Harvard University Press, 1963), chap. 4. Mittelman, "The Politics of Alcohol;" the quotation is from 175. Perry Duis, *The Saloon: Public Drinking in Chicago and Boston, 1880–1920* (Urbana: University of Illinois Press, 1983). The social function of the turn-of-the-century saloon is described in John Koren, *Economic Aspects of the Liquor Problem* (Boston: Houghton Mifflin Company, 1899), chap. 8.

15. See especially Dannenbaum, *Drink and Disorder*; Lender and Martin, *Drinking in America*, chap. 3; Leonard Ellis, "Men Among Men: An Exploration of All-Male Relationships in Victorian America" (doctoral diss., Columbia University, 1982), chap. 3.

16. Duis, *The Saloon*, provides illustrative detail from Chicago and Boston; in Boston, unlike most cities, wholesalers—that group about which so little is known—owned the largest groups of saloons. Baron, *Brewed in America*, especially chap. 30.

17. See in general, Timberlake, *Prohibition and the Progressive Movement*, chap. 4. Peter H. Odegard, *Pressure Politics, The Story of the Anti-Saloon League* (New York: Columbia University Press, 1928), 40. "Good Advice," *Bar and Buffet*, August 1906, 8. Thomas J. Noel, *The City and the Saloon: Denver, 1858–1916* (Lincoln: University of Nebraska Press, 1982), chap. 5, documents the social mobility of one set of saloon men. Neil F. Deighan, "Address," *Beverage Business*, April 1939, 4. H. F. Willkie, *Beverage Spirits in America—A Brief History* (New York: The Newcomen Society, 1947), 26.

18. Year Book of the United States Brewers' Association, 1909, chap. 6. In 1912, the trade paper, the *Liquor Dealer*, 13 April 1912, 1, endorsed an editorial from the Baltimore *Star*, "Lesson for the Saloon," advocating "close the dives where young men (and young women) are rendered outcasts from respectable society. Stop the places that bring disrepute upon the whole business by selling to minors, catering to intoxicated persons, maintaining 'back rooms' and gambling devices. . . ."

19. Lender and Martin, *Drinking in America*, 106. Duis, *The Saloon*, 72. Quotations are from "Church News," *Bar and Buffet*, June 1907, 17.

20. Jon M. Kingsdale, "The 'Poor Man's Club': Social Functions of the Urban Working-Class Saloon," *American Quarterly* 25 (1973): 472–89. Duis, *The Saloon*; Rosenzweig, *Eight Hours*; Elliott West, *The Saloon on the Rocky Mountain Mining Frontier* (Lincoln: University of Nebraska Press, 1979); Noel, *The City and the Saloon*, especially 99. The classic primary source is Royal L. Melendy, "The Saloon in Chicago," *American Journal of Sociology* 6 (1900–1901): 289–306, 433–64.

21. See, for example, Kingsdale, "The 'Poor Man's Club,' " 485–88. West, *The Saloon*, especially chap. 1, 146; Elliott West, "Men, Whisky and a Place to Sit," *American History Illustrated*, July 1981, especially 12; *Liquor Trades' Review*, 1898, passim; *Bar and Buffet*, April 1907, 12. As Bordin, *Woman and Temperance*, 7–8, points out, women in fact had a special stake in fighting drink because the effects of social disabilities on females made them particularly vulnerable to men's drinking. See also Chapter 10, below.

22. David W. Detjen, *The Germans in Missouri, 1900–1918; Prohibition, Neutrality, and Assimilation* (Columbia: University of Missouri Press, 1985), especially 186. Melendy, "The Saloon in Chicago," 462 (pasteurized milk did not come in until later, and even clean, unadulterated milk was hard to find in the cities). See, for example, James E. Brady, "Father George Zurcher: Prohibitionist Priest," *Catholic Historical Review* 62 (1976): 424–33. Paul J. Freund, "Polish-American Drinking, Continuity and Change," in *The American Experience with Alcohol: Contrasting Cultural Perspectives*, ed. Linda A. Bennett and Genevieve M. Ames (New York: Plenum Press, 1985), 77–92. Gary Ross Mormino, *Immigrants on the Hill: Italian-Americans in St. Louis, 1882–1982* (Urbana: University of Illinois Press, 1986), especially chap. 5.

23. Timberlake, *Prohibition*, chap. 4. Noel, *The City and the Saloon*, 45, 53. Lender and Martin, *Drinking in America*, especially 96. Contemporary denunciation is exemplified in "The Peasant Saloon-Keeper—Ruler of American Cities," *McClure's Magazine* 31 (1908): 713–14. Duis, *The Saloon*, 164–65.

24. See especially Kerr, *Organized for Prohibition*, chap. 1, especially 15. Duis, *The Saloon*, chap. 9.

25. Noel, *The City and the Saloon*, 116–17. Duis, *The Saloon*, 230.

26. *Liquor Trades' Review*, 4 January 1898, 6. Timberlake, *Prohibition and the Progressive Movement*, 103.

27. Mark Haller, "Urban Vice and Civic Reform: Chicago in the Early Twentieth Century," in *Cities in American History*, ed. Kenneth T. Jackson and Stanley K. Schultz (New York: Alfred A. Knopf, 1972), 290–305; Duis, *The Saloon*, especially 251–53. West, *The Saloon*, emphasizes how quickly class distinctions developed among western drinking places.

28. Lewis A. Erenberg, *Steppin' Out: New York Nightlife and the Transformation of American Culture, 1890–1930* (Westport, Ct.: Greenwood Press, 1981).

29. Ibid. Harold B. Segel, *Turn-of-the-Century Cabaret: Paris, Barcelona, Berlin, Munich, Vienna, Cracow, Moscow, St. Petersburg, Zurich* (New York: Columbia University Press, 1987).

30. Segel, *Turn-of-the-Century Cabaret*; Lewis A. Erenberg, "From New York to Middletown: Repeal and the Legitimization of Nightlife in the Great Depression," *American Quarterly* 38 (1986): 761–78. As Haller, "Urban Vice and Civic Reform," 297–301, points out, the reality of cabarets was usually a good deal sleazier than the ideal. "Night Clubs of Today Seen Best," *Beverage Retailer Weekly*, 3 January 1938, 2. The impact of the night-club ideal was particularly effective among African-Americans who were coming into northern cities; see Denise Herd, "Ambiguity in Black Drinking Norms," in *The American Experience with Alcohol*, ed. Bennett and Ames, especially 158–63, 166.

31. Melendy, "The Saloon in Chicago," 305.

32. Duis, *The Saloon*, 64–65. William R. Leach, "Transformations in a Culture of Consumption: Women and Department Stores, 1890–1925," *Journal of American History* 71 (1984): 329.

33. As Sinclair, *Prohibition*, 238–41, points out, one of the successes of Prohibition was that after repeal, those who drank continued, on the whole, to be disproportionately the upper classes rather than the workers and their families, an image fostered and encouraged intensely, as I have noted, by the ever more popular motion pictures. Martin and Lender, *Drinking in America*, 153. Ridgely Hunt and George S. Chappell, eds., *The Saloon in the Home: Or, A Garland of Rumblossoms* (New York: Coward-McCann, 1930). Lowell Edmunds, *The Silver Bullet: The Martini in American Civilization* (Westport, Ct.: Greenwood Press, 1981), especially 27, 30. *New Yorker*, 13 January 1934, 45. Don Masson, "On Reading the Ads," *Spirits*, January 1934, 43–44. Robin Room, "The Movies and the Wettening of America: The Media as Amplifiers of Cultural Change," *British Journal of Addiction* 83 (1988): 11–18.

34. Kingsdale, "The 'Poor Man's Club,' " 488–89. Heckman, "Prohibition Passes," chap. 9. See, for example, Thomas C. Cochran, *The Pabst Brewing Company: The History of an American Business* (New York: New York University Press, 1948), 380–81. Room, "The Movies." Whereas Pabst had advertised drinking in a respectable family setting just as prohibition was ending—one ad shows a little girl serving beer to a middle-aged man— by the late 1930s, Pabst was advertising, "Where the smart world sets the pace, Pabst gets the call," naming such settings as the Waldorf-Astoria, on the *Normandie*, at the Stork Club and the Royal Hawaiian, and the "swank Miami shoreline." Examples are from *Delineator*, October 1933, 79 and *New Yorker*, 25 March 1939, 36–37. St. Louis *Post-Dispatch*, 18 January 1935, 3B.

35. See especially David Fogarty, "From Saloon to Supermarket: Packaged Beer and the Reshaping of the U.S. Brewing Industry," *Contemporary Drug Problems* 12 (1985): 541–92, especially 547, 581; the change took place over a long period of time: in 1961, 43 per cent of American supermarkets handled beer; by 1984, it was 72 per cent.

36. Aaron and Musto, "Temperance and Prohibition in America," 168–71. John D. Rockefeller, Jr., "Foreword," in Raymond B. Fosdick and Albert L. Scott, *Toward Liquor Control* (New York: Harper and Brothers, 1933), x. Alcoholic-beverage merchandisers had great reason to want the marketing of their products to be in private hands; when wines, previously available in state stores, were permitted in supermarkets in Idaho in 1971, sales jumped by 283 per cent the first year, and other dramatic increases under similar circumstances occurred in Maine and Montana; Michael Jacobson, Robert Atkins, and George Hacker, *The Booze Merchants: The Inebriating of America* (Washington: CSPI Books, 1983), 137. Robert F. Burk, *The Corporate State and the Broker State: The Du Ponts and American National Politics, 1925–1940* (Cambridge, Mass.: Harvard University Press, 1990), chaps. 5–6, 109–10, 120, describes Pierre Du Pont's plan for a centralized business; because the repeal effort had already gotten away from him, it is uncertain how important this scheme and his courting of brewer August Busch and other powers in the alcohol business was.

37. Austin Kerr is currently preparing to publish an account of the business after repeal that will show how fully the producers controlled federal appointments and policy. In 1935, a fund-raiser noted that "so many rich people who have made contributions of ten thousand dollars a clip for the repeal of the Eighteenth Amendment, claiming that they did so not because they wanted their liquor but because they wanted to promote true temperance," would not give money for practical moderation efforts; Everett Colby to John D. Rockefeller, Jr., quoted in Ron Roizen, "The American Discovery of Alcoholism, 1933–1939" (doctoral diss., University of California, Berkeley, 1991), chap. 3.

38. Larry D. Quinn, *Politicians in Business: A History of the Liquor Control System in Montana* (Missoula: University of Montana Press, 1970), 9. Leonard V. Harrison and Elizabeth Laine, *After Repeal: A Study of Liquor Control Administration* (New York: Harper and

Brothers, 1936), especially 25–26, 35. "One Liquor Vendor for Every 189 Persons," *Liquor Industry News*, 15 December 1935, 7.

39. James T. Hathaway, "The Evolution of Drinking Places in the Twin Cities: From the Advent of White Settlement to the Present" (doctoral diss., University of Minnesota, 1982), 245. Jacob Ruppert, "One Year After Repeal," reprinted in *Modern Brewery Age*, September-October 1983, MS38.

40. See, for example, William L. Downard, *The Cincinnati Brewing Industry: A Social and Economic History* (Athens: Ohio University Press, 1973), 130–31; John C. Eigel, "Surviving Prohibition in Milwaukee," *Historical Messenger of the Milwaukee County Historical Society* 33 (1977): 118–20. Mark H. Haller, "Bootleggers as Businessmen: From City Slums to City Builders," in *Law, Alcohol, and Order: Perspectives on National Prohibition*, ed. David E. Kyvig (Westport, Ct.: Greenwood Press, 1985), 139–57; the quote is from 155. See, for example, on the Bronfmans' background, James H. Gray, *Booze: The Impact of Whiskey on the Prairie West* (Toronto: Macmillan of Canada, 1972); Peter C. Newman, *Bronfman Dynasty: The Rothschilds of the New World* (Toronto: McClelland and Stewart, 1978). Quinn, *Politicians in Business*, 42. In the notes to Chapter 2, citing Allan S. Everest, *Rum Across the Border: The Prohibition Era in Northern New York* (Syracuse: Syracuse University Press, 1978), I noted that New York State police found that regardless of the alcoholic-beverage trade, people who were bootlegging were invariably also into other illegal activities. See Hathaway, "The Evolution of Drinking Places," 269–75, for a local example.

41. Harrison and Laine, *After Repeal*, 69. Hathaway, "The Evolution of Drinking Places," 40. Pierre Du Pont, radio address, July 1934, quoted in ibid. "Discrimination and Retaliation Among the States," *Repeal Review*, October-December 1939, 25. The continuity between the AAPA and the notorious Liberty League, which turned out to be an extremist group, is well known. As late as 1940 a repeal propagandist was blaming Prohibition for softening America for "communism, socialism, pacifism, and acquiescence to dictatorship . . . ;" Elizabeth Livingston, "To Insure Domestic Tranquility," *Repeal Review*, April-June 1940, 5. Burk, *The Corporate State*, discusses the issue in context.

42. Glenn O'Brien, "How to Make a Fortune After Legalization," *High Times*, July 1976, 44–45. "After Legalization, What Happens to Dealers?" *High Times*, August/September 1975, 6. In identifying Forcade, I am following Patrick Anderson, *High in America: The True Story Behind NORML and the Politics of Marijuana* (New York: The Viking Press, 1981), 174 and passim.

43. Following the usual pattern in government-business relations, control officials acted in concert with manufacturers and purveyors. The extent to which control officials allied with the alcoholic-beverage business appears transparently in their many public statements; see, for example, the collection in "Proposal to Increase the Federal Tax on Distilled Spirits," *Repeal Review*, January-March 1938, 8–9. Federal appointees were conspicuously drawn from the ranks of prominent repealers. The wets even went to the point of wanting to amend the Twenty-First Amendment to prevent state governments from forbidding their citizens to obtain liquor. They obviously thought better of the idea and went about achieving the result in other ways, particularly through changes in regulations and national advertising. See, for example, "Discrimination and Retaliation," *Repeal Review*, April-June 1938, 14–15. "Report of the Panel," in *Alcohol and Public Policy: Beyond the Shadow of Prohibition*, ed. Mark H. Moore and Dean R. Gerstein (Washington: National Academy Press, 1981), 63. Fletcher Dobyns, *The Amazing Story of Repeal: An Exposé of the Power of Propaganda* (Chicago: Willett, Clark and Company, 1940), especially 99–100. Stewart Berkshire, "Uniform Control and Taxation of Alcoholic Beverages," *Quarterly Journal of Studies on Alcohol* 1 (1940): 561. Alfred R. Oxenfeldt, *Industrial Pricing and Market Practices* (New York: Prentice-Hall, 1951), 456, noted that the whiskey in-

dustry actually encouraged government regulation because it made the industry appear more respectable. And since the regulators were so responsive to alcoholic-beverage businesses, the regulation could hardly be considered unfriendly as in some other cases. Instances of local corruption are detailed in Hathaway, "The Evolution of Drinking Places," vol. 2, passim.

44. See, for example, John Burnham, "Beer and the Publisher," *National Printer-Journalist*, March 1933, 50. "Liquor and the Newspapers," *Christian Century* 52 (1935): 1228. Harrison and Laine, *After Repeal*, 163. Early marketing is described in "Your Advertising Picture," *Spirits*, May 1934, 50, 66.

45. See, for example, "Drys Open Fight on Liquor Ads in Broadcasts," *Editor & Publisher* 1 April 1939: 13, "552 Dailies Bar Hard-Liquor Ads; 178 Even Ban Beer Copy," *Editor & Publisher*, 18 December 1937, 5, 28; "Give Credit Where Credit Is Due," *Repeal Review*, October-December 1938, 33; "Tunney Hits Liquor Ads, Urges Industry Aid Press," *Editor & Publisher*, 29 October 1938, 22; Henry Bretzfield, *Liquor Marketing and Liquor Advertising: A Guide for Executives and Their Staffs in Management, Sales and Advertising* (New York: Abelard-Schuman, 1955), 16. It did take some years for the *Saturday Evening Post* (the 1950s) and a few other major publications to come around and cash in on the advertising dollars; "Brewing Industry Led Way for Satevepost to Accept Alcoholic Beverage Advertising," *Brewery Age*, 15 September 1958, 1.

46. "Tunney Hits Liquor Ads." "Liquor and the Magazines," *Christian Century* 59 (1942): 518. Arnold H. Pulda, " 'Better Todays': The American Public Culture in the 1930s" (doctoral diss., University of North Carolina, 1978), 10–11. Cochran, *Pabst*, 385, notes that Pabst marketing targeted women as early as 1933—when beer appeared as a grocery item. Francis A. Soper, "Liquor Advertising," *Signs of the Times*, 30 April 1946, 5.

47. See, for example, William Rufus Scott, *Revolt on Mount Sinai: The Puritan Retreat from Prohibition* (Pasadena: The Author, 1944); Edgar T. Reeves, Jr., "The Louisa Plan for Defeating Local Prohibition," *Liquor Store & Dispenser*, February 1947, 35–41, which featured the standard tactics of using prominent citizens, an unfavorable stereotype of Prohibition, and the psychiatric approach to alcoholism, that is, portraying it as an individual, not a social, problem. See Distilled Spirits Institute, Incorporated, *Annual Report*, passim, and *Repeal Review*, passim.

48. Eugene V. Rostow and Thorsten Sellin, "Self-Regulation in the Liquor Industry," *Quarterly Journal of Studies on Alcohol* 3 (1942): 124–37. See, for example, "Watch Your Step Mr. Retailer," *Liquor Store & Dispenser*, February 1936, 43; "Gallup Survey Indicates Rise in Prohibition Sentiment," *Beverage Business*, January 1939, 5 (drinking by the young and drunk driving had alarmed members of the public); "Obey the Law! Palmer Tells Brewers in L.A.," *Liquor Industry News*, 15 November 1935, 2; "Board Aims Rap at L.A. House Gambling," *Liquor Industry News*, 15 January 1936, 8; "The Lewd Show," *Beverage Business*, October 1939, 7. *Brewers Almanac*, 1949, 109–10; 1953, 7. Cochran, *The Pabst Brewing Company*, 370–71; Baron, *Brewed in America*, especially 328–31; Carl W. Badenhausen, "Brewers Use Newspaper Ads to Tell Story of Self-Regulation," *Editor & Publisher*, 28 December 1940, 8. The brewers employed a large staff and effective local organizations to assist in industry regulation, and the distillers at one point, in 1939, contemplated regulations so stringent that salesmen would not be permitted to entertain buyers or to sell more than a customer's normal requirements. "Sturges and the Institute," *Beverage Business*, December 1939, 2. "Successful Merchandising," *Liquor Store & Dispenser*, December 1934, 13.

49. "Propaganda Drive to Take Beer Foundation's $1,000,000 a Year," *Editor & Publisher*, 15 May 1937, 10; and, in general, issues of *Repeal Review*. Elizabeth Livingston, "General Report to Members," *Repeal Review*, October-December 1937, 7, commented that it was only within the year that organs of public opinion began to take seriously the dangers

of not controlling alcohol—that is, the return of Prohibition because of the failure of repeal, parallel to the "failure" of Prohibition. The wet campaign, including the "citizens' committees" established to promote the enforcement of liquor control—at the instance of the Distilled Spirits Institute and the beer wholesalers, as it turned out—can be followed in the *Repeal Review*.

50. See, for example, "The Outlook for 1939," *Repeal Review*, October-December 1938, 10; Mrs. John S. Sheppard, "The Value of the Word 'Temperance,'" *Repeal Review*, October-December 1938, 23–24; Mrs. John S. Sheppard, "A New Responsibility Rests on Administrators," *Repeal Review*, April-June 1937, 3–4; "U.S., Never Wetter, Is Getting Drier," *Business Week*, 20 August 1938, 26–27.

51. A summary is in Lender and Martin, *Drinking in America*, 172–204.

52. Details and documentation appear in Jay L. Rubin, "The Wet War: American Liquor Control, 1941-1945," in *Alcohol, Reform and Society; The Liquor Issue in Social Context*, ed. Jack S. Blocker, Jr. (Westport, Ct.: Greenwood Press, 1979), 235–58; the quotation is from 243. Baron, *Brewed in America*, 331–36. Alvin Griesedieck, "Beer and Brewing in a Nation at War," *Quarterly Journal of Studies on Alcohol* 3 (1942): 293–301. John W. Riley and Charles F. Marden, "The Social Pattern of Alcoholic Drinking," *Quarterly Journal of Studies on Alcohol* 8 (1947): 272. *Distilled Spirits Industry* gave a public-relations version of events during the war. Efforts to counter dry agitation appear in various trade publications and the *Repeal Review*. Cochran, *The Pabst Brewing Company*, 397. Baron, *Brewed in America*, 331–36. Oxenfeldt, *Industrial Pricing*, 451–64, 475. National Archives Record Group 136, Agricultural Marketing Service, citation courtesy of K. Austin Kerr. The pro-business policies of the war effort are described in part in John Morton Blum, *V Was for Victory: Politics and American Culture During World War II* (New York: Harcourt Brace Jovanovich, 1977 [1976]).

53. Randolph W. Childs, *Making Repeal Work* (Philadelphia: Pennsylvania Alcoholic Beverage Study, Inc., 1947), was published as late as 1947. Carson, *The Social History of Bourbon*, 221. Oxenfeldt, *Industrial Pricing*, chap. 9. Baron, *Brewed in America*, 337–48. "A Small Brewer Salutes Repeal," *Modern Brewery Age*, September-October 1983, MS-90. See, for example, *Distilled Spirits Council Annual Report*, 1948–1949; Marty Jezer, *The Dark Ages—Life in the United States*, 1945–1960 (Boston: South End Press, 1982), 136–37. Baron, *Brewed in America*, 340–45.

54. Schenley Industries, Inc., *Annual Report*, 1949, especially 6, 11. Richard Bunce, "From California Grapes to California Wine: The Transformation of an Industry, 1963-1979," *Contemporary Drug Problems* 10 (1981): 55–74. Jacobson, Atkins, and Hacker, *The Booze Merchants*, detail modern industry ownership ties, as do John Cavanagh and Frederick F. Clairmonte, *Alcoholic Beverages: Dimensions of Corporate Power* (London: Croom Helm, 1985).

55. Frank Kane, *Anatomy of the Whisky Business* (Manhasset, N.Y.: Lake House Press, 1965), especially 106–7. Whalen, "The American Liquor Industry," especially 230–31. Jack H. Hornsby and Thomas S. Harrington, *Successful Liquor Retailing* (New York: Greenburg, 1947), especially 113 and 118, which is quoted.

56. Bretzfield, *Liquor Marketing*, especially 148.

57. The propaganda barrage appeared as early as the June 1942 issue of *Beverage Business*. "Off and Running," *Liquor Store*, June 1956, 52. Norman K. Denzin, "Notes on the Criminogenic Hypothesis: A Case Study of the American Liquor Industry," *American Sociological Review* 42 (1977): 907, maintains that the industry from the beginning of the post-1933 period attempted to emphasize home consumption to get away from off-premises patterns of consumption that might bring back the saloon image; moreover, and in particular, home consumption emphasized individual, as opposed to merchandiser, responsibility for misuse of alcohol (see below in this chapter).

58. Hathaway, "The Evolution of Drinking Places," especially 254–55, 260–62, 278, 316, 318–21. See, for example, "The Liquor Store Modernization Boom," *Liquor Store*, January 1963, 18–19; "Hospitality Unlimited," *Liquor Store*, October 1966, 25–27. *Liquor Store*, April 1960, 44–A; September 1977, unpaginated ad. Advertising personnel may or may not have been paid for including drinking as an incidental aspect of upscale life; in a *New Yorker*, 1 August 1983, back-cover ad for AT&T, for example, drinks showed up as a conspicuous prop.

59. "Watch Your Step Mr. Retailer." As early as 1949, Pierre Du Pont was being told bluntly that no anti-liquor legislation would get a hearing in Congress; John J. Williams to Pierre Du Pont, 14 July 1949, Reel 5, AAPA Papers. For example, Kane, *Anatomy of the Whisky Business*, especially chap. 14. Quinn, *Politicians in Business*, 90–91, noticed how much more aggressive vendors became in the 1950s. George B. Hindle, quoted in David B. Gibson, "A Few Warm Weather Thoughts," *Brewers Journal*, June 1952, 13. Robert Smith Bader, *Prohibition in Kansas: A History* (Lawrence: University Press of Kansas, 1986), especially 235. The armed services constituted a continuing base for encouraging and popularizing the use of alcoholic beverages, even using distribution of kegs of beer for purposes of social control; see Larry A. Ingraham, *The Boys in the Barracks: Observations on American Military Life* (Philadelphia: Institute for the Study of Human Issues, 1984), especially 113. "Gallup Poll Shows Sharp Rise in Drinking Adults," *Modern Brewery Age*, 20 June 1960, 4. The longer-term trends in Gallup polls showed less reliable short-term statistics but suggested a substantial increase in numbers of drinkers (changes in amounts consumed did not necessarily correspond) in the 1960s, to almost 70 per cent of the adult population. George Gallup, Jr., *The Gallup Poll, Public Opinion 1984* (Wilmington: Scholarly Resources, Inc., 1985), 179.

60. John J. Daly, quoted in Jacob J. Glaser, "Legal Side of the News," *Bar and Grill Journal*, April 1937, 15. See, for example, *Three Rings*, May 1953, 23. "Dry Group Polls Press on Liquor Ad Use," *Editor & Publisher*, 3 March 1945, 65.

61. "Episcopal Church Backs Social Drinking in Report Issued at General Convention," *Modern Brewery Age*, 20 October 1958, 1.

62. Robert McBride, "Industry Structure, Marketing, and Public Health: A Case Study of the U.S. Beer Industry," *Contemporary Drug Problems* 12 (1985): 593–620. A brief discussion of the non-price competition determinants of advertising is in Walter Adams, *The Structure of American Industry*, 4th ed. (New York: Macmillan, 1971), 212–14. The place of advertising appears clearly in such industry publications as *Liquor Store*; see, for example, Alynn Shilling, "Profit Promotions," *Liquor Store*, December 1956, 31. Meyer Katzper, Ralph Ryback, and Marc Hertzman, "Alcohol Beverage Advertisement and Consumption," *Journal of Drug Issues* 8 (1978): 339–53. See, for example, "$15 Million Ads Whet U. S. Appetite for Wine," *Editor & Publisher*, 22 March 1947, 52; "Rheingold's Sales Growth Parallels Use of Dailies," *Editor & Publisher*, 27 October 1951, 54–55; Bunce, "From California Grapes to California Wine." John Thaddeus Whalen, Jr., "The American Liquor Industry" (doctoral diss., University of California, Berkeley, 1964), 208, 223. For the recent period, see Jacobson, Atkins, and Hacker, *The Booze Merchants*. Cavanagh and Clairmonte, *Alcoholic Beverages*, who take up Miller on 4, 56–57. The controversies over alcoholic-beverage advertising appeared in countless contemporary accounts through the years, such as "Senate Group Weighs Liquor Ad Controls," *Editor & Publisher*, 1 May 1948, 12; "Drys Assail 'Glamor' in Liquor Advertising," *Editor & Publisher*, 14 January 1950, 11; "Liquor Ad Bans," *Broadcasting*, 26 April 1948, 26; Peter Grier, "Critics Say It's Time to Regulate Those Alcohol Ads," *Christian Science Monitor*, 14 June 1983, 2. Neil F. Deighan, quoted in "National Council Recognized by Federal Alcohol Administration," *Beverage Business*, November 1938, 8; "Industry Report," *Liquor Store*, January 1966, 3. The voluntary codes were revealing in that one type of beverage maker

(beer and spirits) could tout lifestyle, but that same content was proscribed for wine merchandisers; Jacobson, Atkins, and Hatcher, *The Booze Merchants*, 10–11. And of course many advertisers did not observe the codes anyway.

63. See especially Jacobson, Atkins, and Hacker, *The Booze Merchants*; the quotations are from 20 and 99. Katzper, Ryback, and Hertzman, "Alcohol Beverage Advertisement." Robert McBride, "Industry Structure, Marketing, and Public Health: A Case Study of the U.S. Beer Industry," *Contemporary Drug Problems* 12 (1985): 604–9, 614. Cavanagh and Clairmonte, *Alcoholic Beverages*; on 26–28, they point out the importance of putting alcohol in the general framework of liquid consumables.

64. "Beer Advertising in Good Company," *Brewers Journal*, June 1952, 14. "Pabst Launches Summer 'Sell' Program," ibid. "Liquor Marketing Report to Retailers," *Liquor Store Magazine*, September 1977, 16–18.

65. See especially William H. Boyenton, "Enter the Ladies—86 Proof: A Study in Advertising Ethics," *Journalism Quarterly* 14 (1967): 445–53. Hornsby and Harrington, *Successful Liquor Retailing*, 13. "Lift Ban on Women in Liquor Commercials," *Modern Brewery Age*, 3 November 1958, 1, tied the revision to the change in the *Saturday Evening Post* policy. The progress of spirits radio advertising can be followed for example in *Modern Brewery Age*, 3 November 1958, 1; 30 March 1959, 1; 24 August 1959, 1.

66. Cavanagh and Clairmonte, *Alcoholic Beverages*, especially 5–6, 134–35, place marketing to vulnerable people in context. See, for example, Childs, *Making Repeal Work*, 7–8. Jacobson, Atkins, and Hacker, *The Booze Merchants*, especially chaps. 5 and 6. Gloria Steinem, "Sex, Lies and Advertising," *Ms.*, July/August 1990, 18–28, tells her side of the *Ms.* story. J. L. Fitzgerald and H. A. Mulford, "The Prevalence and Extent of Drinking in Iowa, 1979," *Journal of Studies on Alcohol* 42 (1981): 38–47.

67. See Phyllis H. Williams and Robert Straus, "Drinking Patterns of Italians in New Haven: Utilization of the Personal Diary as a Research Technique," *Quarterly Journal of Studies on Alcohol* 11 (1950): 618–29; Bennett and Ames, *The American Experience*, especially Richard Stivers, "Historical Meanings of Irish-American Drinking," 122–26. For example, Raul Caetano, "Acculturation and Drinking Patterns Among U.S. Hispanics," *British Journal of Addiction* 82 (1987): 789–99. Lizabeth Cohen, "Encountering Mass Culture at the Grassroots: The Experience of Chicago Workers in the 1920s," *American Quarterly* 41 (1989): 6–33. Bretzfield, *Liquor Marketing*, 88–89. Seagram had started a Negro Historical Calendar in 1968. Jacobson, Atkins, and Hacker, *The Booze Merchants*, chap. 3; the quote is from 33–34. Powermaster, a new brew, caused scandal in 1991: Paul Farhi, "Surgeon General Hits New Malt Liquor's Name, Ads," *Washington Post*, 26 June 1991, A1, A4. This controversy proceeded at a time when there were widespread press reports that African-Americans on average drank less and abstained more than the population in general.

68. A brief history of the six-pack appears in "Beer Celebrates a 30th Anniversary," *Liquor Store Magazine*, March 1963, 24. See, for example, "Sizes Are Getting Larger," *Liquor Store Magazine*, March 1969, 42; *Life*, 16 May 1960, 8. Jerry Della Femina, *From Those Wonderful Folks Who Gave You Pearl Harbor: Front-Line Dispatches from the Advertising War* (New York: Simon and Schuster, 1970), 128–35.

69. Robert H. Miles, *Coffin Nails and Corporate Strategies* (Englewood Cliffs, N.J.: Prentice-Hall, 1982), 167–68. Examples include "Beer's Future Looks Good, But More Advertising Needed, Wholesalers Told," *Advertising Age*, 9 November 1953, 48; Chris Bohlman, quoted in " '33' Aiming at 18–34 Bracket," *Modern Brewery Age*, 10 September 1979, 2; Joe Kroyzend, "Just Thinkin' Out Loud," *Modern Brewery Age*, November 1955, 58; "Liquor Scope," *Liquor Store Magazine*, October 1969, 8; Frank Haring, "High School Drinkers," *Liquor Store*, May 1954, 30; "PAL Boxing Bouts to Be Televised from Gym at Philadelphia Naval Base," *Brewers Journal*, June 1952, 46. "It's Miller Time in Teen

Movie," *Tobacco and Youth Reporter*, Summer 1987, 5; other issues of this newsletter contain many additional examples. The Center for Science in the Public Interest was most active in exposing the tactics employed by alcoholic-beverage vendors; see, for example, David Clark Scott, "How Spirits Industry Takes Advantage of Changing Tastes," *Christian Science Monitor*, 29 July 1983, 10–11; Breed, De Foe, and Wallack, "Drinking in the Mass Media," 660; Jacobson, Atkins, and Hacker, *The Booze Merchants*, especially chap. 4; the quotation is from 49.

70. See especially Charles Atkin, John Hocking, and Martin Block, "Teenage Drinking: Does Advertising Make a Difference?" *Journal of Communication*, Spring 1984, 157–67.

71. McBride, "Industry Structure," 601, 615. Examples are from *Colliers*, 11 March 1950, 35; *Beer Distributor*, June 1966, 35.

72. *Life*, 17 September 1965, 5; and see in general Boyenton, "Enter the Ladies." Compare "A New Low in Advertising," *Beverage Business*, March 1939, 10, denouncing "the ugly, disgusting advertisement of a certain brewer" involving "a sign which for generations has been known among mariners as an invitation to depravity;" in a later time such an ad would have been praised for cleverness. Jacobson, Atkins, and Hacker, *The Booze Merchants*, chap. 7.

73. *Chicago Tribune*, 27 July 1956, 16. See, for example, "See Rise in Beer Sales Due to TV," *Modern Brewery Age*, 9 September 1960, 3. Dennis T. Lowry, "Alcohol Consumption Patterns and Consequences on Prime Time Network TV," *Journalism Quarterly* 58 (1981): 3–8, 37. Warren Breed and James R. DeFoe, "The Portrayal of the Drinking Process on Prime-Time Television," *Journal of Communication*, Winter 1981, 58–67. Shaearon A. Lowery, "Soap and Booze in the Afternoon: An Analysis of the Portrayal of Alcohol Use in Daytime Serials," *Journal of Studies on Alcohol* 41 (1980): 829–38.

74. See, for example, regarding glamorous drinking scenes in the movies clearly of interest to merchandisers, *Liquor Industry News*, 1 December 1935, 6. Jacobson, Atkins, and Hacker, *The Booze Merchants*, 70–73. "Beer Brands in the Movies," *Modern Brewery Age*, 3 September 1979, 2. See, for example, Richard A. Filloy, "Of Drink and Detectives: The Genesis and Function of a Literary Convention," *Contemporary Drug Problems* 13 (1986): 249–71.

75. See especially Harold W. Pfautz, "The Image of Alcohol in Popular Fiction: 1900–1904 and 1946–1950," *Quarterly Journal of Studies on Alcohol* 23 (1962): 131–46; Warren Breed, James R. De Foe, and Lawrence Wallack, "Drinking in the Mass Media: A Nine-Year Project," *Journal of Drug Issues* 14 (1984): 655–64; Room, "The Movies and the Wettening of America," 11–18.

76. Boyenton, "Enter the Ladies," 451.

77. Examples include Christopher Sower, "Teen-Age Drinking as Group Behavior," *Quarterly Journal of Studies on Alcohol* 20 (1959): 655–60; Robert D. Russell, in *Quarterly Journal of Studies on Alcohol* 28 (1967): 549, quoting *Time*, 1965; Warren Breed and James R. De Foe, "Themes in Magazine Alcohol Advertisements: A Critique," *Journal of Drug Issues* 9 (1979): 511–22; Joseph R. Gusfield, "The Structural Context of College Drinking," *Quarterly Journal of Studies on Alcohol* 22 (1961): 428–43; C. Norman Alexander, Jr., and Ernest Q. Campbell, "Peer Influences on Adolescent Drinking," *Quarterly Journal of Studies on Alcohol* 28 (1967): 444–53; Breed, De Foe, and Wallack, "Drinking in the Mass Media," especially 656–57.

78. "A New California Moderation League Launches Campaign," *Liquor Industry News*, 15 February 1936, 3. See *Repeal Review* in general for details. An excellent institutional history is in Blocker, *American Temperance Movements*, 145–60.

79. A sociological account is Craig Reinarman, "The Social Construction of an Alcohol Problem: The Case of Mothers Against Drunk Drivers and Social Control in the 1980s," *Theory and Society* 17 (1988): 91–120, who dissects clearly the economic motives of not

only the media but also the attorneys, counseling programs, and tax-deductible enter-
tainment-industry segments in allying with the alcoholic-beverage marketers to support
MADD. See, for example, "Students Against Driving Drunk," *Modern Brewery Age*,
September-October 1983, MS-76, subtitled, "How wholesalers can get a program started
in their state. . . ." The issues are reviewed in summary fashion in Philip J. Cook, review
of Laurence, Snortum, and Zimring, eds., *Social Control of the Drinking Driver*, in *Science*
241 (1988): 603–4. Revelations of the alcoholic-beverage industry contributions eventually
caused some reaction in the groups.

80. Quite aside from industry funding, there were excellent intellectual reasons why phys-
iologists, especially, took an interest in alcohol-related problems—for example metabo-
lism. And the disease concept of alcoholism had some roots in traditional temperance
concern with the alcohol habit. Nevertheless, industry support raised serious questions,
at the very least, not least those in Reinarman, "The Social Construction." See Norman
Giesbrecht and Kai Pernanen, "Sociological Perspectives on the Alcoholism Treatment
Literature Since 1940," in *Recent Developments in Alcoholism*, ed. Marc Galanter (London:
Plenum Press, 1987), 5: 135–74. Extensive background and discussion is summarized in
Thomas D. Watts, ed., *Social Thought on Alcoholism: A Comprehensive Review*, ed. Thomas
D. Watts (Malabar, Fla.: Robert E. Krieger Publishing Company, 1986), especially Robert
E. Tournier, "The Medicalization of Alcoholism: Discontinuities in Ideologies of De-
viance," 39–51.

81. Roizen, "The American Discovery of Alcoholism," especially chaps. 5, 8; this work
brings in the complex context in which the scientists fell into taking alcoholic-beverage
industry money, in which the industry was taking a chance also, but one that paid off
handsomely in the end. For a time the dry forces backed the scientists in the belief that
scientific truth would support them, but they soon found that the questions researched
were limited to those that helped the alcoholic-beverage industry, namely, individuals
with alcohol problems. "Valuable Work on Alcoholic Problems," *Liquor Store & Dispenser*, December 1944, 31. Harrison M. Trice and Paul M. Roman, *Spirits and Demons
at Work: Alcohol and Other Drugs on the Job*, 2d ed. (Ithaca: Cornell University New York
State School of Industrial and Labor Relations, 1978), in commenting on "The Alcoholism
Industry," 11–12, speculate that "the emergence of the illegal drug problem may have
inadvertently made problem drinking more respectable . . ." by pushing alcoholics up
above the addicts on the social-status scale. Joseph R. Gusfield, "Prevention: Rise, Decline, and Renaissance," in *Alcohol, Science, and Society Revisited*, ed. Edith Lisansky
Gomberg, Helene Raskin White, and John A. Carpenter, (Ann Arbor: University of
Michigan Press, 1982), 402–25, comments from another point of view on this remarkable
post-repeal shift.

82. Mark Keller, "The Disease Concept of Alcoholism Revisited," *Journal of Studies on
Alcohol* 37 (1976): 1694–717, an account now revised in part and extended in Roizen, "The
American Discovery of Alcoholism," who notes (chap. 3) that in 1935 the Council for
Moderation had to drop the word "temperance" from the letterhead, for fear of offending
the repeal forces. "New Program Launched by Distilled Spirits Institute," *Beverage
Business*, January 1940, 14. See, for example, the early volumes of *Quarterly Journal of
Studies on Alcohol*, including 1 (1940): 591, 595, showing the place of industry representatives in the meetings of the Research Council on Problems of Alcohol. Randolph W.
Childs, *Making Repeal Work* (Philadelphia: Pennsylvania Alcoholic Beverage Study, Inc.,
1947), 256. Dry workers, as Roizen, "The American Discovery of Alcoholism," notes,
started dropping out of the alcohol-research group when it began taking beverage-in-
dustry money, and they even began to lose their initial rapport with the therapy-research
movement when a Yale group accepted money from a distiller in 1943; the breach was
complete by 1949. A thorough review of the disengagement of the drys is Jay L. Rubin,

"Shifting Perspectives on the Alcoholism Treatment Movement, 1940–1955," *Journal of Studies on Alcohol* 40 (1979): 376–86; the quote is from 384. Trice and Roman, *Spirits and Demons at Work*, especially 37.

83. Even the churches were called on to deal with the individual alcohol addict; see Blocker, *American Temperance Movements*, 149–50; Seward Hiltner, abstracted in *Quarterly Journal of Studies on Alcohol* 3 (1942): 147–48; Alson J. Smith, "The Church and the Alcoholic," *Christian Century* 61 (1944): 301-2, who characterized alcoholism as "a religious problem, that is, a problem of the whole personality." Thomas F. McCarthy, quoted in "Industry Viewpoint Broadcast," *Liquor Store & Dispenser*, March 1947, 31. See, similarly, the brewers' "Positive Posture" program that put a strong emphasis on "Beer does not abuse people; people abuse beer"; *Brewers Almanac*, 1972, 10. "On the Alcoholism Front," *American Journal of Public Health* 43 (1953): 655, and other contemporary items suggest how the individual approach was taken into the public-health field; the American Medical Association, *Digest of Official Actions* 2 (1959–1968): 38, even made the approach official in 1967. Joseph Hirsch, quoted in "Industry Report," *Liquor Store Magazine*, March 1969, 15. Cf. Joseph Hirsch, *The Problem Drinker* (New York: Duell, Sloan and Pearce, 1949), especially 137-38. The most sophisticated form of this argument was to demonstrate by cross-cultural and psychological studies that ethanol did not account for any particular pattern of behavior and then to show that in American culture the ascription of negative effects to alcohol permitted people to blame the substance rather than the individual; see, for a summary, Barbara Critchlow, "The Powers of John Barleycorn: Beliefs About the Effects of Alcohol on Social Behavior," *American Psychologist* 41 (1986): 751–64. Such a view would contrast with the nineteenth-century idea of a person enslaved to alcohol, that is, with the self damaged; see, for example, Louis J. Kern, *An Ordered Love: Sex Roles and Sexuality in Victorian Utopias—The Shakers, the Mormons, and the Oneida Community* (Chapel Hill: University of North Carolina Press, 1981), 27-28. Harry Gene Levine, "What Is an Alcohol-Related Problem? (Or, What Are People Talking About When They Refer to Alcohol Problems?)," *Journal of Drug Issues* 14 (1984): 45–60, sketches the strategy followed beginning in the 1960s to emphasize the normality of alcohol use.

84. See especially Howard A. Mulford, "Drinking and Deviant Drinking, U.S.A., 1963," *Quarterly Journal of Studies on Alcohol* 25 (1964): 634–50; Giorgio Lolli, *Social Drinking: How to Enjoy Drinking Without Being Hurt by It* (Cleveland: The World Publishing Company, 1960), especially 122; Gusfield, "Prevention: Rise, Decline and Renaissance," 402–25.

85. See especially Blocker, *American Temperance Movements*, 146–49, 150–54; Mark Keller, "Alcohol Problems and Policies in Historical Perspective," in *Law, Alcohol, and Order*, ed. Kyvig, 162–70. Morris E. Chafetz and Marc Hertzman, "Alcohol Abuse and Alcoholism: A New Era in an Old Campaign," *Journal of Drug Issues* 5 (1975): 201-6. Dwight Anderson, "Alcohol and Public Opinion," *Quarterly Journal of Studies on Alcohol* 3 (1942): 376–92, successfully urged the use of the term "alcoholic" in place of the more stigmatizing "drunkard." Much of this emphasizing of the disease model in midcentury and after—including the decriminalization of drunkenness—was in at least partial opposition to some social-science researchers who emphasized that drinking patterns and drunken comportment derived from social conditioning and especially from the immediate social group, not from disease determinants. Lorin R. Daggett and Edward J. Rolde, "Decriminalization of Drunkenness," *Journal of Studies on Alcohol* 41 (1980): 819–28. See the summary, Stanton Peele, "The Cultural Context of Psychological Approaches to Alcoholism," *American Psychologist* 39 (1984): 1337-51.

86. Roizen, "The American Discovery of Alcoholism," passim. No one has traced the effect of the post-repeal repealers' campaigns on school materials. Gail Milgram, "A Historical

Review of Alcohol Education Research and Comments," *Journal of Alcohol and Drug Education* 21 (1976): 1–16. See, for example, "Alcoholism Education Focuses on Colleges," *Modern Brewery*, 8 October 1979, 1; E. J. Cecil, "Washington Report," *Liquor Store Magazine*, October 1977, 22. An article, "Educating the Consumer," *Modern Brewery Age*, September-October 1983, MS78–84, turned out to mean the *young* consumer. The authors of one authoritative publication, for example, denied that drinking was anything but an individual problem, and they included a segment on "components of responsible drinking skills"; *Youth, Alcohol, and Social Policy*, ed. Howard T. Blane and Morris Chafetz (New York: Plenum Press, 1979), especially 314–15, 385.

87. Scott, "How Spirits Industry," 11. "Liquor Today," *Liquor Store Magazine*, January 1973, 6. Patricia A. Whately, "*Los Angeles Times* and *New York Times*, 1950–1958 and 1970–1978: Did Alcohol Related Coverage Change?" (Master's thesis, California State University, Fullerton, 1979).

88. Oxenfeldt, *Industrial Pricing*, chap. 9, describes midcentury industry pressures. See especially Denzin, "Notes on the Criminogenic Hypothesis"; the quotes are from 910 and 919; and Jonathan Rubinstein, *City Police* (New York: Farrar, Straus and Giroux, 1973), especially 419–29, for local-level operations.

89. One approach to a summary is Gomberg, White, and Carpenter, *Alcohol, Science, and Society Revisited*.

FOUR: *Smoking*

1. Among at least some German-American brewers, such a secure world also existed in that part of the alcoholic-beverage industry, but it was complicated by powerful outside disapproval. Wine makers were always even closer to the prosocial tobacco model, but the contrast between the two industries still existed.

2. William Arthur Cullman, "The Marketing of Tobacco Products" (doctoral diss., Ohio State University, 1951), 12. "Tobacconalia," *Knickerbocker* 59 (1859): 528. See, for example, Jack Larkin, *The Reshaping of Everyday Life* (New York: Harper and Row, 1988), 166–69.

3. Patrick G. Porter, "Advertising in the Early Cigarette Industry: W. Duke, Sons and Company of Durham," *North Carolina Historical Review* 48 (1971): 35. George S. Chappell, *Evil Through the Ages: An Outline of Indecency* (New York: Frederick A. Stokes Company, 1932), 286, recalled that when he was young, a naughty grocer boy had given him a card from a package of Sweet Caporal cigarettes; it pictured a Miss Pauline Hall with a "nifty velvet cap and winsome face . . . hour-glass shaped torso . . . splendiferous legs!"—and the latter actually shown, contrary to mores of that time.

4. See Jack J. Gottsegen, *Tobacco, A Study of Its Consumption in the United States* (New York: Pitman Publishing Corporation, 1940), especially 2–13, 36–40, 113–31, 141–42. Nannie M. Tilley, *The R. J. Reynolds Tobacco Company* (Chapel Hill: The University of North Carolina Press, 1985), 156. A general work is Joseph C. Robert, *The Story of Tobacco in America* (New York: Alfred A. Knopf, 1952). The classic guide to literature on tobacco is Jerome E. Brooks, *Tobacco, Its History Illustrated by the Books, Manuscripts and Engravings in the Library of George Arents, Jr.*, 5 vols. (New York: The Rosenbach Company, 1937–1942).

5. Robert Sobel, *They Satisfy: The Cigarette in American Life* (Garden City, N.Y.: Anchor Press/Doubleday, 1978); the quotation is from 9–10; Gottsegen, *Tobacco*, 10, 131, 145.

6. See especially Richard B. Tennant, *The American Cigarette Industry: A Study in Economic Analysis and Public Policy* (New Haven: Yale University Press, 1950), 3–25; Sobel, *They Satisfy*.

7. See, for example, John Bain, Jr., *Tobacco in Song and Story* (New York: The New York Public Library, 1953 [1906]). John Fiske, *Tobacco and Alcohol* (New York: Leypoldt and Holt, 1869), 81.

8. Leonard K. Hirshberg, "The Truth About Tobacco," *Harpers Weekly*, 4 January 1913, 12. G. L. Hemminger, quoted in Hamilton, *This Smoking World*, 21.

9. *New York Times*, quoted in Richard B. Tennant, *The American Cigarette Industry, A Study in Economic Analysis and Public Policy* (New York: Archon Books, 1971 [c. 1950]), 133.

10. There was an abundance of material denouncing cigarettes; for a typical statement from a solid citizen, see D. H. Kress, "The Cigarette as Related to Moral Reform," *Interstate Medical Journal* 23 (1916): 485–89. "Cigarettes vs. Automobiles," *American Journal of Public Health* 5 (1915): 1193. Lucy Page Gaston, "The Cigarette Evil and Its Suppression," *Juvenile Court Record*, March 1906, 24. Perry R. Duis, "Cigarettes and Sin," *Chicago* 10 (1983): 142–45. See, for example, Charles Alma Byers, "A City Fights the Cigarette Habit," *American City* 14 (1916): 369–70; *Tobacco*, 7 July 1899, 6; *Tobacco Leaf*, 7 February 1906, 5; William W. Young, *The Story of the Cigarette* (New York: D. Appleton and Company, 1916), chap. 15.

11. *Tobacco*, 5 July 1889, 2. "Cigarettes to Minors," *Tobacco*, 7 June 1889, 4.

12. "The License Question Again," *Tobacco*, 10 September 1906, 6. "Cigar Store Wooden Indians," *Tobacco*, 1 February 1923, 25. *Tobacco*, 1 May 1919, 8. And see, for example, *Tobacco*, 29 September 1899, 4; "Oregon Trade News," *Tobacco*, 4 August 1899, 8; "Chicago Trade Shows Vitality," *Tobacco*, 10 September 1908, 4. It may be that gambling became more of a problem for tobacco retailers after the saloons closed in the 1920s, but the cigar store was well on the way to extinction by then as other outlets took over retailing; see "Come Seben, Come 'Leben!" *Tobacco*, 1 September 1927, 6.

13. Sobel, *They Satisfy*, 52–56. Gordon L. Dillow, "Thank You for Not Smoking, The Hundred-Year War Against the Cigarette," *American Heritage*, February/March 1981, 94–107. Ronald J. Troyer and Gerald E. Markle, *Cigarettes: The Battle Over Smoking* (New Brunswick: Rutgers University Press, 1983), 33–39.

14. "The Cigarette Laws of 1910," *Tobacco*, 26 July 1889.

15. See especially Robert, *The Story of Tobacco*, 230–35, and Tilley, *The R. J. Reynolds Tobacco Company*, 210–20; and Sobel, *They Satisfy*, 66–86. Other accounts appear in works cited above.

16. Tilley, *The R. J. Reynolds Tobacco Company*, 210–21, 224; Sobel, *They Satisfy*, especially 77–78, 80–81. The profusion of tobacco ads in Chicago newspapers, for example, "from four to six in every edition," was noted in *Tobacco*, 1 May 1919, 20.

17. Sobel, *They Satisfy*, 83–88. See, for example, such serviceman-oriented publications as "A Smoke Barrage," *Home Sector*, 20 March 1920, 16. William D. Parkinson, quoted in "An 'Essay' on Tobacco," *Tobacco*, 12 February 1925, 10.

18. Young, *The Story of the Cigarette*, 223. *Tobacco*, 17 April 1919, 17.

19. See, for example, C. A. Barney and Co., *The Tobacco Industry, Annual Review*, 1928–1929 (New York: C. A. Barney and Co., 1928), 22; "The Worm Turns," *American Journal of Public Health* 19 (1929): 658–59.

20. See the discussion in chapter 1 and citations in note 13, above; Robert, *The Story of Tobacco*, 245–54. "Anti-Tobacco Day," *Tobacco*, 31 March 1921, 6. Examples include "Eloquent and Well Considered Address of President Eisenlohr," *Tobacco*, 20 May 1920, 7, 17, 37; "The Anti-Tobacco Campaign," *Tobacco*, 30 April 1925, 20; "Philadelphia Manufacturers Have Xmas Worry," *Tobacco*, 3 December 1925, 19. Secondary accounts include Sobel, *They Satisfy*, 87–89; Troyer and Markle, *Cigarettes*, 41–45.

21. See, for example, "San Francisco News Notes," *Tobacco*, 10 March 1921, 17; William G. Shepherd, "Lady Nicotine—Next?" *Home Sector*, 20 March 1920, 9–10, 38–39.

22. See, for example, Tilley, *The R. J. Reynolds Tobacco Company*, 335. William K. Anderson, "Will They Force Us to It?" *Christian Century* 46 (1929): 1576–77. *The Lantern* [Ohio State University], 6 October 1930, 4. Some account of the manipulations of the 1920s and 1930s is in Edward L. Bernays, *Biography of an Idea: Memoirs of Public Relations Counsel* (New York: Simon and Schuster, 1965), 372–400.

23. A good summary of the scholarship is Michael Schudson, "Women, Cigarettes, and Advertising in the 1920s," in *Mass Media Between the Wars: Perceptions of Cultural Tension 1918–1941*, ed. Catherine L. Covert and John D. Stevens (Syracuse: Syracuse University Press, 1984), 71–83. President's Research Committee on Social Trends, *Recent Social Trends in the United States*, 2 vols. (New York: McGraw-Hill Book Company, 1933), 2: 903, dated the first "tentative" ads in which women held cigarettes to 1919. Troyer and Markle, *Cigarettes*, 41–42. Susan Cunningham, "Not Such a Long Way, Baby: Women and Cigarette Ads," American Psychological Association *Monitor*, November 1983, 15. Paula S. Fass, *The Damned and the Beautiful: American Youth in the 1920's* (New York: Oxford University Press, 1977), 292–300.

24. See, for example, "Feminine Appeal a Success in Marlboro Campaign," *Tobacco*, 28 April 1927, 25. *Tobacco*, 12 August 1899, 23. Fass, *The Damned and the Beautiful*, especially 295. Frank Leighton Wood, "Is Youth Becoming More Immoral?" *Facts of Life* 1 (1937): 141–42.

25. "Science Studies Women," *Tobacco*, 4 December 1924, 20. "Lindbergh Smokes Cigarette to Prove He's No 'Tin Saint,' " *New York Times*, 27 August 1927, 11. Sobel, *They Satisfy*, 95–105. Michael Schudson, *Advertising, The Uneasy Persuasion: Its Dubious Impact on American Society* (New York: Basic Books, Inc., 1984), chap. 6. Fass, *The Damned and the Beautiful*, 292–300; Fass notes that separate standards for women were part of the more general double standard of morality. There was always the possibility that smoking might become sexually differentiated—cigarettes for women, cigars for men; see, for example, "Cigarettes and the Girl," *Tobacco*, 4 August 1927, 20. Cigarettes in fact came to mean not a dual standard but a single standard for both men and women—the formerly male standard.

26. Anderson, "Will They Force Us to It?" 1576. Robert, *The Story of Tobacco*, 254, claims opposition was dead by that year.

27. Tennant, *The American Cigarette Industry*, 141–42, notes that advertising may not have been effective in inducing women to smoke, because British women took the habit up earlier and faster; the real significance of Tennant's observation is, of course, that Americans resisted the change because of their moral beliefs, and the actions of the advertisers were necessary to effect the market growth in the United States. A. E. Hamilton, *This Smoking World* (New York: The Century Company, 1927), 17–18. *Life* 75 (1920): 711.

28. Troyer and Markle, *Cigarettes*, 44–47. Edgar Dale, *The Content of Motion Pictures* (New York: Macmillan, 1935), 173. Schudson, *Advertising, The Uneasy Persuasion*, 101.

29. Giles Playfair, *Atlantic*, April 1948, quoted in Elizabeth M. Whelan, *A Smoking Gun: How the Tobacco Industry Gets Away with Murder* (Philadelphia: George F. Stickley Co., 1984). Susan Wagner, *Cigarette Country: Tobacco in American History and Politics* (New York: Praeger Publishers, 1971), chap. 4. See earlier in this chapter.

30. American Tobacco Company, *"Sold American!"—The First Fifty Years* ([New York]: The American Tobacco Company, 1954), 84. The very large number of wholesalers in the business did almost no advertising; Cullman, "The Marketing of Tobacco Products," 217–18. Indeed, some wholesalers started to drop cigarettes because of low markup as the manufacturers did more and more direct sales to distributors such as supermarkets; see Harry B. Patrey and Joseph Kolodny, *Successful Methods of Wholesale Tobacco Distribution* (New York: Foresight Publications, 1957). Cullman (128) found that only drugs and cereals had a higher percentage of cost spent on national advertising than did cigarettes; Leonard Garland Gaston, "The Tobacco Industry and Its Customers" (Master's

thesis, Ohio State University, 1964), 27, 154, found that by 1960 the industry was the largest advertiser proportional to receipts. Tilley, *The R. J. Reynolds Tobacco Company*, 332, 342–43. Gottsegen, *Tobacco*, 49–54, 60–71.

31. *Louisville Times*, quoted in *Tobacco*, 4 June 1925, 10.

32. "Attacks Explained," *Tobacco*, 22 May 1919, 10. Carl Avery Werner, in *Tobacco Leaf*, 15 September 1923, 6. Rockford, Illinois, *Gazette*, quoted in *Tobacco*, 14 February 1929, 16. See, for example, *Tobacco*, March 1925. George Francis Kerr, "The Remarkable Increase in Cigarette Consumption and the Cause," *Tobacco*, 24 April 1924, 17. Schudson, *Advertising, The Uneasy Persuasion*, 178–207, argues that the democratic nature of cigarette smoking and the convenience of that form of tobacco were the elements that made it so important in the consumer culture; my comments above suggest that there were more primary elements.

33. See, for example, Roland Marchand, *Advertising the American Dream: Making Way for Modernity, 1920–1940* (Berkeley: University of California Press, 1985), especially chap. 6; he gives striking examples, and more can be found in runs of major interwar magazines. The example is from *New Yorker*, 18 May 1940, 1.

34. See, for example, Tilley, *The R. J. Reynolds Tobacco Company*, 337–40; *Motivation in Health Science* (New York: Columbia University Press, 1948), 49–50.

35. Just by taking a formerly male role and entering the workplace operated, as during World War II especially, to make women take up the male custom of smoking; see John C. Maxwell, Jr., "Trends in Cigarette Consumption," in *Banbury Report: A Safe Cigarette?*, ed. Gio B. Gori and Fred G. Bock (Cold Spring Harbor, N.Y.: Cold Spring Harbor Laboratory, 1980), 326. Gottsegen, *Tobacco*, 185, 188. American Tobacco Company, *"Sold American!"* 94. Sobel, *They Satisfy*, chap. 8. Cullman, "The Marketing of Tobacco Products," 56.

36. American Tobacco Company, *"Sold American!"* 86.

37. Cullman, "The Marketing of Tobacco Products," especially 51. "The Tobacco Habits of the American Male," *Tobacco Leaf*, 8 January 1949, 1.

38. See, for example, the summary and context in A. Lee Fritschler, *Smoking and Politics: Policymaking and the Federal Bureaucracy* (New York: Appleton-Century-Crofts, 1969), 23, and ibid., 4th ed. (Englewood Cliffs, N.J.: Prentice-Hall, 1989), 10.

39. Tennant, *The American Cigarette Industry*, gives a comprehensive picture of the industry in 1950. Another one, and more revealing in many ways, is Cullman, "The Marketing of Tobacco Products," including clear evidence of the profitability of cigarettes to retailers; see especially 205–6, 236–46. See also Philip Lynn Shepherd, "Sooold American!!! A Study of the Foreign Operations of the American Cigarette Industry" (doctoral diss., Vanderbilt University, 1983), which contains substantial analysis of the business and takes up (870–73) the sugggestion that the market for cigarettes was peaking "naturally" in the postwar period. Sobel, *They Satisfy*, 183–87. Ray Jones, "Television Is Revising Our Adv. Technique," *Tobacco Leaf*, 28 February 1953, 8, 32–33. "Chain Grocers Profit Most on Cigarettes," *Tobacco Leaf*, 18 August 1951, 1. And see the trade papers of this period in general.

40. Cullman, "The Marketing of Tobacco," especially 146–52, chap. 5.

41. Troyer and Markle, *Cigarettes*, especially 52, date the end of unquestioned cigarette acceptance at 1953. John C. Burnham, "American Physicians and Tobacco Use: Two Surgeons General, 1929 and 1964," *Bulletin of the History of Medicine* 63 (1989): 1–31. Indeed, to some extent the argument was carried on between two versions of consumer-culture narcissism. The anti-tobacco people appealed to personal-health and fitness concerns, and the tobacco users and sellers appealed to self-indulgence. Both were therefore appealing to self-centeredness, the one for preserving self, the other for gratifying self. In this sense, both were operating within the same general framework. Shepherd, "Sooold

American!!!" Sobel, *They Satisfy*. The more conspicuous examples include Maureen Neuberger, *Smoke Screen: Tobacco and the Public Welfare* (Englewood Cliffs, N.J.: Prentice-Hall, 1963); Wagner, *Cigarette Country*; Thomas Whiteside, *Selling Death: Cigarette Advertising and Public Health* (New York: Liveright, 1971); Kenneth Michael Friedman, *Public Policy and the Smoking-Health Controversy: A Comparative Study* (Lexington, Mass.: Lexington Books, 1975); Whelan, *A Smoking Gun*, 75–76. The politics are dealt with in Fritschler, *Smoking and Politics*. See especially James Overton, "Diversification and International Expansion: The Future of the American Tobacco Manufacturing Industry, with Corporate Profiles of the 'Big Six,' " in *The Tobacco Industry in Transition: Policies for the 1980s*, ed. William R. Finger (Lexington, Mass.: Lexington Books, 1981), 162–163, who puts the whole into a business context.

42. Appealing to youth is covered in the standard exposés, which are cited in previous notes. By 1986, there was even a special publication, *Tobacco and Youth Reporter*, crusading on this particular subject but with material on other related scandals, such as the targeting of minority groups; the publication contains many colorful examples of tobacco-company actions from the 1980s that can illustrate points made in this and following paragraphs. Whiteside, *Selling Death*, 29. Cullman, "The Marketing of Tobacco," 188n. See, for example, *Wall Street Journal*, quoted in *Norr Newsletter*, January 1956, 3. *Tobacco Leaf*, 4 April 1953, back cover; by that date, of course, wholesalers were deep into sundries as well.

43. See, for example, "The 'Kid' Smoker Problem," *Tobacco Leaf*, 9 December 1950, 4. Cullman, "The Marketing of Tobacco," 115, 224–25.

44. Wagner, *Cigarette Country*, 144. Whiteside, *Selling Death*, 2–3.

45. Tilley, *The R. J. Reynolds Tobacco Company*, 501, portrays the campaign as deliberate.

46. "Words and Meaning," *Newsweek*, 26 August 1963. Wagner, *Cigarette Country*, 221. "Cigarette Ads Aimed at Youth," American Psychological Association *Monitor*, November 1987, 34. Anne Browder, quoted in Whelan, *A Smoking Gun*, 186. Peter Bart, "Tobacco Troubles," *Saturday Review*, 10 August 1963, 45, 52. Gaston, "The Tobacco Industry," 65. Numerous other examples occur in anti-tobacco publications and public hearings. The ban on television advertising was evaded in various ways from the beginning; see, for example, "Broadcast Ad Ban on Cigarets—It's Inconsistent and Doesn't Even Work," *Advertising Age*, 28 August 1972, 4. Gaston, "The Tobacco Industry," 79, noted that the ad ban in college newspapers did not stop Max Schulman's supposed humor column from appearing courtesy of Philip Morris.

47. See, for example, Whelan, *A Smoking Gun. Rolling Stone*, 3 February 1983, 15.

48. Whelan, *A Smoking Gun*, 185–86.

49. "On the Feeling of 'Guilt' Among Smokers," *Norr Newsletter*, August-September 1956, 7; "Why Do People Smoke?" *Tobacco Leaf*, 15 November 1952, 4. Joseph D. Matarazzo and George Saslow, "Psychological and Related Characteristics of Smokers and Non-smokers," *Psychological Bulletin* 5 (1960): 493–513, summarized more conventional psychological and public-health research on smokers and found that in general they were in the more vulnerable parts of the population that might be expected to react to external cues. Smokers were particularly apt to drink coffee and use alcoholic beverages.

50. Robert H. Moser, "The New Seduction," *JAMA* 230 (1974): 1564.

51. See, for example, Michael L. Smith, "Selling the Moon: The U.S. Manned Space Program and the Triumph of Commodity Scientism," in *The Culture of Consumption: Critical Essays in American History, 1880–1980*, ed. Richard Wightman Fox and T. J. Jackson Lears (New York: Pantheon Books, 1983), 185; John G. Blair, "Cowboys, Europe and Smoke: Marlboro in the Saddle," in *The American West as Seen by Europeans and Americans*, ed. Rob Kroes (Amsterdam: Free University Press, 1989), 360–83; Robert Glatzer, *The New Advertising: The Great Campaigns from Avis to Volkswagen* (New York: Citadel

Press, 1970), 121–34. A great deal of investigation showed that by the 1970s, with proper demographic controls, smoking behavior was no longer distinguishing gender as both men and women tended toward "masculine" standards; see, for example, Raymond Bossé and Charles L. Rose, "Smoking Cessation and Sex Role Convergence," *Journal of Health and Social Behavior* 17 (1976): 53–61. Whiteside, *Selling Death*, 22–23, 51. On the masculine appeal, see chapter 10, below.

52. *Ms.*, November 1972, 52.

53. Pierre Martineau, "Cigarettes—A Psychological Study of Their Role in American Life," *Michigan Business Papers* 27 (1953): 10–17.

54. "Cigarette Smokers Use Brands Whose Ads They Don't Like," *Tobacco Leaf*, 20 December 1952, 5. Schudson, *Advertising, the Uneasy Persuasion*, argues that the intentions of the advertisers were not necessarily linked to their effects; the matter, as I shall explain in chapter 10, was more complicated than that.

55. Whiteside, *Selling Death*, 21, 49.

56. See especially Robert H. Miles and Kim S. Cameron, *Coffin Nails and Corporate Strategies* (Englewood Cliffs, N.J.: Prentice-Hall, 1982). Shepherd, "Sooold American!!!" especially 964–67. Frederick F. Clairmonte, "The Transnational Tobacco and Alcohol Conglomerates," *New York State Journal of Medicine* 83 (1983): 1322–23. The complexity of the economics and particularly marketing and supply is explored suggestively in Paul R. Johnson, *The Economics of the Tobacco Industry* (New York: Praeger, 1984).

57. Cigarette marketers were led into an advertising strategy that became convoluted. The cigarette advertisers found themselves by the health-conscious 1970s deviant but attempting to appeal to rebelliousness against older standards so as to play down the idea that unhealthy behavior was now deviant.

58. Richard Tyson and Jay R. Walker, *How to Stop Smoking Through Meditation* (Chicago: Playboy Press, 1976). The authors did of course point out that there was evidence that smoking might affect one's sex life (13).

FIVE: *Taking Drugs*

1. An authoritative overview showing a cyclical pattern in acceptance of and rejection of drugs is David F. Musto, "Opium, Cocaine and Marijuana in American History," *Scientific American*, July 1991, 40–47. I shall go on to argue in this chapter that such cycles worked themselves out in specific institutions and group interests. Many myths, in fact, came to surround the deviant substances. At the turn of the twentieth century, for example, knowledgeable people generally believed that cocaine use was making black southerners and city delinquents wildly dangerous. (Whether or not cocaine made people dangerous, most blacks could not have afforded the stuff, and in fact virtually none of them used it—a much smaller proportion than in the white population.) Later, people who used marijuana and LSD believed that they could partake of these substances forever without adverse effects on their health. Such beliefs, positive and negative, distract from actual events, however much they contributed to differences of opinion about the deviant status of drug taking. David Musto, *The American Disease: Origins of Narcotic Control* (New Haven: Yale University Press, 1973), especially 7–8.

2. There are excellent standard sources on which I have drawn freely; special points taken from them are of course noted appropriately: David T. Courtwright, *Dark Paradise: Opiate Addiction in America Before 1940* (Cambridge, Mass.: Harvard University Press, 1982); H. Wayne Morgan, *Drugs in America: A Social History, 1800–1980* (Syracuse: Syracuse University Press, 1981); and Musto, *The American Disease*. See also Gregory A.

Austin, *Perspectives on the History of Psychoactive Substance Use* (Rockville, Md.: National Institute on Drug Abuse, 1978).

3. *North American Review* and *Boston Medical and Surgical Journal*, quoted in Morgan, *Drugs in America*, 6–7.

4. See, for example, H. Wayne Morgan, "Introduction," in *Yesterday's Addicts, American Society and Drug Abuse, 1865–1920*, ed. H. Wayne Morgan (Norman: University of Oklahoma Press, 1974), 6–8. The important English background is treated in Terry M. Parssinen, *Secret Passions, Secret Remedies: Narcotic Drugs in British Society, 1820–1930* (Philadelphia: Institute for the Study of Human Issues, 1983). William Rosser Cobbe, *Doctor Judas, A Portrayal of the Opium Habit* (Chicago: S. C. Griggs and Company, 1895), 152. Cobbe goes on (153) to denounce addiction to cigarettes without opium as well. The tactic of lacing tobacco products with addictive substances plagued the early cigarette industry; see, for example, "Perils of Adulterated Snuff," *Tobacco*, 7 May 1908, 1; Harvey W. Wiley, "A Dinner for the Other Fellow," *Good Housekeeping* 58 (1914): 831, which concluded sarcastically with "Cigarettes (with two parts per million of opium)."

5. See particularly Courtwright, *Dark Paradise*, especially chap. 1, and Morgan, *Drugs in America*.

6. Courtwright, *Dark Paradise*, especially chap. 2; he disagrees with Musto, *The American Disease*, 1–2, who discounts the veterans.

7. Morgan, *Drugs in America*, chap. 2; the quotation is from 27. Courtwright, *Dark Paradise*, chap. 2.

8. Morgan, *Drugs in America*, chap. 2, who emphasizes the role of scientific medicine; the quote is from 101; Courtwright, *Dark Paradise*, especially 47–52; the quote is from 51.

9. Neil Larry Shumsky, "Tacit Acceptance: Respectable Americans and Segregated Prostitution, 1870–1910," *Journal of Social History* 19 (1986): 666–77. Morgan, *Drugs in America*, 35–37. Courtwright, *Dark Paradise*, 67–78; the quote is from 71.

10. Cobbe, *Doctor Judas*, 124, 130.

11. Courtwright, *Dark Paradise*, especially 113–14. Morgan, *Drugs in America*, 90. The two substances always had some elements in common.

12. Musto, *The American Disease*, chaps. 1–5, has details of economic interests' maneuvering; see also Morgan, *Drugs in America*, 102–7. Caffeine replaced the cocaine in Coca-Cola in 1903.

13. The changing pattern of drug use is described in Morgan, *Drugs in America*, especially 91–96; and Courtwright, *Dark Paradise*, especially 83–84, 98–114; I am following Courtwright here. David F. Musto, "America's First Cocaine Epidemic," *Wilson Quarterly*, Summer 1989, 59–65.

14. See previous note and Musto, "Opium, Cocaine." *Bohemian* 16 (1909): 550. Perry M. Lichtenstein, "Narcotic Addiction," *New York Medical Journal* 100 (1914): 962.

15. Morgan, *Drugs in America*, 125–28, 143–45; the quotation is from 96. Courtwright, *Dark Paradise*, 115–16, 124–25, 143–44. Lester Grinspoon and Peter Hedblom, *The Speed Culture: Amphetamine Use and Abuse in America* (Cambridge, Mass.: Harvard University Press, 1975), 20. Joseph L. Zentner, "Barbiturate Drugs and the Criminal Sanction," *Contemporary Drug Problems* 5 (1976): 32–35.

16. See, for example, the suggestive British case detailed in Terry Parssinen and Karen Kerner, "An Historical Fable for Our Time: The Illicit Traffic in Morphine in the Early Twentieth Century," *Journal of Drug Issues* 11 (1981): 45–60. Courtwright, *Dark Paradise*, 83–85; Morgan, *Drugs in America*, 128.

17. Stephanie W. Greenberg and Freda Adler, "Crime and Addiction: An Empirical Analysis of the Literature, 1920–1973," *Contemporary Drug Problems* 3 (1974): 221–70.

18. In a comprehensive survey of the health interests of high-school students at the end of the 1940s, the number-one interest named by students was "Habit Forming Substances."

The authors who reported the survey noted that although alcohol and tobacco were involved, a special factor was the fact that "marijuana is now receiving a great deal of attention, since it is so important a factor in juvenile delinquency"—an additional media scare that developed in the 1940s and early 1950s. See especially Joseph Zentner, "Prominent Features of Opiate Use in America During the Twentieth Century," *Journal of Drug Issues* 5 (1975): 103; Parssinen, *Secret Passions*, 119–21; Joseph E. Lantagne, "Health Interests of 10,000 Secondary School Students," *Research Quarterly* 23 (1952): 331–35.

19. Morgan, *Drugs in America*, 145–46. Arnold Abrams, John H. Gagnon, and Joseph J. Levin, "Psychosocial Aspects of Addiction," *American Journal of Public Health* 58 (1968): 2142–55. Larry Sloman, *Reefer Madness: The History of Marijuana in America* (Indianapolis: Bobbs-Merrill, 1979), especially chaps. 8 and 9; this work is based in part upon retrospective reminiscences that undoubtedly exaggerated earlier drug use. It is striking, for example, how strongly a member of the advanced artistic groups in the West still considered drug taking deviant in the late 1950s: William Karl Thomas, *Lenny Bruce: The Making of a Prophet* (Hamden, Ct.: Archon Books, 1989), 15 and passim. Martin A. Lee and Bruce Shlain, *Acid Dreams: The CIA, LSD, and the Sixties Rebellion* (New York: Grove Press, 1985), show that there was some continuity from the earlier bohemian jazz-slumming drug use to the 1960s bohemians, with the involvement of another non-mainstream group, the CIA and associated figures. Dennis Berrett, "Coverage by Five National Magazines of the Growth of the Use of Drugs in America" (Master's thesis, Brigham Young University, 1969).

20. See previous note. Jerome Lionel Himmelstein, "From Killer Weed to Drop-Out Drug: The Marihuana Problem in America" (doctoral diss., University of California, Berkeley, 1979), especially 213–14. "My Son Was Caught Using Narcotics," *Saturday Evening Post*, December 10, 1960, 32–33, 112, 114.

21. Harrison Pope, Jr., *Voices from the Drug Culture* (Boston: Beacon Press, 1971), 82–83.

22. Himmelstein, "From Killer Weed," especially 5, 215, 87–92. Berrett, "Coverage by Five National Magazines." See, for example, "Narcotics: Slum to Suburb," *Newsweek*, 22 February 1965, 68A–68C.

23. Himmelstein, "From Killer Weed," especially 215–17, 87–92. On the radical opposition to legalization, see Timothy Miller, *The Hippies and American Values* (Knoxville: University of Tennessee Press, 1991), 31. William Braden, "LSD and the Press," in *The Manufacture of News: Social Problems, Deviance and the Mass Media*, ed. Stanley Cohen and Jock Young (London: Constable, 1973), 208. See the further discussion of the press, below.

24. Morgan, *Drugs in America*, 153–54. Deborah Ruth Maloff, "The Construction of a Heroin Problem, 1969–74" (doctoral diss., George Washington University, 1982), especially 55–63.

25. Miller, *The Hippies*, 25–27. See, for example, "Panel Workshop: Multiple Substance Abuse—The New Face of Addiction," *Contemporary Drug Problems* 6 (1976): 239–304; Glenn F. Murray, "The Cannabis-Cocaine Connection: A Comparative Study of Use and Users," *Journal of Drug Issues* 14 (1984): 665–75; Nicholas J. Kozel and Edgar H. Adams, "Epidemiology of Drug Abuse: An Overview," *Science* 234 (1986): 970–74. Allan Y. Cohen, "The Psychedelic Experience," in *Drug Abuse in Today's Society*, ed. Arthur Tye, William M. Dickson, and Robert A. Buerki (Columbus: Ohio State University, 1970), 119–20. The war-on-drugs policies are traced in John C. McWilliams, "Through the Past Darkly: The Politics and Policies of America's Drug Wars," *Journal of Policy History* 3 (1991): 356–92.

26. See previous note. R. K. Siegel, "New Trends in Drug Use Among Youth in California," *Bulletin on Narcotics* 37 (1985): 7–17.

27. Musto, *The American Disease*, 2, and discussion of the drugged society below in this chapter.

28. Grinspoon and Hedblom, *The Speed Culture*, 21–24, summarize one extended scandal. Another summary indictment is John Rublowsky, *The Stoned Age: A History of Drugs in America* (New York: G. P. Putnam's Sons, 1974), 24–26, 178ff. Cohen, "The Psychedelic Experience," 95–96. Great Lakes Products, Inc., and the Chemsearch Corporation, "A Statement of Fact . . . ," (n.p., [1986]), pamphlet in the vertical file of the Kinsey Institute for Research in Sex, Gender, and Reproduction, Bloomington, Indiana.

29. Musto, *The American Disease*, especially chap. 3. Craig Reinarman, "Constraint, Autonomy, and State Policy: Notes Toward a Theory of Controls on Consciousness Alteration," *Journal of Drug Issues* 13 (1983): 19. Physician groups were usually not supportive of any controls, especially by the 1940s, when ideology complicated their perceived interests. Compare Sloman, *Reefer Madness*, 196–97.

30. Joseph Nawrozki and Ralph Whitehead, quoted in Robert Bomboy, *Major Newspaper Coverage of Drug Issues* (Washington: The Drug Abuse Council, Inc., 1974), 27.

31. Full details appear in *Community and Legal Responses to Drug Paraphernalia*, National Institute on Drug Abuse, Services Research Report, DHEW Publication No. (ADM)80–963 (Washington: National Institute on Drug Abuse, 1980). See also Sloman, *Reefer Madness*, chap. 19. Bud Bogart, "Ten Years High! The Forcade Be With You," *High Times*, June 1984, 94. *High Times*, Spring 1975, 18. John Mack Carter, "The Magazine of High Society," *Folio*, June 1976, 68–69, emphasizes the many business ties of *High Times*, including the fact that it got its start among attendees at a boutique trade show that attracted many paraphernalia merchants.

32. Susan Wagner, *Cigarette Country: Tobacco in American History and Politics* (New York: Praeger, 1971), 231. *Rolling Stone*, 7 June 1973, 41. There were persistent rumors that big U.S. tobacco companies had prepared for the legalization of marijuana by buying large areas of marijuana fields in Mexico; such apocryphal and obviously believable tales were always denied by the companies. William Novak, *High Culture: Marijuana in the Lives of Americans* (New York: Alfred A. Knopf, 1980), 159, 165. Sloman, *Reefer Madness*; the quotation is from 334–35.

33. See especially Robert B. McBride, "Business as Usual: Heroin Distribution in the United States," *Journal of Drug Issues* 13 (1983): 147–66; John Lieb and Sheldon Olson, "Prestige, Paranoia and Profit: On Becoming a Dealer of Illicit Drugs in a University Community," *Journal of Drug Issues* 6 (1976): 356–67. James T. Carey, *The College Drug Scene* (Englewood Cliffs, N.J.: Prentice-Hall, 1968), especially chaps. 4 and 5.

34. See especially Lieb and Olson, "Prestige, Paranoia," and Patricia A. Adler and Peter Adler, "Shifts and Oscillations in Deviant Careers: The Case of Upper-Level Drug Dealers and Smugglers," *Social Problems* 31 (1983): 195–207; and Carey, *The College Drug Scene*. The researchers discovered that dealers found themselves unable to leave their work because they were reluctant to give up their affluent standard of living—or their expensive drug habits.

35. See especially McBride, "Business as Usual," and the previous note. Patrick Anderson, *High in America: The True Story behind NORML and the Politics of Marijuana* (New York: The Viking Press, 1981), 10–13, describes power figures in government and the media who were at least touched by the drug culture at one point in the 1970s. Grinspoon and Hedblom, *The Speed Culture*, 25–26.

36. Major publishers also advertised in the publications devoted to illegal drugs. *Rolling Stone*, 21 December 1968, 16–17.

37. See the discussion below, in this chapter. See, for example, Richard H. Blum et al., *Horatio Alger's Children* (San Francisco: Jossey-Bass Inc., 1972). The volume of such literature is very great, starting with the much-cited Joan Didion, *Slouching Towards*

Bethlehem (New York: Farrar, Straus and Giroux, 1968), 84–128. See especially Miller, *The Hippies,* chap. 2. Marsha Rosenbaum, "Becoming Addicted: The Woman Addict," *Contemporary Drug Problems* 8 (1979): especially 144–45. Carey, *The College Drug Scene.* George Gerbner, "Deviance and Power: Symbolic Functions of Drug Abuse," in *Deviance and Mass Media,* ed. Charles Winick (Beverly Hills: Sage Publications, 1978), 21–23, points out that the campus was not the center of drug use; such accounts as David E. Smith and John Luce, *Love Needs Care: A History of San Francisco's Haight-Ashbury Free Medical Clinic and Its Pioneer Role in Treating Drug-Abuse Problems* (Boston: Little, Brown and Company, 1971), underline the multiple kinds of rebelliousness that drug taking involved. Moreover, there were limits to what even rebels were willing to do, at least in the earlier years; Sam Sloan, "Inside an Orgy," in *Sex Marchers,* ed. Jefferson Poland and Sam Sloan (Los Angeles: Elysium Inc., 1968), 109–10, claimed that drugs were unusual among multiple-partner orgy participants. The basis for drug taking as a rebellious, sanctioned act is described in Douglas Clark Kinder, "Shutting Out the Evil: Nativism and Narcotics Control in the United States," *Journal of Policy History* 3 (1991): 468–93.

38. Abrams, Gagnon, and Levin, "Psychosocial Aspects," 2147–48. Rosenbaum, "Becoming Addicted," 159. And, for example, Richard E. Clark, Albert Kowitz, and Diane Duckworth, "The Influence of Information Sources and Grade Level on the Diffusion and Adoption of Marihuana," *Journal of Drug Issues* 5 (1975): 177–88. One collection is Robert H. Coombs, Lincoln J. Fry, and Patricia G. Lewis, *Socialization in Drug Abuse* (Cambridge, Mass.: Schenkman Publishing Company, 1976). The cases and observations in Pope, *Voices from the Drug Culture,* chaps. 1–8, underline both the criminal and rebellious elements involved in young people's participation.

39. Gregory R. Staats, "Effects of Supply, Secrecy, and Immorality on Marijuana Use: An Examination of the Becker Hypothesis," *Contemporary Drug Problems* 6 (1977): 437–49. For the individual, being addicted came to be, perversely, a career—with steady advances in status, the ultimate stages of which, aside from conspicuous consumption, were dealing and going to prison. Dedication to one's addiction and nourishing it came to resemble the normal work-ethic preoccupations and efforts. The classic article, but a late one, is Robert H. Coombs, "Drug Abuse as a Career," *Journal of Drug Issues* 11 (1981): 369–85. National Commission on Marihuana and Drug Abuse, *Marihuana: A Signal of Misunderstanding* (Washington: U. S. Government Printing Office, 1972), 36–41, profiles different degrees of involvement, a scheme that others have adopted to cover all drug involvements.

40. Siegel, "New Trends in Drug Use," 9–11; Lieb and Olson, "Prestige, Paranoia and Profit," especially 358–59, 365; Carey, *The College Drug Scene.* It was customary to differentiate between the irresponsible pusher and the friendly and trustworthy dealer—so by the use of language, proponents of drugs avoided suggesting that sellers were pushers.

41. Carey, *The College Drug Scene.* See, for example, James D. Orcutt and Donald A. Biggs, "Perceived Risks of Marijuana and Alcohol Use: Comparisons of Non-Users and Regular Users," *Journal of Drug Issues* 3 (1973): 355–60; Arthur Stickgold and Alan Brovar, "Undesirable Sequelae of Drug Abuse Education," *Contemporary Drug Problems* 7 (1978): especially 101.

42. Deborah Maloff et al., "Informal Social Controls and Their Influence on Substance Use," *Journal of Drug Issues* 9 (1979): 161–73. See, for example, Bill Graham, in Peter Joseph, *Good Times: An Oral History of America in the Nineteen Sixties* (New York: William Morrow and Company, 1974), 348–49. Bruce had been arrested already in 1961 on drug charges; *Village Voice,* 15 February 1962, 7. Anderson, *High in America,* 25. *High Times,* December/January 1975–1976, 21. Jerald W. Cloyd, *Drugs and Information Control: The Role of Men and Manipulation in the Control of Drug Trafficking* (Westport, Ct.: Green-

wood Press, 1982), 85. *Easy Rider* of course was mostly about marijuana use, but it opened with a scene depicting cocaine dealing.

43. The initial incisive analysis was Norman E. Zinberg, "Why Now? Drug Use as a Response to Social and Technological Change," *Contemporary Drug Problems* 1 (1972): 747–82. See, for example, *Journal of Drug Issues* 6 (1976): v–vi, 1–104, which includes company responses and bibliography. Robert Seidenberg, "Advertising and Drug Acculturation," in Coombs, Fry, and Lewis, *Socialization in Drug Abuse*, 19–25. Joel Fort, *The Pleasure Seekers: The Drug Crisis, Youth and Society* (Indianapolis: Bobbs-Merrill, 1969), 194–95.

44. See, for example, Nicholas Johnson, "Junkie Television," *Journal of Drug Issues* 4 (1974): 227–28, as well as the rest of the issue, cited above. Gene Bylinsky, "A Preview of the 'Choose Your Mood' Society," *Fortune*, March 1977, 220–27; the quote is from 220.

45. Miller, *The Hippies*, 76–77. See, for example, Elaine S. Schwartz, Sanford J. Feinglass, and Carol Drucker, "Popular Music and Drug Lyrics: Analysis of a Scapegoat," in *The Media and Drug Abuse Messages*, ed. N. R. Benchley and Peter G. Hammond (Washington: Special Action Office for Drug Abuse Prevention, 1974), 25–39, especially 31–33 (the authors are naively legalistic in their interpretations). Charles Perry, *The Haight-Ashbury: A History* (New York: Random House, 1984), emphasizes the affinity of rock and roll with drug taking and drug advocacy; as the case of "Rainy Day Women" (the correct title) shows, people at the time read a drug message into rock and roll even when it may not have been there (148). Novak, *High Culture*, 161. Clyde Davis, quoted in *Rolling Stone*, 23 November 1967, 6; the correct title of the other song is "The Times They Are A'Changin'." Anderson, *High in America*, 53–54. Herbert I. London, *Closing the Circle: A Cultural History of the Rock Revolution* (Chicago: Nelson-Hall, 1984), especially 111, 116. Chester White Flippo, "Rock Journalism and *Rolling Stone*" (Master's thesis, University of Texas, 1974), 18. *Rolling Stone*, 7 December 1968, 4; 17 September 1970, 54; 1 October 1970, 18 ("Dope Notes").

46. Later memories attributing drug use to the beat existence are not confirmed by contemporary evidence. Jack Kerouac, *On the Road* (New York: Buccaneer Books, 1957), 7, 9, 107, 119, 120–21, 123, 129, 143, 151–52, 201, 230–34. Perry, *The Haight-Ashbury*, especially 5, 248, distinguishes the Beats from the Hippies, who believed less in the hard work of creativity and more in self-indulgence than the Beat Generation. Smith and Luce, *Love Needs Care*, 86, believe that it was in 1963 that many Beats tried to transfer "their dependence on alcohol into a dependence on marijuana." That same year, Don Carpenter, "Obituary for a Hipster," *Village Voice*, 28 February 1963, 6, spoke of marijuana use among bohemians as a thing of the past. In the late 1950s, *Village Voice* writers tended to label the Beats as drug users in part because of simple stereotyping of bohemians, in part because of the conspicuous marijuana advocacy of Allen Ginsberg; see, for example, *Village Voice*, 15 October 1958, 9.

47. See especially Miller, *The Hippies*, and the account in William L. O'Neill, *Coming Apart: An Informal History of America in the 1960's* (New York: Quadrangle/The New York Times Book Company, 1971), chap. 8, and the chronology of Perry, *The Haight-Ashbury*. As notes below will suggest, there is a substantial antiquarian literature on the 1960s and on drug use in that era. Charles W. Lidz, Andrew L. Walker, and Leroy C. Gould, *Heroin, Deviance and Morality* (Beverly Hills: Sage Publications, 1980), 66. Dean Latimer, quoted in *High Times*, June 1984, 33–34. Smith and Luce, *Love Needs Care*, especially 94–127.

48. Zinberg, "Why Now?" puts the problem in a more general cultural context. Miller, *The Hippies*, especially chap. 2.

49. Alfred R. Lindesmith, "Our Immoral Drug Laws," *Nation* 186 (1958): 558–62. See, similarly, Herbert Berger and Andrew A. Eggstrom, "Should We Legalize Narcotics?" *Coronet*, June 1955, 30–35. William Butler Eldridge, *Narcotics and the Law: A Critique of*

the American Experiment in Narcotic Drug Control (New York: American Bar Foundation, 1962), especially chap. 3. Himmelstein, "From Killer Weed to Drop-Out Drug," 185–86.

50. One history with details of developments is in Rufus King, *The Drug Hang-Up: America's Fifty-Year Folly* (New York: W. W. Norton and Company, 1972), especially chaps. 14–26. Barbara Lynn Kail, "Current Social Thought on Alcohol and Marijuana: A Quantitative Exploration," in *Social Thought on Alcoholism: A Comprehensive Review*, ed. Thomas D. Watts (Malabar, Fla.: Robert E. Krieger Publishing Company, 1986), 109–11, comments on the slowness with which marijuana entered the medical model.

51. See, for example, Darold A. Treffert et al., "A Holistic Model for Drug Treatment Evaluation," *Journal of Drug Issues* 6 (1976): 196–206.

52. King, *The Drug Hang-Up*, 246. A scholarly version was Richard J. Bonnie and Charles H. Whitebread II, *The Marijuana Conviction: A History of Marijuana Prohibition in the United States* (Charlottesville: University Press of Virginia, 1974). *High Times*, February 1984, 81.

53. Jane Newitt, Max Singer, and Herman Kahn, "Some Speculations on U.S. Drug Use," in *Socialization in Drug Abuse*, ed. Coombs, Fry, and Lewis, 418–19.

54. A summary account is in W. David Watts, Jr., *The Psychedelic Experience: A Sociological Study* (Beverly Hills: Sage Publications, 1971), 225–31. Timothy Leary, *Flashbacks, An Autobiography* (Los Angeles: J. P. Tarcher, Inc., 1983), provides his own version of events; and Lee and Shlain, *Acid Dreams*, still another. Perry, *The Haight-Ashbury*, emphasizes the role of Ken Kesey in the San Francisco area. Richard Bunce, "Social and Political Sources of Drug Effects: The Case of Bad Trips on Psychodelics," *Journal of Drug Issues* 9 (1979): especially 222–30. Cohen, "The Psychedelic Experience," 95–121. Norman Hartweg, "Moment," *Los Angeles Free Press*, 23 July 1965, 3. Another public leader was Ken Kesey, publicized especially in Tom Wolfe, *The Electric Kool-Aid Acid Test* (New York: Bantam Books, 1969 [c. 1968]). "Playboy Interview: Timothy Leary," *Playboy*, September 1966, 93–112, 250–56. Many literary people knew also Aldous Huxley, *The Doors of Perception, and Heaven and Hell* (New York: Harper and Brothers, 1956). Miller, *The Hippies*, 29 and chap. 2.

55. Bonnie and Whitebread, *The Marijuana Conviction*, 223–26. Anderson, *High in America*, 53–54. Novak, *High Culture*, 169. The Beatles song was "Happiness Is a Warm Gun" (1968).

56. A narcotics-bureau memorandum reported, "According to a newspaper report, this is not a formal organization and it does not have any officers.... On December 27, 1964, GINSBERG and [others] marched in front of the Department of Welfare Building, East 9th St. and Avenue C, with signs reading 'Smoke Pot, It's Cheaper and Healthier Than Liquor' and 'Pot Is a Reality Kick.' Sloman, *Reefer Madness*, 221. Ginsberg, who aggressively violated many social norms, was, as I have noted, an early, public proponent of selective drug taking; to what extent he influenced—or alienated—others is not known. He appears frequently in Lee and Shlain, *Acid Dreams*.

57. Sloman, *Reefer Madness*, chap. 21. Anderson, *High in America*, especially 4, 13, 45, 58, 73, 79, 169–71, 174–81. Bogart, "Ten Years High!" 28, 93–94. A magazine and other advocacy groups also appeared about the same time. *The Marijuana Review* was published from 1969 to 1973. As I shall note again, supposed harmlessness was part of the propaganda of marijuana advocates.

58. Anderson, *High In America*, 41–43.

59. Berrett, "Coverage by Five National Magazines." Jerome L. Himmelstein, "The Continuing Career of Marijuana: Backlash ... Within Limits," *Contemporary Drug Problems* 15 (1986): 7. Ronald Bayer, "Liberal Opinion and the Problem of Heroin Addiction: 1960–1973," *Contemporary Drug Problems* 4 (1975): 93–112. Anderson, *High in America*. Hartweg, "Moment"; there had been ads for buttons reading "Let's Legalize Pot" and the like

about three months earlier. The *Berkeley Barb*, another underground pioneer, was equally backward until the end of 1965; homosexual rights, for example, by contrast were already high on the underground agenda, but grass still referred to lawn (*Berkeley Barb*, 13 August 1965). Sloman, *Reefer Madness*, 373, in effect discounts his source, who was in fact accurate. Anti-drug stories that did appear were sometimes planted by law-enforcement agencies.

60. The earlier *Village Voice* was not sufficiently deviant in outlook to act as the model for what became the underground press. See especially Robert J. Glessing, *The Underground Press in America* (Bloomington: Indiana University Press, 1970). Cf. Raymond Mungo, *Famous Long Ago: My Life and Hard Times with Liberation News Service* (Boston: Beacon Press, 1970), which details the confusion at that time between left-wing politics and drug taking and the underground press. Gerhard J. Hanneman, "Communicating Drug-Abuse Information Among College Students," *Public Opinion Quarterly* 37 (1973): 171–91. By 1968 there was already a directory of the underground press. The Establishment campaign against the underground press, which included violence, harassment, and other dirty tricks, is detailed in Geoffrey Rips et al., *The Campaign Against the Underground Press* (San Francisco: City Lights Books, 1981); the frequent use of illegal drugs made underground journalists particularly vulnerable to harassment.

61. Marion Magid, "The Death of Hip," *Esquire*, June 1965, 89–103, 138. The first mention of drugs in the *Berkeley Barb* came on 7 September 1965 and was taken from a regular media report of a drug raid on a neighboring campus. *The Psychedelic Review* appeared from 1963 to 1969.

62. Carey, *The College Drug Scene*, 147. People who worked with drug users were astonished by the high number of unfavorable physical reactions, even to marijuana—contrary to drug-culture myth; see Smith and Luce, *Love Needs Care*, 15–16 and passim. John Sinclair, "The Marijuana Revolution," *Marijuana Review*, January-June 1971, 9. Miller, *The Hippies*, chap. 2.

63. Glessing, *The Underground Press*, especially 116–19.

64. "Life on Two Grains a Day: The Heroin Epidemic Spreads into the High Schools," *Life*, 20 February 1970, 24–32. Musto, "Opium, Cocaine," 46–47. For example, Michael P. Rosenthal, "The Legislative Response to Marihuana: When the Shoe Pinches Enough," *Journal of Drug Issues* 7 (1977): 61–77. Larry A. Ingraham, *The Boys in the Barracks: Observations on American Military Life* (Philadelphia: Institute for the Study of Human Issues, 1984), especially 144–45. Wayne L. Lucas, "Changes in Social and Attitudinal Dimensions of Marijuana Abstainers: 1969 to 1976," *Journal of Drug Issues* 11 (1981): 399–414. Reinarman, "Constraint, Autonomy, and State Policy," 11; Anderson, *High in America*, 101. Paul J. Goldstein, *Prostitution and Drugs* (Lexington, Mass.: Lexington Books/D.C. Heath and Company, 1979), 122–23.

65. For example, Harrison M. Trice and Janice M. Beyer, "A Sociological Property of Drugs: Acceptance of Users of Alcohol and Other Drugs Among University Undergraduates," *Journal of Studies on Alcohol* 38 (1977): 58–74. Himmelstein, "The Continuing Career of Marijuana," 1–7.

66. See, for example, Peter Lloyd, in *Good Times: An Oral History of America in the Nineteen Sixties*, ed. Peter Joseph (New York: William Morrow and Company, 1974), 137–38; Lloyd D. Johnston and Patrick M. O'Malley, "Why Do the Nation's Students Use Drugs and Alcohol? Self-Reported Reasons from Nine National Surveys," *Journal of Drug Issues* 6 (1976): 29–66; Manuel Ramos and Leroy C. Gould, "Where Have All the Flower Children Gone? A Five-Year Follow-Up of a Natural Group of Drug Users," *Journal of Drug Issues* 8 (1978): 75–84; Lee N. Robins, "A Follow-Up Study of Vietnam Veterans' Drug Use," *Journal of Drug Issues*, Winter 1974, 61–63; Bayer, "Liberal Opinion"; David E. Smith, "The Free Clinic Movement in the United States: A Ten Year Perspective (1966–1976)," *Journal of Drug Issues* 6 (1976): 348–49; Robert C. Peterson, "Decriminalization

of Marijuana—A Brief Overview of Research-Relevant Policy Issues," *Contemporary Drug Problems* 10 (1981): 265–75. K. Murphy, in *High Times*, February 1984, 7. A revealing local history is Smith and Luce, *Love Needs Care*. Novak, *High Culture*, especially 157, 164, comments on the changing generations of drug users.

67. Himmelstein, "The Continuing Career of Marijuana," especially 10. See, for example, Barbara Lynn Kail, "Current Thought on Alcohol and Marijuana: A Quantitative Exploration," *Journal of Drug Issues* 15 (1985): 111–17. Bunce, "Social and Political Sources," especially 229–30.

68. Ralph Bell, "The Effect of Community Type on the Use and Availability of Marijuana Among Illinois Adults," *Journal of Drug Issues* 14 (1984): 611–21. Leon Gibson Hunt and Carl D. Chambers, *The Heroin Epidemics: A Study of Heroin Use in the United States, 1965–75* (New York: Spectrum Publications, 1976).

69. Peter Kerr, "The Unspeakable Is Debated: Should Drugs Be Legalized?" *New York Times*, 14 May 1988, 1, 24. Schmoke's remarks were made at the April United States Conference of Mayors.

70. One of the very best informed and most reasonable statements was that of Murray E. Jarvik, "The Drug Dilemma: Manipulating the Demand," *Science* 250 (1990): 387–92. Patrick A. Langan, "America's Soaring Prison Population," *Science* 251 (1991): 1568–73, maintained that drugs were not a major factor in overpopulating prisons. A summary is David T. Courtwright, "Drug Legalization, the Drug War, and Drug Treatment in Historical Perspective," *Journal of Policy History* 3 (1991): 393–414.

71. Allen Ginsberg, quoted in *Oracle*, 14 January 1967, 17.

72. See, for example, Watts, *The Psychedelic Experience*, 190; Nathan Adler, *The Underground Stream: New Life Styles and the Antinomian Personality* (New York: Harper and Row, 1972), 89–91; Reinarman, "Constraint, Autonomy," 10–11; Erich Goode, *The Marijuana Smokers* (New York: Basic Books, 1970), especially 73–74; Pope, *Voices from the Drug Culture*; Robert M. Veatch, "Value Foundations for Drug Use," *Journal of Drug Issues* 7 (1977): 253–62. Timothy Leary, quoted in *Oracle*, undated [1967], 31. Lidz, Walker, and Gould, *Heroin, Deviance and Morality*, especially 93. From at least one point of view, represented by a social-psychological approach, so much had American society changed by 1990 that *not* experimenting with drug use was abnormal for young people; Jonathan Shedler and Jack Block, "Adolescent Drug Use and Psychological Health," *American Psychologist* 45 (1990): 612–30, although it should be noted that the conclusions were based only on a sample from the San Francisco Bay area.

S I X : *Gambling*

1. John Snyder, "Introduction," in John Philip Quinn, *Fools of Fortune, Or, Gambling and Gamblers, Comprehending a History of the Vice in Ancient and Modern Times, and in Both Hemispheres: An Exposition of Its Alarming Prevalence and Destructive Effects; with an Unreserved and Exhaustive Disclosure of Such Frauds, Tricks and Devices as Are Practiced by "Professional" Gamblers, "Confidence Men," and "Bunko-Steerers"* (Chicago: The Anti-Gambling Association, 1892), 29–30. Foster Rhea Dulles, *America Learns to Play: A History of Popular Recreation, 1607–1940* (New York: Peter Smith, 1952 [c. 1940]), 154, who in general provides a context for the history of gambling as recreation. Darrell W. Bolen, "Gambling: Historical Highlights and Trends and Their Implications for Contemporary Society," in *Gambling and Society: Interdisciplinary Studies on the Subject of Gambling*, ed. William R. Eadington (Springfield, Ill.: Charles C. Thomas, 1976), 18–19. Ted Ownby, *Subduing Satan: Religion, Recreation, and Manhood in the Rural South, 1865–1920* (Chapel Hill: University of North Carolina Press, 1990), who shows how important gambling

was in that society, notes in particular (86–87) how cockfighting declined because of crooked and rigged contests.

2. See especially John M. Findlay, *People of Chance: Gambling in American Society from Jamestown to Las Vegas* (New York: Oxford University Press, 1986), chap. 1. Other general works on which I have drawn include Herbert Asbury, *Sucker's Progress: An Informal History of Gambling in America from the Colonies to Canfield* (New York: Dodd, Mead and Company, 1938), and Henry Chafetz, *Play the Devil: A History of Gambling in the United States from 1492 to 1955* (New York: Clarkson N. Potter, 1960). A brief account is Fact Research, Inc., "Gambling in Perspective: A Review of the Written History of Gambling and an Assessment of its Effect on Modern American Society," in Commission on the Review of the National Policy Toward Gambling, *Gambling in America* (Washington: U. S. Government Printing Office, 1976), Appendix 1, 1–101; the report of the Commission in general contains much historical summary. John Samuel Ezell, *Fortune's Merry Wheel: The Lottery in America* (Cambridge, Mass.: Harvard University Press, 1960), has been supplemented by Charles T. Clotfelter and Philip J. Cook, *Selling Hope: State Lotteries in America* (Cambridge, Mass.: Harvard University Press, 1989), especially part 1. T. H. Breen, "Horses and Gentlemen: The Cultural Significance of Gambling Among the Gentry of Virginia," in *Sport in America: New Historical Perspectives*, Donald Spivey (Westport, Ct.: Greenwood Press, 1985), 3–24, and David K. Wiggins, "Leisure Time on the Southern Plantation: The Slaves' Respite from Constant Toil, 1810–1860," in ibid., 36–37. David Hackett Fischer, *Albion's Seed: Four British Folkways in America* (New York: Oxford University Press, 1989), 343, 360–64.

3. See especially Chafetz, *Play the Devil*, 44–50. Findlay, *People of Chance*, especially 27–30, found that early Americans were relatively moderate gamblers compared to their English counterparts. Ann Vincent Fabian, "Rascals and Gentlemen: The Meaning of American Gambling, 1820–1890" (doctoral diss., Yale University, 1982), particularly explores the ambivalence; a partial version of this is Ann Fabian, *Card Sharps, Dream Books, & Bucket Shops: Gambling in 19th-Century America* (Ithaca: Cornell University Press, 1990).

4. Asbury, *Sucker's Progress*; Findlay, *People of Chance*, especially 32–33; Chafetz, *Play the Devil*, especially 29, 42. Ezell, *Fortune's Merry Wheel*, especially 33–34. The quotations are from the New York *Tribune*, 24 March 1877, 2, and 6 April 1877, 2.

5. Findlay, *People of Chance*, emphasizes the frontier connection; see also 81–82. Asbury, *Sucker's Progress*, 229. Fabian, "Rascals and Gentlemen," passim and especially 64–66. Karen Halttunen, *Confidence Men and Painted Women: A Study of Middle-Class Culture in America, 1830–1870* (New Haven: Yale University Press, 1982), 16–20.

6. Findlay, *People of Chance*, especially 83, 100–104. Quinn, _Fools of Fortune, 185.

7. Andrew Steinmetz, *The Gaming Table, Its Votaries and Victims: In All Times and Countries, Especially in England and in France*, 2 vols. (London: Tinsley Brothers, 1870), 1: 221–22.

8. "Gambling," *Godey's Lady's Book* 71 (1865): 428. Late in the twentieth century, the unstructured nature of a gambler's life still disturbed both critics and gamblers themselves; see David M. Hayano, *Poker Faces: The Life and Work of Professional Card Players* (Berkeley: University of California Press, 1982), 136–39. Asbury, *Sucker's Progress*, 78–87. William Christie MacLeod, "The Truth About Lotteries in American History," *South Atlantic Quarterly* 35 (1936): 201–11, details the legislation and the corrupting influence of business contractors in public wagering. Ezell, *Fortune's Merry Wheel*. Paul Boster, "Georgia Plays the Numbers: A History of Lotteries in Georgia," *Atlanta Historical Journal* 24 (1985–1986): 95–104. Mark H. Haller, "Bootleggers and American Gambling, 1920–1950," in Commission on the Review of the National Policy Toward Gambling, *Gambling in America*, Appendix 1, 104–8.

9. Mason Long, *The Life of Mason Long, The Converted Gambler: Being a Record of His Experience as a White Slave; A Soldier in the Union Army; A Professional Gambler; A Patron of the Turf; A Variety Theater and Minstrel Manager; And, Finally, A Convert to the Murphy Cause, And to the Gospel of Christ* (Fort Wayne, Ind.: Mason Long, 1883), 159–60. Fabian, "Rascals and Gentlemen," repeatedly mentions the risqué aspects of gamblers' narratives.

10. Leonard Ellis, "Men Among Men: An Exploration of All-Male Relationships in Victorian America" (doctoral diss., Columbia University, 1982), especially 66–73, 107–19; the quote is Henry C. Alley, 116.

11. New York *Tribune*, 26 February 1876, 5. The system of policy betting, aimed particularly at the poor, is described in detail in the *National Police Gazette*, 16 October 1845, 54.

12. J. H. Green, quoted in Fabian, "Rascals and Gentlemen," 58; see also 66–68.

13. See, for example, Quinn, *Fools of Fortune*, 186; Fabian, *Card Sharps, Dream Books*, especially 188–200. Mark H. Haller, "Policy Gambling, Entertainment, and the Emergence of Black Politics: Chicago from 1900 to 1940," *Journal of Social History* 24 (1991): 719–39.

14. Haller, "Bootleggers and American Gambling," 106–8. Barton Wood Currie, "The Transformation of the Southwest Through the Legal Abolition of Gambling," *Century* 75 (1908): 905–10.

15. Jacob A. Riis, "The Gambling Mania," *Century* 73 (1907): 926.

16. Chafetz, *Play the Devil*, 413–14 and, for example, 195. Quoted in Stephen Longstreet, *Win or Lose: A Social History of Gambling in America* (Indianapolis: Bobbs-Merrill, 1977), 214.

17. Asbury, *Sucker's Progress*, 419–20.

18. See, for example, repeated comments throughout *Home Sector*, 1919–1920. Chafetz, *Play the Devil*, 387. There was racetrack betting in Kentucky in 1906. John A. Lucas and Ronald A. Smith, *Saga of American Sport* (Philadelphia: Lea and Febiger, 1978), 321–22. Because of differing definitions and uncertain legal status in the face of court challenges, it is extremely difficult to chart exactly when racetrack betting developed; this summary is based on *New York Times* reports, including 1 January 1936, 38, and 23 May 1937, 4: 10.

19. Eadington, *Gambling and Society*, 5, who notes that this lottery movement was paralleled elsewhere in the world. Clotfelter and Cook, *Selling Hope*, especially 3, 22–24, 144–47, 201.

20. Fact Research, Inc., "Gambling in Perspective." James David Fairbanks, "Politics, Economics and the Public Morality: State Regulation of Gambling, Liquor, Divorce and Birth Control" (doctoral diss., Ohio State University, 1975), 170. Clotfelter and Cook, *Selling Hope*, 147–50, show that the need for revenue was not a valid argument for instituting state lotteries in the late twentieth century.

21. Lucas and Smith, *Saga of American Sport*, 52.

22. Noah Webster, *A Dictionary of the English Language*, 2 vols. (London: Black, Young, and Young, 1832), vol. 2, unpaginated. *The Modern Eclectic Dictionary of the English Language* (New York: P. F. Collier and Son, 1905). *The Slang Dictionary* (London: Chatto and Windus, 1913) noted that sport was "an American term for a gambler or turfite—more akin to our sporting man than to our sportsman."

23. Devol, *Forty Years a Gambler*, passim. Richard H. Thornton, *An American Glossary*, 2 vols. (Philadelphia: J. B. Lippincott Company, 1912), 2: 839, citing *Harper's Weekly*, 1861.

24. And, as will be suggested below, not just to gambling; one of the early meanings of "sport" was copulation, and people at the turn of the century knew that a "sporting house" was not just a place where followers of athletic contests gathered. *Slang and Its Analogues: Past and Present, A Dictionary, Historical and Comparative of the Heterodox*

Speech of All Class of Society for More than Three Hundred Years, ed. John Stephen Farmer and W. E. Henley, 7 vols. ([London:] Printed for Subscribers Only, 1890–1904), 6: 321.

25. Benjamin G. Rader, *American Sports from the Age of Folk Games to the Age of Spectators* (Englewood Cliffs, N.J.: Prentice-Hall, 1983), especially 25–26, 30–34. See also Elliott J. Gorn, *The Manly Art: Bare-Knuckle Prize Fighting in America* (Ithaca: Cornell University Press, 1986), especially chap. 4, for the many hidden social agendas involved in the rise of sports. Melvin L. Adelman, *A Sporting Time: New York City and the Rise of Modern Athletics, 1820–70* (Urbana: University of Illinois Press, 1986), 38, 88, 101, etc., notes the early ties to gambling and the toleration of upper-class sporting men for gambling. Haller, "Bootleggers and American Gambling," 106, points out the important role of Irish ethnics in pre-World War I gambling, along with their role in urban politics. Oliver Wendell Holmes, *The One Hoss Shay With Its Companion Poems, How the Old Horse Won the Bet and the Broomstick Train* (Boston: Houghton Mifflin and Company, 1892), 31–57. Thorstein Veblen, *The Theory of the Leisure Class: An Economic Study of Institutions* (New York: New American Library, 1953 [c. 1899]).

26. See especially Gorn, *The Manly Art*. *New York Tribune*, 28 October 1876, 8; 13 February 1894, 9. Frank Luther Mott, *A History of American Magazines, 1865–1885* (Cambridge, Mass.: Harvard University Press, 1938), 3: 222. Each sport, it should be clear, like horse racing, boxing, and baseball, had a unique history and changing relationship to gambling and betting.

27. Rader, *American Sports*, especially 97–105. James Turner, *Reckoning with the Beast: Animals, Pain, and Humanity in the Victorian Mind* (Baltimore: Johns Hopkins University Press, 1980), 28–29. Gorn, *The Manly Art*; the quote is from 130.

28. Rader, *American Sports*. Gorn, *The Manly Art*.

29. See especially Gorn, *The Manly Art*, and Jeffrey T. Sammons, *Beyond the Ring: The Role of Boxing in American Society* (Urbana: University of Illinois Press, 1988).

30. See especially Donald J. Mrozek, *Sport and American Mentality, 1880–1910* (Knoxville: The University of Tennessee Press, 1983), chap. 3. Adelman, *A Sporting Time*, especially 9–10, 284–85.

31. See, for example, the *National Police Gazette* in the late nineteenth century; Gorn, *The Manly Art*; and Rader, *American Sports*. The role of the so-called police gazettes was ambiguous; they pioneered both sexual and crime material as well as sports material; see, for example, Frank Luther Mott, *A History of American Magazines, 1850–1865* (Cambridge, Mass.: Harvard University Press, 1938), 187, 333–35. Haller, "Bootleggers and American Gambling," especially 122–24, details some of the connection between journalism and gangsters in the gambling business. H. Roy Kaplan, "The Convergence of Work, Sport, and Gambling in America," *Annals of the American Academy of Political and Social Science* 445 (1979): 30–31.

32. Mark Sullivan, *Our Times: The United States, 1900–1925*, 6 vols. (New York: Charles Scribner's Sons, 1926–1935), 6: 589. See particularly Benjamin G. Rader, *In Its Own Image: How Television Has Transformed Sports* (New York: The Free Press, 1984), especially 196–97, 201–2; Kaplan, "The Convergence of Work, Sport, and Gambling," 24–38; and Patrick Dale Gammill, "The Evolution of Spectator Sports and the Emergence of the Garrison State: The Nixon Sports Campaign" (doctoral diss., University of Texas, 1982); the quotation is from 196.

33. Devol, *Forty Years a Gambler*, is the classic, but it can be supplemented by the modern clinical literature on compulsive gamblers. Hayano, *Poker Faces*, is a modern example. See *Gamblers World*, 1973–1974.

34. This subject comes up again below, in Chapter 10. See, among other publications, Jean-Cristophe Agnew, "The Consuming Vision of Henry James," in *The Culture of Consumption: Critical Essays in American History, 1880–1980*, ed. Richard Wightman Fox and

T. J. Jackson Lears (New York: Pantheon Books, 1983), 68–75. For a contemporary example, see the account of the wealthy at the races, Joseph Freeman Marsten, "The Sport of Kings in America," *Munsey's Magazine* 28 (1902): 161–71, especially the almost casual note on gambling, 171.

35. Haller, "Bootleggers and American Gambling," passim. Bolen, "Gambling: Historical Highlights," 11, 17.

36. See especially Mark H. Haller, "Bootleggers as Businessmen: From City Slums to City Builders," in *Law, Alcohol, and Order: Perspectives on National Prohibition*, ed. David E. Kyvig (Westport, Ct.: Greenwood Press, 1985), 139–57; Haller, "Bootleggers and Gambling"; James Schwoch, "The Influence of Local History on Popular Fiction: Gambling Ships in Los Angeles, 1933," *Journal of Popular Culture* 20 (1987): 103–11; Findlay, *People of Chance*, 110–99. Dulles, *America Learns to Play*, 343–44. Clotfelter and Cook, *Selling Hope*, especially 38–41.

37. Haller, "Policy Gambling"; Ivan Light, "Numbers Gambling Among Blacks: A Financial Institution," *American Sociological Review* 42 (1977): 893–904. Dulles, *America Learns to Play*, 342–43. Ezell, *Fortune's Merry Wheel*, especially chap. 14. Catharine Brody, "With Benefit of Clergy," *Collier's*, 7 May 1938, 14, 42, 44. Clotfelter and Cook, *Selling Hope*, 38–41. Fairbanks, "Politics, Economics," 168–69. A later contemporary description is John A. Gardner, "Public Attitudes toward Gambling and Corruption," *Annals of the American Academy of Political and Social Science* 374 (1967): 125–26.

38. Fabian, "Rascals and Gentlemen," 331. Anthony Comstock, *Traps for the Young* (Cambridge, Mass.: Harvard University Press, 1967 [c. 1883]), 94–95. And see note 2, above.

39. Commission on the Review of the National Policy Toward Gambling, *Gambling in America*, 146–47. Exemptions had begun as early as 1964. Clotfelter and Cook, *Selling Hope*, especially 5–8, 22–23, 30–31. Fairbanks, "Politics, Economics," 168. *Gaming Business Magazine*, January 1984, 34.

40. Vicki Abt, James F. Smith, and Eugene Martin Christianson, *The Business of Risk: Commercial Gambling in Mainstream America* (Lawrence: University Press of Kansas, 1985), 15.

41. See especially both Fairbanks, "Politics, Economics," chap. 5, and Abt, Smith, and Christianson, *The Business of Risk*. Recollection quoted to show how he was socialized into accepting gambling by Hayano, *Poker Faces*, 144, with corrected punctuation.

42. See, for example, Hayano, *Poker Faces*.

43. John Richard O'Hare, *The Socio-Economic Aspects of Horse Racing* (Washington: Catholic University of America Press, 1945), 108–10; Fairbanks, "Politics, Economics," 177–78. I have not attempted in this brief survey to explore the details of different ethnic customs in the realm of betting.

44. See, for one example, Wallace Turner, *Gamblers' Money: The New Force in American Life* (Boston: Houghton Mifflin Company, 1965).

45. See, for example, *Gaming Business Magazine*, passim. Brody, "With Benefit of Clergy," 42, 44. Clotfelter and Cook, *Selling Hope*, especially 128, 158. Chafetz, *Play the Devil*, 380–81, 417. A poolroom could mean either a bookmaker's establishment or a place in which a form of billiards was played, or, presumably, both.

46. Haller, "Policy Gambling," describes a whole neighborhood of entertainment in Chicago that developed around gambling. O'Hare, *The Socio-Economic Aspects*, 55–56; Fairbanks, "Politics, Economics," 181. Rienzi W. Jennings, *Legalized Racing with Pari-Mutuel Wagering—A Potential Tax Source for Tennessee* (Memphis: Memphis State University Bureau of Business and Economic Research, 1972), 46. Philip G. Satre, quoted in *Gaming Business Magazine*, April 1984, 69. Holiday Inns eventually moved to sell off the hotel (*sic*) operations of the business, a deal completed in 1989, according to press reports.

47. See especially the details in Findlay, *People of Chance*, chaps. 4–6; Haller, "Bootleggers as Businessmen"; Haller, "Bootleggers and Gambling." Gerald D. Nash, *The American West Transformed: The Impact of the Second World War* (Bloomington: Indiana University Press, 1985), 84–87. As early as 1931, the mayor of Reno defended not only the easy divorce law but also legalized drinking, prostitution, and gambling—and tied them all together; Phillip I. Earl, "The Legalization of Gambling in Nevada, 1931," *Nevada Historical Society Quarterly* 24 (1981): 39–50.

48. "C-Store Lottery Promos Thriving," *Gaming & Wagering Business*, December 1985, 14; Lesa Ukman, "Sponsorship: A New Tool for the Industry," ibid., 27; "GB International Expo I," *Gaming Business Magazine*, March 1984, 3, 45. Alec Boatman, "Boxing Fans Are a Horse of a Different Color," *Gaming Business Magazine*, September 1984, 49.

49. Editorial, *Gaming & Wagering Business*, November 1984, 4. Saul E. Leonard, "1984: It Won't Be as Orwell Envisioned," *Gaming Business Magazine*, January 1984, 95. See especially Clotfelter and Cook, *Selling Hope*, 6–7, 203–12, 232.

50. Chafetz, *Play the Devil*, 448. Maureen Kallick et al., *A Survey of American Gambling Attitudes and Behavior* (Ann Arbor: Survey Research Center, Institute for Social Research, University of Michigan, 1979). Bolen, "Gambling: Historical Highlights," 19–20. Kaplan, "Work, Sport, and Gambling," 31. Patricia Helsing, "Gambling—The Issues and Policy Decisions Involved in the Trend Toward Legalization—A Statement of the Current Anachronism of Benign Prohibition," in *Gambling in America*, Appendix 1, 774. Clotfelter and Cook, *Selling Hope*, confirm the ways in which gambling engendered even more gambling but note (131–33) that it might be possible that the numbers games were slowed by state lottery numbers games, although they were skeptical.

51. W. B. Curtis, "The Increase of Gambling and Its Forms," *Forum* 12 (1891): 292. "Is Bingo Gambling When Church-Sponsored?" *Literary Digest* 125 (1938): 33. Heywood Broun, quoted in David P. Campbell, "Who Wants to Be a Professional Gambler?" in *Gambling and Society*, ed. Eadington, 265.

52. Abt, Smith, and Christianson, *The Business of Risk*, 145. "Balanced Budgets: Bad News for Gaming Bills," *Gaming Business Magazine*, January 1984, 13. I have not attempted to summarize numerous comments from the media of the late 1980s and later about the lamentable conditions then prevailing in Atlantic City.

53. Howard J. Klein, review of Sternlieb and Hughes, *The Atlantic City Gamble*, in *Gaming Business Magazine*, January 1984, 37, which also summarizes many modern arguments. Quinn, *Fools of Fortune*, 70. Clotfelter and Cook, *Selling Hope*, 8.

54. See especially Felicia Campbell, "Gambling: A Positive View," in *Gambling and Society*, ed. Eadington, 218–28, especially 223.

55. The example quoted is Iago Galdston, "The Psychodynamics of the Triad, Alcoholism, Gambling, and Superstition," *Mental Hygiene* 35 (1951): 589–98; the quotation is on 594. Modern examples include "Non-Compulsive Behavior," *Gaming & Wagering Business*, December 1985, 4; John Bales, "Losses Heavy Under Legalized Gambling," American Psychological Association *Monitor*, May 1984, 25–26, which explicitly parallels alcohol and gambling addiction. A recent summary is Cecil P. Peck, "Risk-Taking Behavior and Compulsive Gambling," *American Psychologist*, April 1986, 461–65.

SEVEN: *Sexual Misbehavior*

1. Gary W. Potter, *The Porn Merchants* (Dubuque, Iowa: Kendall/Hunt Publishing Company, 1986), especially chap. 4.

2. David Flaherty, "Law and Enforcement of Morals in Early America," *Perspectives in American History* 5 (1971): 201–53. Emil Oberholzer, Jr., *Delinquent Saints: Disciplinary*

Action in the Early Congregational Churches of Massachusetts (New York: Columbia University Press, 1956). A general synthesis is John D'Emilio and Estelle B. Freedman, *Intimate Matters: A History of Sexuality in America* (New York: Harper and Row, 1988). See also Thomas L. Altherr, *Procreation or Pleasure? Sexual Attitudes in American History* (Malabar, Fla.: Robert E. Krieger Publishing Company, 1983). The historiography of the history of sexuality is discussed in John C. Burnham, *Paths into American Culture: Psychology, Medicine, and Morals* (Philadelphia: Temple University Press, 1988), chaps. 7 and 8. Roger Thompson, *Sex in Middlesex, Popular Mores in a Massachusetts County, 1649–1699* (Amherst: University of Massachusetts Press, 1986). Edmund S. Morgan, "The Puritans and Sex," *New England Quarterly* 15 (1942): 591–607.

3. See previous note; Thompson, *Sex in Middlesex*, 43; and David H. Flaherty, *Privacy in Colonial New England* (Charlottesville: University Press of Virginia, 1972).

4. See especially the classic account of Arthur W. Calhoun, *A Social History of the American Family*, 3 vols. (New York: Barnes and Noble, 1960 reprint), vol. 1; the quotation is from 321. D'Emilio and Freedman, *Intimate Matters*, 10–11. David Hackett Fischer, *Albion's Seed: Four British Folkways in America* (New York: Oxford University Press, 1989), stresses the geographical diversity of sexual standards and practices, based in part on differences in migrants' origins in different British localities.

5. Quoted in Calhoun, *A Social History*, 1: 315–16.

6. A survey of sexual behavior and reactions to it, in a general social context, is in Jack Larkin, *The Reshaping of Everyday Life*, 1790–1840 (New York: Harper and Row, 1988), especially 191–203. The perception of the sinfulness of nonreproductive sexual activity is emphasized as such in Vern L. Bullough and Martha Voght, "Homosexuality and Its Confusion with the 'Secret Sin' in Pre-Freudian America," *Journal of the History of Medicine and Allied Sciences* 28 (1973): 143–55. A general survey of public discussions is Sidney Ditzion, *Marriage, Morals and Sex in America: A History of Ideas* (New York: Bookman Associates, 1953). See Morgan, "The Puritans and Sex," and Thompson, *Sex in Middlesex*, 22.

7. See, for example, the summary of the change, in a sophisticated context, in Carroll Smith-Rosenberg, "Sex as Symbol in Victorian America," *Prospects* 5 (1980): 51–70. Nancy F. Cott, "Passionlessness: An Interpretation of Victorian Sexual Ideology, 1790–1850," *Signs* 4 (1978): 219–36. D'Emilio and Freedman, *Intimate Matters*, cover most developments, including the importance of urban centers. John Spurlock, "The Free Love Network in America, 1850–1860," *Journal of Social History* 21 (1988): 765–78, portrays the small free-love group as an aspect of the quest for purity and individuality in a reform context.

8. Robert H. Wiebe, *The Search for Order, 1877–1920* (New York: Hill and Wang, 1967), xiii–xiv. Steven E. Brown, "Sexuality and the Slave Community," *Phylon* 42 (1981): 1–10.

9. G. Stanley Hall, *Life and Confessions of a Psychologist* (New York: D. Appleton and Company, 1923), 133–34.

10. The social-class aspects of behavior patterns are taken up below.

11. See, for example, Daniel Scott Smith and Michael S. Hindus, "Premarital Pregnancy in America 1640–1917: An Overview and Interpretation," *Journal of Interdisciplinary History* 5 (1975): 537–70. Martin Bauml Duberman, " 'Writhing Bedfellows': 1826; Two Young Men from Antebellum South Carolina's Ruling Elite Share 'Extravagant Delight,' " *Journal of Homosexuality* 6 (1980–1981): 85–101.

12. See, for example, G.J. Barker-Benfield, *The Horrors of the Half-Known Life: Male Attitudes Toward Women and Sexuality in Nineteenth-Century America* (New York: Harper and Row, 1976), especially 175–88. Charles E. Rosenberg, "Sexuality, Class and Role in 19th-Century America," *American Quarterly* 25 (1973): 131–53, makes the case for a functional interpretation of Victorian sexual attitudes. Paul Boyer, *Urban Masses and Moral*

Order in America, 1820–1920 (Cambridge, Mass.: Harvard University Press, 1978), shows the way in which Victorian attitudes were in fact in many ways a reaction against industrialism. Lee A. Gladwin, "Tobacco and Sex: Some Factors Affecting Non-Marital Sexual Behavior in Colonial Virginia," *Journal of Social History* 12 (1978): 57–75, for example, found that illegitimacy rates correlated with class and contraceptive practices in eighteenth-century Virginia, not attitude or behavior, and the increase in permissive attitudes before evangelicalism came in was independent of industrialization. Karen Lystra, *Searching the Heart: Women, Men, and Romantic Love in Nineteenth-Century America* (New York: Oxford University Press, 1989), has provided a comprehensive and authoritative revision of the literature and a portrait of the place of love and sex among the middle classes.

13. Boyer, *Urban Masses and Moral Order*. G. Edward Stephan and Douglas R. McMullin, "Tolerance of Sexual Nonconformity: City Size as Situational and Early Learning Determinant," *American Sociological Review* 47 (1982): 411–15.

14. Early steps in commercialization are explored in Timothy J. Gilfoyle, "Strumpets and Misogynists: Brothel 'Riots' and the Transformation of Prostitution in Antebellum New York City," *New York History* 68 (1987): 45–65. David W. Rose, "Prostitution and the Sporting Life Aspects of Working Class Culture in Nineteenth Century Wheeling," *Upper Ohio Valley Historical Review* 16 (1987): 7–31, provides a stunningly detailed account of the evolution of one urban center.

15. See especially Timothy Gilfoyle, "The Urban Geography of Commercial Sex: Prostitution in New York City, 1790–1860," *Journal of Urban History* 13 (1987): 371–93. D'Emilio and Freedman, *Intimate Matters*, 130–38. William W. Sanger, *The History of Prostitution: Its Extent, Causes and Effects Throughout the World* (New York: Eugenics Publishing Company, 1939 reprint [c. 1858]), 521 (punctuation altered slightly).

16. Richard Christian Johnson, "Anthony Comstock: Reform, Vice, and the American Way" (doctoral diss., University of Wisconsin, 1973), especially 54, 98–103. Untitled broadside catalog, Collection VFM 3449, Ohio Historical Society, Columbus. Courtesy of Amos Loveday.

17. Robert E. Riegel, "Changing American Attitudes Toward Prostitution (1800–1920)," *Journal of the History of Ideas* 29 (1968): 437–38. Neil Larry Shumsky, "Tacit Acceptance: Respectable Americans and Segregated Prostitution, 1870–1910," *Journal of Social History* 19 (1986): 664–679. Sanger, *History of Prostitution*, especially 457, 459.

18. Ibid., especially 606, 563. Riegel, "Changing American Attitudes," 438–439. Kevin F. White, "The Flapper's Boyfriend: The Revolution in Morals and the Emergence of Modern American Male Sexuality, 1910–1930" (doctoral diss., Ohio State University, 1990), chap. 5.

19. Samuel Paynter Wilson, *Chicago by Gaslight* ([Chicago: The author], [1890]), 23. See, for example, Richard Tansey, "Prostitution and Politics in Antebellum New Orleans," *Southern Studies* 18 (1980): 449–79. Claudia D. Johnson, "That Guilty Third Tier: Prostitution in Nineteenth-Century American Theaters," *American Quarterly* 27 (1975): 575–84; the quotations are from 581 (William Evarts) and 583 (Robert Turnbull).

20. They also differentiated themselves along economic lines according to clienteles and fees charged. See in general Marion S. Goldman, *Gold Diggers and Silver Miners: Prostitution and Social Life on the Comstock Lode* (Ann Arbor: University of Michigan Press, 1981); Anne M. Butler, *Daughters of Joy, Sisters of Misery: Prostitutes in the American West, 1865–90* (Urbana: University of Illinois Press, 1985).

21. Keith Thomas, "The Double Standard," *Journal of the History of Ideas* 20 (1959): 195–216. The quotation is from Marian J. Morton, "Seduced and Abandoned in an American City: Cleveland and Its Fallen Women 1869–1936," *Journal of Urban History* 11 (1985):

448. George W. Peck, *Peck's Bad Boy and His Pa*, [3rd] ed. (Chicago: Stanton and Van Vliet Co., 1900).

22. B. O. Flower, "Prostitution Within the Marriage Bond," *Arena* 13 (1895): 59–73. And see, for example, such works as Samuel Paynter Wilson, *Chicago and Its Cess-Pools of Infamy*, 16th. ed. (Chicago: Samuel Paynter Wilson, [1910?]). When a physician attempted to conceptualize sexual misbehavior that occurred (as was commonplace) in a charitable home for boys, he found that the activities were carried out as sexual favors prostituted for gain; Randolph Winslow, "Report of an Epidemic of Gonorrhea Contracted from Rectal Coition," *Medical News* 49 (1886): 180–82. Carroll Smith-Rosenberg, *Disorderly Conduct: Visions of Gender in Victorian America* (New York: Oxford University Press, 1985), takes up many aspects of the history of Victorian sexual roles.

23. See especially Butler, *Daughters of Joy*. Ruth Rosen, *The Lost Sisterhood: Prostitution in America, 1900–1918* (Baltimore: Johns Hopkins University Press, 1982), especially 72, notes that in the practice as described in reports in the early twentieth century, the prostitutes usually did not get to keep the money they took in, and the large profits went to others working the system.

24. See especially Goldman, *Gold Diggers and Silver Miners*. Another example, of a special group with which the economic aspect was clear, is Lucie Cheng Hirata, "Free, Indentured, Enslaved: Chinese Prostitutes in Nineteenth-Century America," *Signs* 5 (1979): 3–29. Elizabeth Jane Greiner, "Saxton Street: The Reconstruction of a Red Light Community, 1906–1913" (Master's thesis, Ohio State University, 1987).

25. White, "The Flapper's Boyfriend," gives the best description of the complex changes of the 1910–1940 era.

26. John C. Burnham, "The Progressive Era Revolution in American Attitudes Toward Sex," *Journal of American History* 59 (1973): 885–908; the story is continued in Fred D. Baldwin, "The Invisible Armor," *American Quarterly* 16 (1964), 432–44; and David J. Pivar, "Cleansing the Nation: The War on Prostitution, 1917–21," *Prologue* 12 (1980): 29–40. The fate of pornography is taken up later in this chapter.

27. See particularly Louis J. Kern, *An Ordered Love: Sex Roles and Sexuality in Victorian Utopias—The Shakers, the Mormons, and the Oneida Community* (Chapel Hill: University of North Carolina Press, 1981), especially 32–33; William G. Shade, "A 'Mental Passion': Female Sexuality in Victorian America," *International Journal of Women's Studies* 1 (1978): 13–29; Peter Gardella, *Innocent Ecstasy: How Christianity Gave America an Ethic of Sexual Pleasure* (New York: Oxford University Press, 1985); Paula S. Fass, *The Damned and the Beautiful: American Youth in the 1920's* (New York: Oxford University Press, 1977), especially chap. 6, who summarizes much other literature. James Reed, *The Birth Control Movement and American Society: From Private Vice to Public Virtue*, 2d ed. (Princeton: Princeton University Press, 1983). Lystra, *Searching the Heart*, especially 8, 59–60, points out that romantic love, with sexuality implicit, replaced religious practices and attitudes as part of secularization. Michael Gordon, "From an Unfortunate Necessity to a Cult of Mutual Orgasm: Sex in American Marital Education Literature, 1830–1940," in *Studies in the Sociology of Sex*, ed. James M. Henslin (New York: Appleton-Century-Crofts, 1971), 53–77. The social-science material is summarized in John Modell, *Into One's Own: From Youth to Adulthood in the United States, 1920–1975* (Berkeley: University of California Press, 1989), especially chap. 3. A general description of one version of the change is in Lary May, *Screening Out the Past: The Birth of Mass Culture and the Motion Picture Industry* (New York: Oxford University Press, 1980).

28. Gordon S. Haight, "Male Chastity in the Nineteenth Century," *Contemporary Review* 219 (1971): 252–62. Overall, as many medical writers observed, Americans also had much lower rates of venereal-disease incidence than Europeans—an unusually concrete confirmation of otherwise rather elusive trends.

29. D'Emilio and Freedman, *Intimate Matters*, 181–88. Kathy Peiss, " 'Charity Girls' and City Pleasures: Historical Notes on Working-Class Sexuality, 1880–1920," in *Powers of Desire: The Politics of Sexuality*, ed. Ann Snitow, Christine Stansell, and Sharon Thompson (New York: Monthly Review Press, 1983), 74–87; this material is put into context in Kathy Peiss, *Cheap Amusements: Working Women and Leisure in Turn-of-the-Century New York* (Philadelphia: Temple University Press, 1986). Joanne J. Meyerowitz, *Women Adrift: Independent Wage Earners in Chicago, 1880–1930* (Chicago: University of Chicago Press, 1988), chap. 5.

30. William Foote Whyte, "A Slum Sex Code," *American Journal of Sociology* 49 (1943): 24–31. Modell, *Into One's Own*, emphasizes that by at least the 1920s, most young black people followed patterns remarkably different from the rest of the population taken as a whole.

31. Alfred C. Kinsey, Wardell B. Pomeroy, and Clyde E. Martin, *Sexual Behavior in the Human Male* (Philadelphia: W. B. Saunders Company, 1948), especially 374–84.

32. May, *Screening Out the Past*, provides one version of the way in which dissenting groups affected the media. Mark Haller, "Urban Vice and Civic Reform," in *Cities in American History*, ed. Kenneth T. Jackson and Stanley K. Schultz (New York: Alfred A. Knopf, 1972), 291–94, describes the "streets" and the youngsters and others in them vividly.

33. David M. Schneider and Raymond T. Smith, *Class Differences and Sex Roles in American Kinship and Family Structure* (Englewood Cliffs, N.J.: Prentice-Hall, 1973); the quotation is from 3.

34. W. F. Robie, *Rational Sex Ethics, A Physiological and Psychological Study of the Sex Lives of Normal Men and Women, with Suggestions for a Rational Sex Hygiene with Reference to Actual Case Histories* (Boston: Richard G. Badger, 1918), 296. Martin E. Marty, *Health and Medicine in the Lutheran Tradition: Being Well* (New York: Crossroad, 1983), 38–40, explores some of the later writings tolerant of masturbation. Lois Skinner Prator, "A Review and Analysis of Investigational Literature Dealing with Sex Information, Attitudes and Practices in the United States from 1920 to 1940" (Master's thesis, University of Colorado, 1942), especially 112–15. Gordon, "From an Unfortunate Necessity."

35. The best summary of these pressures is Christine Clare Simmons, " 'Marriage in the Modern Manner': Sexual Radicalism and Reform in America, 1914–1941" (doctoral diss., Brown University, 1982). Simmons emphasizes the activities of radicals and can be supplemented by other writers, particularly Gardella, *Innocent Ecstasy*, and Elaine Tyler May, *Great Expectations: Marriage and Divorce in Post-Victorian America* (Chicago: University of Chicago Press, 1980); and D'Emilio and Freedman, *Intimate Matters*. Lystra, *Searching the Heart*, especially 30–31, notes the essentially antisocial rebelliousness implicit in traditional romantic love. Gordon, "From an Unfortunate Necessity," especially 68–73. See, for example, Kern, *An Ordered Love*, 8–9. Christina Simmons, "Modern Sexuality and the Myth of Victorian Repression," in *Passion and Power: Sexuality in History*, ed. Kathy Peiss and Christina Simmons (Philadelphia: Temple University Press, 1989), 157–77, comments on efforts to promote fulfillment in marriage. See Chapters 9 and 10, below. The new ideal of youth as a sexual athlete, beginning especially in the 1920s, was of course another factor, and for this and other points, I have depended upon White, "The Flapper's Boyfriend."

36. John F. Kasson, *Amusing the Million: Coney Island at the Turn of the Century* (New York: Hill and Wang, 1978); the quote is from 41. Peiss, *Cheap Amusements*, particularly shows the interplay between commercialization and culture. D'Emilio and Freedman, *Intimate Matters*, 194–201.

37. Some account is given in Baldwin, "The Invisible Armor." The official policy of leading officials was to urge and favor continent behavior and clean living.

38. Richard C. Robertiello, "The Decline and Fall of Sex," *Journal of Sex Research* 12 (1976): 70–73, comments on the strength of nonconventional and otherwise-neglected sexual

interests in otherwise quite unexceptional people. Ben Hecht, *Fantazius Mallare: A Mysterious Oath* (Chicago: Covici-McGee, 1922), 12–13.

39. See especially Bullough and Voght, "Homosexuality and Its Confusion" and E. Anthony Rotundo, "Romantic Friendship: Male Intimacy and Middle-Class Youth in the Northern United States 1800–1900," *Journal of Social History* 23 (1989): 1–25. See also George Chauncey, Jr., "From Sexual Inversion to Homosexuality: The Changing Medical Conceptualization of Female 'Deviance,' " in *Passion and Power*, ed. Peiss and Simmons, 87–117. Thomas A. Seboek, "Fetish," *American Journal of Semiology* 6 (1989): 51–66.

40. Christina Simmons, "Companionate Marriage and the Lesbian Threat," *Frontiers* 4 (1979): 54–59; Smith-Rosenberg, *Disorderly Conduct*, 35–36ff; and see the dissent of George Chauncey, Jr., "Christian Brotherhood or Sexual Perversion? Homosexual Identities and the Construction of Sexual Boundaries in the World War One Era," *Journal of Social History* 19 (1985): 189–211, who argues that there were lower-class identities available all along but notes, nevertheless, that a new emphasis on the homoerotic act in the early twentieth century, rather than the role, involved large numbers of men in an awareness of deviance that had not theretofore been present.

41. See, for example, the connection between urban transients and the impersonal city in Edward T. Stone, "Porn in Philly, 1912," *American Heritage*, October 1976, 92–93. A parallel account but with very different emphases is in D'Emilio and Freedman, *Intimate Matters*, especially 241. White, "The Flapper's Boyfriend," especially 123–28, emphasizes the role of Bernarr Macfadden's publications.

42. See in general Joseph Lieberman, "The Emergence of Lesbians and Gay Men as Characters in Plays Produced on the American Stage from 1922 to 1954" (doctoral diss., CCNY, 1981), which is much more comprehensive than the title suggests and summarizes other research. Burnham, "The Progressive Era Revolution"; Edward L. Bernays, *Biography of an Idea: Memoirs of Public Relations Counsel* (New York: Simon and Schuster, 1965), 53–62.

43. May, *Screening Out the Past*. Lillian Schlissel, paper presented at meetings of the American Studies Association, San Antonio, 1975. Lieberman, "The Emergence of Lesbians," especially chap. 4. *Nation* 137 (1933): 497. The book never appeared. See, in general, Carol M. Ward, *Mae West: A Bio-Bibliography* (Westport, Ct.: Greenwood Press, 1989).

44. Lester A. Kirkendall, *Sex Adjustments of Young Men* (New York: Harper and Brothers, 1940), 126–28.

45. Granville W. Larimore and Thomas H. Sternberg, "Does Health Education Prevent Venereal Disease?" *American Journal of Public Health* 35 (1945): 799–804. Allan M. Brandt, *No Magic Bullet: A Social History of Venereal Disease in the United States Since 1880* (New York: Oxford University Press, 1985).

46. Ibid., especially 161, 174. I am following Brandt's analysis here.

47. John Costello, *Love, Sex and War: Changing Values, 1939–45* (London: Collins, 1985), provides a comprehensive summary of evidence that values changed; the quote is from 149.

48. Brandt, *No Magic Bullet*, 170–73. Some of the confusion is indicated in the withdrawal of medical elements from venereal-disease control in the army after World War II; see "Changing Attitude of the Army with Regard to Venereal Diseases," *American Journal of Public Health* 38 (1948): 1150–52. Kinsey, Pomeroy, and Martin, *Sexual Behavior in the Human Male*; Alfred C. Kinsey et al., *Sexual Behavior in the Human Female* (Philadelphia: W. B. Saunders Company, 1953). Reed, *The Birth Control Movement*, 311–66.

49. See, for a perceptive summary, Regina Markell Morantz, "The Scientist as Sex Crusader: Alfred C. Kinsey and American Culture," *American Quarterly* 29 (1977): 563–89. Some press comment is summarized in Donald G. Hileman, "The Kinsey Report: A Study of Press Responsibility," *Journalism Quarterly* 30 (1953): 434–47.

50. Edwin M. Schur, *The Americanization of Sex* (Philadelphia: Temple University Press, 1989), 59. Gordon, "From an Unfortunate Necessity," especially 69, traces the mutual-orgasm cult back to the 1920s and 1930s marital-education literature. Richard S. Musser, Jr., "Newspaper Treatment of Dr. Alfred C. Kinsey's Sexual Research" (Master's thesis, Indiana University, 1974).

51. Arthur H. Hirsch, *Sexual Misbehavior of the Upper Cultured* (New York: Vantage Press, 1955), found that since 1930 the middle-class leaders had been moving toward a much more tolerant sexual standard, and he cited, for example, schoolteachers whose personal moral behavior was no longer adequate cause for dismissal (especially 79, 83–87).

52. A revealing and often perceptive summary of the folklore and journalism coverage of changing standards from the 1940s to the 1970s—with a chronology—as well as a contemporary document arguing for the existence of a revolution is Allan Sherman, *The Rape of the A*P*E*, The Official History of the Sex Revolution, 1945–1973: The Obscening of America* (Chicago: Playboy Press, 1973). Another approach is Joseph E. Scott, "An Updated Longitudinal Content Analysis of Sex References in Mass Circulation Magazines," *Journal of Sex Research* 22 (1986): 385–92, which especially documented growing tolerance during the entire half century.

53. One brief treatment is Herbert I. London, *Closing the Circle: A Cultural History of the Rock Revolution* (Chicago: Nelson-Hall, 1984), 22–25. Larry M. Lance and Christina Y. Berry, "Has There Been a Sexual Revolution? An Analysis of Human Sexuality Messages in Popular Music, 1968–1977," *Journal of Popular Culture* 15 (1981): 155–64. This subject is taken up again in Chapter 9 in a more general context, where specific examples are given.

54. David Boroff, "Sex: The Quiet Revolution," *Esquire*, July 1961, 95–99.

55. See, for example, *Sex in the 60s: A Candid Look at the Age of Mini-Morals*, ed. Joe David Brown (New York: Time-Life Books, 1968). Rebecca Leigh Clark, "Changing Perceptions of Sex and Sexuality in Traditional Women's Magazines, 1900–1980" (doctoral diss., Arizona State University, 1987), surveys much of the research on media coverage of sexuality: in the traditional women's magazines, although traditional themes persisted, there was a dramatic increase in the amount of material about sexuality in the mid twentieth century, and extramarital sexuality for the first time came in for serious discussion at about the same time as an option, however undesirable. John Wilcock, "Other Scenes," *Berkeley Barb*, 22 April 1966, 7. Jefferson Poland, "Picketing for Sex," in *Sex Marchers*, ed. Jefferson Poland and Sam Sloan (Los Angeles: Elysium, Inc., 1968), 11–31, gives a partial chronology of his activity in sexual-freedom advocacy activities beginning in 1962–1963. In the early years, he and others understood the movement to be traditionally bohemian rebelliousness and without the mass and lower-order support that the media later picked up.

56. Lillian Faderman, *Odd Girls and Twilight Lovers: A History of Lesbian Life in Twentieth-Century America* (New York: Columbia University Press, 1991), 192 and elsewhere comments on the crucial role of mainstream media in the 1960s. Barbara Ehrenreich, Elizabeth Hess, and Gloria Jacobs, *Re-Making Love: The Feminization of Sex* (Garden City, N.Y.: Anchor Press/Doubleday, 1986), identified a real revolution in women's sexual experiences and, to some extent, aspirations; the quote is the title of chap. 3. See the summary of evidence and interpretation in Modell, *Into One's Own*, especially 39–40, chap. 7. Richard Sennett, *The Fall of Public Man: The Forces Eroding Public Life and Burdening the Modern Psyche with Roles It Cannot Perform* (New York: Alfred A. Knopf, 1976), 7, comments: "Victorian eroticism involved social relationships, sexuality involves personal identity."

57. See, for example, *Playboy*, January 1965, 3, and December 1956, 3; Milton Moskowitz, "Newsstand Strip-Tease," *Nation*, 20 July 1957, 24; Robert Love, "The Retreat of the

Skin Mags," *Washington Journalism Review*, November 1981, 33–35. Jean Marie McMahon, "*Playgirl*: New Player, Old Game" (Master's thesis, University of Oregon, 1976), especially 21–23. The circulation of *Playboy* was between six and seven million in the 1970s; an extraordinary number of people, however, on the average saw each copy. Timothy Miller, *The Hippies and American Values* (Knoxville: University of Tennessee Press, 1991), 60–61, affirms the influence of *Playboy* even on cultural "revolutionaries."

58. Benjamin De Mott, "The Anatomy of Playboy," *Commentary* 34 (1962): 111–19.

59. Paul Gebhard, quoted in "Think Clean," *Time*, 3 March 1967, 76. Theodore Roszak, quoted in Bernard Gendron, *Technology and the Human Condition* (New York: St. Martin's Press, 1977), 120. See the similar interpretation in Schur, *The Americanization of Sex*, 84–90; and Peter Michelson, "The Pleasures of Commodity, Or How to Make the World Safe for Pornography," in *The Pornography Controversy: Changing Moral Standards in American Life*, ed. Ray C. Rist (New Brunswick: Transaction Books, 1975), 140–58.

60. See previous note. *Playboy*, January 1956, 27.

61. Harvey Cox, quoted in Edwin G. Warner, "Bunnies and Playmates," in *Sex in the '60s*, ed. Brown, 40. See especially Bradley Greenberg and Sandra Kahn, "Blacks in *Playboy* Cartoons," *Journalism Quarterly* 47 (1970): 556–57; M. J. Sobran, Jr., "The Sage and Serious Doctrine of Hugh Hefner," *National Review*, 1 February 1974, 133–36. Hefner tried to express his views in a series of articles in the magazine in 1962–1963. Among contemporary descriptions was "Merchants of Raunchiness," *Time*, 4 July 1977, 69–70.

62. Joel Howell pointed this shift out to the writer and very graciously furnished an unpublished account of the change. See also Robert P. Snow, "Vicarious Behavior: Leisure and the Transformation of *Playboy* Magazine," *Journal of Popular Culture* 3 (1969): 428–40. In an editorial comment, *Playboy*, March 1956, 3, 5, for example, an indignant moralist was told, "... what you're objecting to isn't the action but the mere mention of it. You're not only against sexual shenanigans, you're against joking about them"—invoking the use of humor to confirm deviance boundaries in this early stage.

63. See, for example, *Playboy*, May 1965, 51. Content analysis kindly supplied by Joel Howell.

64. See especially, Snow, "Vicarious Behavior." Allan Taber, "A Value Comparison of Products Pictured in *Playboy* and *Esquire*," *Journalism Quarterly* 44 (1967): 738–40. Any number of commentators have remarked on the Hefner lifestyle. Earlier advertisers included most conspicuously men's clothing and accessories (including a gun rack) and records/record equipment as well as some alcoholic-beverage, cigarette, and self-improvement-program vendors.

65. See, for example, Tony Schwartz with Martin Kasindorf, "Playboy's Quarter Century," *Newsweek*, 1 January 1979, 68. Mike Roberts, "Anal Intercourse: Through the Back Door," *Hustler*, July 1975, 27.

66. Dennis R. Hall, "A Note on Erotic Imagination: *Hustler* as a Secondary Carrier of Working-Class Consciousness," *Journal of Popular Culture* 15 (1983): 150–56. William E. Brigman, "Pornography as Political Expression," *Journal of Popular Culture*, Fall 1983, 129–34; variations of this idea appear throughout the issues of *Maledicta*. *Hustler*, July 1975, 11; cf. Chris Paul and Michael Foldes, "Hustler Interview with Hustler Editor and Publisher Larry C. Flynt," *Hustler*, July 1975, 65–70.

67. One report was Alan Devoe, "Any Sex Today?" *American Mercury* 41 (1937): 175–78. See especially Joan Hoff, "Why Is There No History of Pornography?" in *For Adult Users Only: The Dilemma of Violent Pornography*, ed. Susan Gubar and Joan Hoff (Bloomington: Indiana University Press, 1989), 17–46; Paul P. Somers, Jr., and Nancy Pogel, "Pornography," in *Concise Histories of American Popular Culture*, ed. M. Thomas Inge (Westport, Ct.: Greenwood Press, 1982), 271–79; *The Report of the Commission on Obscenity and Pornography* (New York: Bantam Books, 1970), 1–26; Al Di Lauro and Gerald Rabkin, *Dirty Movies: An Illustrated History of the Stag Film, 1915–1970* (New York: Chelsea

House, 1976); Di Lauro and Rabkin emphasize the lower-middle-class/working-class nature of the old stag films.

68. There is an extensive literature on late-twentieth-century pornography; see, for example, Rist, *The Pornography Controversy*. Summaries appear in *Pornography: Research Advances and Policy Considerations*, ed. Dolf Zillmann and Jennings Bryant (Hillsdale, N.J.: Lawrence Erlbaum Associates, 1989), with historical material particularly in Dan Brown and Jennings Bryant, "The Manifest Content of Pornography," 3–24. On earlier socialization, see John H. Gagnon and William Simon, "Pornography—Raging Menace or Paper Tiger?" in ibid., 90–94. The extent to which the new entrepreneurs preceded Hefner and the extent to which he inspired them is uncertain. The first of the new arcade booths (which facilitated masturbation) for the viewing of movies, for example, appeared at just about the same time. Di Lauro and Rabkin, *Dirty Movies*, 100–101, 105, 117. An account of mostly small-time activity that was just entering a transitional stage is James Jackson Kilpatrick, *The Smut Peddlers* (Garden City, N.Y.: Doubleday and Company, 1960). At one point, pornographers overproduced for the market, in classic economic terms. Daniel Eisenberg, "Toward a Bibliography of Erotic Pulps," *Journal of Popular Culture* 15 (1982): 175–84. Stephen Grover, "Pornography Business Experiences a Decline Despite Liberal Laws," *Wall Street Journal*, 12 August 1971, 1, 23.

69. See especially *Report of the Commission*; Tony Schwartz, "The TV Pornography Boom," *New York Times Magazine*, 13 September 1981, 44, 120–36; Jack McIver Weatherford, *Porn Row* (New York: Arbor House, 1986); commercial written pornography had no limits on what could be described. Journalistic status reports include "The Porno Plague," *Time*, 5 April 1976, 58–63, and "The War Against Pornography," *Newsweek*, 18 March 1985, 58–67. The quote is from D'Emilio and Freedman, *Intimate Matters*, 328. Potter, *The Porn Merchants*, details the business and the ties to organized crime. Andrew Ross, *No Respect: Intellectuals & Popular Culture* (New York: Routledge, 1989), chap. 6.

70. "Skin Trouble," *Time*, 11 September 1975, 50. Weatherford, *Porn Row*, 204–5. On drugs and sexual experience, see, for example, "Provo," "Harold Hemphill and His Psychedelic Lingam . . . ," *Intercourse*, Spring 1968, [2]. Edward W. Barrett, "Sex, Death and Other Trends in Magazines," *Columbia Journalism Review*, July/August 1974, 25. N. Sixx, quoted in Tipper Gore, *Raising PG Kids in an X-Rated Society* (Nashville: Abingdon Press, 1987), 54.

71. See, for example, *The Report of the Commission*, especially 18–19; Potter, *The Porn Merchants*; Gubar and Hoff, *For Adult Users Only*, passim; Berkeley Kaite, "Reading the Body Textual: The Shoe and Fetish Relations in Soft and Hard Core," *American Journal of Semiotics* 6 (1989): 91n; Joseph W. Slade, "Violence in the Hard-Core Pornographic Film: A Historical Survey," *Journal of Communication*, Summer 1984, 148–63; C. Everett Koop, "Report of the Surgeon General's Workshop on Pornography and Public Health," *American Psychologist* 42 (1987): 945; Di Lauro and Rabkin, *Dirty Movies*, especially 97. Susan Franzblau, Joyce N. Sprafkin, and Eli A. Rubinstein, "Sex on TV: A Content Analysis," *Journal of Communication*, Spring 1977, 164–210, found that on television "aggressive touching" rather than overt depictions most often carried the content that connected violence and sex. Weatherford, *Porn Row*, especially 169, 198–99. Compare Herbert A. Otto, " 'The Pornographic Fringeland' on the American Newsstand," *Journal of Human Relations* 12 (1964): 375–90, who dates some change to about 1958. John G. Cawelti, *Adventure, Mystery and Romance: Formula Stories as Art and Popular Culture* (Chicago: University of Chicago Press, 1976), 14; and setting the cultural context, John Cawelti, "Pornography, Catastrophe, and Vengeance: Shifting Narrative Structures in a Changing American Culture," in *The American Self: Myth, Ideology, and Popular Culture*, ed. Sam B. Girgus (Albuquerque: University of New Mexico Press, 1981), 182–92. Lazlo Kurti, "Dirty Movies—Dirty Minds: The Social Construction of X-Rated Films," *Journal*

of Popular Culture, Fall 1983, 187–92; and in general the special section, 123–92 of this issue. Irene Diamond, "Pornography and Repression: A Reconsideration," *Signs* 5 (1980): 686–701. Schur, *The Americanization of Sex*, 113–35. Ross, *No Respect*, chap. 6, considers especially the recent commercial and political aspects. Evidence compiled from the anti-pornography standpoint is in Franklin Mark Osanka and Sara Lee Johann, *Sourcebook on Pornography* (Lexington, Mass.: Lexington Books, 1989).

72. Gendron, *Technology and the Human Condition*, chap. 7, in particular distinguishes com-mercialized, lower-class advocacy from idealistic reform. The same theme was early pursued by Bill Manville, "Saloon Society," *Village Voice*, 13 January 1960, 13, in contrasting the slumming upper crust, who patronizingly hired a beatnik, with the more sexually proper if slightly unconventional bohemians. The nineteenth-century free-love idealists are described and put in context in John C. Spurlock, *Free Love: Marriage and Middle-Class Radicalism in America, 1825–1860* (New York: New York University Press, 1988); see also Hal D. Sears, *The Sex Radicals: Free Love in High Victorian America* (Lawrence: The Regents Press of Kansas, 1977); Hubert Charles Newland, *The Change in Attitude Towards Sex Freedom as Disclosed by American Journals of Opinion During the Years* 1911 *to* 1930 (Chicago: The University of Chicago Libraries, 1935), 1–2. Poland and Sloan, *Sex Marchers*, describes a late version. "*Hustler* Sexplay Agreement," *Hustler*, July 1974, 21; this material was of course ambiguous in that it could be read at least in part as humorous—but it need not be.

73. Steven Marcus, "Pornotopia," *Encounter*, August 1966, 9–18. Sherman, *The Rape of the A*P*E**, 85–86.

74. Bradley Smith, *The American Way of Sex: An Informal Illustrated History* (New York: Two Continents Publishing Company, 1978), 239–43. An earlier projection into the future is found in George S. Chappell, *Evil Through the Ages: An Outline of Indecency* (New York: Frederick A. Stockes Company, 1932).

75. See, for example, Joseph E. Scott and Jack L. Franklin, "Sex References in the Mass Media," *Journal of Sex Research* 9 (1973): 196–209; Steven M. Lovelady, "Top Nudie Film-Maker, Russ Meyer, Scrambles to Outshock Big Studios," *Wall Street Journal*, 24 April 1968, 1, 25; Bradley S. Greenberg et al., "Sexual Intimacy on Commercial TV During Prime Time," *Journalism Quarterly* 57 (1980): 211–15; Barry S. Sapolsky, "Sexual Acts and References on Prime-Time TV: A Two-Year Look," *Southern Speech Communication Journal* 47 (1982): 212–26. Joyce N. Sprafkin and L. Theresa Silverman, "Update: Phys-ically Intimate and Sexual Behavior on Prime-Time Television, 1978–79," *Journal of Communication* 31 (1981): 34–40, found a dramatic increase in just three years.

76. Alan Kreizenbeck, "Soaps: Promiscuity, Adultery and 'New Improved Cheer,' " *Journal of Popular Culture*, Fall 1983, 175–81; the quote is from 181. See, for example, James A. Wechsler and August Heckscher, "Can Newspapers Survive Without Sex?" *Saturday Review of Literature*, 24 June 1950, 8–39; "How 'Does She ... or Doesn't She?' Began the Era of the Permissive Pun," *Campaign*, 22 May 1970, 17–18; "Sexy Does It," *Newsweek*, 15 September 1986, 62–64.

77. See, for example, L. E. Luehrs, "Moral and Psychologic Aspects of the Control of Venereal Disease," *New York State Journal of Medicine* 46 (1946): 1451–54; John A. Court-right and Stanley J. Baran, "The Acquisition of Sexual Information by Young People," *Journalism Quarterly* 57 (1980): 107–14; Sapolsky, "Sexual Acts," 213; Judith Blake, "The Teenage Birth Control Dilemma and Public Opinion," *Science* 180 (1973): 708–13. One type of change is charted in Daniel Yankelovich, *New Rules: Searching for Self-Fulfillment in a World Turned Upside Down* (New York: Bantam Books, 1982 [c. 1981]), especially 96–98; and much of the literature is summarized in Modell, *Into One's Own*, although he interprets it primarily in the from-the-bottom-up mode, which, as I shall remark again, is anachronous for the mid and late twentieth century.

78. Little is known about this really important population group; see especially Laud Humphreys, "Impersonal Sex and Perceived Satisfaction," in *Studies in the Sociology of Sex*, ed. Henslin, 351–74, who raises the possibility quite seriously that in fact some people for unknown reasons have unusually strong sexual drives that would require some institutional adjustment. Such special population elements had the same goal as the sensationalistic and cynical media and advertising people: to convince as many Americans as possible that everybody was doing everything frequently—and the latter groups of course were involved in selling goods that would contribute to the practices, from dirty books and bar services to all consumables that might be associated with a lifestyle out of *Playboy* or one of the even less subtle agents of pornography.

79. Scott and Franklin, "Sex References in the Mass Media," found that after midcentury, there was a striking increase in mass-media references to birth control and homosexuality, in both cases increasingly tolerantly or favorably mentioned. Schur, *The Americanization of Sex*, especially chap. 3, provides a detailed description of commercialization of all kinds from the late 1980s. People in the sex-therapy movement were direct descendants (if not the same personnel, including Kinsey) of the sexual liberals. Many advocated some use of the commercial pornography by then available. See, for example, Arnold Birenbaum, "Revolution without the Revolution: Sex in Contemporary America," *Journal of Sex Research* 6 (1970): 257; Allan C. Carlson, "Families, Sex, and the Liberal Agenda," *Public Interest*, Winter 1980, 77; Ellen Ross, " 'The Love Crisis': Couples Advice Books of the Late 1970s," *Signs* 6 (1980): 109–22, who pointed out (116) the curious tendency of "experts" to describe sexual relationships in contractual terms; "The Second Sexual Revolution," *Time*, 24 January 1964, 59; André Béjin, "The Decline of the Psycho-Analyst and the Rise of the Sexologist," in *Western Sexuality: Practice and Precept in Past and Present Times*, ed. Philippe Ariès and André Béjin (New York: Basil Blackwell, 1985), 181–200; Constance Holden, "Sex Therapy: Making It as a Science and an Industry," *Science* 186 (1974): 330–34.

80. Carol Thurston, *The Romance Revolution: Erotic Novels for Women and the Quest for a New Sexual Identity* (Urbana: University of Illinois Press, 1987). Ross, *No Respect*, chap. 6. Faderman, *Odd Girls*, especially chaps. 9–11, describes conflicts in one group over male models of sexuality.

81. Tom Burke, "The New Homosexuality," *Esquire*, December 1969, 178, 304–18, noted the connection between heterosexual "perversions" and homosexual advocates. Jefferson Poland, "Picketing for Sex," in Poland and Sloan, *Sex Marchers*, 18. See, for example, Betty Fang, "Swinging: In Retrospect," *Journal of Sex Research* 12 (1976), 220–37; Joseph N. Sorrentino, *The Moral Revolution* (Los Angeles: Nash Publishing, 1972), 3–12. John Leo et al., "Sexes: The Revolution is Over," *Time*, 9 April 1984, 74–83; the authors in fact suggested, despite the title, how little the trend to quantity and variety was in fact diminishing. Ehrenreich, Hess, and Jacobs, *Re-Making Love*, exemplified persistent advocacy in the 1980s (they appealed to one version of feminism).

82. See especially Ersel LeMasters, *Blue-Collar Aristocrats: Life Styles at a Working-Class Tavern* (Madison: University of Wisconsin Press, 1975). Martin S. Weinberg and Colin J. Williams, "Sexual Embourgeoisment? Social Class and Sexual Activity: 1938–1970," *American Sociological Review* 45 (1980): 33–48, found persistent class patterns; the use of education as a class measure may explain such findings that are contrary to other evidence. Ehrenreich, Hess, and Jacobs, *Re-Making Love*, 196. Ross, *No Respect*, 169, has described how in the 1960s commercialized "camp" "helped to overturn legitimate definitions of taste and sexuality." Faderman, *Odd Girls*, 203.

83. See especially James Kent Willwerth and Stefan Kanfer, "Rebels and Swingers," in *Sex in the '60s*, ed. Brown, 28–34; D'Emilio and Freedman, *Intimate Matters*, 290–91, 304–5. William J. Helmer, "New York's 'Middle Class' Homosexuals," *Harpers*, March 1963,

85–92. Dan E. Beauchamp, *The Health of the Republic: Epidemics, Medicine, and Moralism as Challenges to Democracy* (Philadelphia: Temple University Press, 1988), 218–23, describes the homoerotics' role as an erotic extreme. James T. Hathaway, "The Evolution of Drinking Places in the Twin Cities: From the Advent of White Settlement to the Present," 2 vols. (doctoral diss., University of Minnesota, 1982), vol. 2, especially 309–13, emphasizes the entrance of unattached females into essentially male territory as a profitable development for bar owners. "Dating Bars," *Time*, 17 February 1967, 47, noted the continuity with "the old-style pickup bar." Airline stewardesses were the apocryphal spur to the development of the singles' bar, in another account; John Kronenberger, "The Singles Scene," *Look*, 6 February 1968, 80. Craig Reinarman and Barbara Critchlow Leigh, "Culture, Cognition, and Disinhibition: Notes on Sexuality and Alcohol in the Age of AIDS," *Contemporary Drug Problems* 14 (1987): 452, noted that patrons of bars, according to general belief, had no right to resent sexual approaches made to them.

84. D'Emilio and Freedman, *Intimate Matters*, especially 234–35, 305–6; the quote is from 328. Schur, *The Americanization of Sex*, and Ehrenreich, Hess, and Jacobs, *Re-Making Love*, especially chap. 4, comment on the sexual-hardware business from different points of view.

85. Edward J. Mishan, "Making the World Safe for Pornography," *Encounter*, March 1972, 11. Schur, *The Americanization of Sex*, summarizes developments as of the late 1980s.

86. Schur, *The Americanization of Sex*, particularly works out "commoditization." Wendell Stacy Johnson, *Living in Sin: The Victorian Sexual Revolution* (Chicago: Nelson-Hall, 1979), 189.

E I G H T : *Swearing*

1. I do not take up directly here one aspect of harmful words, sexual violence; see, for example, Barbara Lawrence, "Four-Letter Words Can Hurt You," in *Philosophy & Sex*, ed. Robert Baker and Frederick Elliston (Buffalo: Prometheus Books, 1975), 31–33.

2. Charles H. Hall, "Swearing and Cursing," in Samuel Fallows et al., *Hot Shot Fired at Fashion's Follies and Society's Abominations: Portrayed by Eminent Thinkers and Writers* (Chicago: Standard Publishing Co., 1889), 124. Grady McWhiney, *Cracker Culture: Celtic Ways in the Old South* (Tuscaloosa: The University of Alabama Press, 1988), 174, notes that what he characterizes as the Celtic tradition of excessive use of offensive language caused the most comment by visitors to the antebellum South and symbolized to them what they believed was the generally immoral style of life of southerners who disdained "Yankee ways."

3. Allen Walker Read, "British Recognition of American Speech in the Eighteenth Century," *Dialect Notes* 6 (1933): 328–39. H. L. Mencken, "American Profanity," *American Speech* 19 (1944): 245–46. That there were any changes in early customs is dubious, but in a sermon in 1686, New England divine Joshua Moodey testified that "Cursing and Swearing begin to grow common in this Land. It was not so in our first Dayes. I lived near twenty years in this Country before I heard an Oath or a Curse. But now as you pass along in the Streets, you may hear Children curse and swear, and take the great and dreadful Name of God in vain . . . ;" Joshua Moodey, quoted in Ronald A. Bosco, "Lectures at the Pillory: The Early American Execution Sermon," *American Quarterly* 30 (1978): 166, italics omitted.

4. See previous note.

5. G.T.W. Patrick, "The Psychology of Profanity," *Psychological Review* 8 (1901): 114–15. A more elaborate, and of course later, analysis is in Ashley Montagu, *The Anatomy of Swearing* (New York: Collier Books, 1973 [c. 1967]), especially 103–6.

6. Ibid., 124–25.

7. Clara Ann Bowler, "Carted Whores and White Shrouded Apologies: Slander in the County Courts of Seventeenth-Century Virginia," *Virginia Magazine of History and Biography* 85 (1977): 411–26. Charles P. Flynn, "Sexuality of Insult Behavior," *Journal of Sex Research* 12 (1976): 1–13.

8. The scholarly journal devoted to swearing recognizes in the title, *Maledicta*, the element of aggression and insult as well as desire to shock that exists in the use of offensive language. Renatus Hartog and Hans Fantel, *Four-Letter Word Games, The Psychology of Obscenity* (New York: M. Evans and Company, 1967), especially 32–34.

9. Quoted in Lewis O. Saum, *The Popular Mood of Pre-Civil War America* (Westport, Ct.: Greenwood Press, 1980), 136.

10. Mencken, "American Profanity," 242. H. L. Mencken, *The American Language, An Inquiry into the Development of English in the United States*, 4th ed. (New York: Alfred A. Knopf, 1937), 300–18.

11. Most of the scholarship on swearing lies in the fields of linguistics and folklore, and particularly for the nineteenth century, such expertise is not very helpful to the social historian. W. H. Luckenbach, *The Folly of Profanity* (Philadelphia: Lutheran Publication Society, 1884), 131.

12. Chillicothe Association for Promoting Morality and Good Order, *Addresses of the Chillicothe Association for Promoting Morality and Good Order to Their Fellow-Citizens, On Profane Swearing, The Violation of the Sabbath, and the Intemperate Use of Ardent Spirits* (Chillicothe: John Andrews, 1815), especially 16.

13. Ibid., especially 5.

14. Richard B. Stott, *Workers in the Metropolis: Class, Ethnicity, and Youth in Antebellum New York City* (Ithaca: Cornell University Press, 1990), 260–64; the quote is on 261. See, for example, "Profanity Among Boys," *New York Times*, 30 June 1909, 6. Some early legislation is described in David H. Flaherty, *Privacy in Colonial New England* (Charlottesville: University Press of Virginia, 1972), 179–84. "Breach of the Peace," *University of Pennsylvania Law Review* 84 (1935): 101–2.

15. The more general context is explored in John C. Burnham, "The Progressive Era Revolution in American Attitudes Toward Sex," *Journal of American History* 59 (1973): 885–908; and in John D'Emilio and Estelle B. Freedman, *Intimate Matters, A History of Sexuality in America* (New York: Harper and Row, 1988), 156–67. Leonard Ellis, "Men Among Men: An Exploration of All-Male Relationships in Victorian America" (doctoral diss., Columbia University, 1982), especially 48–50. D.W. Maurer, "Language and the Sex Revolution: World War I Through World War II," *American Speech* 51 (1976): 5. Ted Ownby, *Subduing Satan: Religion, Recreation, and Manhood in the Rural South, 1865–1920* (Chapel Hill: University of North Carolina Press, 1990), especially 39–41, 49–50.

16. Edwin P. Whipple, "The Swearing Habit," *North American Review* 140 (1885): especially 536–37.

17. Quoted in David J. Rothman, *Conscience and Convenience: The Asylum and Its Alternatives in Progressive America* (Boston: Little, Brown and Company, 1980), 223–24.

18. See, for example, Brander Matthews, "The Function of Slang," *Harper's Monthly Magazine* 87 (1893): 304–12. Lucia Gilbert Runkle, "Slang," *St. Nicholas* 11 (1884): 908. Ellen Burns Sherman, "A Study in Current Slanguage," *Critic* 31 (1897): 153. *Education* 19 (1899): 309, carried a poem, "Slang," by Edward Wm. Dutcher:

> If we go racing through the realms of thought
> On donkey steeds in fancy colors wrought,
> Like clowns who make contortions with the tongue,
> To win applause the sordid crowds among,

> We miss the true, ideal companionship,
> The sweet communion of heart and lip.

As late as 1926 serious researchers could assume that slang indicated bad character; Gladys C. Schwesinger, "Slang as an Indication of Character," *Journal of Applied Psychology* 10 (1926): 245–63. Edward Sagarin, *The Anatomy of Dirty Words* (New York: Lyle Stuart, 1962), 36–42, considered "dirty words" not only closely related to blasphemy but also a subset of slang.

19. Burges Johnson, "The Every-Day Profanity of Our Best People," *Century Magazine* 92 (1916): 311.
20. Patrick, "The Psychology of Swearing," 126–127. Sherman, "A Study." William James, "The Moral Equivalent of War," *International Conciliation* 27 (1910): 3–20. Other cultural analysis might well bring in the primitivism that was influencing at least literature in this period.
21. "Profanity as a Resource," *Atlantic Monthly* 86 (1900): especially 860; "Profanity: A Lost Art," ibid., 109 (1912): 570–72. Johnson, "The Every-Day Profanity," 312–13. "Damn Not Profane in New Jersey," *New York Times*, 23 March 1910, 13.
22. Philadelphia *Evening Public Ledger*, quoted in "Are We Growing Profane?" *Literary Digest* 59 (1918): 33–34. Anonymous, quoted in Burges Johnson, *The Lost Art of Profanity* (Indianapolis: Bobbs-Merrill, 1948), 30–31.
23. "Are We Growing Profane?"
24. See Chapter 1, above; Frederick Lewis Allen, *Only Yesterday, An Informal History of the Nineteen-Twenties* (New York: Harper and Row, 1964 [c. 1931]), especially 92–94. Paul S. Boyer, *Purity in Print: The Vice-Society Movement and Book Censorship in America* (New York: Charles Scribner's Sons, 1968), gives a rich and insightful account of what eventually appeared to be inevitable progress; the quote is from 125.
25. See especially Maurer, "Language and the Sex Revolution," 5–15. David Stenn, *Clara Bow, Runnin' Wild* (New York: Doubleday, 1988), 80–82.
26. Rupert Wilkinson, *American Tough, The Tough-Guy Tradition and American Character* (Westport, Ct.: Greenwood Press, 1984), analyzes the tradition that flowered in the gangster era and especially brings out the element of mastery in the stereotype. See also Chapter 10, below.
27. Boyer, *Purity in Print*, gives many details of one set of controversies and much of the background besides; the skit is described on 193. A good example is a well-known paper, Allen Walker Read, "An Obscenity Symbol," *American Speech* 9 (1934): 264–78. See, for example, the early-twentieth-century classic, Margaret Mead, *Coming of Age in Samoa, A Psychological Study of Primitive Youth for Western Civilisation* (New York: William Morrow and Company, 1961 [1928]), especially 136–38.
28. Boyer, *Purity in Print*. William Safire, "Unwed Words," *New York Times Magazine*, 11 August 1985, 9. For example, "Keeping Down the Tide of Profanity," *Literary Digest*, 11 July 1936, 28; "Pink Cards for Purple Talk," *Newsweek*, 23 September 1940, 54.
29. Boyer, *Purity in Print*. Maurer, "Language and the Sex Revolution," is just one such commentator.
30. Bernard DeVoto, "The Easy Chair," *Harper's Magazine*, December 1948, 98–101. Quoted in John Costello, *Love, Sex and War: Changing Values, 1939–1945* (London: Collins, 1985), 115.
31. Mencken, "American Profanity," 247n. Maurer, "Language and the Sex Revolution." Clearly popularization in the 1940s did not imply a date of origin of any term.
32. DeVoto, "The Easy Chair," 101–2.
33. Walter Allen, "The Writer and the Frontiers of Tolerance," in *"To Deprave and Corrupt ...": Original Studies in the Nature and Definition of Obscenity*, ed. John Chandos (New

York: Association Press, 1962), 149–50. Sagarin, *The Anatomy of Dirty Words*, 168. Cath-erine Hughes, "Art and Responsibility," *Catholic World* 209 (1969): 210–12. One incisive summary is in Paul P. Somers, Jr., and Nancy Pogel, "Pornography," in *Concise Histories of American Popular Culture*, ed. M. Thomas Inge (Westport, Ct.: Greenwood Press, 1982), 273–74. I note the case of Lenny Bruce below, in another context.

34. Joseph E. Scott and Jack L. Franklin, "Sex References in the Mass Media," *Journal of Sex Research* 9 (1973): 196–209. Lee H. Smith, "Is Anything Unprintable?" *Columbia Journalism Review*, Spring 1968, 19–23.

35. Later commentators tended to read back into the late 1950s and early 1960s underground newspeople's later flagrant printing of the most offensive language imaginable. Donna Lloyd Ellis, "The Underground Press in America: 1955–1970," *Journal of Popular Culture* 5 (1971): 102–5. Robert J. Glessing, *The Underground Press in America* (Bloomington: Indiana University Press, 1970), especially 114–15. *Berkeley Barb*, 8 October 1965, 1. Smith, "Is Anything Unprintable?" Boyer, *Purity in Print*, xiv.

36. See especially Richard R. Cole, "Top Songs in the Sixties: A Content Analysis of Popular Lyrics," *American Behavioral Scientist* 14 (1971): 394–95; Ellis, "The Underground Press," 116. Other examples were cited in Chapter 7, above, in connection with the growth of pornography and pornographic attitudes. British groups most popular among American youngsters, like the Rolling Stones, tended much more and much earlier than American counterparts to introduce offensive language. See, for example, United States Senate, Committee on Commerce, Science, and Transportation, 99th Congress, First Session, Hearings on "Contents of Music and the Lyrics of Records," 19 September 1985 (Wash-ington: U. S. Government Printing Office, 1985). Studies showed that young fans indeed knew and repeated the words to songs; "Samples of Violent Music Lyrics," *NCTV News*, April-June 1990, 2–3.

37. James H. Smylie, "Prudes, Lewds and Polysyllables," *Commonweal* 89 (1969): 671–73. Paul Cameron, "Frequency and Kinds of Words in Various Social Settings, Or What the Hell's Going On?" *Pacific Sociological Review* 12 (1969): 101–4. Larry A. Ingraham, *The Boys in the Barracks: Observations on American Military Life* (Philadelphia: Institute for the Study of Human Issues, 1984), passim.

38. John Ciardi, "Shock Language," *Saturday Review*, 20 August 1966, 15. And, for example, "Damning Blasphemy," *Time*, 16 May 1969, 72. Kathleen Molz, "The Public Custody of the High Pornography," *American Scholar* 36 (1966–1967): 93–103.

39. Somers and Pogel, "Pornography." Maurice Girodias, "More Heat Than Light," in *"To Deprave and Corrupt,"* ed. Chandos, 125–37.

40. See, for example, Albert Goldman, "The Comedy of Lenny Bruce," *Commentary* 36 (1963): 312–17.

41. See W. J. Rorabaugh, *Berkeley at War: The 1960s* (New York: Oxford University Press, 1989), especially 38–41, and contemporary press reports, especially *Los Angeles Free Press*, 19 March 1965, 3; *Berkeley Barb*, 22 October 1965, 8. The *New York Times* referred to "the *filthy* speech movement"; locals used "*foul* speech" as a parody on "free speech."

42. Ethel Grodzins Romm, "***** Is No Longer a Dirty Word," *Esquire*, April 1969, 135–36. For example, "X-Rated Expletives," *Time*, 20 May 1974, 72–73.

43. Smylie, "Prudes, Lewds." Bobby Seale, quoted in J. Dan Rothwell, "Verbal Obscenity, Time for Second Thoughts," *Western Speech* 35 (1971): 234.

44. Henry Woodward Hulbert, "Profanity," *Biblical World* 42 (1920): 74.

45. Mark Rudd, "Symbols of the Revolution," in Jerry L. Avorn et al., *Up Against the Ivy Wall, A History of the Columbia Crisis* (New York: Atheneum, 1970), 292–93; blanks provided by the present author. See, for example, Gail Sears Petrich, "An Empirical Study of Predictors of Obscene Language" (Master's thesis, Ohio State University, 1975), 11.

46. Leo Marx, " 'Noble Shit': The Uncivil Response of American Writers to Civil Religion in America," *Massachusetts Review* 14 (1973): 709–39. Rothwell, "Verbal Obscenity."

47. David L. Paletz and William F. Harris, "Four-Letter Threats to Authority," *Journal of Politics* 37 (1974): 955–79. Geoffrey Pearson, *The Deviant Imagination: Psychiatry, Social Work and Social Change* (New York: Holmes and Meier Publishers, 1975), chap. 4; Rubin is quoted on 84. Timothy Miller, *The Hippies and American Values* (Knoxville: University of Tennessee Press, 1991), 117–18, describes one context.

48. Paletz and Harris, "Four-Letter Threats." Gary R. Shroat, "Swive Diascatesis!" *Maledicta* 7 (1983): 74; Shroat attributes the idea to Lenny Bruce.

49. See, for example, Haig A. Bosmajian, *Dissent: Symbolic Behavior and Rhetorical Strategies* (Boston: Allyn and Bacon Inc., 1972), 303. Montagu, *Anatomy of Swearing*, 72–73. Joyce Brothers, "What Dirty Words Really Mean," *Good Housekeeping*, May 1973, 62–66.

50. George Steiner, "Über Pornographie," *Der Monat*, November 1966, 14. Harry M. Clor, "Obscenity and Freedom of Expression," in *Censorship and Freedom of Expression, Essays on Obscenity and the Law*, ed. idem. (Chicago: Rand McNally College Publishing Company, 1971), 109. See, for example, David Rankin, "A State of Incivility," *Newsweek*, 8 February 1988, 10.

51. The examples are from Wilkinson, *American Tough*, 89; and Hartogs and Fantel, *Four-Letter Word Games*, chap. 1.

52. Bob Greene, "Little Shocks Viewers Now," syndicated column, *Columbus Dispatch*, 28 January 1990, 3D.

53. Greil Marcus, *Lipstick Traces: A Secret History of the Twentieth Century* (Cambridge, Mass.: Harvard University Press, 1989), 2–3, puts the incident in context.

NINE: *The Coopting Process*

1. There was always a danger that any specific program alternative to Prohibition might be far more extreme; see, for example, David T. Courtwright and Shelby Miller, "Progressivism and Drink: The Social and Photographic Investigations of John James McCook," in *Social Thought on Alcoholism: A Comprehensive Review*, ed. Thomas D. Watts (Malabar, Fla.: Robert F. Krieger Publishing Company), 101–3.

2. As already noted, this book does not attempt to deal with the so-called organized-crime aspect of the minor vices such as is suggested so richly in Gary W. Potter, *The Porn Merchants* (Dubuque, Iowa: Kendall/Hunt Publishing Company, 1986). Crime syndicates and groups of course had many ties to legitimate businesses, and, again, I am not attempting to open that subject.

3. Virgil G. Eaton, "How the Opium Habit is Acquired," reprinted in *Yesterday's Addicts: American Society and Drug Abuse, 1865–1920*, ed. H. Wayne Morgan (Norman: University of Oklahoma Press, 1974), 182–83. John Thaddeus Whalen, Jr., "The American Liquor Industry" (doctoral diss., University of California, Berkeley, 1964), 8. See, for example, *Life*, 7 October 1957, 118. Robert McBride, "Industry Structure, Marketing, and Public Health: A Case Study of the U.S. Beer Industry," *Contemporary Drug Problems* 12 (1985): 601, listed as industries with direct ties to beer: "agriculture, glass, can manufacturing, machinery, transportation, and finance. . . . restaurant, tourism, hotel, and airline industries, supermarkets, grocery stores, convenience stores—and even gas stations."

4. The ownership patterns in relevant industries may also have accelerated direct influence such as that associated with Pierre Du Pont; Alfred R. Oxenfeldt, *Industrial Pricing and Market Practices* (New York: Prentice-Hall, 1951), 457, notes that in the alcoholic-beverage industry the major firms were relatively less publicly held and the officers were more deeply involved than in most U.S. companies. The modern ties and especially the impact

of conglomerate arrangements in the 1970s period are detailed in John Cavanagh and Frederick F. Clairmonte, *Alcoholic Beverages: Dimensions of Corporate Power* (London: Croom Helm, 1985).

5. The sources of these casual figures are Cathy Griggers, "Bearing the Sign in Struggle: Pornography, Parody, and Mainstream Cinema," *American Journal of Semiotics* 6 (1989): 98; Nina Youngstrom, "Debate Rages On: In- or Outpatient?" American Psychological Association *Monitor*, October 1990, 19.

6. Richard Butsch, "Introduction: Leisure and Hegemony in America" and "Home Video and Corporate Plans: Capital's Limited Power to Manipulate Leisure," in *For Fun and Profit: The Transformation of Leisure into Consumption*, ed. idem. (Philadelphia: Temple University Press, 1990), 3–27 and 215–35.

7. Fred A. Beal, *Proletarian Journey: New England, Gastonia, Moscow* (New York: Hillman-Curl, Inc., 1937), 33.

8. See, for example, Kathy Peiss, *Cheap Amusements: Working Women and Leisure in Turn-of-the-Century New York* (Philadelphia: Temple University Press, 1986), especially 30.

9. David McReynolds, "The Gay Underground—A Reply to Mr. Krim," *Village Voice*, 25 March 1959, 4; obvious error corrected.

10. Paul J. Goldstein, *Prostitution and Drugs* (Lexington, Mass.: Lexington Books/D. C. Heath and Company, 1979), found that real latter-day prostitutes sometimes did and sometimes did not have a deviant identity—and the accompanying panoply of deviant behaviors. Dean Latimer, quoted in *High Times*, June 1984, 34–35.

11. Clinton R. Sanders, "Doper's Wonderland: Functional Drug Use by Military Personnel in Vietnam," *Journal of Drug Issues*, Winter 1973, 73.

12. A standard, typical analysis is Bernard Barber, *Social Stratification* (New York: Harcourt, Brace and World, 1957), especially 314–16. Some of the implications and complications not taken up here can be found in works such as David M. Schneider and Raymond T. Smith, *Class Differences and Sex Roles in American Kinship and Family Structure* (Englewood Cliffs, N.J.: Prentice-Hall, 1973), and Margo Anderson, "The Language of Class in Twentieth-Century America," *Social Science History* 12 (1988): 349–75. It is striking, for example, how risktaking and criminality tend to appear in the same young people; Richard Freeman, quoted in *Reporting from the Russell Sage Foundation*, June 1990, 7.

13. The standard primary account is Malcolm Cowley, *Exile's Return: A Literary Odyssey of the 1920's* (New York: The Viking Press, 1951). Edward Abrahams, *The Lyrical Left: Randolph Bourne, Alfred Stieglitz, and the Origins of Cultural Radicalism in America* (Charlottesville: University Press of Virginia, 1986). Stanley Coben, *Rebellion Against Victorianism: The Impetus for Cultural Change in 1920s America* (New York: Oxford University Press, 1991), describes some of the rebels and 52–54 emphasizes the influence of publishers with economic as well as cultural motivations.

14. Robert K. De Arment, *Knights of the Green Cloth: The Saga of Frontier Gamblers* (Norman: University of Oklahoma Press, 1982), 178. Cf. Chapter 6, above, in which the reciprocal connection was noted in Arizona.

15. See, for example, "Flashes," *High Times*, Spring 1975, 6; "Duane H.," "Medical News Review," *Black and Blue*, March 1968, 13; the latter was a chiefly homophile leather/biker publication. Marijuana plants were advertised in *Gay Sunshine*, January 1972, unpaginated.

16. See, for example, Gaye Tuchman, *Making News, A Study in the Construction of Reality* (New York: The Free Press, 1978), especially 183–84; Sanford Sherizen, "Social Creation of Crime News: All the News Fitted to Print," in *Deviance and Mass Media*, ed. Charles Winick (Beverly Hills: Sage Publications, 1978), especially 207–8.

17. Alexander Saxton, "Problems of Class and Race in the Origins of the Mass Circulation Press," *American Quarterly* 36 (1984): 211–34. James L. Crouthamel, "James Gordon Bennett, the *New York Herald*, and the Development of Newspaper Sensationalism,"

New York History 54 (1973): 294–316. Michael Schudson, *Discovering the News: A Social History of American Newspapers* (New York: Basic Books, 1978). Dan Schiller, *Objectivity and the News: The Public and the Rise of Commercial Journalism* (Philadelphia: University of Pennsylvania Press, 1981), especially 53, 67–72. People at that time and later recognized the ambiguity that moralistic attacks on the upper classes presumably should have reinforced bourgeois, evangelistic standards but in fact offered not only titillation but alternate role models, namely, misbehaving social leaders—everybody does it. R. Laurence Moore, "Religion, Secularization, and the Shaping of the Culture Industry in Antebellum America," *American Quarterly* 41 (1989): 216–42, explores the complications but takes the point of view of uplifters rather than the underworld.

18. Saxton, "Problems of Class and Race." Schiller, *Objectivity and the News*, especially chaps. 4–6.

19. Schudson, *Discovering the News*, especially chaps. 2 and 3; Dreiser is quoted on 86.

20. W. W. Ramsay, "Newspaper Responsibility in Relation to Temperance," *Methodist Review* 77 (1895): 568–80. Frank L. Mott, "The Magazine Revolution and Popular Ideas in the Nineties," *Proceedings of the American Antiquarian Society* 64 (1954): 209–14.

21. See, for example, the broad approach taken by Robert Sobel, *The Manipulators: America in the Media Age* (Garden City, N.Y.: Anchor Press/Doubleday, 1976). Neil Postman, *Amusing Ourselves to Death: Public Discourse in the Age of Show Business* (New York: Viking Penguin, 1985), does the same with some twists.

22. In one striking example, during the 1950s, motion-picture makers made films based on current novels and used the content of the novels to justify their violating previous norms; Richard Maltby, *Harmless Entertainment: Hollywood and the Ideology of Consensus* (Metuchen, N.J.: The Scarecrow Press, 1983), 73–74.

23. John Burnham, "Beer and the Publisher," *National Printer Journalist*, March 1933, 50. In addition to material cited in earlier chapters, see, for example, Ernest Gordon, "Does Luce's $17,700,000 Intake from Liquor Render Him Immune to Decency and Conscience?" reprinted in *Congressional Record*, 96 (6 January 1950), A52–A54. Luce's own mother irritated him by objecting to the alcoholic-beverage ads in his magazines (information courtesy of James L. Baughman). Another example is J. Anthony Lukas, "High Rolling in Las Vegas," in *Stop the Presses, I Want to Get Off! Inside Stories of the News Business from the Pages of [More]*, ed. Richard Pollack (New York: Random House, 1975), 218–31. There were of course occasions on which news coverage was, at least for short periods of time, independent of overt advertising influence, but they were not characteristic. Edward O. Fritts, quoted in *New York Times*, 8 February 1985, C32.

24. See, for example, Patricia A. Whately, "*Los Angeles Times* and *New York Times*, 1950–1958 and 1970–1978: Did Alcohol-Related Coverage Change?" (Master's thesis, California State University, Fullerton, 1979), 7; James W. Tankard, Jr., and Kate Peirce, "Alcohol Advertising and Magazine Editorial Content," *Journalism Quarterly* 59 (1982): 302–5. In the 1950s, the brewers were even using professional journalism journals for institutional advertising "to respect the other fellow's preference for a glass of beer;" *Quill*, May 1954, 15.

25. *Tobacco and Youth Reporter*, Autumn 1990, 5; other examples are found throughout that publication.

26. See, for example, James P. Forkan, "Print Media Use by Cigarets Grows in Spite of Bans by Some Publishers," *Advertising Age*, 9 June 1969, 4, which covers alcohol as well. Ads in the *New Yorker* over many years give a good sample of presumably incidental use of the bad habits.

27. The underground newspapers in their early days utilized this ploy very effectively to publicize unpopular and fringe points of view.

28. See, for example, "Advertising," *Brewers Almanac*, 1958, 4.

29. "1961 Edgar Award Winners," *Liquor Store*, May 1962, 50–51.

30. See especially, and in context, Donald W. Goodwin, *Alcohol and the Writer* (Kansas City: Andrews and McMeel, 1988), 204–6. Stanley Walker, "Decline of the Newspaper Souse," *American Mercury* 46 (1939): 449; Ted Joseph, "A Study of Alcohol Use by Reporters and Editors," *Newspaper Research Journal* 4 (1983): 3–8.

31. Patrick Anderson, *High in America: The True Story Behind NORML and the Politics of Marijuana* (New York: The Viking Press, 1981), 10–15, 17–23.

32. Daniel J. Czitrom, *Media and the American Mind: From Morse to McLuhan* (Chapel Hill: University of North Carolina Press, 1982), especially chap. 2. Lary May, *Screening Out the Past: The Birth of Mass Culture and the Motion Picture Industry* (New York: Oxford University Press, 1980). Stephen Vaughn, "Morality and Entertainment: The Origins of the Motion Picture Production Code," *Journal of American History* 77 (1990): 39–65. Carolyn See, "The American Dream Cheat," in *Tough Guy Writers of the Thirties*, ed. David Madden (Carbondale: Southern Illinois University Press, 1968), 201. Marlou Belyea, "The Joy Ride and the Silver Screen: Commercialized Leisure, Delinquency and Play Reform in Los Angeles, 1900–1980" (doctoral diss., Boston University, 1983).

33. Czitrom, *Media and the American Mind*. May, *Screening Out the Past*. Sobel, *The Manipulators*, 172. Maltby, *Harmless Entertainment*, especially 134–36. Leonard J. Leff and Jerold L. Simmons, *The Dame in the Kimono: Hollywood, Censorship, and the Production Code from the 1920s to the 1960s* (New York: Grove Weidenfeld, 1990).

34. See, for example, David Karnes, "The Glamourous Crowd: Hollywood Movie Premieres Between the Wars," *American Quarterly* 38 (1986): especially 562–63; "Paging Mr. Robin Hood," *North American Review* 239 (1935): 1–3. See in general Maltby, *Harmless Entertainment*.

35. Czitrom, *Media and the American Mind*, especially 51–52. *Mass Media Between the Wars: Perceptions of Cultural Tension*, ed. Catherine Covert and John D. Stevens (Syracuse: Syracuse University Press, 1984). John L. Caughey, "Artificial Social Relations in Modern America," *American Quarterly* 30 (1978): 70–89.

36. This literature was extensive and of course much contested by selfishly interested parties and their allies. See, for example, Fredric Wertham, *Seduction of the Innocent* (New York: Rinehart and Company, 1954), especially 257, and generations of good social-science research, finally followed in the newsletter of the National Coalition on Television Violence, *NCTV News*. The original classic was Wilbur Schramm, Jack Lyle, and Edwin B. Parker, *Television in the Lives of Our Children* (Stanford: Stanford University Press, 1961). Marvin E. Wolfgang, "Delinquency in Two Birth Cohorts," *American Behavioral Scientist* 27 (1983): 75–86, found that the generation turning 18 in 1963 were decidedly less violent—although about as delinquent—than those turning 18 in 1976. Perhaps the most startling example was the study that found that boxing matches heavily publicized on television led consistently to a sharply increased number of homicides; David P. Phillips, "The Impact of Mass Media Violence on U. S. Homicides," *American Sociological Review* 48 (1983): 560–68. When, after the first years of television, violent dramas came on the scene, they replaced in large part the violent sports that had been so popular, such as wrestling; Benjamin G. Rader, *In Its Own Image: How Television Has Transformed Sports* (New York: The Free Press, 1984), 37.

37. See, for example, Charles R. Hearn, *The American Dream in the Great Depression* (Westport, Ct.: Greenwood Press, 1977), 122–27. Fairfax M. Cone, *The Blue Streak: Some Observations, Mostly About Advertising* (n.p.: Crain Communications, 1973), 2–3.

38. Czitrom, *Media and the American Mind*, especially 190–91. *Development of Antisocial and Prosocial Behavior: Research, Theories, and Issues*, ed. Dan Olweus, Jack Block, and Marian Radke-Yarrow (Orlando: Academic Press, Inc., 1986). See, for example, Erik Barnouw, *The Sponsor: Notes on a Modern Potentate* (New York: Oxford University Press, 1978),

and such research as Leslie A. Baxter and Stuart J. Kaplan, "Context Factors in the Analysis of Prosocial and Antisocial Behavior on Prime Time Television," *Journal of Broadcasting* 27 (1983): 25–36. Maltby, *Harmless Entertainment*, 312–13. Another level of analysis is suggested by, for example, the evidence of Robert Goldman, "Legitimation Ads, Part I: The Story of the Family, in Which the Family Saves Capitalism from Itself," *Knowledge and Society* 5 (1984), 243–67, that television advertising helped significantly to transform the nuclear family from a social institution to an instrument of consumption.

39. See especially George Lipsitz, " 'Against the Wind': The Class Composition of Rock and Roll Music," *Knowledge and Society* 5 (1984), 269–96, who argues the fundamentally rebellious and subversive nature of much working-class music. The basic source on the indecent aspects of jazz lyrics—much condemned by middle-class blacks at the time—is Guy B. Johnson, "Double Meaning in the Popular Negro Blues," *Journal of Abnormal and Social Psychology* 22 (1927): 12–20. "Rock 'n roll" was also originally a slang term for sexual intercourse; Leff and Simmons, *The Dame in the Kimono*, 214.

40. See Chapter 5 above. Seymour Krim, "Anti-Jazz: Unless the Implications Are Faced," *Village Voice*, 1 January 1958, 10.

41. The sexual content of rock has been mentioned above in Chapters 7 and 8. See, for example, Lipsitz, " 'Against the Wind' "; Herbert I. London, *Closing the Circle: A Cultural History of the Rock Revolution* (Chicago: Nelson-Hall, 1984). Details, including explicit lyrics, are in Tipper Gore, *Raising PG Kids in an X-Rated Society* (Nashville: Abingdon Press, 1987); the incident is described on 17.

42. Bernice Martin, "The Sacralization of Disorder: Symbolism in Rock Music," *Sociological Analysis* 40 (1979): 87–124; the quote is from 104. See, similarly, Timothy Miller, *The Hippies and American Values* (Knoxville: University of Tennessee Press, 1991), chap. 4.

43. London, *Closing the Circle*, especially 25–26 and 37–52, where he emphasizes how conformist early rock was. Chester White Flippo, "Rock Journalism and *Rolling Stone*" (Master's thesis, University of Texas, 1974), 2, 9. B. Lee Cooper, "The Image of the Outsider in Contemporary Lyrics," *Journal of Popular Culture* 12 (1978): 169–70. Simon Frith, *Sound Effects: Youth, Leisure, and the Politics of Rock* (London: Constable, 1983), especially 48–52, 238–39.

44. See especially London, *Closing the Circle*. Dave Marsh, quoted in Flippo, "Rock Journalism," 124. Samuel S. Janus and Cynthia L. Janus, "Children, Sex, Peers, Culture: 1973–1983," *Journal of Psychohistory* 12 (1985): 368–69. Other illustrative studies include James R. Huffman and Julie L. Huffman, "Sexism and Cultural Lag: The Rise of the Jailbait Song, 1955–1985," *Journal of Popular Culture*, Fall 1987, 65–83; and on a powerful combination of rock and television, R. Serge Denisoff, "Ted Turner's Crusade: Economics vs. Morals," *Journal of Popular Culture*, Summer 1987, 27–42.

45. See Chapter 5, above. Martin, "The Sacralization of Disorder," especially 108. See, for example, "Hymning the Joys of Girls, Gunplay and Getting High," *Newsweek*, 2 February 1987, 70–71. "Samples of Violent Music Lyrics," *NCTV News*, April–June 1990, 2–3.

46. James M. Curtis, "Toward a Sociotechnological Interpretation of Popular Music in the Electronic Age," *Technology and Culture* 25 (1984): 91–102. Columbia Records and Tapes advertised starting right out in the first issue of *Hustler* in 1974, along with marketers of erotic books and whiskey. Flippo, "Rock Journalism," especially 8–9, 17, 39–48. An additional demoralizing factor was the notoriously corrupt business practices that marked the rock-and-roll music business—a separate topic not covered in this book. One scandal, for example, was noted in part in "Payola Scandal Prods Record Makers, Stations, to Stiffen Ethics Guidelines," *Wall Street Journal*, 7 August 1973, 1. See also Miller, *The Hippies*, 78, 81.

47. Some of these points are taken up in Flippo, "Rock Journalism," and London, *Closing the Circle*; the quote is from 136. Greil Marcus, *Lipstick Traces: A Secret History of the*

Twentieth Century (Cambridge, Mass.: Harvard University Press, 1989), especially 1–152. Gore, *Raising PG Kids*. Other details are in United States Senate, Committee on Commerce, Science, and Transportation, 99th Congress, First Session, Hearings on "Contents of Music and the Lyrics of Records," 19 September 1985 (Washington: U. S. Government Printing Office, 1985).

48. *Bar and Buffet*, April 1907, 12.
49. Some comment is made in the next chapter on spokespersons for the minor vices who took a prosocial role because it was even more effective than rebelliousness. *Penthouse*, April 1972, 136. Using Santa and other holiday figures to advertise alcoholic beverages was of course a commonplace.
50. Intellectual rebels in the twentieth century are treated to some extent in Christopher Lasch, *The New Radicalism in America (1889–1963): The Intellectual as a Social Type* (New York: Vintage Books, 1967 [c. 1965]), especially 254–56, 286–89.
51. There was a more general shift to unapologetic hedonism as deviancy status changed in some groups; Richard Bunce, "Social and Political Sources of Drug Effects: The Case of Bad Trips on Psychedelics," *Journal of Drug Issues* 9 (1979): 228. See Miller, *The Hippies*, especially 118–19.
52. "Gossiping Guru," *Oracle*, undated, 1967, 24. See the works on the drug culture cited in Chapter 5, above, such as Lewis Yablonsky, *The Hippie Trip* (New York: Pegasus, 1968). Many even "advanced" intellectuals of course distanced themselves from drug slums that they found nevertheless fascinating.
53. See the comment of Cowley, *Exile's Return*, 286, that even in the 1920s "the religion of art had failed when it tried to become a system of ethics. . . ." William Philips, "Writing About Sex," *Partisan Review* 34 (1967): 552.
54. Examples are from Edwin McDowell, "The Critics Descend on Pornotopia," *Wall Street Journal*, 15 May 1973, 24; Charles I. Glicksberg, *The Sexual Revolution in Modern American Literature* (The Hague: Martinus Nijhoff, 1971), 147.
55. Paul Boyer, *Purity in Print: The Vice-Society Movement and Book Censorship in America* (New York: Charles Scribner's Sons, 1968), especially 93–94.
56. Boyer, *Purity in Print*, provides dramatic specifics of reformer efforts. Richard J. Bonnie and Charles H. Whitebread II, *The Marihuana Conviction: A History of Marihuana Prohibition in the United States* (Charlottesville: University Press of Virginia, 1974), 209, who quote the headline. Larry Sloman, *Reefer Madness: The History of Marijuana in America* (Indianapolis: Bobbs-Merrill, 1979), 230–31.
57. *Marijuana Review*, January-March 1969, 5. A typical example is "Legislation Jeopardizes Liquor Ads in Newspaper," *Editor and Publisher*, 3 September 1977, 9. A particularly ironic example was the defense of the American Psychological Association for material in a popular journal; see, "Advertising Policy Adopted for Magazine," American Psychological Association *Monitor*, August 1983, 2; Leonard D. Goodstein, "Across My Desk," ibid., May 1987, 11.
58. Haven Emerson, "Public Health Awaits Social Courage," *American Journal of Public Health* 24 (1934): 1016–17. "Bits & Pieces," *Hustler*, June 1976, 10.
59. "History & Preservation 1984" (Ketchikan, 1984); copy kindly supplied by Ketchikan Public Library.
60. The examples are from Boyer, *Purity in Print*, and John F. Galliher and John R. Cross, *Morals Legislation without Morality: The Case of Nevada* (New Brunswick: Rutgers University Press, 1983), 76–83. James G. Houghland, Jr., James R. Wood, and Samuel E. Mueller, "Organizational 'Goal Submergence': The Methodist Church and the Failure of the Temperance Movement," *Sociology and Sociological Research* 58 (1974): 408–416.
61. Peter Gardella, *Innocent Ecstasy: How Christianity Gave America an Ethic of Sexual Pleasure* (New York: Oxford University Press, 1985), especially 151–61. See also Barbara

Ehrenreich, Elizabeth Hess, and Gloria Jacobs, *Re-Making Love: The Feminization of Sex* (Garden City, N.Y.: Anchor Press/Doubleday, 1986), chap. 5. See, for example, *Swinging World* [Hollywood, California], 1968.

62. Edward A. Ross, *Sin and Society: An Analysis of Latter Day Iniquity* (Boston: Houghton Mifflin Company, 1907), 98. I have not seen an account that speaks to which group abandoned the other, or what other events described in this book caused the split.

63. Undated statement, Sexual Freedom League, San Francisco Chapter.

64. Richard Fantina, "The Fugs," *High Times*, November 1984, 39.

65. The best general treatment is unfortunately focused on political aspects, John D'Emilio, *Sexual Politics, Sexual Communities: The Making of a Homosexual Minority in the United States*, 1940–1970 (Chicago: University of Chicago Press, 1983). A rich account is Lillian Faderman, *Odd Girls and Twilight Lovers: A History of Lesbian Life in Twentieth-Century America* (New York: Columbia University Press, 1991). See, for example, William Barrett, "New Innocents Abroad," *Partisan Review* 17 (1950): 272–91. Douglas Auchincloss, "The Gay Crowd," in *Sex in the '60s: A Candid Look at the Age of Mini-Morals*, ed. Joe David Brown (New York: Time-Life Books, 1968), 66–69. Large numbers of Americans occasionally acted as homophiles, and their senses of identity were at best ambivalent or ambiguous; in any event, precise definitions are beside the point where one is dealing with population groups of unknown size anyway.

66. Faderman, *Odd Girls*, discusses the problematic role of bars. Barrett, "New Innocents Abroad"; Lieberman, "The Emergence of Lesbians," especially 124–57. D'Emilio, *Sexual Politics*.

67. See, for example, in addition to material cited previously, Tom Burke, "The New Homosexuality," *Esquire*, December 1969, 178, 304–18; Morgan Pinney, "Some Thoughts About Gay Life," *Gay Sunshine*, January 1972, 11; "What's This Shit?" *Gay Sunshine*, August-September 1970, 2; Edmund White, "The Political Vocabulary of Homosexuality," in *The State of the Language*, ed. Leonard Michaels and Christopher Ricks (Berkeley: University of California Press, 1980), 244–45; Donal E. J. MacNamara and Edward Sagarin, *Sex, Crime, and the Law* (New York: The Free Press, 1977), 100–101. Faderman, *Odd Girls*, 282. Jim Kepner, "Angles on the News," *Advocate*, June 1969, 25. Especially useful is Diane Taub and Robert G. Leger, "Argot and the Creation of Social Types in a Young Gay Community," *Human Relations* 37 (1984): 181–89. This brief account of course glosses over social-class differences and numerous complicated stances among the developing gay/lesbian activists—and those who were not active.

68. David C. Rowe, Joseph Lee Rogers, and Sylvia Meseck-Bushey, "An 'Epidemic' Model of Sexual Intercourse Prevalences for Black and White Adolescents," *Social Biology* 36 (1989): 127–45.

69. Early examples include Christopher Sower, "Teen-Age Drinking as Group Behavior," *Quarterly Journal of Studies on Alcohol* 20 (1959): 655–63; Everett M. Rogers, "Reference Group Influences on Student Drinking Behavior," *Quarterly Journal of Studies on Alcohol* 19 (1958): 244–54; Joseph R. Gusfield, "The Structural Context of College Drinking," *Quarterly Journal of Studies on Alcohol* 22 (1961): 428–43. K. H. Beck and T. G. Summers, "Social Context of Alcohol Consumption and Sources of Information Among High School Alcohol Abusers," in *Health Education and the Media II*, ed. D. S. Leathar et al. (Oxford: Pergamon Press, 1986), 51–56. See the brief discussion in a historical context in Paul Boyer, *Urban Masses and Moral Order in America*, 1820–1920 (Cambridge: Harvard University Press, 1978), 289, 369n.

70. Daniel J. Boorstin, *The Americans: The Democratic Experience* (New York: Random House, 1973), part 2. *Brewery Age*, 6 April 1959, 3. *The Culture of Consumption: Critical Essays in American History*, 1880–1980, ed. Richard Wightman Fox and T.J. Jackson Lears (New York: Pantheon Books, 1983), especially Christopher P. Wilson, "The Rhetoric

of Consumption: Mass-Market Magazines and the Demise of the Gentle Reader, 1880–1920," 57, and Jean-Christophe Agnew, "The Consuming Vision of Henry James," 67–69. This subject comes up again in the next chapter.

T E N : *Patterns of Convergence in a Complex Society*

1. This closely paraphrases Robert Sobel, *They Satisfy: The Cigarette in American Life* (New York: Doubleday, 1978), 222. There is no attempt here to explore the psychological affinities between the bad habits, particularly as, for example, drug taking and gambling substituted for sexual activity (noted in other connections was the expression "action" for betting, not sex, in some circles).

2. Graham M. Sykes and David Matza, "Techniques of Neutralization: A Theory of Delinquency," *American Sociological Review* 22 (1957): 664–70. Crane Brinton, *The Anatomy of Revolution*, 2d ed. (New York: Vintage Books, 1965), especially 42–47, speaks eloquently of the revolutionary potential of a shift of intellectuals' allegiance to an alternative authority. Paula Fass, *The Damned and the Beautiful: American Youth in the 1920s* (New York: Oxford University Press, 1977), especially 359, suggests that a major aspect of the shift in standards lay in the sense that leading young people had that the old morals were not *their* morals.

3. No attempt is made here to introduce the literature on modern anomie and cultural relativism—much less the idea that the United States had been in a postmodern stage for some time.

4. Richard Stivers, *Evil in Modern Myth and Ritual* (Athens: The University of Georgia Press, 1982), offers one conceptualization of the relation of evil, if not vice, to ritual, including the mass media and advertising.

5. Fred Greenstein, "New Light on Changing American Values: A Forgotten Body of Survey Data," *Social Forces* 42 (1964): 441–50. There is a large literature on the effects of prosocial television; see, for example, Edmond M. Rosenthal, "Pro-Profit Conquers Pro-Social in Nework Kids' Programs," *Television/Radio Age*, 18 August 1975, 26–28, 88–93; *Development of Antisocial and Prosocial Behavior: Research, Theories, and Issues*, ed. Dan Olweus, Jack Block, and Marian Radke-Yarrow (Orlando: Academic Press, Inc., 1986). Alan Casty, "The Gangster and the Drama of the Thirties," in *Challenges in American Culture*, ed. Ray B. Browne (Bowling Green: Bowling Green University Popular Press, 1970), 224–93. George Grella, "The Gangster Novel: The Urban Pastoral," in *Tough Guy Writers of the Thirties*, ed. David Madden (Carbondale: Southern Illinois University Press, 1968), 186–98, and other essays in the same book.

6. See, for example, the interplay of class, commercialism, and culture in the events described in David A. Macleod, *Building Character in the American Boy: The Boy Scouts, YMCA, and Their Forerunners*, 1870–1920 (Madison: University of Wisconsin Press, 1983), especially 32–36. It of course is not possible in this book to explore the entire cultural and social context within which the minor vice-industrial complex evolved and flourished.

7. See, for example, Jack J. Gottsegen, *Tobacco: A Study of Its Consumption in the United States* (New York: Pitman Publishing Corporation, 1940), 77. The advantage of constant reinforcement appeared in the fact that advertising for consumers, for example, also affected the behavior and attitudes of distributors and retailers; see, for example, Meyer Katzper, Ralph Ryback, and Marc Hertzman, "Alcohol Beverage Advertisement and Consumption," *Journal of Drug Issues* 8 (1978): 347, which (339–353) speaks to the whole issue.

8. "STAT Campaign Cuts Illegal Sale of Tobacco to Minors in Half," *Tobacco and Youth Reporter*, Autumn 1988, 1.

9. See, for example, standard works such as *The Culture of Consumption: Critical Essays in American History, 1880–1980*, ed. Richard Wightman Fox and T. J. Jackson Lears (New York: Pantheon Books, 1983); John F. Kasson, *Amusing the Million: Coney Island at the Turn of the Century* (New York: Hill and Wang, 1978); and David Karnes, "The Glamorous Crowd: Hollywood Movie Premieres Between the Wars," *American Quarterly* 38 (1986): especially 562–64. Lary May, *Screening Out the Past: The Birth of Mass Culture and the Motion Picture Industry* (New York: Oxford University Press, 1980), 200–201. Kathy Peiss, *Cheap Amusements: Working Women and Leisure in Turn-of-the-Century New York* (Philadelphia: Temple University Press, 1986), especially 186–88, emphasizes the commercialization of leisure and fulfillment in consumption. Tom Jones Parry, "Beer Dispensing Is a Business—Not a Racket," *Beer Distributor*, July 1935, 12–14. London, *Closing the Circle*, 37–52, notes that although the lyrics of rock tunes did not shift to pro-abuse substance and anti-work until the 1960s, from the beginning all rock was aimed commercially and stylistically, both, at children of the consumer society. In 1979, beer merchandisers objected to realism in the movies that connected drinking to violence and drunk driving and wanted beer instead to appear only in a setting of pleasant fantasy; Debbie Kasdan, "Beer Brands in the Movies," *Modern Brewing Age*, 3 September 1979, 2.

10. See especially Kasson, *Amusing the Million*; William R. Leach, "Transformations in a Culture of Consumption: Women and Department Stores, 1890–1925," *Journal of American History* 71 (1984): 319–42, especially 336; Daniel Horowitz, *The Morality of Spending: Attitudes Toward the Consumer Society in America, 1875–1940* (Baltimore: The Johns Hopkins University Press, 1985), especially 134–35, 162–71; Roland Marchand, *Advertising the American Dream: Making Way for Modernity, 1920–1940* (Berkeley: University of California Press, 1985), especially 284; May, *Screening Out the Past*.

11. See, for example, Michael D. Newcomb, P. M. Bentler, and Caroline Collins, "Alcohol Use and Dissatisfaction with Self and Life: A Longitudinal Analysis of Young Adults," *Journal of Drug Issues* 16 (1986): 480–81. The authors note the use of abuse substances to counteract subjective feelings of being personally defective.

12. May, *Screening Out the Past*, makes the connection in a specific context. The depersonalization of commoditized sex is taken up in Edwin Schur, *The Americanization of Sex* (Philadelphia: Temple University Press, 1988). Lawrence Birken, *Consuming Desire: Sexual Science and the Emergence of a Culture of Abundance, 1871–1914* (Ithaca: Cornell University Press, 1988), presents a very complex and sophisticated account.

13. Donald J. Mrozek, *Sport and American Mentality, 1880–1910* (Knoxville: University of Tennessee Press, 1983), chap. 4. For *Playboy*, see Chapter 7 above. Tom Burke, "The New Homosexuality," *Esquire*, December 1969, 178, 304–18.

14. As noted in Chapter 3, leisure appeared as such after the drinking and socializing of the early-nineteenth-century workplace moved into a separate time and place. Richard Butsch, ed., *For Fun and Profit: The Transformation of Leisure into Consumption* (Philadelphia: Temple University Press, 1990), explores some of the significance of the commercialization of leisure. Roy Rosenzweig, *Eight Hours for What We Will: Workers and Leisure in an Industrial City, 1870–1920* (Cambridge: Cambridge University Press, 1983); and especially Francis G. Couvares, *The Remaking of Pittsburgh: Class and Culture in an Industrializing City, 1870–1930* (Cambridge: Cambridge University Press, 1983). Leonard Ellis, "Men Among Men: An Exploration of All-Male Relationships in Victorian America" (doctoral diss., Columbia University, 1982), 80–85. Because for so long the culture valued work, the growing importance of leisure-time activities was neglected by both contemporaries and later historians.

15. Ibid. Kasson, *Amusing the Million*; the quotation, from George Elliott Howard, is on 105. Joseph Buchanan, quoted in David Brundage, "The Producing Classes and the Saloon:

Denver in the 1880s," *Labor History* 26 (1985): 43. For example, Macleod, *Building Character in the American Boy*, shows how the forces of decency turned to the arena of leisure and recreation to try to recapture young people.

16. Gilman M. Ostrander, *American Civilization in the First Machine Age: 1890–1940* (New York: Harper and Row, 1970), 69; the figure for alcoholic-beverage expenditures, at least, was undoubtedly understated. Jon M. Kingsdale, "The 'Poor Man's Club': Social Functions of the Urban Working-Class Saloon," *American Quarterly* 25 (1973): 472–89. Rosenzweig, *Eight Hours*; and especially Kasson, *Amusing the Million*. See also chapter 7, above.

17. See especially Perry Duis, *The Saloon: Public Drinking in Chicago and Boston, 1880–1920* (Urbana: University of Illinois Press, 1983), and Kasson, *Amusing the Million*. Ted Ownby, *Subduing Satan: Religion, Recreation, and Manhood in the Rural South, 1865–1920* (Chapel Hill: University of North Carolina Press, 1990), spells out in detail the struggle over leisure space in the small towns of the South. See also chapter 3, above. Ian R. Tyrrell, *Sobering Up: From Temperance to Prohibition in Antebellum America, 1800–1860* (Westport, Ct.: Greenwood Press, 1979), pays particular attention to social-class relationships in the formative period of the mobilizing of the proponents of the minor vices. Gustavus Myers, *Ye Olden Blue Laws* (New York: The Century Co., 1921), tied contemporary Sunday blue laws to the Puritan past. In the nineteenth century, as I noted above, violating Sunday laws was usually considered part of the constellation of minor vices. With secularization, the issue was subordinated to the other, more specific, vices. The example is from Mark H. Haller, "Urban Vice and Civic Reform: Chicago in the Early Twentieth Century," in *Cities in American History*, ed. Kenneth T. Jackson and Stanley K. Schultz (New York: Alfred A. Knopf, 1972), 295. See especially Daniel J. Czitrom, *Media and the American Mind: From Morse to McLuhan* (Chapel Hill: University of North Carolina Press, 1982); Kasson, *Amusing the Million*; Lewis A. Erenberg, *Steppin' Out: New York Nightlife and the Transformation of American Culture, 1890–1930* (Westport, Ct.: Greenwood Press, 1981); Couvares, *The Remaking of Pittsburgh*; Rosenzweig, *Eight Hours*. Ellis, "Men Among Men," 166–67, notes that women grouped together in homes but still shared a bucket of beer sent up from the public saloon of the men. Don C. Kirschner, "The Perils of Pleasure: Commercial Recreation, Social Disorder and Moral Reform in the Progressive Era," *American Studies* 21 (1980): 27–42, especially 28–29. Marlou Belyea, "The Joy Ride and the Silver Screen: Commercial Leisure, Delinquency and Play Reform in Los Angeles, 1900–1980" (doctoral diss., Boston University, 1983). Some of the historical issues are taken up in Michael Denning, "Cheap Stories: Notes on Popular Fiction and Working Class Culture in Nineteenth-Century America," *History Workshop Journal* 22 (1986): 1–17.

18. Joseph Lieberman, "The Emergence of Lesbians and Gay Men as Characters in Plays Produced on the American Stage from 1922 to 1954" (doctoral diss., City University of New York, 1981), 23.

19. Rosenzweig, *Eight Hours*, especially 5, 222–27, chap. 8. Couvares, *The Remaking of Pittsburgh*. May, *Screening Out the Past*. This shift in the consumer culture, in which consumers lost power to largely national commercial hegemonic groups, especially in the period of the 1920s, is taken particularly from Lawrence Greenfield, "Toys and the Toy Industry as Socializing Agents in the Culture of Consumption" (doctoral diss., Ohio State University, 1991). Lizabeth Cohen, "Encountering Mass Culture at the Grassroots: The Experience of Chicago Workers in the 1920s," *American Quarterly* 41 (1989): 6–33, shows how working-class ethnics up until sound movies in the 1930s used the new media to resist acculturation, much less uplift. Gareth Stedman Jones, "Class Expression versus Social Control? A Critique of Recent Trends in the Social Theory of 'Leisure,'" *History Workshop*, Autumn 1977, 162–70, is a good example of commentators who have tried to

make a choice on the social control issue, missing the point that the rise of popular culture changed the social relationships.

20. See, for example, Abram Lipsky, "The Political Mind of Foreign-Born Americans," *Popular Science Monthly* 85 (1914): 397–403. Jack Larkin, *The Reshaping of Everyday Life* (New York: Harper and Row, 1988), 151. A classic essay giving more general cultural background is Martha Wolfenstein, "The Emergence of Fun Morality," *Journal of Social Issues* 7 (1951): 15–25. Peter A. Lupsha, "American Values and Organized Crime: Suckers and Wiseguys," in *The American Self: Myth, Ideology, and Popular Culture*, ed. Sam B. Girgus (Albuquerque: University of New Mexico Press, 1981), 144–54. Daniel Yankelovich, *New Rules: Searching for Self-Fulfillment in a World Turned Upside Down* (New York: Bantam Books, 1982 [c. 1981]), especially 187. Later in the century, with ever more leisure time available, people who were "bored" found from the media that drinking and associated activities would entertain them, and the fear of boredom became a major selling point for advocates of the attractive vices; James D. Orcutt, "Contrasting Effects of Two Kinds of Boredom on Alcohol Use," *Journal of Drug Issues* 14 (1984): 161–73.

21. I use here the words of Norman H. Clark, *Deliver Us from Evil: An Interpretation of American Prohibition* (New York: W. W. Norton and Company, 1976), 50. See the summary in Richard B. Stott, *Workers in the Metropolis: Class, Ethnicity, and Youth in Antebellum New York City* (Ithaca: Cornell University Press, 1990), 270–71. A powerful specific description is in David W. Rose, "Prostitution and the Sporting Life Aspects of Working Class Culture and Sexuality in Nineteenth Century Wheeling," *Upper Ohio Valley Historical Review* 16 (1987): 7–31. See particularly Elliot J. Gorn, *The Manly Art: Bare-Knuckle Prize Fighting in America* (Ithaca: Cornell University Press, 1986), especially 140–43, 192–93. David G. Pugh, *Sons of Liberty: The Masculine Mind in Nineteenth-Century America* (Westport, Ct.: Greenwood Press, 1983), chap. 4, identifies in the late-twentieth-century "cult of manliness": savagery, working-class attitudes, and independent individualism as well as traditional machismo.

22. Dwight B. Heath, "In Other Cultures, They Also Drink," in *Alcohol, Science and Society Revisited*, ed. Edith Lisansky Gomberg, Helene Raskin White, and John A. Carpenter (Ann Arbor: University of Michigan Press, 1982), 74. Ellis, "Men Among Men," especially chaps. 1–3. The connection between manliness and the minor vices in the rural South is a theme in Ownby, *Subduing Satan*. John M. Findlay, *People of Chance: Gambling in American Society from Jamestown to Las Vegas* (New York: Oxford University Press, 1986), 25–26. Arthur M. Sutherland, "The Psychological Aspects of Cancer of the Lung," in *Pulmonary Carcinoma: Pathogenesis, Diagnosis, and Treatment*, ed. Edgar Mayer and Herbert C. Maier (New York: New York University Press, 1956), 444. See, for example, media advertising in *Liquor Store and Dispenser*, later *Liquor Store*; in an ad in *Liquor Store*, May 1966, 324, *Sports Illustrated* claimed to reach "beer-serving households more efficiently" than other magazines read primarily by men. Arden G. Christen and Ben Z. Swanson, "Orally Used Smokeless Tobacco as Advertised in the Metamorphic Trade Cards of 1870–1890," *Bulletin of the History of Dentistry* 31 (1983): 82–87. Jack Gould, "For TV in 1957: A Viewer's Resolutions," *New York Times*, 30 December 1956, magazine section, 9. Bobbie Jacobsen, *The Lady Killers: Why Smoking Is a Feminist Issue* (London: Pluto Press, 1981), especially 60–61, provides one example.

23. See especially Edward K. Strong, *Vocational Interests of Men and Women* (Stanford University: Stanford University Press, 1943); Joseph H. Pleck, *The Myth of Masculinity* (Cambridge, Mass.: The MIT Press, 1981), 88–89; and, for example, Peter Shaw, "The Tough Guy Intellectual," *Critical Quarterly* 8 (1966): 13–28. *Sault Ste. Marie News*, quoted in *Tobacco*, 18 June 1925, 8. Simon Frith, *Sound Effects: Youth, Leisure, and the Politics of Rock* (London: Constable, 1983), 85–88. Kingsley Widmer, "The Way Out: Some Life-Style Sources of the Literary Tough Guy and the Proletarian Hero," in *Tough Guy*

Writers of the Thirties, ed. David Madden (Carbondale: Southern Illinois University Press, 1968), especially 3–11, traces the influence of the hobo—a prototypical marginal, lower-order figure—in American ideas of desirable masculinity. Many other essays in that book are suggestive also. Warren I. Susman, *Culture and History: The Transformation of American Society in the Twentieth Century* (New York: Pantheon Books, 1984), 129–30. Anne Robinson Taylor, "The Virginal Male as Hero in American Films," *Southwest Review* 63 (1978): 317–29. Pugh, *Sons of Liberty*.

24. The involvement of the American Legion is additionally suggested in William Pencak, *For God and Country, The American Legion, 1919–1941* (Boston: Northeastern University Press, 1989), especially 95–97, 100, 131–37. See, for example, Roland Marchand, "Visions of Classlessness, Quests for Dominion: American Popular Culture, 1945–1960," in *Reshaping America: Society and Institutions, 1945–1960*, ed. Robert Bremner and Gary Reichard (Columbus: Ohio State University Press, 1982), 172; John Walsh, "Survey Shows Freshmen Shift on Careers, Values," *Science* 219 (1983): 822. One of the nastiest aspects of the latter-day misogyny was blaming women—and children!—for social problems because mothers did not bring children up properly; see, for example, W. Norton Grubb and Marvin Lazerson, *Broken Promises: How Americans Fail Their Children* (New York: Basic Books, Inc., 1982), especially 33–36.

25. Some history of American women as moralists is found in Nancy F. Cott, "Passionlessness: An Interpretation of Victorian Sexual Ideology, 1790–1850," *Signs* 4 (1978): 219–36; and Ann Douglas, *The Feminization of American Culture* (New York: Alfred A. Knopf, 1977). Barbara Leslie Epstein, *The Politics of Domesticity: Women, Evangelism, and Temperance in Nineteenth-Century America* (Middletown: Wesleyan University Press, 1981), elucidates the explicitly anti-male themes in reform. Belyea, "The Joy Ride," especially 367–70, provides vital evidence and analysis. Raymond Bossé and Charles L. Rose, "Smoking Cessation and Sex Role Convergence," *Journal of Health and Social Behavior* 17 (1976): 53–61. One classic statement about the new hero was Norman Mailer, "The White Negro," reprinted in *The Beat Generation and the Angry Young Men*, ed. Gene Feldman and Max Gertenberg (New York: Dell Publishing Co., 1958), 371–94. See also such witnesses as David E. Smith and John Luce, *Love Needs Care: A History of San Francisco's Haight-Ashbury Free Medical Clinic and Its Pioneer Role in Treating Drug-Abuse Problems* (Boston: Little, Brown and Company, 1971), 82–83.

26. See, for example, Herbert A. Otto, " 'The Pornographic Fringeland' on the American Newsstand," *Journal of Human Relations* 90 (1964): 375–90; Jean Marie McMahon, "*Playgirl*: New Player, Old Game" (Master's thesis, University of Oregon, 1976); Ann Barr Snitow, "The Front Line: Notes on Sex in Novels by Women, 1969–1979," *Signs* 5 (1980): 702–18.

27. José Ortega y Gasset, *The Revolt of the Masses*, trans. anon. (New York: W. W. Norton and Company, 1932). Marvin E. Wolfgang, "Real and Perceived Change in Crime and Punishment," *Daedalus* 107 (1978): 154. Belyea, "The Joy Ride," gives a vivid description of how reverse diffusion worked out in practice. Joanne J. Meyerowitz, *Women Adrift: Independent Wage Earners in Chicago, 1880–1930* (Chicago: University of Chicago Press, 1988), especially 116, provides a striking specific example of this phenomenon in describing the spread of lower-order standards among working and other women in the early twentieth century. Marchand, "Visions of Classlessness," 166, describes the process as "leveling down," but he is concerned mostly with style.

28. Deanne I. Wolcott, Fawzy I. Fawzy, and Robert H. Coombs, "Reinforcing Networks: The Medical Pharmaceutical, Mass Media and Paraphernalia Establishments," *Journal of Drug Issues* 14 (1984): 223–31.

29. Marchand, "Visions of Classlessness," 167–70. Lesa Ukman, "Event Marketing," *Gaming & Wagering Business*, December 1985, 27. McBride, "Industry Structure," 615–16, connects

lifestyle advertising directly to alcohol-related problems such as operating machinery while drinking.

30. See, for example, two educators' attempt to use students' backgrounds and subjective feelings as a basis for standards in Gwendolyn D. Scott and Mona W. Carlo, *On Becoming a Health Educator* (Dubuque, Iowa: Wm. C. Brown Company, 1974). Kenneth Auchincloss, "1984 Scrapbook," *Newsweek*, 24 December 1984, 50.

31. See, for example, Bruce Lohof, "The Higher Meaning of Marlboro Cigarettes," *Journal of Popular Culture* 3 (1969): 441–50. Patrick Anderson, *High in America: The True Story Behind NORML and the Politics of Marijuana* (New York: The Viking Press, 1981), 106.

32. Basic sources on "victimless crime" include the pioneer work, Edwin M. Schur, *Crimes Without Victims: Deviant Behavior and Public Policy* (Englewood Cliffs, N.J.: Prentice-Hall, 1965), and Gilbert Geis, *Not the Law's Business? An Examination of Homosexuality, Abortion, Prostitution, Narcotics and Gambling in the United States* (Rockville, Md.: National Institute of Mental Health, Center for Studies of Crime and Delinquency, 1972). Or it may be that the argument involved an extremely legalistic point of view: the victim or victims may be so remotely or indirectly affected that they would have no standing as complainants in a court of law, or the victims may suffer just as members of the society that is damaged, not as individuals. In the late twentieth century, adults could not sue, for example, because they were offended by language overheard, although some people tried to make a case for passive-smoking damage and the way in which sexual misbehavior increased everyone's insurance rates. No attempt is made here to summarize the large abstract literature on the broader social and moral questions involved, such as the right to privacy or the work that John Stuart Mill sparked on the issue of liberty; the proponents of the minor vices invoked all such materials freely in their arguments. A subset was the idea of overcriminalization, the idea from the 1960s that too many matters were subject to criminal legal penalties; see, for example, Richard J. Bonnie and Charles H. Whitebread II, *The Marihuana Conviction: A History of Marihuana Prohibition in the United States* (Charlottesville: University Press of Virginia, 1974), 226; Sanford H. Kadish, "The Crisis of Overcriminalization," *Annals of the American Academy of Political and Social Science* 374 (1967): 157–70.

33. *Journal of Commerce*, quoted in "The Temperance Reform," *Bonfort's Wine and Spirit Circular* 26 (1886): 88. Jeffrey T. Sammons, "America in the Ring: The Relationship Between Boxing and Society, Circa 1930–1980" (doctoral diss., University of North Carolina, 1982), 24–27. "Testimony of Larry A. Schott," *Contemporary Drug Problems* 8 (1979): 444.

34. Not least among their concerns were technical liabilities. For many years after repeal, for example, alcoholic-beverage merchandisers worked to alter laws that embodied generations of common sense so that the dispenser of a beverage could be held responsible for the subsequent actions of a drinker. See, for example, *Modern Brewery Age*, 15 June 1959, 3, concerning a success in North Carolina.

35. See, for example, Paul J. Freund, "Polish-American Drinking: Continuity and Change," in *The American Experience with Alcohol: Contrasting Cultural Perspectives*, ed. Linda A. Bennett and Genevieve M. Ames (New York: Plenum Press, 1985), 86–87; Lawrence J. Hatterer, *The Pleasure Addicts: The Addictive Process—Food, Sex, Drugs, Alcohol, Work, and More* (South Brunswick: A. S. Barnes and Company, 1980). Janice M. Irvine, "Disorders of Desire: The Professionalization of Sexology" (doctoral diss., Brandeis University, 1984), 6–7.

36. Laurence London, "Editor's Page," *Contemporary Drug Problems* 8 (1979): 435–36.

37. P. J. O'Rourke, "Dirty Words," *Rolling Stone*, 25 September 1983, 62.

38. Richard J. Bonnie, "Discouraging Unhealthy Personal Choices: Reflections on New Directions in Substance Abuse Policy," *Journal of Drug Issues* 8 (1978): 199–219. *Libertarian*, Fourth Quarter 1923, 10.

39. See, for example, "The Washington Hearings on Cigarette Labelling," *Time*, 27 March 1964, 79–80. *Paraphernalia and Accessories Digest*, quoted in National Institute on Drug Abuse, *Community and Legal Responses to Drug Paraphernalia*, DHEW Publication No. (ADM) 80–963, (Washington: Government Printing Office, 1980), 13.

40. "A Youthful Hero," *Lady's Home Magazine* 12 (1858): 232.

41. Charles W. Lidz, Andrew L. Walker, and Leroy C. Gould, *Heroin, Deviance and Morality* (Beverly Hills: Sage Publications, 1980), 139.

42. See especially Amitai Etzioni, "Toward an I and We Paradigm," *Contemporary Sociology* 18 (1989): 171–76. Gregory H. Singleton, *Religion in the City of Angels: American Protestant Culture and Urbanization in Los Angeles, 1850–1930* (Ann Arbor: UMI Research Press, 1979), provides one concrete example of the retreat of good people to an individualistic approach. Ethicists commenting on the bias of individualism include Michael Lynn and Andrew Oldenquist, "Egoistic and Nonegoistic Motives in Social Dilemmas," *American Psychologist* 41 (1986): 529–34. Richard W. Wilsnack and Sharon C. Wilsnack, "Drinking and Denial of Social Obligations among Adolescent Boys," *Journal of Studies on Alcohol* 41 (1980): 1118–33. Richard Sennett, *The Fall of Public Man* (New York: Alfred A. Knopf, 1977), confirms the death of public responsibility and explores many ramifications of the change.

43. A. T. Poffenberger, "Motion Pictures and Crime," *Scientific Monthly* 12 (1921): 336–37.

44. See, for statistics on heavy users (in 1962 half of all beer-drinking households used 88 per cent of all beer), Michael Schudson, *Advertising, The Uneasy Persuasion: Its Dubious Impact on American Society* (New York: Basic Books, Inc., 1984), 26–27. Charles Winick and Paul M. Kinsie, *The Lively Commerce: Prostitution in the United States* (Chicago: Quadrangle Books, 1971), 223. Geis, *Not the Law's Business?* 215. *Time*, 11 January 1971, 54. For a 1980s example, see "Creating a Mass Market for Wine," *Business Week*, 15 March 1982, 108–18.

45. See, for example, Schur, *Crimes without Victims*, 172–73. Harrison Pope, Jr., *Voices from the Drug Culture* (Boston: Beacon Press, 1971), 72.

46. Wertham, *Seduction of the Innocent*, 259.

47. Dwight Macdonald, "A Theory of Mass Culture," in *Mass Culture: The Popular Arts in America*, ed. Bernard Rosenberg and David Manning White (New York: The Free Press, 1957), 66; Joshua Meyrowitz, "The Adultlike Child and the Childlike Adult: Socialization in an Electronic Age," *Daedalus* 113 (1984): 19–48, which is put into context in Joshua Meyrowitz, *No Sense of Place* (New York: Oxford University Press, 1985). Neil Postman, *The Disappearance of Childhood* (New York: Delacorte Press, 1982). Late in the twentieth century, *Tobacco and Youth Reporter* furnished innumerable examples, particularly from the areas of smoking and drinking. See, for example, Stuart Elliott, "Camel's Success and Controversy," *New York Times*, 12 December 1991, D1, 17; "I'd Toddle a Mile for a Camel," *Newsweek*, 23 December 1991, 70; John A. Blatnik, "Making Cigarette Ads Tell the Truth," *Harper's Magazine*, August 1958, 49; Lee H. Smith, "Is Anything Unprintable?" *Columbia Journalism Review*, Spring 1968, 23. On sexualizing the child, see Schur, *The Americanization of Sex*, 166–78.

48. Bruno Lessing, "Smoking," *Times* [Detroit], 2 January 1926. See, for example, James Gilbert, *A Cycle of Outrage: America's Reaction to the Juvenile Delinquent in the 1950's* (New York: Oxford University Press, 1986), especially chap. 12 and postscript. The ways in which Americans were destroying traditional childhood were complex and go far beyond the brief allusion above; see, for examples of suggestive scholarship, William Graebner, "Coming of Age in Buffalo: The Ideology of Maturity in Postwar America,"

Radical History Review 34 (1986): 53–74; and Ann Douglas, "The Dream of the Wise Child: Freud's 'Family Romance' Revisited in Contemporary Narratives of Horror," *Prospects* 9 (1984): 293–348.

49. Mary de Young, "Ethics and the 'Lunatic Fringe': The Case of Pedophile Organizations," *Human Organization* 43 (1984): 72–74. National Institute on Drug Abuse, *Community and Legal Responses*, 13.

50. See, for example, Paul L. Berkman, "Life Aboard an Armed-Guard Ship," *American Journal of Sociology* 51 (1946): 380–87; Henry Elkin, "Aggressive and Erotic Tendencies in Army Life," *American Journal of Sociology* 51 (1946): 408–22.

51. Stivers, *Evil in Modern Myth and Ritual*, 9–13, points out that the electronic media made an oral culture, regressing to preliterate modalities. One curious phenomenon indicative of the loss of kidding boundary-setting was the death of the ritual male dirty joke sometime around 1960. That kind of boundary confirmation was no longer very acceptable.

52. The stake of the alcoholic-beverage marketers is suggested in Claude M. Steele and Robert A. Josephs, "Alcohol Myopia: Its Prized and Dangerous Effects," *American Psychologist* 45 (1990): 921–33.

53. A striking example of the social costs is given in the description of the late stages of the development of black political power in Mark H. Haller, "Policy Gambling, Entertainment, and the Emergence of Black Politics: Chicago from 1900 to 1940," *Journal of Social History* 24 (1991): especially 733–34.

Epilogue

1. See, for example, Frederick Clairmonte, "The Transnational Tobacco and Alcohol Conglomerates: A World Oligopoly," *New York State Journal of Medicine* 83 (1983): 1322; and John Cavanagh and Frederick F. Clairmonte, *Alcoholic Beverages: Dimensions of Corporate Power* (London: Croom Helm, 1985), 105 and context. Louis Kraar, "Seagram Tightens Its Grip on Du Pont," *Fortune*, 16 November 1981, 75–76. *Tobacco and Youth Reporter*, Summer 1987, 5.

2. Daniel Yankelovich, *New Rules: Searching for Self-Fulfillment in a World Turned Upside Down* (New York: Bantam Books, 1982 [c. 1981]). See especially "Seven New Deadly Sins," *Life*, 7 November 1969, 46, in which the editors, without much theological savvy, tried to substitute a new set of sins for the traditional seven, including the substitution of "Prudery" as a sin for the traditional "Lust." The relaxed informality and escape from authority of non-middle-class lifestyles was intimately associated with beer drinking; see, for example, Marty Jezer, *The Dark Ages—Life in the United States 1945–1960* (Boston: South End Press, 1982), 136.

3. See, for example, L. Johnston, P. O'Malley, and J. Buchman, *Drug Use, Drinking and Smoking: National Survey Results from High School, College, and Young Adults Populations, 1975–1988* (Rockville, Md.: National Institute on Drug Abuse, 1989), especially 135–41; Trish Hall, "A New Temperance Is Taking Root in America," *New York Times*, 15 March 1989, A1, C6.

4. See, for example, James T. Hathaway, "The Evolution of Drinking Places in the Twin Cities: From the Advent of White Settlement to the Present" (doctoral diss., University of Minnesota, 1982), especially 304–5. Jack S. Blocker, Jr., *American Temperance Movements: Cycles of Reform* (Boston: Twayne Publishers, 1989), 157–60, 163–67. Kim Foltz et al., "Alcohol on the Rocks," *Newsweek*, 31 December 1984, 52–54. Sometimes the efforts of the proponents of the minor vices brought possibly unintended consequences, for the

violence spawned at the least by television—a whole subject in itself—was not necessarily a part of the goal of all advocates of the bad habits.

5. Specific examples include Gilbert Geis, *Not the Law's Business? An Examination of Homosexuality, Abortion, Prostitution, Narcotics and Gambling in the United States* (Rockville, Md.: National Institute of Mental Health, Center for Studies of Crime and Delinquency, 1972), 197–98; Charles Winick and Paul McKinsie, *The Lively Commerce: Prostitution in the United States* (Chicago: Quadrangle Books, 1971), 223–25; Patricia A. Adler and Peter Adler, "Shifts and Oscillations in Deviant Careers: The Case of Upper-Level Drug Dealers and Smugglers," *Social Problems* 31 (1983): 195–207, especially 201. Edwin M. Schur, *Crimes Without Victims: Deviant Behavior and Public Policy* (Englewood Cliffs, N.J.: Prentice-Hall, 1965), 6–7: "One must be on guard against assuming that, because a law does not prevent certain acts from occurring, it is therefore without effect." Those who claimed that prohibitory laws were "failures" because there were violations consistently refused to set up a standard by which success or failure could be judged, whether in the 1920s or the 1970s. This refusal makes it hard to take their arguments seriously, because it puts them in such an extreme idealistic position.

6. Troy S. Duster, *The Legislation of Morality: Law, Drugs, and Moral Judgment* (New York: The Free Press, 1970). Comparative studies are cited in Thomas Dull and David J. Giacoppassi, "An Assessment of the Effects of Alcohol Ordinances on Selected Behaviors and Conditions," *Journal of Drug Issues* 16 (1986): 512. Ross Homel, *Policing and Punishing the Drinking Driver: a Study of General and Specific Deterrence* (New York: Springer-Verlag, 1988), especially 269–72. On availability and sanction, an early example is Harris E. Hill, "The Social Deviant and Initial Addiction to Narcotics and Alcohol," *Quarterly Journal of Studies on Alcohol* 23 (1962): 570–71.

7. Kenneth E. Warner, "Cigarette Smoking in the 1970's: The Impact of the Antismoking Campaign on Consumption," *Science* 211 (1981): 729–30. Tom W. Smith, "The Use of Public Opinion Data by the Attorney General's Commission on Pornography," *Public Opinion Quarterly* 51 (1987): 260. See, similarly, *The Liquor Handbook 1984* (New York: Jobson Publishing Corp., 1984), 12: "A number of factors . . . have converged to create new consumer attitudes, and therefore new marketing conditions." (Courtesy of Austin Kerr.)

8. Those who wish to could probably substitute the word *hegemony* for *dominance* without distorting what happened; I am simply trying to avoid unnecessary ideology. Richard Butsch, "Introduction: Leisure and Hegemony in America," in *For Fun and Profit: The Transformation of Leisure into Consumption,* ed. idem. (Philadelphia: Temple University Press, 1990), especially 18–19, describes an interactive hegemony similar to that I found, although I hope that I have made clear that as the twentieth century progressed, there was much more from-the-top-down manipulation on behalf of the minor vices than earlier.

Acknowledgments

The Ohio State University has provided substantial research support for the writing of this book, including a Faculty Professional Leave, during which some of the research was carried out, and a Special Research Assignment for drafting most of Chapter 10 and revising the whole manuscript. Additional financial and other kinds of support were provided by Marjorie A. Burnham. Milton and Diana Engel generously and repeatedly furnished the author a place to stay while he was using the Library of Congress.

Library staff were as usual both helpful and indispensable, and the author is greatly indebted to them not only at The Ohio State University, where Robert Thorson took special pains, but at the Library of Congress and the Alfred C. Kinsey Institute for Research in Sex, Gender, and Reproduction at Indiana University, as well as at institutions that loaned books or assisted with illustrations. Unless otherwise noted, illustrations are from The Ohio State University Libraries regular collections.

Innumerable colleagues have encouraged and advised me as this book has developed, and I am grateful to them all. Especially did I impose on Mark H. Haller, Bert Hansen, and B. Edward McClellan in the early stages and receive counsel from Lewis Bateman at a late stage. Benjamin Rader was encouraging at all stages.

My colleague Austin Kerr has been continually supportive and inspiring as my writing proceeded and deserves special acknowledgment and thanks for continual counsel and for his constructive reading of a draft of the manuscript.

For detailed comments from a complete reading of a draft, I am also extremely grateful to Paul Boyer, Wesley Chambers, Norman H. Clark, Daniel M. Fox, Niko Pfund, James Reed, John E. Sauer, and an anonymous referee, all of whom carried collegiality far beyond ordinary duty. I am most fortunate to have benefited from their numerous suggestions and insights, and I wish to recognize the contribution of each one for constructive suggestions and corrections as well as general observations.

In addition, Ronald D. Gibbs, Mark H. Haller, Susan M. Hartmann, Mark Lender, Neil Larry Shumsky, Warren Van Tine, Lois and Robert Whealey, Kevin F. White, and another anonymous referee were kind enough to comment in a particularly penetrating way on draft chapters, and to them all I am also deeply grateful. They have saved me from many errors and suggested many improvements.

As is customary, many other kind colleagues have contributed thoughts, especially when some of the ideas were presented to research seminars at the Research School of the Social Sciences at Australian National University, at the University of New Mexico Department of History, and at the University of Kansas Department of History.

It is only fair to observe, finally, that I was unable to take all the suggestions of my colleagues. But I still recognize and remain grateful for their generosity.

Index